BUSINESS
DATA PROCESSING
with BASIC
and FORTRAN

second edition

Mike Murach

SCIENCE RESEARCH ASSOCIATES, INC.
Chicago, Palo Alto, Toronto, Henley-on-Thames, Sydney, Paris
A Subsidiary of IBM

Library of Congress Cataloging in Publication Data

Murach, Mike.
    Business data processing with BASIC and FORTRAN.

    Includes index.
    1. Basic (Computer program language) 2. FORTRAN
(Computer program language) I. Title.
HF5548.5.B3M87   001.6′424   76–40245
ISBN 0–574–21115–2

We gratefully acknowledge the following for their permission to reprint or adapt the materials listed:

Reprinted by permission of International Business Machines Corporation: figures 1–3, 1–5, 2–11, 3–5, 3–11, 4–1, 4–2, 5–1, 5–3, 5–4, 5–6, 5–8, 5–9, 5–11, 5–12, 7–6, 13–1, 13–3, 13–5, 14–5, 15–1, 15–9, 15–10, 15–11, 15–13, 15–16, 15–17, 15–20, 16–2, 16–11, 19–1, 19–2, C–1, C–2, C–3, and C–4; also, forms GX24-6599, GX20-1816, GX20-1702, GX20-8021, GX28-7327, GX21-9090, GX21-9092, GX21-9093, and GX21-9094.

Courtesy of the Univac Division of Sperry Rand Corporation: figures 1–1 and 11–6.

Courtesy of The National Cash Register Company: figures 1–4, 12–8, 15–7, and 16–9.

Courtesy of Control Data Corporation: figures 6–4 and 15–14.

Courtesy of The Burroughs Corporation: figures 7–8, 15–8, and 16–10.

Courtesy of Teletype Corporation: figure 16–3.

Courtesy of Singer Business Machines: figures 15–2 and 15–21.

Courtesy of Mohawk Data Sciences Corporation: figure 15–3.

Courtesy of United California Bank: figure 15–15.

Courtesy of Digitronics Division of Iomec Inc.: figure 15–18.

Courtesy of Datapoint Corporation: figures 17–1 and 17–2.

CONTENTS

Preface for Instructors

Business Data Processing with BASIC and FORTRAN, second edition, is designed for a one-semester course in business data processing. Because of its emphasis on the design of business systems (probably more than any other introductory text), I think it is particularly suited for the business curriculum. In addition, it contains sections on BASIC and FORTRAN, so a language can be taught as part of the introductory course.

This is a revised edition of *Business Data Processing and Computer Programming* (1973). During revision, I have put my major efforts toward improving the educational effectiveness of the book. In particular, I have made significant changes in the first four chapters, which should be a definite improvement of this section over the first edition.

On the other hand, the changes in content in this revision are few. I have added material on system design and analysis (chapter 3), structured programming (chapter 9), and minicomputers (chapter 17). I have presented BASIC in section 5. I have de-emphasized punched-card equipment to reflect its obsolescence; specifically, it is mentioned only in the optional chapter on punched-card systems (chapter 13). And the section on FORTRAN has been extensively revised to improve its effectiveness.

Features

One of the features of this book is its approach, sometimes called *modular design.* After reading the first four chapters (section 1), the student may proceed with any of the other sections. In particular, the book is organized as follows:

SECTION	CHAPTERS	SECTION NAME	PREREQUISITE SECTION	DESIGN
1	1–4	Introductory Concepts	—	Sequential
2	5–7	Card, Tape, and Direct-Access Concepts	1	Random
3	8–10	Programming and Software Concepts	1	Random
4	11–18	Auxiliary Subjects	1	Random
5	19–20	BASIC	1	Sequential
6	21–22	FORTRAN	1	Sequential

This means that the chapters in sections 1, 5, and 6 should be studied in sequence, and that the chapters in sections 2, 3, and 4 may be studied randomly. Within these limitations, you are free to choose the sequence of instruction and to emphasize what you think is best for your course. Although you will probably not have time to cover all 22 chapters, you will be able to select those that are most appropriate for your class.

I might add that, although many books are advertised as modular, few actually are. In most cases, a few alternative paths through the book are given to support the claim of modularity, but these seem to be after-thoughts, rather than an integral part of the book's design. To be truly modular, I think the essence of the subject should be presented in the first section of the book, and all subsequent modules should need only this first section as a prerequisite.

A second feature of this text is its content. If I may be critical for a moment, much of the content in other introductory data-processing text-books is irrelevant: the abacus and Pascal's adding machine, how the print chain of a 1403 works, how the sense wire in core memory works, flip-flop circuits, complement arithmetic, binary addition and subtraction, hexadecimal multiplication—all of these are irrelevant to the needs of the programmer, system analyst, or businessman. They are doubly irrelevant for the introductory student.

In contrast, the content of this book has been selected on the basis of relevancy. To begin the selection, I first asked "In today's world, what is the minimum a person should know about computing?" In my opinion, chapters 1–4 provide the answer to that question. I then added to this core content by asking, "What additional material is relevant to the layman, businessman and woman, system analyst, or programmer?" Sections 2, 3, and 4 are made up of the material I think is most meaningful to them. Finally, since I believe that programming is enlightening, I have included sections on BASIC and FORTRAN.

Needless to say, my decisions are open to dispute. For instance, you may question the chapter on CPU concepts and overlap (chapter 14) or the chapter on punched-card systems (chapter 13). You may even question whether the material on program design (chapter 9) shouldn't be deferred to a later course. (I question some of this material myself, and I welcome your comments.) Regardless of the disputes, however, I strongly feel that relevancy should be a primary factor in deciding which text to use for an introductory course.

A third feature of the book is that the relationships between equipment, application, system design, and programming are continually shown. Two just criticisms of previous books are that (1) they are equipment oriented, and (2) they don't show these relationships. In this book, however, equipment, applications, system design, and programming are introduced in the first four chapters. Thereafter, all subjects are described in their proper context. Equipment is never described without relating it to applications, system design, and programming. Similarly, system design techniques are never discussed without relating them to applications and equipment. To paraphrase Jacques Barzun in *The American University*—technique without purpose never introduced anybody to anything but boredom.

A fourth feature worth noting is the organization within the individual chapters. As a chapter progresses, it becomes more detailed and more rigorous. Thus, you, as the instructor, can adjust the text to the capabilities of the class by making assignments that cover less than a complete chapter. For example, chapter 6 is divided into three topics:

Topic 1   Tape Characteristics
Topic 2   Tape System Design
Topic 3   Programming and System Considerations

Topic 1 includes everything the traditional textbook normally covers in regard to magnetic tape; in topic 2, the equipment is related to applications and system design; then, the programming and system complications that are peculiar to tape systems are discussed in topic 3. Depending on the capabilities of the class and the emphasis of the course, you can assign only topic 1, topics 1 and 2, or the entire chapter.

A final feature of this book is that the student begins learning about computers right from the start. This may seem to be a trivial point, but there is no better way to kill the enthusiasm of an introductory data-processing class than to begin with a subject other than computers (as many textbooks do). To a student, it seems, business data processing means computers (and I'm inclined to agree with them). Later in the semester, you can assign chapter 12, Manual and Mechanical Methods of Processing Data, and chapter 13, Punched-Card Systems, to give some perspective.

Conclusion

Available with this text are a Student Workbook, an Instructor's Guide, and a set of masters for making overhead projector foils (OPF's). The workbook is a no-nonsense, no-busywork (no multiple-choice, no true/false, no matching) soft-cover book that consists of behavioral objectives, practice problems and case situations, solutions and explanations for immediate feedback, and problems for classroom or laboratory solution. (A complete description and explanation of its contents is given in the Instructor's Guide.)

The Instructor's Guide includes behavioral objectives for each chapter, answers to the questions given for each topic in this text, progress tests based on the objectives, model test answers, and solutions to the unanswered workbook problems. The OPF master set consists of many of the text illustrations, plus supporting materials.

Although the contents of this package may resemble those of competing products, I think you'll find a new emphasis throughout, a new dedication to education. I also think you'll find greater flexibility when using this product than when using any other. Finally, because of its relevancy, I think you'll experience greater classroom interest with this text than you have had with any previous text. In any event, I welcome your comments, criticisms, suggestions, or questions.

Mike Murach
Fresno, California

Introduction for Students

Before you can really understand computer systems, you must be familiar with four somewhat independent areas of knowledge. You must understand the capabilities of the computing *equipment*. You must understand how *programs* are used to direct the operation of a computer and what the processing limitations of a program are. You should be familiar with data-processing *applications*—the uses to which a computer is put. And finally, you need to know how the equipment and programs are coordinated through a system of procedures; this is commonly referred to as *system design,* or *system analysis*.

The first four chapters of this book introduces you to all four areas of knowledge. In my opinion, these chapters contain the basic, minimum information that anyone should know about computing. Once you have mastered them, any mystery about computer systems should be dispelled. You can then build on this base of knowledge by reading the remaining chapters.

This book is designed for a person with no previous exposure to computer systems. As a result, it begins at the beginning. Before you start to use this book, however, there are several things that you should know about it.

1. This text is designed so that the chapters don't necessarily have to be read in sequence. They are grouped into five sections, as shown in this table:

SECTION	CHAPTERS	SECTION TITLE	PREREQUISITE SECTION	DESIGN
1	1–4	Introductory Concepts	—	Sequential
2	5–7	Card, Tape, and Direct-Access Concepts	1	Random
3	8–10	Programming and Software Concepts	1	Random
4	11–18	Auxiliary Subjects	1	Random
5	19–20	BASIC	1	Sequential
6	21–22	FORTRAN	1	Sequential

This means that you may read any section after completing section 1. It also means that the chapters in sections 1, 5, and 6 should be read in sequence, but the chapters in sections 2, 3, and 4 can be read in the sequence that most interests you. For instance, you may want to study BASIC immediately after section 1. Or you may want to read the chapter on minicomputers in section 4 immediately after section 1.

If you are studying this book on your own, you may want to read the chapters in sequence. But don't hesitate to jump around in the text. Whenever your interest in a subject is aroused, read the appropriate chapter. There is no greater assurance that learning will take place than by studying a subject in search of an answer.

2. At the end of each topic or chapter are lists consisting of the new terms. The intent is not that you should be able to define these words, but that you understand them. After you read a topic, glance at the list and note any word whose meaning is unclear to you. Then reread the related material. Once the terms are fixed in your mind, continue on.

3. Following the terminology lists are questions. These are intended to get you involved. If there is one message coming from research in education, it is that meaningful learning depends on what the learner does—not on what he sees, hears, or reads. In general, these questions are designed to force you to think about the material in the chapter from a different perspective.

SECTION ONE

INTRODUCTORY CONCEPTS

This section tries to give you a basic understanding of computer systems. Once you complete it, you should understand how computer systems can make mistakes, how programmers create programs, and why managers decide to purchase computer systems in the first place.

1 AN INTRODUCTION TO ELECTRONIC DATA PROCESSING

TOPIC 1
PREVIEW

As you read this book, you will of course learn what data processing means and what it involves. As a preliminary definition, though, you should know that *data processing* refers to a sequence of operations, often mathematical, that are performed on facts and figures. *Business data processing* refers to the processing of business facts and figures.

Data processing can be accomplished by clerks using pencil and paper, by clerks using mechanical devices like adding machines and typewriters, or by electronic machines like computers. In a small business, data processing is likely to be handled by one or more clerks with the aid of some simple mechanical devices. A large business is likely to use many methods of processing data, ranging from pencil and paper to a large computer. A *data-processing—* or *DP—system* is made up of the people, equipment, and procedures that process data.

Business data processing is an important subject, because it greatly affects a company's operations. Consider, for example, that one out of six persons in industry today does clerical work. This means that data processing (or paperwork) is one of the major costs of running a business. Reducing this expense can have a significant effect on profits.

Furthermore, opportunities for cost reduction are often greater in clerical areas than in other areas of business. Cost reductions of 10 percent and more in selected data-processing areas are not in the least unrealistic. This doesn't necessarily imply a move toward automation; it only means eliminating or improving inefficient clerical procedures that too often develop as an institution grows.

One chemical company, for example, decided to study its business forms as a possible area for cost reduction. The company was using over 15,000 different forms. Many of these duplicated functions, were difficult to use, or were obsolete. By consolidating, eliminating, and redesigning forms, the total number was reduced to 11,000 and the resultant cost savings was over $250,000 per year. One expert in the control of business forms estimates that a company that has never conducted a program for forms control can cut printing costs by a minimum of 20 percent, to say nothing of reduced clerical costs.

Other companies have had similar successes as a result of improving data-processing procedures. One company reduced its order-processing personnel from 275 to 145 in one year's time without affecting the quality of service. Another company reduced paperwork by 70 percent and clerical costs by $40,000 per year when its management reporting system was redesigned. And a large manufacturer eliminated 400 expediters and 200 clerks by installing an automated production-control system.

But costs are only part of the story. Data processing can be the cause of many common business problems. Late or incomplete shipments of merchandise, overbilling customers, excessive accounts receivables, idle assembly lines—all of these may result from a faulty data-processing system. At its worst, an ineffective DP system can burden sales and technical personnel with paperwork, lose sales through poor customer service, and destroy employee morale.

Management expects a data-processing system to provide them with information. This aspect has been emphasized so much lately that data processing is now also being referred to as *information processing,* and data-processing systems as *information systems.* By providing current information, a data-processing system can assist a manager in making decisions such as whether or not to market a new product, in what areas advertising funds should be used, and to what extent a company can reasonably increase its indebtedness. If the information helps management make better decisions, the increased revenue and decreased expenses resulting from these decisions can well be the most important benefit of a company's data-processing system.

Although business data processing may not include the use of computers, this book is about data-processing systems that do. Such systems are called *computer,* or *electronic data-processing* (EDP), *systems.* EDP systems already dominate DP activities in companies with over 500 employees, and it seems certain that they will also dominate those in smaller companies. In recent years computers that cost less than $1000 a month to lease have become common, so any company with over 100 employees is a likely prospect for a computer system. And since companies with fewer than 100 employees can either share a computer or rent a service, computer processing is an important consideration for yet thousands of other companies.

HOW THIS TEXT IS ORGANIZED

Before you can really understand EDP systems, you must be familiar with four different areas of knowledge. (In my opinion, this is the primary difficulty in learning about computers.) First, you must understand the capabilities of the computing equipment, or *hardware.* Second, you should be familiar with *computer applications*—that is, the uses of a computer. Third, you will have to understand how the hardware is coordinated with people through a system of procedures—this is commonly referred to as *system design and analysis.* And finally, you should know something about *programming*—specifically, how *programs* are used to direct the operation of a computer, and what the processing limitations of individual programs are.

Section 1 of this book gets you started in all four of these areas. In the remainder of this chapter, you will be introduced to hardware. Then, chapter 2 will introduce you to applications and systems flow, chapter 3 to system design and analysis, and chapter 4 to programming.

After section 1, you may proceed with any of the other sections. If you check the table of contents, you will see that section 2 emphasizes hardware and system flow; section 3 delves into programming; section 4 is a collection of auxiliary subjects that encompasses programming, systems design, hardware, and applications; and so on. If you complete all of the book's sections, you will undoubtedly know more about EDP systems than most of today's businesspeople do.

SUMMARY   A data-processing system is the collection of procedures, people, and equipment manipulating facts and figures. An EDP system is a data-processing system centered around the computer.

TERMINOLOGY

data processing	information system
business data processing	computer system
data-processing system	electronic data-processing system
DP system	EDP system
information processing	

QUESTIONS

1. Why do you think there is more emphasis on data processing today than there was 25 years ago?

2. What is the primary reason that businesses install EDP systems?

3. What are some of the inefficient systems you encounter in your daily life?

4. Which systems that you encounter strike you as very efficient?

5. Of the inefficient and efficient systems you named in questions 3 and 4, which ones do you think are computerized?

TOPIC 2
AN INTRODUCTION TO
HARDWARE

Before you begin the study of computer applications, system design, or programming, you should become familiar with some of the terms associated with various types of computer systems. This chapter, then, provides that base of terminology.

To begin with, a *computer* is a machine that accepts input data, processes it, and gives output data. For example, a computer can read sales data from punched cards, process this data, and provide output in the form of a printed sales report. A computer can also accept many other forms of input, such as magnetic tapes or checks recorded in magnetic ink, and give many other forms of output, such as data on magnetic disks or displays on television-like devices. Because a computer's processing depends on the sequence of instructions (the program) that it is given prior to doing a job, a computer can process data in an almost endless variety of ways.

In general, a computer, also referred to as a *computer system,* consists of one or more input devices, one or more output devices, and a *central processing unit (CPU).* A small system consists of a CPU and only a few *input/output (I/O) devices,* while a large system consists of a CPU and dozens of I/O devices. Theoretically, at least, the components of a computer system are chosen to fulfill the needs of the user; the system should be large enough to do all the jobs required by the user but not so large that processing capacity goes to waste.

Some of the smallest computer systems consist of four components: a card reader for input, a card punch and a printer for output, and a CPU for processing. These components are shown in figure 1-1. Because the punched card is its only input, a system like this is often called a *card system.* The standard punched card, which can hold up to 80 characters of data, is described in detail in chapter 5.

Although the four components shown in figure 1-1 can be physically separate, they are connected electronically by cables that are usually placed under a raised floor. During operation, the four components work together. When punched-card data is read by the card reader, it is transferred to the storage of the CPU, where it can be processed. When data is printed on the printer or punched into cards by the card punch, the data is transferred from the storage of the CPU to the output device. All operations—input, processing, and output—take place under control of instructions stored in the CPU.

The *card reader* of a computer system usually has one input hopper and one or more output stackers, depending on the model of the device. As the cards are read, one at a time, they pass from the input hopper to one of the stackers. Although some card readers can read over 2000 cards

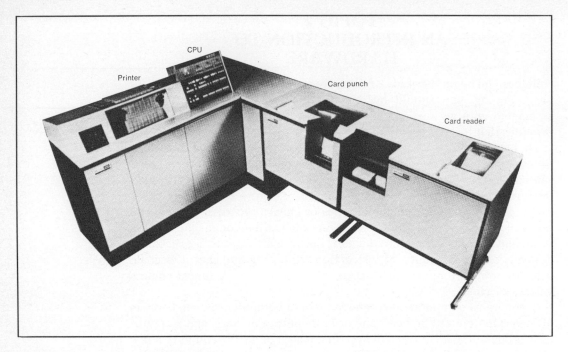

FIGURE 1-1   A card computer system

per minute, a card reader in a card system is more likely to read from 200 to 600 cards per minute.

A *card punch,* which looks very much like a card reader, also has one input hopper and one or more output stackers. Although both the punch and the reader may be separate physical units, they are often combined into one unit. In most cases, however, even when combined into one unit, they continue to operate separately. As a rule, card punches operate somewhat slower than card readers—typically, in the range of 100 to 300 cards per minute.

Printer speeds for card systems commonly range from 300 to 600 lines per minute. So that a printer can operate at such high speeds, it prints on continuous, rather than cut, forms. *Continuous forms* are attached to each other in a continuous band of paper, as illustrated in figure 1-2. They are fed through the printer by a mechanism that fits into the tiny holes on both sides of the forms. After the forms are printed, the sides can be removed and the forms themselves separated, usually at perforations. Because a printer can be adjusted to forms of many widths and lengths, it can be used to print very small forms such as mailing labels as well as sixteen-inch wide management reports.

A printer also has the capability of skipping to appropriate lines before printing. For example, in preparing the monthly statement illustrated in

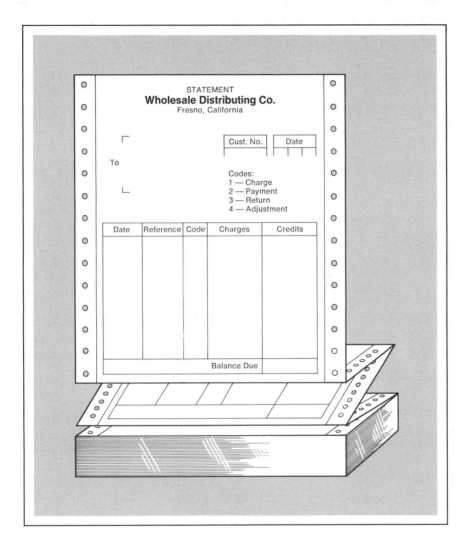

FIGURE 1-2   A continuous-form statement

figure 1-2, the printer skips to the top of the form before printing the customer's name and address, to the body of the form before printing detailed information about the amounts billed and payments received, and to the total line of the form before printing the balance owed. This capability is commonly called *forms control*. By using forms control, a computer system can meet the printing requirements of almost all business forms.

The CPU is usually a large rectangular unit. It controls the operations of the entire computer system by executing the instructions given it in the form of *programs*. The CPU contains control circuitry so that it can execute a variety of instructions. It also contains storage, so it can store the programs while they are executed. As records are read from input devices, they too are stored in the storage area of the CPU.

In many ways, it is the stored program that gives a computer its unique abilities. By loading different programs into a CPU's storage, a computer's operations can be changed dramatically from one application to another. Thus it is possible for a computer to print payroll checks as one program is executed, and then—when a second program is executed—to print invoices. (In chapter 4 you will learn how the programs are actually created, through the discipline of programming.)

On the front of the CPU you will often find a panel of lights, dials, and operational keys. This panel (if present) is called the *console* of the system. It is used by the computer operator or by the computer-repair personnel.

On many systems you will also find a typewriter-like device called the *console typewriter*. It is usually located near the console of the system. In normal operation, a listing of all programs that are run is printed by the console typewriter. This listing will give starting and ending times for each job. If there is an operational problem, a message will be printed on the typewriter, and the computer operator may be called upon to enter a coded response through the keyboard of the console typewriter.

When an institution outgrows a card system, it usually moves up to a *tape system* or a *direct-access system*. A tape system uses magnetic tape as its primary input and output. The magnetic tape is a long strip of plastic tape that is wound on a reel—just like on a tape recorder. When the reel of tape is mounted on a tape I/O device, data can be read from or written on the tape at speeds much faster than those of card or printing operations. Although a large number of tapes can be used on a single computer system, a typical tape system, as shown in figure 1-3, consists of a CPU, a card reader, a card punch, a printer, and four tape units called *tape drives*.

Direct-access systems use direct-access devices as the primary input and output of the system. The most widely used direct-access device, the *magnetic disk,* consists of several platters (disks) stacked on a central spindle. The unique characteristic of a direct-access device is that any one of the records stored on the device can be accessed without reading the other records. For example, one model disk can store approximately 44,000 100-character records; yet, any one of these records can be accessed and read in an average of about 88/1000 second. Contrast this with magnetic tape, in which the first 5999 records on a tape must be read before the six-thousandth record can be read. Although a direct-access system can have many direct-access devices attached to it, a small system such as the one in figure 1-4 consists of a CPU, a card reader, a printer, and two disk units called *disk drives*. A direct-access system that uses disk I/O is commonly referred to as a *disk system*.

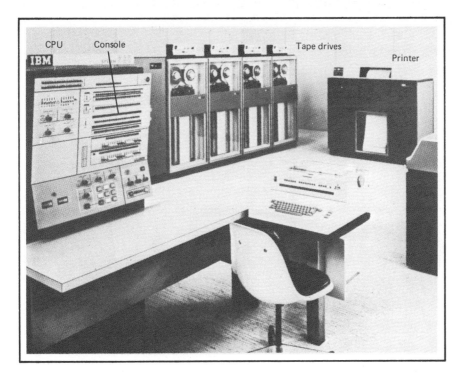

FIGURE 1-3   A tape system

As a company expands its EDP operations, it moves to larger, faster computers. This can mean replacing its existing I/O devices with faster ones. It can also mean increasing the total number of I/O devices attached to the CPU. Or it can mean switching to a system with a faster, more powerful CPU plus faster I/O devices. Figure 1-5, for example, shows a computer system consisting of a CPU, card reader, card punch, three printers, eight tape drives, and two types of direct-access devices (an eight-module disk device plus a single-module one). This might be classified as a medium-sized computer system.

To identify a specific computer system, it is common to give the manufacturer's name and the model number of the CPU. For example, one computer is referred to as a Burroughs B2800 or just B2800, where Burroughs Corporation is the manufacturer and B2800 is the model number. Another computer is referred to as an IBM System/360 Model 25, where IBM (International Business Machines) is the manufacturer and System/360 Model 25 specifies the model. The computer in figure 1-1 is a Univac 9200 (Univac is the computer division of Sperry Rand); the computer in figure 1-3 is an IBM System/360 Model 40; and figure 1-4 shows an NCR (National Cash Register Company) Century 100 computer.

To more specifically identify a computer, the type of system and the major I/O components are commonly stated. For example, you might

FIGURE 1-4   A small disk system

hear a programmer describe his company's system as an "HIS (Honeywell Information Systems) 115 disk system." Or you might hear a system designer describe a system as a "Model 135 System/370 with eight tape drives and five disk modules."

DISCUSSION

It should be clear by now that computer systems vary tremendously as to the components that make them up, their capabilities, . . . and their price. A small card system may rent for as little as $1000 per month, while a large direct-access system may cost well over $100,000 per month. Purchase prices for computer systems vary accordingly; generally, they are about forty-five times as much as the monthly rental price. (In most cases, the computer user has the option of either renting or buying a computer system.)

FIGURE 1-5   A medium-sized computer system

Before a computer can be used to process data, it must be given a detailed sequence of instructions called a program. In other words, the equipment (or *hardware*) must be combined with programs (or *software*). A separate program is required for each job that a computer does; thus, a typical computer installation has hundreds of different programs. Because of the time required to write programs, about as much money is spent for programming as is spent for computer rental.

Before a program can be *executed* by a computer system, it must be *loaded* into the CPU. From an operator's point of view, this process is generally quite simple. To load and execute a program on a typical disk system, for example, the operator performs steps something like these:

1. He or she inserts the appropriate continuous form in the printer and pushes the printer's start button.
2. If cards are to be punched by the program, he puts blank cards in the card punch and pushes the start button on the punch.
3. He mounts whatever tapes are going to be used on the appropriate tape drives, mounts whatever disk packs are going to be used on the appropriate disk drives, and pushes the start buttons on these devices.
4. He puts one or more *job-control cards* in the card reader; these cards indicate what program is to be loaded and executed. If the program

is supposed to read input cards, the operator puts the input (data) cards on top of the job-control cards. Then, he pushes the start button on the card reader.

Once these operations are performed, the computer system loads and executes the program specified by the job-control cards. It can do this because all programs are stored on one of the system's magnetic disks. After it reads the job-control cards, the computer searches for the appropriate program on the disk, loads it (reads it) into the storage of the CPU, and executes it.

To illustrate the procedures for loading and executing a program on a combined disk and tape system, assume that a computer is to prepare payroll checks from two input tapes—one containing weekly payroll data and one containing year-to-date totals. The operator begins by mounting the required tapes on the appropriate tape drives and pushing the start buttons. Next, he or she adjusts the continuous-form payroll checks in the printer and pushes its start button. Finally, he puts the job-control cards for the check-writing program in the card reader. When he pushes the start button on the card reader, the computer system loads the program from the disk and executes it, thus reading the input tapes and printing the payroll checks.

Two striking features or even the simplest computer system are the speed and accuracy with which it can process data. The speed can be broken down into I/O speed and CPU speed. In the check-writing program just described, for example, suppose there are 2400 records of 100 characters each on each of the input tapes and that 3 lines are to be printed on each payroll check (a total of 7200 lines for the 2400 employees). At a printing speed of 600 lines per minute, it would take 12 minutes to print the 2400 checks. As for reading the input tapes, a typical tape drive would read the 2400 records in less than a minute.

CPU speeds, on the other hand, are commonly measured in microseconds (millionths of a second) and even nanoseconds (billionths of a second). One medium-sized computer, for instance, can do 100,000 additions in a second. That's one every 10 microseconds. If the CPU of the disk system requires an average of 50 microseconds per instruction and 400 instructions per employee, that's only 1/50 second per employee, or 48 seconds of processing time for all 2400 employees.

As for a computer's accuracy, electronic checking circuitry is built into all I/O devices as well as the CPU to make sure that all errors are caught. A card reader, for example, doesn't simply read a card. If it did, a faulty reading mechanism might cause inaccurate data to be read into the CPU. Instead, most card readers read data twice, at two different reading stations. The data that is read at the first reading station is compared with the data read at the second station. If the two readings aren't the same, an error is detected and the computer system stops. Similarly, electronic checking circuitry is built into the CPU, printer, card punch, tape drives, disk drives, and all other I/O units that may be attached to a system. As a result, computer errors that go undetected by a modern computer system are extremely rare. Upon investigation, errors that are blamed on the computer can be traced to errors in system design, programming, or operating procedure.

SUMMARY

1. A computer, or a computer system, is made up of a CPU and at least one input and one output device.

2. The three basic types of computer systems are card, tape, and direct-access. Their identification is determined by the primary form of I/O devices used.

3. Because checking circuitry is built into all the components of a computer system, an undetected computer error is extremely rare. For all practical purposes, a computer processes data with 100 percent accuracy.

TERMINOLOGY

computer
computer system
central processing unit
CPU
input/output device
I/O device
card system
card reader
card punch
printer
continuous form
forms control
program

console
console typewriter
tape system
tape drive
direct-access system
magnetic disk
disk drive
disk system
hardware
software
loading a program
executing a program

QUESTIONS

1. What type of computer does your school have? Identify it and name its components.

2. What different types of continuous forms do you think your school's computer system uses? Which ones have you encountered?

3. Do you believe the statement that for all practical purposes the hardware in a computer system performs with 100 percent accuracy? What other hardware systems have you read about that perform with great accuracy?

2 AN INTRODUCTION TO APPLICATIONS AND SYSTEMS FLOW

TOPIC 1
AN INTRODUCTION TO
APPLICATIONS

A *computer application* is a problem or operation to which a computer system can be applied. Since billing is a business operation that can be carried out by a computer system, billing is a computer application. Similarly, sales reporting and inventory control are computer applications.

Although applications vary depending on the type of business involved, there are eight accounting applications that are common to most businesses. This topic will introduce you to five of these: order writing, billing, accounts receivable, inventory control, and sales analysis. (Chapter 11 will introduce you to the three others and give a survey of other kinds of computer applications.) The five applications presented in this chapter will be used as a basis for illustrating many system concepts throughout the remainder of this book.

As you read about the applications in this topic, you should (1) become familiar with the input and output documents used, and (2) note how each application can affect profits. In business terminology, *document* refers to any form or report. Thus, an invoice, a routing slip, and a profit-and-loss statement are all documents.

If you have some business background and you are already familiar with these applications, you may want to check the summary and terminology list at the end of this topic before starting. They will help you determine whether you should read, browse, or skip this topic.

ORDER WRITING

When customers place an order with a company, they do it in several ways. They can telephone the order to the company; they can give the order to a salesperson; they can mail in their own purchase order; or they can send the order in by telegram. This original order, known as the *customer order* (or *sales order*) is the input document of the *order-writing* application. An example of a customer order is given in figure 2-1.

The output document of the order-writing application is a *shipping order* such as the one illustrated in figure 2-2. In preparing the shipping order, customer codes, names, and addresses are usually checked against customer master files; item codes, descriptions, and prices are usually checked against item master files; and, in some cases, particularly for a new acount, a customer's credit may be checked. If a company has many items in its product line, they may be rearranged on the shipping order into a sequence that corresponds to the sequence of items in the shipping department; the warehouse locations of the items may also be printed on the shipping order. Such aids to order pickers increase their efficiency by as much as 20 to 30 percent.

Customer Order

Wholesale Distributing Co.
Fresno, California

Sold To _ALLWORTHY EQUIPMENT_
2446 SIMPSON STREET
TURLOCK, CA. 95380

Order No. 22109		New customer Credit OK	
Date 10-2-77	Cust. order No. Q 29 H273	Salesman No. 16	Cust. No. 1257

Quantity	Item Number	Description	Unit Price
15	11141	½ INCH ADJ. WRENCH	2.75
3	12303	ECONOMY ¼ INCH DRILL	11.29
5	21214	6 PC. OPEN END SET	10.49

Shipping instructions VIA TRUCK	Order taker gm

FIGURE 2-1 A customer order

The shipping order is normally prepared in several copies, one of which is called the picking copy and is sent to the shipping department to be used for picking the order. A second copy may be sent to the customer as an acknowledgment that the order has been received; another copy may be enclosed with the shipment as a packing slip. A fourth copy may be retained in the data-processing department as an office copy.

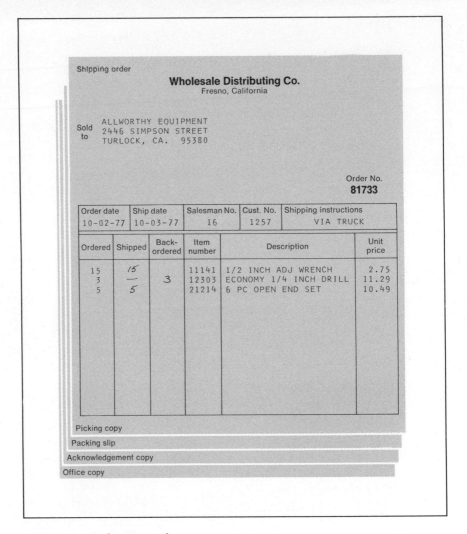

FIGURE 2-2   A shipping order

As an order is filled, the order picker indicates in the back-ordered column of the picking copy which items are not in stock and therefore can't be delivered. These items, called *back-ordered items*, or *back orders*, will be shipped to the customer when they become available. In figure 2-2, the order picker has back-ordered 3 Economy 1/4-Inch Drills, thus indicating that they aren't in stock. When the order picker has finished, the picking copy is returned to the data-processing department so that the customer's bill can be prepared.

The objective of the order-writing application is simply to prepare the shipping order as accurately and rapidly as is practical since both accuracy and speed can affect profits. An inaccurate shipping order, for example, can mean that the wrong items or quantities are shipped to a customer or that the order is delivered to the wrong address. Since all of these conditions affect customer satisfaction, inaccurate shipping orders can eventually mean lost sales.

Because the speed of an order-writing application determines to a certain extent how fast orders are shipped, it too can affect customer satisfaction. If it takes two weeks from receipt of a customer order until a shipping order reaches the warehouse, one-week deliveries are of course impossible. Since the sales in many industries are dependent on fast deliveries—as in the toy industry during the Christmas season—order-writing speed can be critical to a company's sales. On the other hand, in some mail-order businesses where fast deliveries aren't expected, an order-writing delay of a day or two has no effect on sales.

BILLING

After the shipping order is returned to the data-processing department, the customer's *bill,* or *invoice,* must be prepared. The input document of the *billing* application is the shipping order; the output document is the bill. The goal of the application is to quickly and accurately prepare the bills.

If you compare the bill in figure 2-3 with the shipping order in figure 2-2, you can see that the primary difference between the two documents is that the *line items* on the bill are *extended.* The term *line item* refers to each of the lines that describes a type of item sold; the bill illustrated has three line items. To get the *extension* of each line item, the quantity shipped is multiplied by the unit price. Thus, the extension of the first line item is $41.25, of the third line item, $52.45.

At least two copies of an invoice are normally prepared: the original for the customer and the copy for the office file. Other copies may be prepared for use in keeping track of back orders, sales commissions, or amounts owed to the company.

As with most applications, both speed and accuracy are critical in billing. An inaccurate bill can result in overcharging or undercharging a customer. An incorrect address can mean delays in getting the bill to the customer.

Speed in billing is important because it affects the amount of money owed to a company. To appreciate this, suppose that a company ships an average of $20,000 of merchandise per day and bills the customers for the merchandise 10 days after shipping. If the customers pay their bills an average of 30 days after receiving them, approximately $800,000 will be owed to the company at any one time. (10 days plus 30 days equals 40 days; 40 times $20,000 equals $800,000).

Invoice — Customer copy

Wholesale Distributing Co.
Fresno, California

Sold to
ALLWORTHY EQUIPMENT
2446 SIMPSON STREET
TURLOCK, CA. 95380

PAGE 01

Invoice No.
55423

Invoice No.	Invoice date	Salesman No.	Customer No.	Terms
55423	10-05-77	16	1257	2%/10 — NET/30

Shipped	Back-ordered	Item number	Description	Unit price	Amount
15		11141	1/2 INCH ADJ WRENCH	2.75	41.25
	3	12303	ECONOMY 1/4 INCH DRILL	11.29	
5		21214	6 PC OPEN END SET	10.49	52.45

BACK-ORDERED PORTION OF THIS ORDER
TO BE SHIPPED WITHIN 21 DAYS.

Invoice total 93.70

FIGURE 2-3 An invoice

Now suppose the company reduces the delay in billing from 10 days to 2. Then, approximately $640,000 will be owed at any one time, a difference of $160,000. At 5 percent interest, this difference in uncollected debts would mean $8,000 in increased company profits. Even more than the interest, though, it would mean $160,000 is available for expansion: developing new products or markets, buying new equipment, or financing new buildings.

Depending on the company, billing may or may not be an important application. If, for example, a company writes only a few invoices a day with only a few line items per invoice, billing can be done easily with a typewriter and a calculator. On the other hand, a company that does many thousands of line items of billing per day would very likely profit by an automated billing system.

ACCOUNTS RECEIVABLE

Accounts receivable refers to the amounts owed to a company by its customers (accounts). The accounts receivable application is concerned with keeping records of the amounts owed and providing information that will help a company control the amounts owed.

The input documents for the accounts receivable application are invoices, payment vouchers (records of payment), and credit and debit memos (records of adjustments to a customer's account). The output documents are (1) individual customer records, such as the one in figure 2-4, showing at least the present balance owed and, often, the individual charges and credits; (2) monthly statements, such as the one in figure 1-2, reminding customers of their debts; and (3) management reports such as the aged trial balance and delinquent-account list in figure 2-5. If an account is delinquent, a reminder is usually sent to the customer. If the delinquency continues, the customer is then contacted personally.

The accounts receivable record illustrated in figure 2-4 is called a *ledger card;* it is typical of the records used in a noncomputerized system. The entire file of ledger cards, one per customer, represents the total amount owed to the company. As records of charges and credits are received, they are recorded on the appropriate ledger card and the new balance owed is calculated. This is referred to as *posting accounts receivable.* In contrast, the records of a computerized system, though they contain similar information, are in the form of punched cards, magnetic-tape records, or direct-access records.

To control the amounts owed to a company, management needs information similar to that given in the reports in figure 2-5. The first report, the *aged trial balance,* indicates the amount owed by each customer and the length of time the amounts have been owed. Thus, there is a column for current debts (owed for less than thirty days), plus columns for debts owed over thirty, sixty, and ninety days. The second report, the delinquent-accounts list, shows only those customers with debts older than sixty days. A report such as this can be used for contacting all the delinquent customers.

One of the major differences in accounts receivable systems is whether a customer's payment is applied to specific unpaid invoices or to the balance owed. In general, manufacturers and wholesale distributors are paid by the invoice (called an *open-item* system); retail stores receive payments that are applied to the balance owed (called a *balance-forward* system).

Since accounts receivable records represent money owed to a company, the importance of accuracy within the application is obvious. Besides causing revenue to be lost outright, inaccurate records or statements can be an annoyance to a customer. Similarly, processing

Customer
ALLWORTHY EQUIPMENT
2446 SIMPSON STREET
TURLOCK, CA. 95380

Cust. No. 1257	Salesman CURRIER		Credit limit $3,000.00	
Date	Reference	Charges	Credits	Balance
			Balance forward	212.00
6-06-77	46141	186.02		398.02
6-15-77	47733	711.94		1109.96
6-27-77	48120	945.95		2055.91
6-28-77	11480		212.00	1843.91
7-05-77	48777	77.40		1921.31
7-24-77	50200	388.67		2309.98
7-31-77	12733		1843.91	466.07
8-15-77	51101	568.65		1034.72
9-05-77	51772	106.63		1221.35
9-07-77	51933	363.20		1584.55
9-13-77	52022	676.89		2261.44
9-19-77	53788	475.64		2737.08
9-26-77	14498		568.65	2168.43
10-05-77	55423	93.70		2262.13

FIGURE 2-4   An accounts-receivable ledger card

delays can lead to customer dissatisfaction. If a statement dated April 30 doesn't show payments received on April 29, confusion can result. And if delinquent reminders dated May 15 are sent to customers who paid outstanding balances on May 10, ill will can arise.

On the other hand, an accounts receivable system that is both fast and accurate while providing up-to-date management information can be a significant help in reducing the accounts receivable total. One oil and gasoline company, for example, reports that its accounts receivable total

```
                     DELINQUENT-ACCOUNT LIST

 10-31-77                                                  PAGE 0001

 CUST.      CUSTOMER           --------- LAST 12 MOS. ---------    AMOUNT
  NO.         NAME             TIMES OVER 30 ---- TIMES OVER 60   OVER 60

 1153  ALFIE'S GARDEN SHOP          12                1             70.90
 1257  ALLWORTHY EQUIPMENT           2                1            466.07
 1755  CONSOLIDATED HARDWARE         1                1            102.50
 2501  J. W. MOORE CO.               6                4           1024.12
 2753  LAS VEGAS NURSERY             2                2            108.50

                        AGED TRIAL BALANCE

 10-31-77                                                  PAGE 0001

 CUST.      CUSTOMER          TOTAL     CURRENT    OVER    OVER    OVER
  NO.         NAME           BALANCE                30      60      90

 1057  A & A EQUIPMENT SUPPLY   815.25    815.25
 1153  ALFIE'S GARDEN SHOP    1109.66     742.00   296.76                70.90
 1257  ALLWORTHY EQUIPMENT    2262.13      93.70  1702.36  466.07
 1351  ARNOLD'S BARGAIN BARN   552.93     552.93
 1453  BENGSTON'S SEED STORE   129.00     129.00
 1653  CAMPUS GARDEN SHOP      781.71     781.71
 1755  CONSOLIDATED HARDWARE   915.13     812.63           102.50
 1855  DOWNTOWN HARDWARE CO.  1299.00    1299.00
 2257  GENERAL EQUIPMENT CO.    49.50      49.50
 2501  J. W. MOORE CO.        1737.44     543.00   170.32 1024.12
 2753  LAS VEGAS NURSERY       427.76     319.26                        108.50
 3007  MC CORD'S LUMBER CO.     53.00      53.00
```

FIGURE 2-5   Accounts-receivable reports

was reduced by $400,000 when a better system was installed. The new system not only shortens statement-preparation time from nine days to two, but also provides information that helps to quickly spot and terminate bad credit risks. Under the old system, it would take as long as forty-five days to spot a bad risk—even an intentional offender—but with the new system, it takes less than a week.

INVENTORY CONTROL

An *inventory-control* system has two basic goals. The first is to keep the amount of money invested in inventory as low as possible. This goal is critical to the success of many companies because of the high cost of carrying inventory. For every $100 of inventory carried throughout the year, as much as $30 may be spent on carrying costs such as inventory taxes, insurance, storage, handling, physical deterioration, and the cost of the money invested. Although the rate used for estimating carrying costs varies from company to company, one commonly used figure is 25 percent of the average inventory investment.

To appreciate the significance of this first inventory goal, suppose a company has gross sales of $10 million and an average inventory of $2 million. At a carrying-cost rate of 25 percent, the company spends $500,000 per year to maintain its inventory, or 5 percent of its gross sales. If the average inventory could be reduced by 20 percent ($400,000), profits could be increased by $100,000.

The second goal of an inventory-control system is to improve customer service by avoiding stockouts. One measure of customer service, called the *service level,* is calculated by dividing the value of orders placed into the value of orders filled:

$$\text{Service level} = \frac{\$\text{ Orders filled}}{\$\text{ Orders placed}}$$

If, for example, a company receives orders for $100,000 worth of merchandise but can fill only $80,000 worth because of stockouts, the service level is 80 percent. A service level of 100 percent indicates that all orders were filled from the available stock.

To appreciate the significance of this second goal, suppose a retail grocery chain has a service level of 80 percent. In this particular business, stockouts usually mean lost sales because a buyer normally can find the item in another store. So if a store does an annual business of $8 million at a service level of 80 percent, it would gross $8.5 million at an increased service level of 85 percent. With an average markup of 35 percent, this would result in increased profits of about $175,000 (35 percent of $500,000).

Unfortunately, the two goals of the inventory-control system are contradictory. The one sure way of avoiding stockouts is to keep large inventories. But, if inventories are reduced to keep the money invested as low as possible, stockouts are more likely. The problem of the inventory-control application, then, is to help a company reach the most profitable balance between the two goals—to let the company keep inventories as low as possible while still maintaining an adequate service level.

The input documents of the inventory-control application are records of items sold, returned, received, destroyed, and lost. These records include shipping orders or invoices, return notices, receiving reports, scrap notices, and adjustment slips. The output documents are (1) inventory records, such as the ledger-card record in figure 2-6, and (2) management reports, as illustrated in figure 2-7, that provide control information. These reports should answer questions such as: What items should be reordered? What amounts should be reordered? What items have had unusual increases or decreases in demand? What items are becoming obsolete? What items have a poor service level?

Item No. 21214	Description 6 PC OPEN END SET			Unit cost 8.99	Unit price 10.49	Reorder point 160
Date	Reference	Issues	Receipts	On hand	On order	
6-15-77	47731	3		212		
6-20-77	48111	55		157		
6-27-77	5543			157	250	
7-05-77	48770	3		154	250	
7-06-77	48805	20		134	250	
7-11-77	49001	20		114	250	
7-11-77	49002	5		109	250	
7-13-77	49150	15		94	250	
7-17-77	49244	5		89	250	
7-18-77	77265		250	339		
7-26-77	50499	7		332		
7-27-77	50505	10		322		
8-02-77	50737	5		317		
8-03-77	50800	35		282		
8-08-77	50811	2		280		
8-13-77	50941	10		270		
8-14-77	51009	8		262		
8-15-77	51101	5		257		
8-24-77	51443	20		237		
8-31-77	51667	5		232		
9-04-77	51699	3		229		
9-05-77	51773	10		219		
9-10-77	52001	5		214		
9-11-77	52005	3		211		
9-18-77	53733	2		209		
9-18-77	53737	25		184		
9-20-77	53888	15		169		
9-21-77	53911	4		165		
9-26-77	54299	3		162		
10-05-77	55423	5		157		

FIGURE 2-6   An inventory ledger card

In a typical business, particularly a small business, reducing inventory by 20 percent without decreasing the service level is not in the least unrealistic. Why? Because most businesses do not use modern inventory-management techniques.

To illustrate, consider what takes place in a typical ledger-card system for inventory control. For each item in the product line, a ledger card such as the one in figure 2-6 is kept. As transactions occur, they are posted to the ledger cards and the on-hand balances are brought up to date. This

```
                      SERVICE-LEVEL REPORT FOR MONTH ENDING 10-31-77

                                       ----THIS MONTH----            YTD
ITEM                              VALUE      BACK    SERVICE       SERVICE
NO.       DESCRIPTION            ORDERED   ORDERED    LEVEL         LEVEL

12122     8 AMP BELT SANDER     3,230.50              100.0%        94.4%
12210     JET SCREWDRIVER         428.35    65.90      84.6%        89.2%
12301     1/4 INCH VAR SPEED DRILL 413.25             100.0%        91.0%
12303     ECONOMY 1/4 INCH DRILL   282.25   112.90     60.0%        70.9%
12401     7 INCH POWER SAW      1,523.88              100.0%        98.5%
```

```
MONTH ENDING 10-31-77                                                      PAGE 003

                   MONTHLY SALES BY ITEM

                        -----MONTHLY SALES-----           ---YEAR-TO-DATE SALES---
ITEM                     THIS      LAST     PERCENT      THIS      LAST     PERCENT
NO.    DESCRIPTION       YEAR      YEAR     INC/DEC       YTD       YTD     INC/DEC

21114  11 PC SOCKET SET    402.35    439.49   8.4CR     4,363.95   3,744.95   16.5
21116  19 PC SOCKET/WRENCH SET 125.00  62.50  100.0       625.00     750.00   16.7CR
21210  12 PC BOX END SET   192.50                      2,117.50
21212  6 PC COMBINATION SET 2,783.80 1,355.98 105.3    22,450.00  15,472.54   45.0
21214  6 PC OPEN END SET    734.30    713.32   2.9      8,392.00   8,288.00    1.3
21310  MITER BOX AND SAW    647.40  1,079.00  39.9CR    3,776.50  10,843.95   65.2CR
```

```
                   DAILY REORDER LISTING--10/05/77

ITEM     ITEM                         ON      ON      REORDER
NO.      DESCRIPTION                 HAND    ORDER     POINT

11143    3/4 INCH ADJ WRENCH          55                 60
11222    CAMPER AXE                  107                125
11510    6 VIAL LEVEL                 12      60          75
12110    2 AMP ORBITAL SANDER         21                 28
12303    ECONOMY 1/4 INCH DRILL              125        150
21114    11 PC SOCKET SET             38                 50
21214    6 PC OPEN END SET           157                160
21410    24 PC TAP AND DIE SET        24      30          60
31140    RD POINT DIRT SHOVEL         85                100
```

FIGURE 2-7 Inventory reports

posting to inventory records can be done either manually or by a posting machine, the method usually determined by the number of items in the product line and the number of daily transactions.

Periodically, perhaps once a week, a clerk or manager in the inventory-control department reviews the ledger cards to determine which items should be reordered. If the on-hand balance is below the reorder point, the ledger card is put in the reorder pile. Of course, if an order has already been placed, the item doesn't need to be reordered unless on hand plus on order is below the reorder point. A variation of this system is to compare on hand with the reorder point during the posting operation and if necessary, to place the ledger cards in a reorder pile. Since the ledger card in figure 2-6 shows that on hand is below the reorder point and that a new order hasn't been placed, this item should be reordered.

To determine the reorder point, an inventory-control manager first considers two factors: (1) the clerical time required for posting and reviewing the ledger cards and (2) the *lead time*—the amount of time it takes to receive an order after it has been placed. Suppose, for example, that it takes three working days from the time shipments are made until the issues are actually posted to the ledger cards. Suppose also that it takes three days after posting before the ledger cards are reviewed and new orders are placed. Once the order is placed, the supplier takes three weeks for delivery. In this case, if the average weekly sales for the item is 20, the reorder point must be at least four weeks' usage, or about 80. Thus, the actual on-hand balance will reach zero just as the new order is received.

However, if the sales are above average because of normal fluctuations in demand, a stockout will occur. As a result, some amount of *safety stock* is added to the reorder point. For example, if a one-month supply of the item is used as safety stock (80 units), the reorder point is 160 (80 + 80). Then, the average demand will have to double before a stockout will occur. Incidentally, a typical rule to follow when setting reorder points is to use a one-month supply as safety stock for all inventory items.

The amount that is reordered in a typical system (the order quantity) is also based on a fixed usage, such as a two- or three-month supply. For example, a typical company may have a rule of reordering a three-month supply whenever an order is placed. In figure 2-6, since usage for the last three months has been about 250, 250 units will be reordered. By using a three-month rule for determining order quantity, each item in inventory will have to be ordered about four times per year.

Although a ledger-card system may very well be the most profitable system for a company, there are many ways in which the system just described can be improved. Perhaps the simplest way is to cut the processing and review time so that all transactions are processed and all records are reviewed on a daily basis. By reducing the clerical time, reorder points can be lowered, thus reducing inventory levels without any change in the service level. For example, if the clerical time is reduced by five days (one work week), the reorder point can be reduced by about one week's usage and, thus, the average inventory investment can also be reduced.

Beyond this simple measure, scientific management techniques can be used to determine reorder point and order quantity. To determine order quantity, for example, an arbitrary rule such as the three-month usage rule is rarely the most profitable method. Similarly, there is a better way to determine safety stock and therefore reorder point than by using an arbitrary rule like the one-month usage rule. In general, however, scientific inventory management requires computational power that is practical only when the processing is done by a computer system.

Whether or not a company uses scientific techniques for determining reorder point and order quantity, one message should be clear: It takes information to determine a profitable balance between the conflicting goals of inventory management. To this end, reports such as those in figure 2-7 are helpful. The first report, the daily reorder listing, lists those items that need to be reordered—on hand plus on order is below the reorder point. The second report, called a monthly sales-by-item report, indicates items that are increasing or decreasing in demand. This information will help inventory personnel to pinpoint the items that require a change in reorder point or order quantity. Similarly, the third report, a monthly service-level report, indicates items for which a larger or smaller safety stock should be considered.

In summary, the inventory-control application can be complex, but it can also be the source of the greatest increase in company profits resulting from a changeover to a computerized system. Many computer systems, in fact, have been justified by this application alone. Although the success stories are many, one auto and machine parts distributor typifies what can be accomplished. By using modern management techniques for 30 percent of its 13,000 items (the ones with the largest investments), the company was able to decrease its average inventory investment on those items by 26 percent. At the same time, the service level for those items increased from 94 to 96 percent.

SALES ANALYSIS

The purpose of the *sales-analysis* application is to provide information for management. The input documents are the records of shipments and returns, the invoices, and the return notices. The output documents are sales reports designed to answer questions such as: Who are our most profitable sales people? Should we drop a product from the product line? Should a new product be developed? Where should our advertising dollars be spent?

Figure 2-8 illustrates two typical sales reports. The first shows total sales and gross profit for each salesperson. The fact that the biggest selling salesperson is not the one that brings the largest gross profit to the company indicates that perhaps a different incentive system should be considered. The second report gives the sales for each customer and compares year-to-date sales with the previous year-to-date sales. By studying unusual decreases, a manager can determine sales losses as they develop and take action to recover the lost business.

In some companies, of course, sales analysis is not an important application. For example, if a company has a limited number of products, salesmen, and customers, sales analysis may be a relatively insignificant application. On the other hand, if a company has thousands of items and products, a large sales staff, and several sales offices, sales analysis is likely to be critical. Without adequate information, management can't make effective decisions.

```
                        MONTHLY SALES BY CUSTOMER

MONTH ENDING 10-31-77                                           PAGE 001

                    CUST.     SALES     -------YEAR-TO-DATE SALES-------
     CUST. NAME      NO.    THIS MONTH  THIS YEAR   LAST YEAR    INC/DEC

A & A EQUIPMENT SUPPLY  1057  8,752.98  81,825.44   76,655.62    5,169.82
ALFIE'S GARDEN SHOP     1153    336.29   2,106.90    1,265.99      840.91
ALLWORTHY EQUIPMENT     1257    735.57   8,490.34    9,473.00      982.66CR
ARNOLD'S BARGAIN BARN   1351  3,333.90  44,947.05   25,280.00   19,667.05
BENGSTON'S SEED STORE   1453    415.35  11,458.58   38,857.50   27,398.92CR
CALLEY HARDWARE CO.     1555 16,408.81  90,511.33   86,645.12    3,866.21
```

```
                        MONTHLY SALES BY SALESMAN

   MONTH ENDING 10-31-77                                PAGE 001

                        SALESMAN     NET      COST OF     GROSS
      SALESMAN NAME       NO.       SALES      SALES      PROFIT

      CRAMER               10    25,280.29   19,405.79   5,874.50
      CRAWFORD             13     3,547.25    2,930.83     616.42
      CURRIER              16    18,062.34   14,823.54   3,238.80
      GRAHAM               19    19,746.37   15,839.97   3,906.40
      HEMPHILL             22    35,165.43   29,923.90   5,241.53
      HENNIS               25    32,261.85   25,343.79   6,918.06
      MCDONALD             28    23,726.26   18,793.96   4,932.30
      MASTERS              32    18,777.50   14,990.05   3,787.45
```

FIGURE 2-8   Sales-analysis reports

DISCUSSION

Although we have described the major documents and characteristics of these applications, the descriptions are brief and simplified. As you go from industry to industry and from company to company, there are significant variations in the way that applications are handled. To illustrate, consider the differences in the order-writing, billing, and accounts receivable applications as you go from a wholesale to a retail distributor. First, the retail distributor normally doesn't write an order while the wholesale distributor does. The retail customer selects merchandise and brings it to a checkout counter. Second, a retail store often doesn't prepare a bill if the sale is a cash payment (although some stores do). If the sale is a charge, a bill is written and one copy is handed to the customer. In contrast, the wholesale distributor prepares a bill for each shipment of merchandise. Third, the wholesale distributor keeps accounts receivable records on an open-item basis, the retail distributor on a balance-forward basis. Retail payments are applied to the balance owed, not to individual invoices.

Beyond these variations, there are many others. The formats of the various documents differ from company to company. In some industries, customers will not accept back-ordered items—the sale is simply lost. And many companies combine the order-writing and billing applications so that the shipping order is actually a copy of the bill. To do this, inventory records are checked before preparing the shipping order and bill to determine in advance if an item is available in stock.

Regardless of the procedural variations, these five applications provide you with a good base of knowledge, since they are common to most businesses or other institutions. Manufacturers and wholesale distributors, for example, perform all five. Service businesses do too; although they don't have merchandise, they write service orders and bill for the services. And although they don't keep an inventory of merchandise, they do keep inventories of service parts and maintenance supplies. Retail distributors may not write orders, but they perform the other applications. Similarly, banks, insurance companies, hospitals, and even government agencies perform most of these applications, even though the applications may seem significantly different. A hospital may keep inventory records of available beds; the insurance company's bill is a premium notice; and sales tax payments from businesses are part of the government's accounts-receivable application.

Although the applications are described separately in this chapter, it is important to realize that groups of applications are often closely related. For example, the output of the order-writing application—the shipping order—is the input to the billing application. Similarly, the bill is an input document for the accounts receivable, inventory, and sales-analysis applications. Because these five applications are related in this way, they are often referred to as a family of applications—specifically, the *distribution family of applications.*

The interrelationship of the applications is an important concept, because it helps explain why computer processing of data is economical. Once data is recorded in a machine-readable form, such as the punched card, the data can be processed by the computer to prepare a variety of outputs. In fact, the data that represents one line item on a shipping order can be used to prepare invoices, update inventory records, and print sales reports. By using the same data in several applications, the cost of preparing the output documents is reduced.

In conclusion, the study of computer applications can easily be a subject in itself, for the study of applications is the study of business. Although this topic is about computer applications, we do not mean to imply that a computer is the best processing method for any particular application. The choice of equipment depends on the size of the company, the volumes of data to be processed, and the type of industry, in addition to many other factors.

SUMMARY

1. The distribution family of applications is made up of order writing, billing, accounts receivable, inventory control, and sales analysis. In one form or another, these applications are found in most businesses.

2. Because the applications described in this topic are interrelated, they lend themselves to automated processing. In brief, the data that makes up one line item on an order can be used to prepare invoices, update accounts receivable and inventory records, and print sales reports.

TERMINOLOGY

computer application
document
customer order
sales order
order writing
shipping order
back-ordered item
back order
bill
invoice
billing
line item
extension
accounts receivable

ledger card
posting accounts receivable
aged trial balance
open-item accounts receivable
balance-forward accounts
    receivable
inventory control
service level
lead time
safety stock
sales analysis
distribution family of
    applications

QUESTIONS   1. Some of the major classifications of businesses are manufacturing, wholesale and retail distribution, construction, and service. Which applications of the distribution family of applications would you expect to be critical in each of these industries?

2. Two of the five major causes of business failures (bankruptcies) are receivables difficulties and inventory difficulties. How would you explain this?

TOPIC 2
AN INTRODUCTION TO SYSTEMS FLOW

Now that you know something about hardware and applications, the next step is to learn how the hardware is used for some specific application. As a result, this topic will describe some typical EDP procedures for order writing, billing, inventory control, and accounts receivable. When you finish, you should have a reasonable idea of how computers can be applied to a wide range of applications.

Throughout this topic, assume that a small disk system is used for all applications. This system consists of card reader, card punch, printer, console typewriter, and two disk drives.

A SIMPLE SYSTEM FLOWCHART

To visually present the procedures within an EDP system, system designers often use *system flowcharts* like the one shown in figure 2-9. This flowchart symbolically represents the steps that must be followed to prepare the required output documents from the available input. Although the system flowchart may look somewhat imposing at first, once you are familiar with it, you will find that studying a system flowchart is the easiest way to learn what is happening in a system—far easier than reading a written description.

The symbols used in the system flowchart are summarized in figure 2-10. Thus a trapezoid represents a manual operation; a rectangle represents a processing run on the computer; and so on.

To read a system flowchart, you begin in the upper lefthand corner and follow the flowlines that connect the symbols. As you read, follow the flowlines down and to the right, *except* when arrowheads indicate movement to the left or up. Thus the flowchart in figure 2-9 begins with the customer order and continues with the keypunch operation, transaction cards, and so on. There are only two processing steps in this flowchart, indicated by the numbers 1 and 2 written over the manual operation and processing symbols.

Keypunching and Verifying
(Step 1)

Before a computer can process data, the data must be put in a machine-readable form. The most common way of doing this is to punch the data into cards. The cards can then be read by the card reader of a computer system.

You are probably somewhat familiar with punched cards, but in case you aren't, chapter 5 describes them in detail. For now, it is enough that

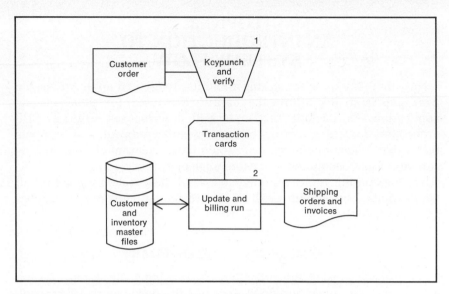

FIGURE 2-9   A system flowchart for a billing application

you know that the most commonly used punched card can store 80 characters of data. Since a character is either a letter, number, or special character (like &, #, and $), 1489 is four characters of information; and JIM DANDY is nine characters (the space counts as a character also). In general, 80 characters is more than enough for the data relating to a single transaction such as a line item of billing.

To record data in punched cards, a *keypunch,* such as the one in figure 2-11, is used. During operation, the keypunch operator places blank cards in the input hopper of the machine and sits at the typewriter-like keyboard. To the left of the operator are printed documents, called *source documents,* from which the data is to be keypunched. As the operator's fingers strike the keys, the corresponding codes are punched into the cards, one character per keystroke. At the end of the job, the newly punched cards are in the stacker on the left of the machine.

During the keypunching operation, some functions take place automatically—for example, feeding cards, skipping over fields that aren't going to be punched, and duplicating data from one card into the following card. This increases the speed at which an operator can keypunch data. Since the automatic functions can be changed quite easily at the beginning of each job, the keypunch can be used to punch cards in any format. On most keypunches, the data that is punched in the card is also printed at the top of the card, so the operator can visually check whatever data has been punched.

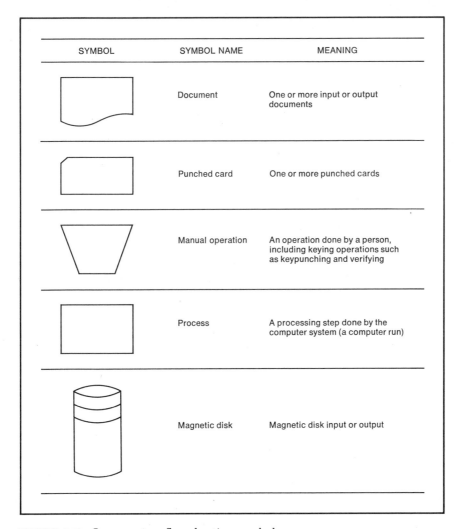

SYMBOL	SYMBOL NAME	MEANING
	Document	One or more input or output documents
	Punched card	One or more punched cards
	Manual operation	An operation done by a person, including keying operations such as keypunching and verifying
	Process	A processing step done by the computer system (a computer run)
	Magnetic disk	Magnetic disk input or output

FIGURE 2-10   Some system flowcharting symbols

Figure 2-12 illustrates the keypunching for one document as required by step 1 of the flowchart in figure 2-9. Here, the source document is the customer order. The data printed at the top of the punched card identifies the data that is punched into it. As you can see, transaction date, customer order number, and customer number are taken from the heading of the source document; the data for each item ordered is taken from the line items of the source document. Although this punched card has room for five line items, only three are shown, since this particular order consists of only three. If there are more than five line items, more

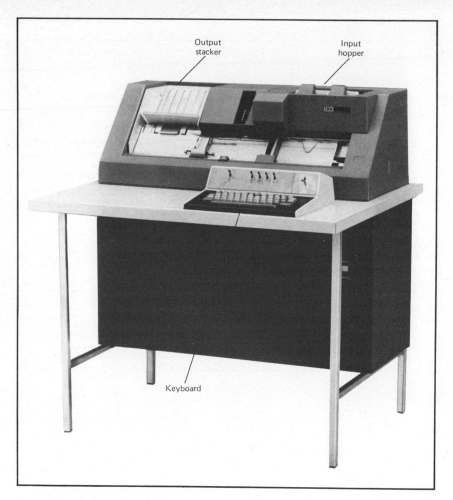

FIGURE 2-11   A keypunch

than one card could be used, with the heading data duplicated from one card to the next. To save keypunching time, only quantity ordered and item number are punched for each line item.

To ensure that the data punched in the cards is accurate, the keypunch operation is usually followed by a verifying operation. The *verifier* can be a separate machine that looks much like a keypunch, or it can be the same machine as the keypunch. In this second case, the machine is changed to verifying mode by the flip of a switch.

Regardless of what type of machine is used, verifying is similar to the keypunching operation. The verifier operator uses the same source documents that were used during keypunching. He or she places the

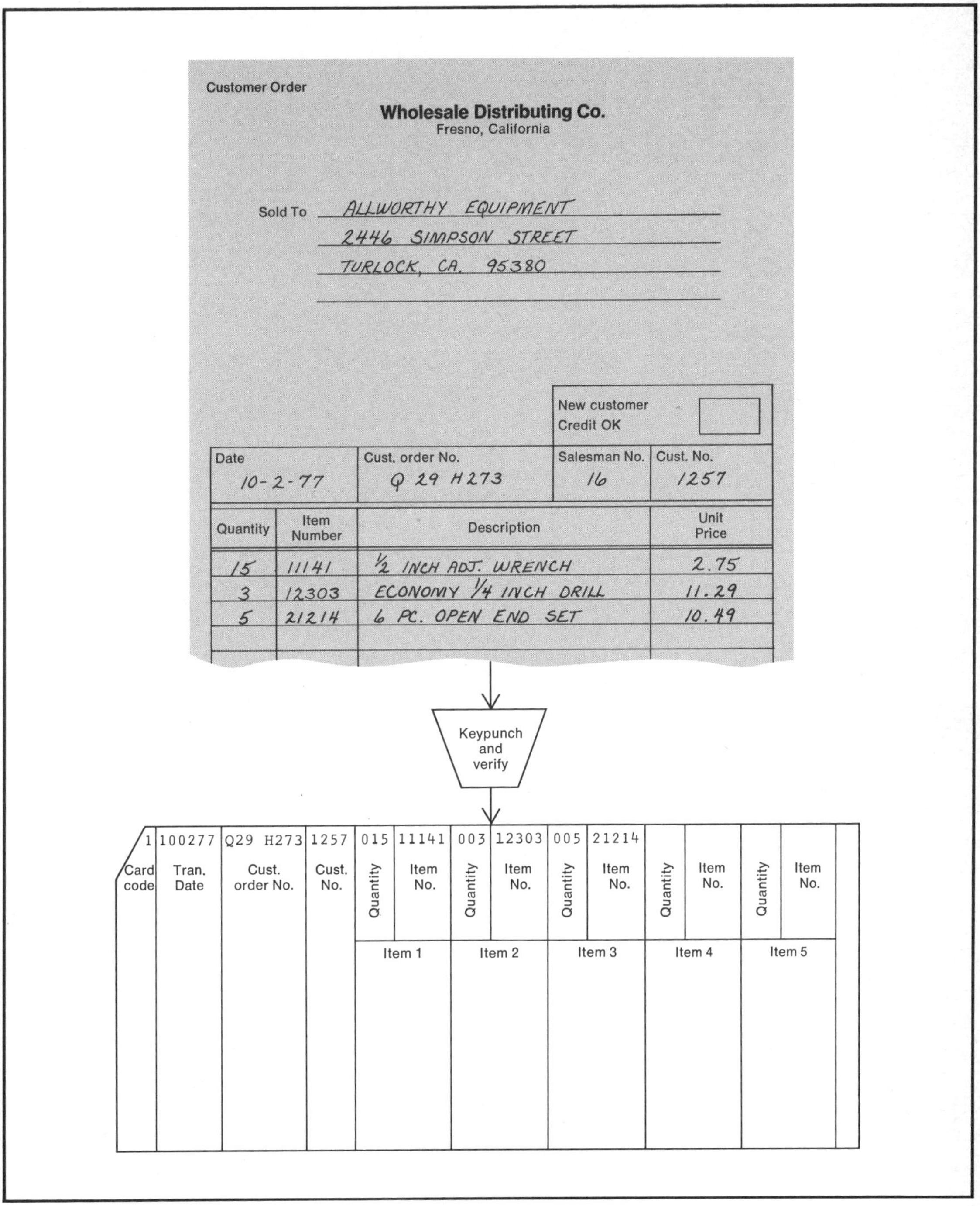

Customer Order

Wholesale Distributing Co.
Fresno, California

Sold To   ALLWORTHY EQUIPMENT

2446 SIMPSON STREET

TURLOCK, CA. 95380

New customer
Credit OK

Date	Cust. order No.	Salesman No.	Cust. No.
10-2-77	Q 29 H273	16	1257

Quantity	Item Number	Description	Unit Price
15	11141	½ INCH ADJ. WRENCH	2.75
3	12303	ECONOMY ¼ INCH DRILL	11.29
5	21214	6 PC. OPEN END SET	10.49

Keypunch
and
verify

1	100277	Q29 H273	1257	015	11141	003	12303	005	21214				
Card code	Tran. Date	Cust. order No.	Cust. No.	Quantity	Item No.	Quantity	Item No.	Quantity	Item No.	Quantity	Item No.	Quantity	Item No.
				Item 1		Item 2		Item 3		Item 4		Item 5	

FIGURE 2-12   Schematic illustration of keypunching and verifying

keypunched cards in the input hopper of the verifier and keys data on the keyboard of the verifier exactly as if operating the keypunch. The difference is that the verifier, instead of punching, checks to see that the holes in the card correspond to the keys that the operator strikes. If all the characters of data that the operator keys for a card agree with the characters already punched in the card, a correct-card notch is cut on the right side of the card indicating that its data has been verified.

Suppose, however, that the verifier operator keys the digit 3 for column 12 of a card, but the column contains the digit 2. (There are 80 *columns* in a typical card, and one character of data can be punched in each column). In this case, the keyboard locks, and an error light turns on. The operator checks the source document to be sure that the digit 3 is correct, pushes a button to release the keyboard, and strikes the digit 3 again. If the character in the card and the character keyed do not agree this time, the keyboard again locks and the error light turns on. The operator then repeats the process one more time to be absolutely sure that the correct character is 3, and, if so, keys it again. If the verifier still detects an error, an error notch is cut over the card column, and the verifier moves on to the next column. Once an error card is detected, a new card is punched, either as part of the verifying operation or as a separate step later on (depending on what type of equipment is used).

In any event, when the keypunch and verify step in the system flowchart is completed, the operator will have a deck of transaction cards that are ready for processing by the computer. Assuming the verifying and correction operation has been done diligently, the cards are error free. And now, the data in these cards, combined with data taken from customer and inventory master files stored on disks, should be all that is needed to print shipping orders and invoices.

The Update and Billing Run

If you look at step 2 in figure 2-9, you will see that it is an update and billing run. A *run* in computer terminology refers to the execution of one of the computer's programs. As a result, a typical system will make many different runs every day: billing runs, payroll runs, accounts receivable runs, etc.

As you can see by the system flowchart, the input to the update and billing run is the deck of transaction cards prepared in step 1. The outputs are shipping orders and invoices (one copy of the invoice form acts as the shipping order; another copy as the invoice). In addition, both customer and inventory master records are updated during this run.

Figure 2-13 describes the data contained in the customer and inventory master records. Each of the items listed for each record is referred to as a *field*. For instance, the customer record contains a customer number field, a customer name field, and a salesman number. It also contains

CUSTOMER MASTER RECORD	INVENTORY MASTER RECORD
Customer Master Record	Inventory Master Record
Customer number	Item number
Customer name	Item description
Customer address	Unit cost
Customer city, state, and zip	Unit price
Salesman number	Date of last transaction
State code	On hand
Credit limit	On order
Sales this month	Reorder point
Sales this year-to-date	Reorder quantity
Open item 1	Sales this month
Invoice date	Sales this year-to-date
Invoice amount	
Open item 2	
Invoice date	
Invoice amount	
Open item 3	
Invoice date	
Invoice amount	
Open item 4	
Invoice date	
Invoice amount	
Open item 5	
Invoice date	
Invoice amount	
Open item 6	
Invoice date	
Invoice amount	
Total owed	

FIGURE 2-13   The fields within the customer and inventory master records

fields for up to six unpaid (open item) invoices. Similarly, each inventory record contains an item number field, an item description field, and so on.

Figure 2-14 gives an example of one invoice prepared during this run. If you compare the output data and the master records with the data in the transaction card in figure 2-12, you can see that the computer takes some data from the transaction card, some from the customer master record, and some from each of three different inventory master records in order to prepare the invoice shown. More specifically, here's what happens as the update and billing run is executed for the transaction card shown in figure 2-12.

1. The transaction card is read.
2. The customer master record corresponding to the customer number in the transaction card (customer number 1257) is accessed

Invoice | Customer copy

Wholesale Distributing Co.
Fresno, California

Sold to
ALLWORTHY EQUIPMENT
2446 SIMPSON STREET
TURLOCK, CA. 95380

PAGE 01

Invoice No.
55423

Invoice No.	Invoice date	Salesman No.	Customer No.	Terms
55423	10-05-77	16	1257	2%/10 — NET/30

Shipped	Back-ordered	Item number	Description	Unit price	Amount
15		11141	1/2 INCH ADJ WRENCH	2.75	41.25
	3	12303	ECONOMY 1/4 INCH DRILL	11.29	
5		21214	6 PC OPEN END SET	10.49	52.45

BACK-ORDERED PORTION OF THIS ORDER
TO BE SHIPPED WITHIN 21 DAYS.

Invoice total 93.70

FIGURE 2-14 A sample invoice prepared by the billing system

from the disk and read into the storage of the CPU. (Remember that a record in a disk file can be accessed in a fraction of a second without reading any of the other records in the file.)

3. The heading portion of the invoice is printed using the data from the customer record, such as name, address, and salesman number. (The page number, invoice number, and invoice date are taken from the storage of the CPU. These items of data were entered into storage at the start of this run.)
4. The inventory master record corresponding to the first item in the transaction card (item number 11141) is accessed from the disk and read into storage of the CPU. Since more than one file can be stored on a single disk drive, both customer and inventory master files can be stored on one disk or they can be on separate disks.
5. The first line item is printed on the invoice. As shown in figure 2-14, the computer must calculate the amount (41.25) by multiplying the

unit price (taken from the inventory record) by the quantity shipped. Before printing the line item, the program checks the on hand field in the inventory master record to make sure that there are enough items available to fill the order.

6. The data in the inventory master record is brought up-to-date (*updated*), and the master record is written back onto the disk in its updated form. Specifically, this program will change the on-hand, date-of-last-transaction, sales-this-month, and sales-this-year-to-date fields in the master record. The on-hand field will be reduced by the quantity shipped. The date-of-last-transaction field will be made equal to the transaction date in the transaction card. And the sales fields will be increased by the amount of the transaction.

7. The inventory master record corresponding to the second item in the transaction card (item number 12303) is accessed from the disk and read into the storage of the CPU. (Here the program checks the on-hand field and finds that three items aren't available, so this line item will be treated as a back order.)

8. The second line item is printed with no amount shown, since the item is back ordered.

9. Inventory master record 12303 is updated and is written back onto the disk file. Since on hand doesn't change— because of the back order—only the date-of-last-transaction field is changed.

10. The inventory master record corresponding to the third item in the transaction card (item number 21214) is accessed from the disk file and read into the storage of the CPU. Then the line item is printed, the master record is updated, and the updated master record is written back onto the disk file.

11. Since there are no more line items, the computer totals the invoice and prints the total line. Since one item has been back ordered, the message in the lower lefthand corner of the invoice is also printed from storage.

12. The customer master record is updated by changing the sales-this-month, sales-this-year-to-date, and one of the open-item fields. If, for example, the customer already has three unpaid invoices, the program will store the invoice date and amount in the fields for the fourth open item. Thus, the customer record contains the pertinent data for all unpaid invoices. After the fields have been updated, the customer master record is written back on the disk in its original location. (Incidentally, the record layout given in figure 2-13 assumes that a customer will never have more than six unpaid invoices at any one time.)

Now you should have a better idea of what's happening as the update and billing run is executed. In brief, at least two master records are read for each transaction card (one customer record and one inventory record for each item ordered). And each master record is written back onto the disk file after it has been updated. As for the data on the invoice, it comes from five different sources: (1) from the transaction card, (2) from the customer master record, (3) from the inventory master records, (4) from computations performed during the execution of the program (like amount and invoice total), and (5) from CPU storage after it has been entered prior to the start of the run (such as the invoice date and the first invoice number).

A MORE COMPLETE SYSTEM
FLOWCHART

Although the flowchart in figure 2-9 gives you a good idea of what happens in an EDP system for billing, inventory, and accounts receivable, it is a simplified one. In actual practice, at least three steps would be added to this system, as shown in the system flowchart in figure 2-15. Here, an editing and sort run is added to the system before the update and billing run. Also, two steps called "balancing to controls" are added (steps 3 and 5).

The Editing and Sort Run

The purpose of an *editing run* is to check the transaction data to make sure that it is acceptable for processing in subsequent computer runs. In figure 2-15, the input to this run is the deck of transaction cards; the outputs are (1) a listing of unacceptable transactions along with control totals, and (2) a transaction file on disk of the acceptable transaction records in customer number sequence. The transaction disk file contains the same data as the transaction card file; however, it is in a form that can be read at high speeds.

During the editing run, the computer will make several checks on the input data. For instance, the computer may check each customer number and item number to make sure they are valid. It can do this by checking the numbers given against a table of valid numbers held in the storage of the CPU. It may also check to make sure that none of the fields contain blanks when they should contain data. If, for example, a quantity is given for item 2, then an item number must also be given. If an unacceptable transaction is found, a message will be printed, and the transaction will not be written on the disk file for subsequent processing.

After editing, the program will sort the transactions into customer-number sequence. (As you will see in chapter 7, sorting transaction records may improve processing efficiency in the update and billing run, even though it doesn't change the function of the run.) From a programming point of view sorting is complex, but from a systems view it simply changes the records in a file from one sequence to another.

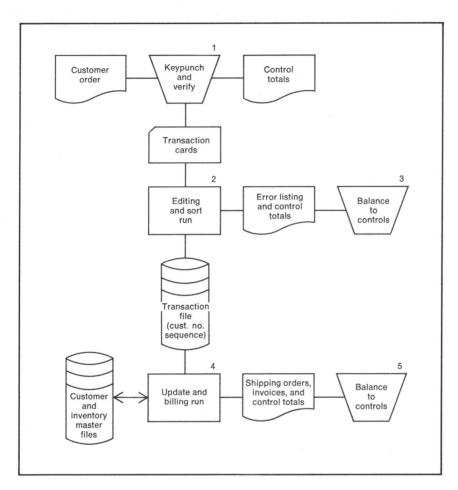

FIGURE 2-15   System flowchart for a more complete billing system

At the end of the editing and sort run, control totals that have been accumulated during the execution of the program are printed at the bottom of the error listing. These totals typically will include (1) the total number of transaction cards processed and (2) the number of transaction cards that were unacceptable for processing. These totals can then be used in step 3.

Balancing to Controls

Control balancing, or *balancing to controls,* is common to all business data processing, whether or not a computer is used. The idea is to compare a control total accumulated at the start of a job with a total accumulated later on. If the totals agree, it is at least some assurance that the processing up to that point has been done accurately.

In figure 2-15, for example, a control total is taken during the keypunch and verify step. This may simply be a count of the number of transaction cards for the day. Then if the control totals printed during the editing run agree with the earlier control totals, it is proof that no cards have been lost during transfer from the keypunch department to the computer system. Since all data has been verified, it is also assurance that the update and billing run should take place without error.

After the update and billing run, control balancing is done again (step 5). Here, control totals accumulated during billing are compared with the earlier control totals. Specifically, the total number of invoices printed can be compared with the total number of source documents entered for keypunching. If these numbers agree, the invoices and shipping orders can be released to the accounts-receivable and shipping departments. Otherwise, the output documents are held until the cause of the imbalance has been discovered.

CONCLUSION

The system just described is still rather simplified. Invoices are rarely as cleancut as the one shown. In actual practice, billing procedures must provide for freight charges, multiple shipping addresses, and so on. Similarly, customer and inventory master records are likely to require additional fields so that they are acceptable for other accounts receivable and inventory runs.

The point of this topic, however, is to give you some insight into how computers are used and controlled within an EDP system. As a result, even though the system desribed was simplified, it still gives a basis for understanding systems flow. So now let's draw some conclusions.

First, in any EDP system there is a phase called *data preparation*. Here, source data is converted into a machine-readable form. In most cases, this means punching and verifying cards, but, as you will see in chapter 15, there are a number of alternatives to keypunching that are becoming more and more popular in recent years.

Second, every EDP system requires files. These can be card files, tape files, or direct-access (disk) files. A *master file* consists of records that contain semipermanent information, such as a customer's name and address or an inventory item's description and unit price. In contrast, a *transaction file* consists of records that contain daily data, such as sales data in a billing application or hours worked in a payroll application.

The data in the files is determined by what documents are to be prepared by the system. In brief, the computer can only print documents based on the data provided to it by available input files. Thus the transaction card must contain the customer order number if it is to be printed on the invoice; the inventory record must contain item description and unit price if it is to be printed on the invoice; and the customer record must contain address and salesman number if it is to be printed on the invoice.

Furthermore, the master records are designed so that they contain all the data necessary for all the runs that they are going to be involved in. For instance, since the customer record is going to be used for statement preparation and management information later on, it contains sales-this-month, sales-this-year-to-date, and open-item fields. As a result, statements and an aged trial balance can be prepared as described by the system chart in figure 2-16. The statement will consist of customer name and address plus a listing of the open items. The aged trial balance will contain customer name, plus sales this month (current charges), plus the amounts owed over 30, 60, and 90 days. Since the open-item fields give both invoice date and amount, the computer can determine the-age of each invoice.

Third, balancing to controls is an important part of any EDP system. It protects against errors in data preparation—as well as programming and operational errors. It does not, however, ensure that a system is error free (no system is).

How could errors creep into the system just described? The primary way is in the data-preparation phase. If the source documents themselves are inaccurate—say an order clerk has recorded a quantity of 21 when he or she meant 12—the billing system in figure 2-15 will never catch the error. Similarly, it is possible that both the keypunch and verifier operators misread a slightly illegible character on the source document in the same way—say a 3 when it should have been an 8—with a resulting

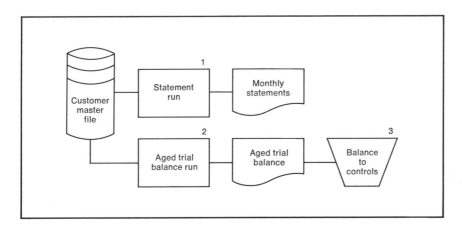

FIGURE 2-16   System flowchart for the preparation of statements and an aged
trial balance

error in the punched card. And it is possible that by pure chance the keypunch operator and verifier operator will make the same mistake on the same card column, although this type of error is rare.

A second source of errors is in programming. Although all programs are tested before they are actually used, a programming error is always a possibility. In fact, some classic blunders have resulted from programming errors. When one state's computer sent $67,000 to welfare recipients no longer eligible for benefits, it was due to a programming error. The program failed to test correctly for the last date on which recipients were eligible for benefits. Although balancing to controls will catch some programming errors, it won't catch them all.

SUMMARY

1. A system flowchart is one of the tools of system design. It symbolically illustrates what takes place within a system.

2. In most systems, keypunching and verifying are part of the data preparation phase of system flow. Once verified, the card file can be read and processed by the computer system at relatively high speeds.

3. All systems require files, both master and transaction files. The data in these files is based on the output requirements of the system.

4. Balancing to controls is a technique that assures the accuracy of an EDP system. It is not foolproof, however, and errors can still enter a system, primarily through data preparation and occasionally through programming.

TERMINOLOGY

system flowchart	update a record
keypunch	editing run
source document	control balancing
verifier	balancing to controls
column in a card	data preparation
computer run	master file
field in a record	transaction file

QUESTIONS

1. Suppose the inventory application requires a daily listing of the items to be reordered (those in which on hand plus on order has fallen below the reorder point). Could this report be prepared from the inventory master file described in figure 2-13? If not, why not? And if so, how?

2. Suppose a sales-analysis application requires a monthly report of sales by customer. This report consists of customer name, sales for the month, year-to-date sales, last year-to-date sales, and the difference

between this year-to-date and last year-to-date amounts. Could this report be prepared from the customer master file described in figure 1-18? If not, why not? And if so, how?

3. Based on the information you have thus far, what is the most likely way errors could creep into the aged trial balance prepared by the system in figure 2-16?

4. Which do you think would be faster: a manual billing system consisting of clerks, calculators, and typewriters, or the EDP system described by the chart in figure 2-15? When speaking of speed, we mean the time that elapses from the moment the customer's order is received until the time the shipping order reaches the shipping department and the invoice reaches the mailing room. Defend your choice.

3 AN INTRODUCTION TO SYSTEMS ANALYSIS AND DESIGN

Now that you have been introduced to hardware, applications, and systems flow, you are ready to learn more about the process of systems analysis and design. As a result, topic 1 of this chapter describes the ten phases commonly performed in the development of a system. Topic 2 presents the tools used by the systems analyst during the development of a system. And topic 3 focuses on cost/benefit analysis, a concept that is essential to effective systems development.

When you complete this chapter, the whole field of EDP should begin to make sense to you. You should understand how companies decide to install computer systems in the first place, why most systems cost more to develop than planned, why the process of systems analysis is critical to the success of any data-processing system.

TOPIC 1
THE PROCESS OF
SYSTEM
DEVELOPMENT

In the field of data processing, the word *system* has several different uses. *The system* can refer to an electronic hardware system (the computer system), a software system (a system of interrelated programs), or a DP system (one that consists of hardware, software, people, and procedures). In the context of systems design and analysis, the third use is the most common; that is, a DP system as opposed to a hardware or software system.

When we speak of *system development,* we mean the development of a DP system. This can be a relatively small task such as modifying a payroll system so that it will handle hourly as well as salaried employees. Or it can be a huge project such as replacing a manual system for billing, inventory, and accounts receivable with a computerized system.

In all cases, however, system development takes place in phases as summarized in figure 3-1. The ten specific phases shown on the left of this figure can be summarized into the five general phases shown on the right. Although some system development projects may not require the ten specific steps, all projects should include definition, analysis, design, implementation, and evaluation.

Problem Definition

In general, system projects are started in response to some problem. For instance, a marketing manager may complain: "Our customers say they need faster delivery. They're losing business because they run out of stock. And that hurts us too."

Specific Phases in System Development	General Phases
1. Problem definition	Definition
2. Data gathering 3. Creation of alternatives 4. Determining feasibility 5. Systems proposal	Analysis
6. Equipment evaluation and selection (if any) 7. System design	Design
8. Program development 9. System implementation and conversion	Implementation
10. System review and followup	Evaluation

FIGURE 3-1   The process of system development

Or a collections manager may say: "Our monthly statements are full of errors. That's why we get so many calls from customers, and that's why my people spend so much time spinning their wheels."

Or a financial manager may declare: "We have too much money tied up in inventory. If we could cut our inventories, maybe then we'd have some money for expansion."

Any of these problems may lead to a systems study that will in turn lead to a system modification or a new system. But note that none of these problem definitions originated in the systems department. Although a systems department may have a task force that seeks out problem areas within a company, new projects often start because of requests from other departments.

A problem may be simple or complex. It may involve some minor part (a *subsystem*) of a larger system. (For instance, the problem of inaccurate statements involves a subsystem of the accounts-receivable system.) Or it may involve a complete reorganization of some major company system (reducing inventories may be that type of problem).

In any event, it is important to identify the objectives of a systems project during the problem-definition phase. For example, the objective for the shipping-delay problem might be stated as: "To reduce the elapsed time between receipt of order and actual shipment to 24 hours or less." On the other hand, the initial objective for a more complex problem like the inventory one may be more tentative: "To determine whether it is feasible to reduce our inventories by 10 percent without reducing customer service."

In the first case, it is assumed that the problem can be solved, so the process of system development is likely to be followed to its conclusion—a systems change. In the second case, a preliminary study is indicated. As a result, only the first four specific phases shown in figure 3-1 may be completed. Then, if the possibility of inventory reduction seems feasible, a more refined objective may be stated and a more detailed systems project started.

Data Gathering

Data gathering refers to the collection of information pertinent to the systems project. In other words, the systems analyst learns more about the problem or application that is under study. If the analyst isn't familiar with the application, he or she will do general research on the application as well as specific research as to how the company handles the application.

To get information, the analyst may read books or reports, go through files, collect forms for later analysis, or interview people. Interviewing is an important skill for the analyst who may interview managers, workers, and sometimes even customers. Often, some of the most important information comes from the low-level employees (the workers). For instance, a receivables clerk may be able to give you information about current practices that even the collections manager may not be aware of.

As information is collected, the analyst will document the important aspects so it can be referred to later on. For this purpose, he or she may use forms, charts, or tables. (In topic 2, these tools of analysis will be described in detail.)

Creation of Alternatives

Once the analyst has a clear idea of the problem, he or she begins to create some possible solutions. In actual practice, these solutions usually begin to form while the initial research (data gathering) is going on. Then, after completing the research, the analyst chooses the most promising alternatives and develops them.

In order to create sound alternatives, the analyst must have a broad background, must be familiar with the many different types of equipment that can be applied to the problem, and must be familiar with the various types of procedures that can be used. From this background, he or she can develop an alternative that is similar to one that some other company or group is using or can create a special or unique solution to his or her company's problem.

It is important to realize that the solutions at this stage are not developed in detail. For instance, although the purchase of new equipment may be indicated in one or more alternatives, it is done in general terms. Then specific purchases can be made later on, in conjunction with the general specifications given here. Similarly, the procedures developed here aren't specific. Although a general logic flow is created for each alternative, specific steps will be determined during the systems-design phase.

Unless the problem is quite limited, analysts should try to develop more than one alternative. This will give them the freedom to explore imaginative solutions rather than taking only the quick and obvious one. It will also give management a broader perspective on the range of available solutions.

Determining Feasibility

In brief, determining feasibility means deciding whether or not a proposed solution will work. A *feasibility study* is one that tries to determine whether a solution will work. More specifically, a feasibility study tries to answer questions like these:

1. Does the proposed system meet the objectives identified in the problem-definition phase?
2. What additional resources (men or machines) will the new system require? What will it cost to run the new system?
3. What will it cost to implement the new system?
4. What benefits will the new system provide? What value can be applied to each of these benefits?
5. What impact will the new system have on the rest of the company?
6. Is it likely that the new system will work as presented?

After the feasibility of each alternative has been studied, the analyst is likely to focus on the most promising solution. It may then be studied in greater detail (more data gathering) to make sure its basic assumptions are correct. Once the analyst feels comfortable with the conclusions, he or she is likely to make a written feasibility report.

The feasibility report should include information about the primary solution as well as the alternatives. The report can be used as a basis for discussing the proposed solution with management—both systems management and the management of the department that initiated the systems study. Based on these discussions, the solution may be modified or some of the conclusions changed. Once there is general agreement between all levels of management, the analyst is ready to begin the systems proposal.

Systems Proposal

The systems proposal is a written presentation of the proposed system selected by the feasibility study. It usually includes a summary of the problem and the proposed solution. In addition, it will give a schedule for completion of the project, a statement of what personnel are required to complete it, and how the results of the project are to be evaluated. It may also state at what point the systems department will turn over the system to the user departments.

In short, the systems proposal is an agreement between the systems department and all affected departments. After all parties review the initial draft of the proposal, modifications may be made to it. When all parties agree to it, the proposal becomes a guideline for the rest of the systems project.

Equipment Evaluation and Selection

Up to this point, the solution has been stated in somewhat general terms. As mentioned before, some type of equipment may have been indicated by the proposal, but specific purchases are not decided on until after the systems proposal is accepted. At this stage, then, the systems department may contact equipment vendors for information and prices concerning specific machines. When a systems proposal involves major equipment purchases, this phase of system development can be a major project in itself.

If the machines can be purchased, leased, or rented at a price that stays within the limits stated in the systems proposal, the project continues as proposed. Otherwise the analyst may be forced to return to the feasibility and systems proposal phases with the unexpected cost data. A good analyst, however, will check prices and capabilities with several vendors during the feasibility analysis to make sure that the cost projections are reasonable. He or she will not only consider the costs at the time of the study but most likely price increases as well.

Systems Design

Up to the time of the systems proposal, analysts have concerned themselves with the *logical design* of the system. Although they have decided what type of equipment should be used, they haven't decided what specific machines should be purchased. Furthermore, they haven't decided what specific procedures should be followed. Instead, they concentrate on general systems flow, the cost of the system, and overall feasibility.

After the systems proposal is agreed to, analysts or systems designers concern themselves with the *physical design* of the system. Here, they create detailed specifications for every aspect of the system. This includes form design, file organization, procedural steps, and so on. If a computer system is to be used, they will chart the steps required for all phases of processing.

Depending on department standards, systems designers may also prepare detailed program specifications for each program required by the new system. These specifications can be passed to the programming department for program development. Systems designers will also prepare a detailed implementation schedule and plan for all stages of implementation.

Program Development

Program development means creating the programs that are required for the new system. This includes testing them to make sure they work as specified. (Program development is covered in more detail in chapter 4.)

System Implementation and Conversion

Implementing a system requires preparation in several areas besides program development. For instance, if new clerical procedures are to be used, the affected personnel must be trained. If new equipment is going to be used, the area that will house the equipment must be prepared. And new equipment will always mean special training for the operators.

In addition, if files are changed from their present to a new form, the data in these files must be converted. This is called *file conversion*. If, for example, a manual file is to be changed to a punched-card file, the relevant data must be keypunched. Similarly, if a card file is going to be converted to a disk file, a program must be written that reads the data from the cards and writes it on disk.

After the people have been trained, the equipment has been installed, and the files have been converted, a *system test* is normally run. This is a test on recent or current data to make sure that the system actually works as intended. If it does, it is time to convert from the old system to the new.

Because *conversion* from one system to another is always somewhat risky, it is common to run both the old and the new systems for a short period after installing the new one. This is referred to as *parallel operation*. Then, if the new system fails because of some unexpected problem, the old one can take over. This is an expensive form of conversion, however, because you double your system cost until the conversion period ends.

In contrast, the old system is dropped and the new one is adopted on the same day when the *direct conversion* method is used. This is the least expensive method but the most risky. It is commonly used when the new system isn't very complex, and the application isn't too critical to the successful operation of the company. (In some cases, there is no choice but to use this method, since the old equipment may no longer be available.)

System Review and Follow-up

After a system has been implemented, it is tempting to forget about it and go on to new problems. However, most systems need follow-up, and all systems should be reviewed.

Follow-up refers to the need for making adjustments to a system. Although analysts try to think of everything when they design a system, they rarely do. As a result, there are usually aspects of the system that can be improved: a form that can be designed for greater efficiency, a procedural step that can be removed because it's unnecessary, or what have you. Sometimes, a system will have some serious shortcomings that must be corrected right away.

The purpose of the review is to determine whether or not the project was successful. Does the system meet the original objectives? Does it perform within the stated budget and performance requirements? Was the project completed on time and within the systems budget? Are there ways in which the new system can be improved?

Reviews like this help improve the procedures for future systems projects. When the follow-up and review period is over and the user department indicates that it accepts the new system, the system development project is officially finished.

DISCUSSION

Although the ten phases in system development are described separately in this topic, they are by no means done one step at a time, as might be implied. Instead there is a continual movement back and forth from one phase to another. For instance, the analyst may come upon data during the data gathering phase that causes him or her to change the objectives of the project. Similarly, if none of the alternatives seems feasible during the feasibility study, the analyst may go back to create new alternatives. Finally, problems encountered during systems design may cause changes in the systems proposal, and problems encountered during implementation may cause changes in the systems design.

You should also be aware that the phases in this topic have been described as they should be done, not necessarily as they are done. In actual practice, only the larger, more sophisticated companies follow formal systems procedures as described above. In many companies, systems development is completely haphazard. Even though systems development may have an enormous effect on the success of a company, many small firms not only do not have a systems department, but they don't even have anyone assigned to systems considerations.

For instance, it was common in the 1960s for representatives of some computer manufacturers to run a systems study for a company. The manufacturer's representative would then make recommendations for

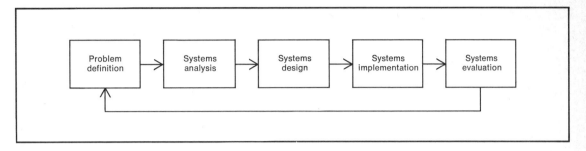

FIGURE 3-2   The continuing nature of system development

systems changes (that always included the installation of some of the manufacturer's equipment). If the company's management accepted the manufacturer's proposal, the manufacturer's representative would guide the design and implementation of the new system.

Because of the natural bias in a situation like this, the best possible system solution was rarely installed. Problem definition and final evaluation were often neglected or glossed over. And there was usually little choice of alternatives in the manufacturer's proposal.

Now, in the 1970s, the system-development process still leaves much room for improvement. In all but a few exceptional user companies, many of the stages of development are done ineffectively. Perhaps the major difficulty, though, is in estimating the cost of implementing the new system, the time required to implement the new system and the cost required to run it once it is implemented. Because the error is usually on the low side, many system projects (perhaps most) end up over budget and behind schedule. And the new system costs far more than expected, even if it does provide the anticipated benefits.

In closing, system development should be thought of as a continual process. No system is ever perfect. It can always be improved. As a result, figure 3-2 is a good representation of the systems process. After problem definition, systems analysis, systems design, and systems implementation, evaluation can lead back to another problem definition. Thus the systems process starts again.

SUMMARY

The process of system development takes place in stages. After problem definition, the systems analysis phase attempts to develop a logical system design for the problem solution. Then, during the systems design phase a physical systems design is developed. After this physical system is implemented, it is evaluated based on the objectives set in the problem definition phase.

TERMINOLOGY

system
system development
subsystem
feasibility study
logical system design
physical system design

file conversion
system test
system conversion
parallel operation
direct conversion

QUESTIONS

1. Sometimes a system doesn't provide the benefits it was supposed to, and a special study is started to find out why. Occasionally, the special study may conclude that the new system is "rotten to the core." What do you suppose this means, and where in the process of system development do you suppose the major mistakes were made?

2. In general, the physical system that is developed during systems design will work and will be implemented. Unfortunately, this doesn't mean that the system will be a success. Why?

TOPIC 2
THE TOOLS OF THE SYSTEMS ANALYST

A *systems analyst* is a person who carries out the tasks required by a system development project. As systems analysts work their way through the various phases of system development, they need to be organized. When they receive new information, they must record it in a way that they can easily review. As they begin to create alternatives, they must record them in a way that can be easily explained and transmitted to other people.

Over the years a number of ways have been developed to record systems information in a manageable form. For instance, record layout forms and print charts have been developed to describe the exact formats of computer input and output. Grid charts and decision tables are often used to summarize relationships that are hard to describe or visualize. And system flowcharts are used to visually present the characteristics of a logical or physical system design.

Record Layout Forms

Record layout forms are used to show the exact format of card, tape, or direct-access records. For instance, the multiple-card layout form in figure 3-3 gives the format of a transaction card that might be used in a billing application. Although the form can be used to describe the layouts for up to six different cards, only one is described in this example. By

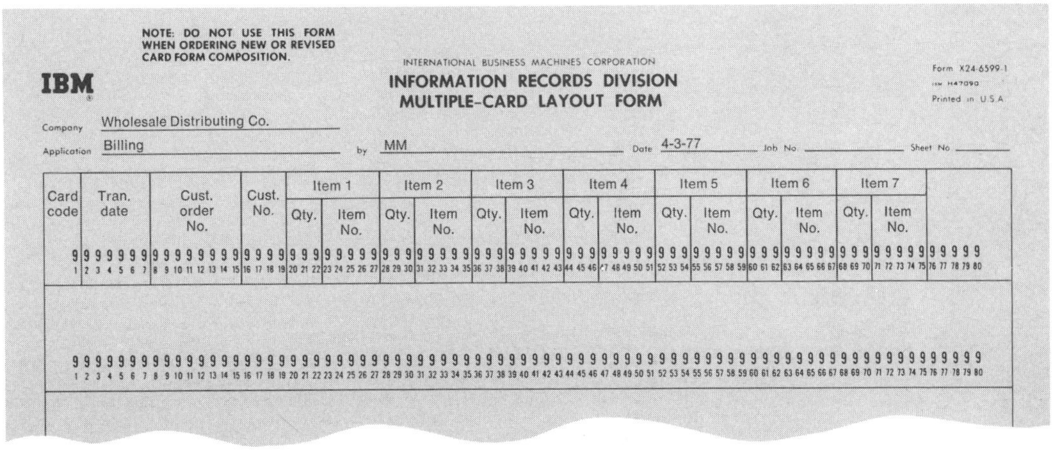

NOTE: DO NOT USE THIS FORM WHEN ORDERING NEW OR REVISED CARD FORM COMPOSITION.

IBM

INTERNATIONAL BUSINESS MACHINES CORPORATION
INFORMATION RECORDS DIVISION
MULTIPLE-CARD LAYOUT FORM

Form X24-6599-1
Printed in U.S.A.

Company Wholesale Distributing Co.
Application Billing by MM Date 4-3-77 Job No. Sheet No.

Card code	Tran. date	Cust. order No.	Cust. No.	Item 1 Qty.	Item 1 Item No.	Item 2 Qty.	Item 2 Item No.	Item 3 Qty.	Item 3 Item No.	Item 4 Qty.	Item 4 Item No.	Item 5 Qty.	Item 5 Item No.	Item 6 Qty.	Item 6 Item No.	Item 7 Qty.	Item 7 Item No.	
1	2–7	8–15	16–19	20–22	23–27	28–30	31–35	36–38	39–43	44–46	47–51	52–54	55–59	60–62	63–67	68–70	71–75	76–80

FIGURE 3-3 A transaction card format described on a multiple-card layout form

studying this form, you can see that the card code is stored in column 1, the transaction date is stored in columns 2-7, the customer order number in columns 8-15, and so on.

A more general record layout form is shown in figure 3-4. Here a master accounts receivable record is described. This record could be stored on tape or a direct-access device. The form could also be used to give the format of a punched card. If you study the form in figure 3-4, you can see that the entire accounts-receivable record is 220 storage positions long. A delete code is stored in relative position 1, customer number is stored in relative positions 2-5, customer name in relative positions 6-27, and so on. The last 18 positions are unused so that they can accomodate future changes to the master records. There are many different kinds of record layout forms. All, however, simply state the precise format of one or more records. As a result, they should be self-explanatory.

Systems analysts may use record layout forms as they design the proposed system. On the other hand, if the system project concerns a system that already exists, they may get copies of the existing record layouts during data gathering. Then, they may be able to use existing records for their system problems or may be called upon to create a new file.

Print Charts

A print chart, like the one in figure 3-5, gives the layout of a printed report or other document. It indicates the print positions to be used for each item of data on the report. It also indicates the headings to be printed. The print chart in figure 3-5 gives the format for an aged trial balance report. This report is supposed to start with a heading in print positions 22-65 that reads AGED TRIAL BALANCE FOR MONTH ENDING XX-XX-XX. The X's indicate where the actual date should be printed. In other words, if the report was for the month of March in the year 1977, the heading would read: AGED TRIAL BALANCE FOR MONTH ENDING 3-31-77.

After the report heading, a number of column headings are shown. Thus, CUST NO, CUSTOMER NAME, CURRENT, and so forth are to be printed over the various columns of data. Beneath these headings, the X's indicate where the actual customer data should be printed. As a result, customer number should print in print positions 1-4 and customer name in positions 7-28. Although ony two lines of customer data are indicated by X's, it is understood that there will be as many customer lines in the report as there are customers with unpaid invoices.

The X's at the bottom of columns headed by CURRENT, OVER 30, OVER 60, and so on, indicate where the final totals should be printed. As a result, this report will show the total amount owed for the current month, the total amount owed over 30 days, etc. The grand total of amounts owed by all customers can then be balanced to daily control sheets to make sure that the report includes all outstanding debts.

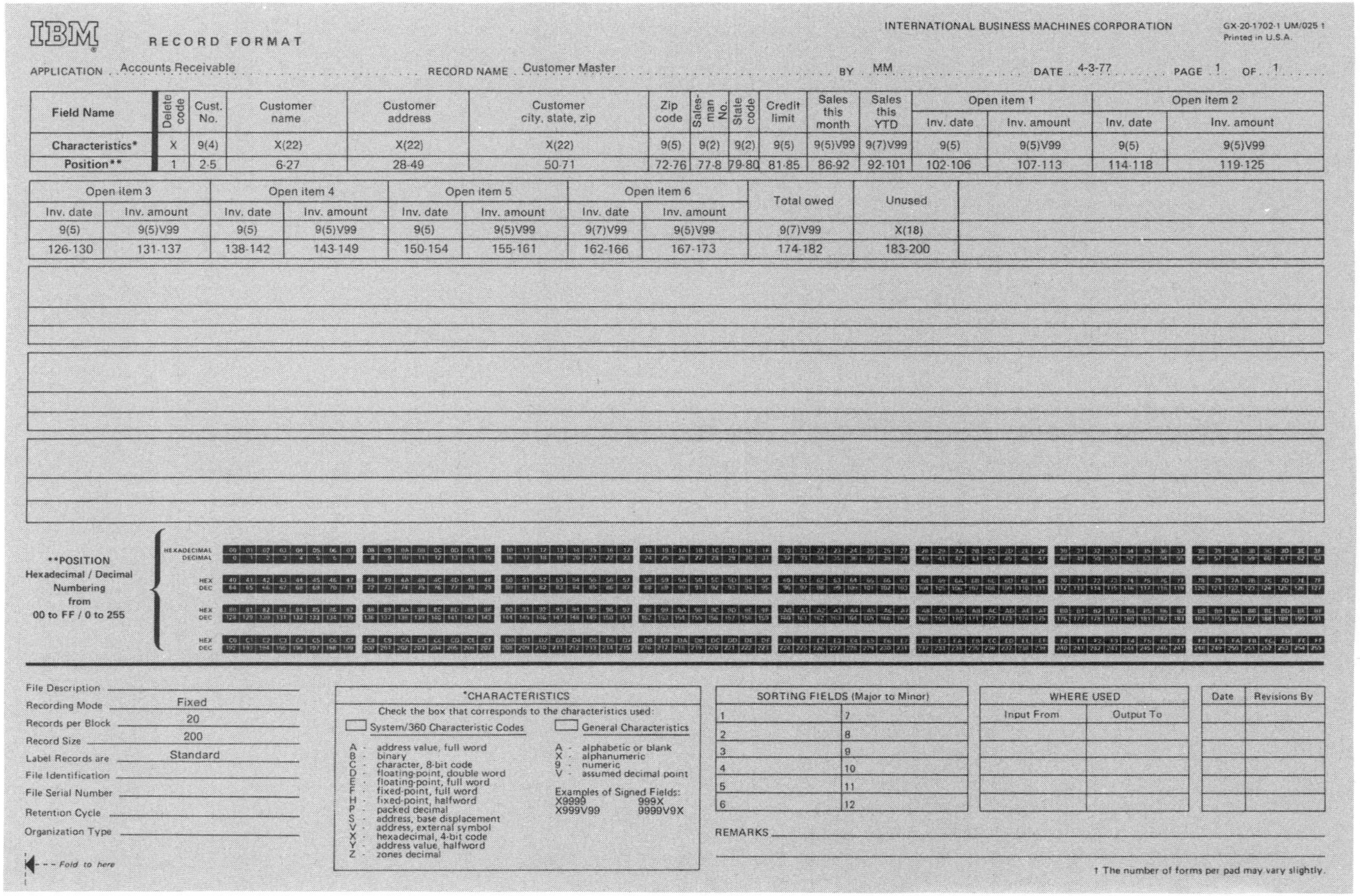

FIGURE 3-4 Customer master record described on record layout form

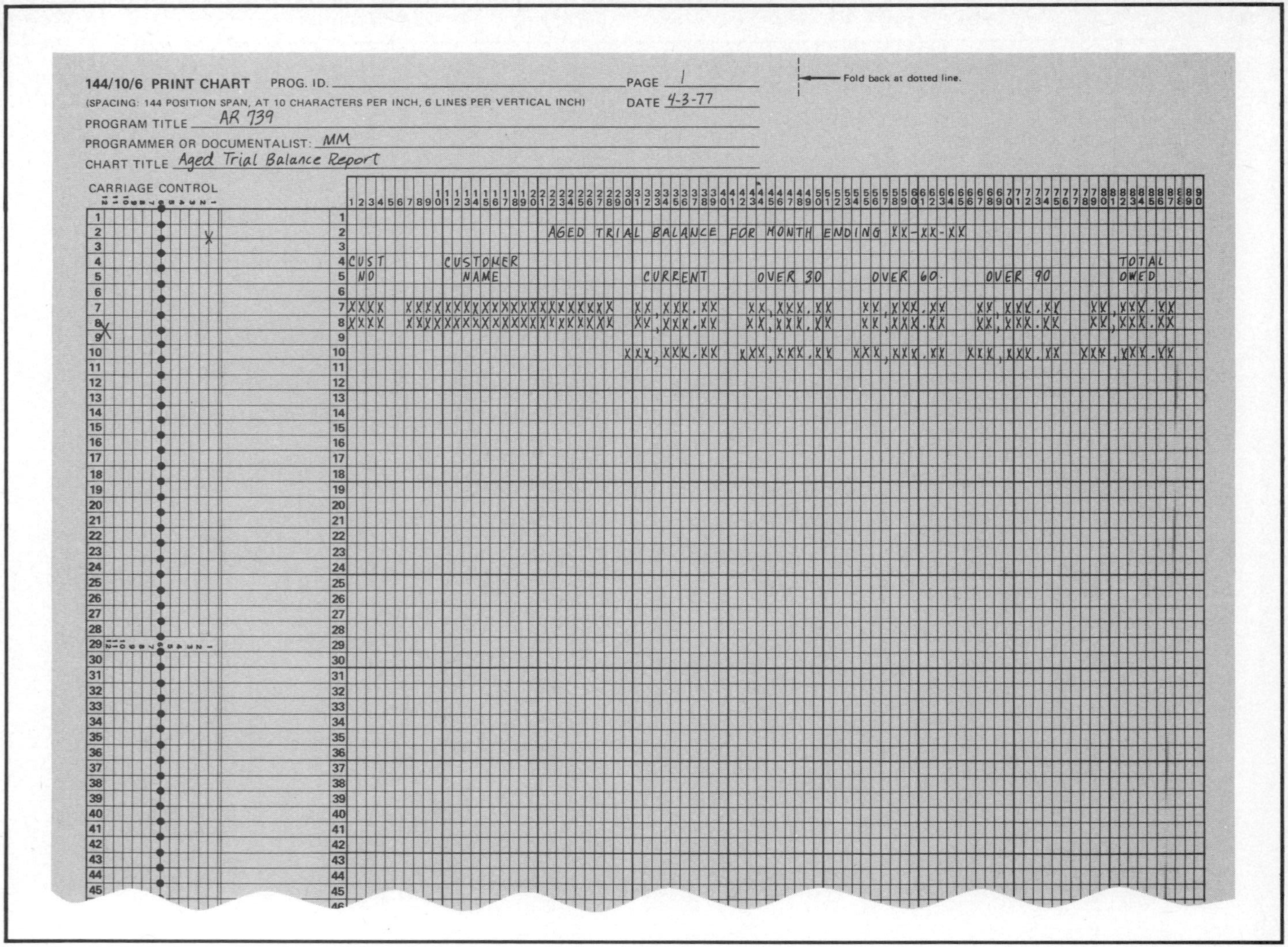

FIGURE 3-5 A print chart for an aged trial balance report

Although the print chart in figure 3-5 shows only 90 print positions from left to right, a complete print chart usually has 132 or more—at least as many as available on the printer being used. A print chart may also show which punches are to be used in the carriage-control tape of the printer as shown on the left of the print chart in figure 3-5. A carriage-control tape is used in some printers to control the movement of the continuous form. In general, a 1-punch in the control tape is used to indicate where the first line on a page should be printed; a 12-punch is used to indicate where the last line on a page should be printed. (Since this is the concern of the programmer, not the analyst, you can forget about the carriage-control portion of the print chart for now.)

In summary, then, a print chart is used to give the format of a document printed by a computer system. X's are used to indicate where variable items of data are to be printed; actual characters are used to show where heading or constant data is to be printed.

Analysts may use print charts in the system-design phase of a project. If so, they will pass the print chart on to the programming department during program development. The programmer assigned to write the program can then use the chart as he or she prepares the program. Analysts may also come into contact with print charts if they are called upon to modify the output of some existing program.

Grid Charts

When the relationships between parts of a system are complex (as they often are), an analyst needs concise summaries. For this purpose, he or she may use a grid chart in one form or another. For instance, the grid chart in figure 3-6 indicates which departments use the documents prepared by the current order writing, billing, and accounts-receivable system. The X's indicate that the sales order is used in the order writing and sales departments; the shipping order in the order writing, shipping, billing, and inventory control departments; and so on. An analyst might use a chart like this to help plan the documents and information flow for the new system.

A grid chart is simply a tabular means of summarizing relationships. Although the one shown in figure 3-6 is done by an artist, they are normally done in a much more informal manner. Unless they are intended for formal presentation, an analyst is likely to draw them freehand on ruled paper.

Decision Tables

A decision table is a tabular summary of the actions to be taken when various combinations of conditions are met. For instance, the decision table in figure 3-7 represents the rules for order approval, based on

Document \ Department	Order writing	Billing	Accounts receivable	Marketing	Shipping	Inventory control
Sales order	X			X		
Shipping order	X	X			X	X
Credit authorization form			X	X		
Invoice		X	X	X		
Delinquent account notice			X	X		
Aged trial balance			X	X		
Monthly statements			X			

FIGURE 3-6   Grid chart showing use of documents by department

various combinations of credit conditions. Here, the Y's mean yes, the N's mean no, and the X's indicate which actions are to be taken.

If you were to put this decision table into words, it would go something like this. Rule 1: If a customer is over his credit limit, has a good or better credit history, and has no unpaid invoice over 60 days old, his order should be approved and then referred to the credit manager. Rule 2: If a customer is over his credit limit, doesn't have a good credit history, and has one or more unpaid invoices over 60 days old, he should be refused credit. From this you can see that it would take some time to cover all eight rules.

Because decision tables are generally easy to follow, they are useful for recording information gathered during research on the old system. They are also useful for summarizing information about the proposed system. In many cases, decision tables are passed on to the programming department for use in program development.

The essential parts of a decision table are shown schematically in figure 3-8. They are the *condition stub,* which describes the conditions, the *action stub,* which describes the possible actions, the *condition entries* (Y or N), and the *action entries* (X's). Each combination of conditions is referred to as a *rule,* so the table in figure 3-8 has eight different rules. To create a decision table, you follow these general steps:

1. List all conditions and actions.
2. Combine actions that give both alternatives for the same condition. For instance, you shouldn't have a condition like "if over credit limit" along with a condition like "if under credit limit." One is enough.

Credit rules for order processing	Decision rules							
	1	2	3	4	5	6	7	8
Conditions								
If over credit limit	Y	Y	Y	Y	N	N	N	N
If credit history is good or better	Y	N	Y	N	Y	N	Y	N
If any invoices are over 60 days old	N	Y	Y	N	N	Y	Y	N
Actions								
Then approve order	X				X			X
Then approve order pending receipt of over 60 day amounts			X			X	X	
Then refer to credit manager			X	X				
Then refuse credit		X		X				

FIGURE 3-7   A decision table that gives the rules for credit authorization

3. Fill in the condition entries (Y or N).
4. Fill in the action entries for each rule with an X.
5. Make sure there are enough rules to cover all possible combinations of conditions. Thus, there should be 4 rules for 2 conditions, 8 rules for 3 conditions, 16 rules for 4 conditions, and so on.
6. If possible, combine rules to simplify the table. This can be done if the action entries for two or more rules are the same and only one set of condition entries differs. For instance, the table in figure 3-7 can be simplified as shown in figure 3-9. Here, the hyphen (-) means that the condition doesn't affect the action (it can be either Y or N).
7. Reorder the table if it will improve clarity.

In some cases, a set of decisions will be so complex that you may want to refer from one table to another. For example, one of the actions of one

Heading	Rule numbers				
Condition stub			Condition entries		
Action stub			Action entries		

FIGURE 3-8   The parts of a decision table

Credit rules for order processing		Decision rules					
		1	2	3	4	5	6
Conditions	If over credit limit	Y	Y	Y	Y	N	N
	If credit history is good or better	Y	N	Y	N	–	–
	If any invoices are over 60 days old	N	Y	Y	N	Y	N
Actions	Then approve order	X					X
	Then approve order pending receipt of over 60 day amounts			X		X	
	Then refer to credit manager			X	X		
	Then refuse credit		X		X		

FIGURE 3-9   A decision table that has combined rules for greater clarity

table may be to follow the rules of a second table. This idea can be carried on so that several tables are interrelated. Remember that the purpose of decision tables is to clarify relationships, so you don't want any one table to become difficult or impossible to follow.

System Flowcharts

In chapter 2 you were introduced to the system flowchart and some of the standard flowcharting symbols. As you may recall, the purpose of the system flowchart is to present symbolically the procedures within a system. To read flowcharts, you start with the symbol in the upper lefthand portion of the chart and continue down and to the right, unless arrowheads indicate movement up or to the left.

Figure 3-10 presents the entire range of symbols you might use when preparing system flowcharts. As you can see, there are specialized symbols for various types of input and output. There are also special symbols for various types of processing. For instance, the inverted triangle indicates that the records from two or more files should be merged; the upright triangle indicates that certain types of records should be selected or extracted from a file. (Although some of these symbols may not mean much to you right now, they will be presented in more detail in chapters where they are applicable.)

As an aid in drawing symbols, an analyst uses a plastic template like the one shown in figure 3-11. By placing a pen or pencil in the symbol to be drawn, the analyst is able to draw a more exact symbol than can be done freehand. Because using the template is somewhat slower than drawing freehand, an analyst is likely to make one or more freehand sketches of a flowchart before using the template to draw a final version.

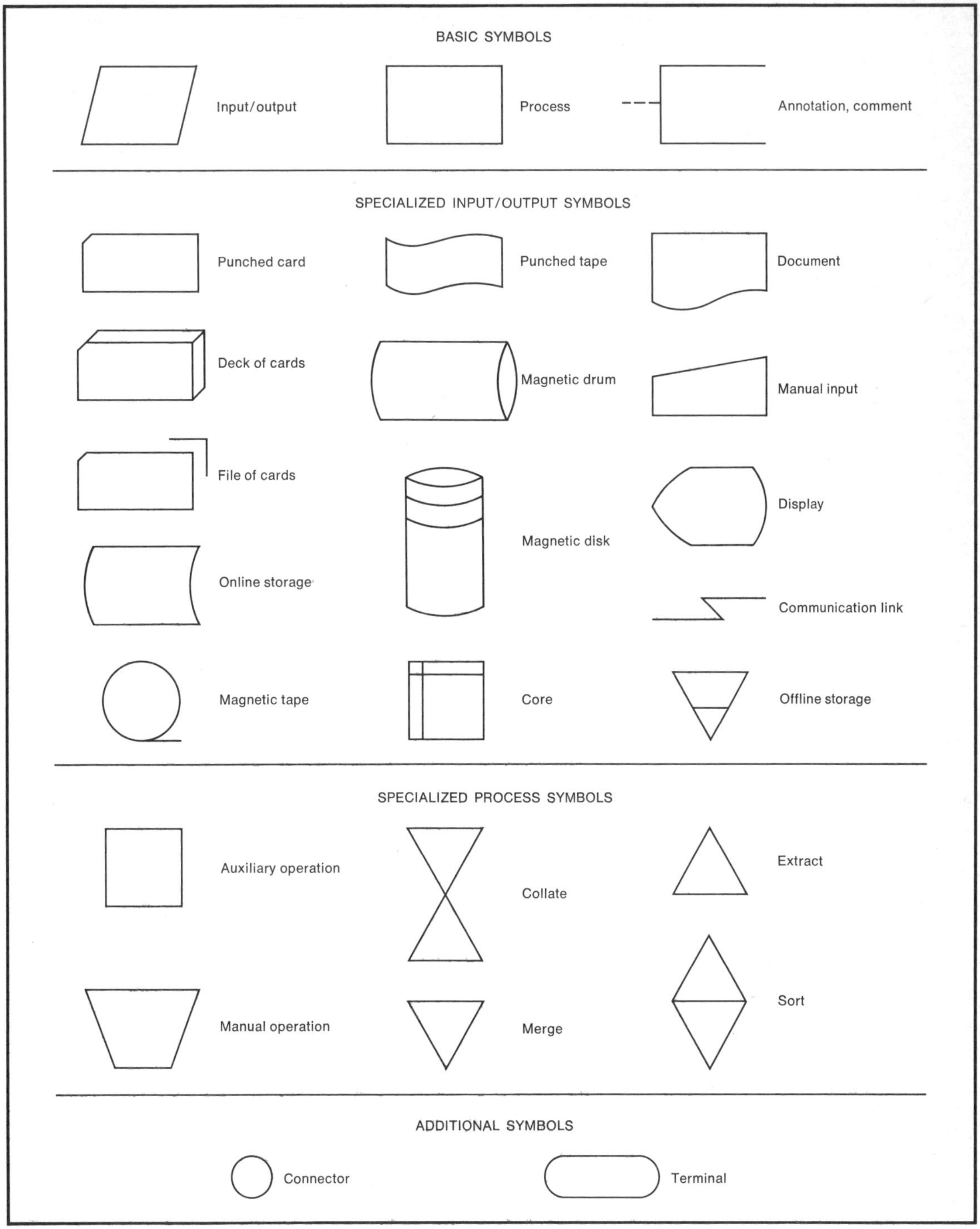

BASIC SYMBOLS

Input/output		Process		Annotation, comment	

SPECIALIZED INPUT/OUTPUT SYMBOLS

Punched card

Punched tape

Document

Deck of cards

Magnetic drum

Manual input

File of cards

Magnetic disk

Display

Online storage

Communication link

Magnetic tape

Core

Offline storage

SPECIALIZED PROCESS SYMBOLS

Auxiliary operation

Collate

Extract

Manual operation

Merge

Sort

ADDITIONAL SYMBOLS

Connector

Terminal

FIGURE 3-10   Standard flowcharting symbols for system flowcharts

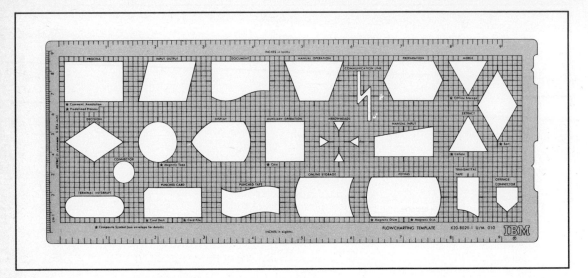

FIGURE 3-11   A flowcharting template

In general, system flowcharts are drawn at two different levels. These are referred to as macro (general) charts and micro (detailed) charts. During systems analysis, when the analyst is concerned with creation of a logical system, he or she will generally use only *macro flowcharts*. For instance, the macro chart in figure 3-12 represents the logical design for a billing system. After step 2, data preparation, the general I/O symbol is used because the analyst doesn't know at this point whether the transaction file will be on cards, tape, or disk (there are data preparation devices that record data on tape or disk rather than in punched cards, as you will discover in chapter 15). Similarly, in step 3, the more general online storage symbol is used for the inventory and customer file, because the analyst doesn't know whether the files will be on tape, disk, or some other direct-access device.

Micro charts are used during system design when every procedural step must be described in detail. Figure 3-13, for instance, might be the micro system chart for the logical system described in figure 3-12. Here, all aspects of the system are accounted for. As you can see, cards are punched in the data-preparation phase. And step 3 in the macro chart becomes three different programs in the micro chart—programs that use both tape and disk I/O.

Although you may not understand all that this flowchart represents right now, it will become clear by the time you finish section 2 of this book. For now, please notice how the offline storage symbol is used to indicate the storage of cards and magnetic tapes after they have been used for transaction data. Also notice how the notation symbol is used in two places to give explanatory information.

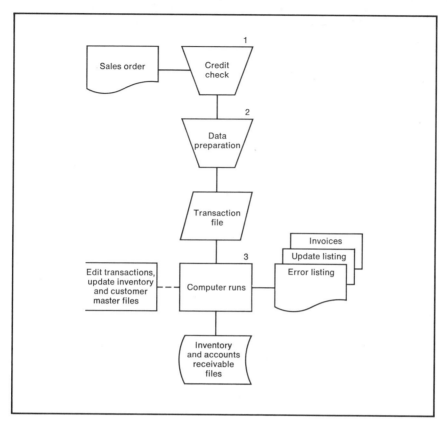

FIGURE 3-12   A macro systems flowchart for a billing application

1. Because of the complexity of most systems, an analyst must stay organized. That's why he or she uses tools like record layout forms, print charts, grid charts, decision tables, and system flowcharts.

2. An analyst prepares system flowcharts at two levels during system development. A macro flowchart is used during systems analysis to describe the logical design of a system; a micro flowchart is used during systems design to describe the physical design of the system.

systems analyst
record layout form
print chart
grid chart
decision table
  condition stub
  action stub

condition entry
action entry
rule
system flowchart
  macro flowchart
  micro flowchart

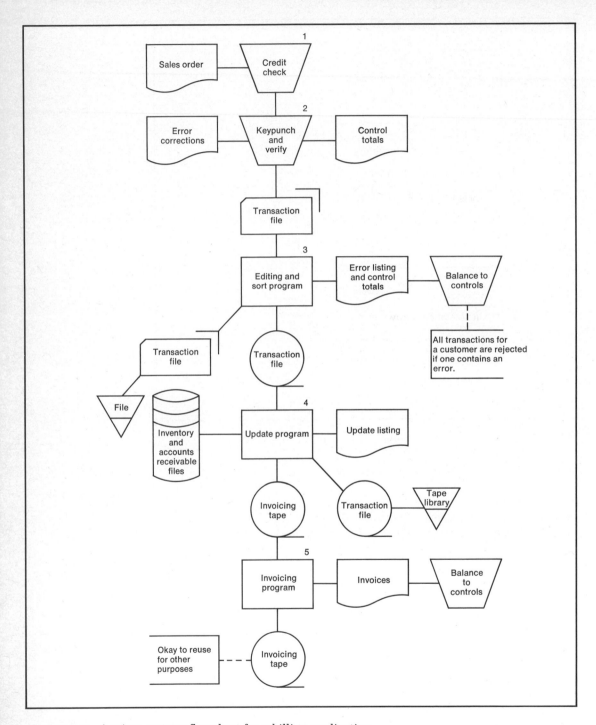

FIGURE 3-13 A micro systems flowchart for a billing application

QUESTIONS

1. In your own words, state rule 3 as presented by the decision table in figure 3-9. Now state rule 4.

2. In general terms, describe what is happening at each step of the system in figure 3-13.

TOPIC 3
COST/BENEFIT
ANALYSIS

Perhaps the most critical phase in the process of system development is determining feasibility. Here, the costs and benefits of the proposed systems must be compared with those of the existing system. Based on this analysis, called *cost/benefit analysis,* the study team decides whether or not one of the proposed systems should be implemented.

This is a critical phase, because there are many possibilities for error. Determining costs and evaluating benefits is an inexact process that relies heavily on estimates. And determining feasibility based on this inexact cost and benefit data is a task that requires experience—as well as wisdom.

In actual practice, cost/benefit analysis takes place at several stages of the systems project. During the feasibility study, before detailed systems design, the cost and benefit values may be rough approximations. If the system looks promising based on this analysis and the detailed systems design is done, a more detailed cost/benefit analysis may take place. Here, the analyst will have more complete data so his or her results should be more precise. If this analysis conflicts with the first analysis, the project may require another feasibility study based on the new results.

DETERMINING COSTS

In any system-development project, there are two types of costs. Development costs are those costs required to design and implement the system; they are one-time costs. Operating costs are those costs required to run the system once system conversion has taken place.

Development Costs

Development costs include the expenses of the systems staff for design and implementation. They include the expenses of the programming staff for program development and file conversion and the expenses for keypunching and computer time as required for program development, file conversion, and parallel operation. They may also include expenses from other departments if they are involved in the project. For instance, if the order department requires retraining, their costs must be included. Or if the user department helps in organizing data for file conversion, that cost must be included.

Development costs include personnel, equipment, and supplies. For example, the chart in figure 3-14 summarizes the development expenses

Project tasks	Systems analysis	Programming	Keypunch	Computer	Supplies	User personnel	Total
Systems design	$ 9,500.						$ 9,500.
Programming development		$7,500.	$ 800.	$2,500.			$10,800.
Operational procedures	$ 1,200.		$1,200.		$1,200.	$ 840.	$ 4,440.
File conversion	$ 1,000.	$ 900.		$ 700.		$1,200.	$ 3,800.
Training	$ 2,000.					$1,500.	$ 3,500.
Parallel operation			$ 300.	$2,000.		$ 500.	$ 2,800.
Final Total	$13,700.	$8,400.	$2,300.	$5,200.	$1,200.	$4,040.	$34,840.

FIGURE 3-14   Development cost summary

for a relatively small systems project. As you can see, the major equipment cost is computer time for program development, file conversion, and parallel operation. Note also that user personnel is involved in creating operational procedures, file conversion, training, and parallel operation.

Development costs are usually difficult to determine, because they are based on estimates of how long it will take to complete the project, how many men are required for the project, and so forth. If the project is complex and the company has no experience with similar projects, the estimated costs may be more of a guess than anything else (a guesstimate). Because of human nature, both estimates and guesstimates tend to be on the low side when the systems staff strongly supports a project, so it is common for a project to end up costing more than expected.

To illustrate, consider what is involved in estimating the cost required for program development in a project that requires several new programs. Here, the cost required to develop each program will vary depending on the length of the program, the complexity of the program, and the ability of the programmer assigned to the job. But at the time of the initial feasibility study, the analyst may not know how many programs are going to be required, may have only a hazy notion of how complex these programs will turn out to be, and will most likely not know who is going to write the programs.

Even after the detailed systems design has been completed, programming estimates are imprecise. One programmer may be able to write a program several times faster than another can. New employees may be assigned to a project, so no past records of their programming speeds exist. And if a new computer system with new programming languages is being installed, it may slow down the entire programming staff. The best estimates are made when a company has considerable data on the programming speeds of its staff over a wide range of projects.

Because of these problems in estimating development costs, estimates are usually done at three levels: the most likely development cost, the minimum cost likely to be achieved, and the maximum cost likely to be experienced. During feasibility analysis, all three costs are considered. In actual practice, the cost of system development is so difficult to estimate that it is not uncommon for development costs to go beyond the maximum cost projection.

Operating Costs

Operating costs, on the other hand, are usually easier to estimate. In general, an analyst estimates the requirements of the new system (personnel, equipment, supplies, and overhead) based on the volumes of data being processed by the current system. He or she is likely to use the system flowchart for the proposed system as a guideline so that nothing is omitted.

For example, if a company prints 3000 payroll checks per month, analysts can estimate keypunch requirements and translate this into personnel as well as equipment costs (keypunch and verifier). Similarly, they can attribute costs to all other steps in the systems flowchart. Finally, they can estimate general costs like the one for supplies and overhead.

When a system is complex, however, operating costs also can be difficult to determine. If operating procedures are unknown at the time of the feasability study, how do you know how many transactions an operator can process in an hour? Or if the volume of transactions is unknown (perhaps the new system offers a capability that wasn't offered by the old system), how do you estimate the workload?

Because of the difficulties in estimating operating costs, three levels of estimates are usually made—just as they are for development costs. For instance, the chart in figure 3-15 brackets the expected operation costs by

Year	Present system	Alternative system		
		Lowest possible estimate	Most likely estimate	Highest possible estimate
1	562,971	391,627	426,793	464,456
2	619,268	411,209	452,400	501,612
3	681,695	431,769	479,544	541,741
4	749,314	453,357	508,317	585,080
5	824,245	522,668	538,816	631,886
Total	3,437,493	2,210,630	2,405,870	2,724,775

FIGURE 3-15   Operating cost summary

using "most likely," "lowest possible," and "highest possible" estimates. Note also that estimates are given over a period of five years, so increases in the volume of data are considered. Regardless of these precautions, however, some enormous mistakes have been made in actual system projects.

EVALUATING BENEFITS

All systems development is intended to improve the operations or effectiveness of a company. In a profit-making organization, new systems are intended to contribute to profits—either by cutting costs or increasing sales. In short, the new system is supposed to provide benefits that compensate for its development cost.

Traditionally, one of the major benefits of a new system was a reduction in operating costs. For instance, a small company might invest $20,000 in a new payroll system if it would lower the cost of preparing the payroll and associated documents by $1000 per month. At that rate, the development cost would be paid for in less than two years.

Unfortunately, the possibilities for reducing operating costs are limited. In many cases, a new system can make a greater contribution to profits by providing other benefits. For instance, the major benefit of an inventory control system may be reduced inventory investment or increased service level. And the major benefit of an accounts-receivable system may be a lower volume of bad debts. Although these benefits are more difficult to evaluate than reduced operating costs, often they are more significant.

In any event, during the feasibility study, the systems analyst must list all possible benefits of the proposed systems and compare them with those of the existing system. For instance, figure 3-16 lists the benefits of a proposed billing and accounts receivable system. After making the list, the analyst tries to determine the effect of each benefit on the company and tries to assign a monetary value to each benefit.

As a guideline for listing benefits, you may want to consider these characteristics of the proposed system: (1) the speed of document preparation, (2) the accuracy of the documents, (3) the quality of the management information provided by the system, (4) the operating cost of the system, and (5) any intangible benefits. In figure 3-16, for example, the analyst has listed three benefits relating to speed, two related to accuracy, five related to management information, and two intangibles. Since this proposed system costs more than the existing system, he hasn't listed reduced operating cost as a benefit.

When it comes to management information, both speed and accuracy affect its quality. A report that represents an accounting period just completed is certainly more valuable than one that is three months old. And accuracy in management reporting speaks for itself.

Benefit	Effect on	Monetary value
Accuracy:		
1. Error reduction in billing from one error per 100 invoices to one per 500 invoices	Customer service	?
2. Error reduction in monthly statements from one error per 500 statements to one per 1000	Customer service	?
3. No discrepancy between book balance and statement balance at month end	Accounting efficiency	?
Speed:		
4. Bills sent out on same day as shipment vs. a seven day billing delay	Accounts receivable	10% of $100,000, or $10,000 per year
5. Statements sent out one day after period closes vs. a seven day delay	Accounts receivable	?
Information:		
6. Improved accuracy on management reports	Management	?
7. Management reports delivered within two days after close of accounting period	Management	?
8. New level of exception reporting	Management	?
9. Over 60 delinquent lists prepared for each salesman within two days after accounting period closes	Accounts receivable	?
10. Bad credit risks reported daily on an exception basis so their orders will not be shipped	Bad debt	20% of $20,000, or $4,000 per year
Intangibles:		
11. Improved employee morale	Employee turnover	?
12. Increased sales due to better customer service	Sales	?

FIGURE 3-16   Benefit evaluation for a billing and accounts-receivable system

When evaluating management information, the concept of *management-by-exception* (or *exception reporting*) must also be considered. The idea here is that a manager doesn't need to know about the conditions that don't require attention; he or she needs to know only about the exceptional conditions. The credit manager needs to know which customers are potential bad debts. The inventory control manager needs to know which items of inventory can have lower reorder points, thus reducing the inventory levels. The sales manager needs to know which salespeople are no longer producing. When a system does a good job of exception reporting, the managers should become more effective.

As for *intangible benefits,* these are benefits that are assumed to exist but can't be proven. For instance, studies of attitudes have shown that employees tend to be more satsified with their work when their department runs efficiently. If many customers are calling in because their invoices or statements are incorrect, it eventually affects the morale of the employees. As a result, a more efficient system should improve employee morale. But it can't be proven, and certainly not before the system is installed. Similarly, improved customer service should eventually increase sales. Although this can't be proven, it is a reasonable assumption.

Assigning Monetary Values

Because cost/benefit analysis considers a system's effect on profits, every effort must be made to assign dollar values to benefits. If this is done thoroughly and accurately, the eventual decision is sure to be improved. Unfortunately, it is often difficult to assign a monetary value to a benefit, and in some cases it is nearly impossible.

What, for example, is the value of increasing billing accuracy from 98 to 99 percent? Or what is the value of improved exception reporting? If the decisions made by the managers aren't improved, or if managers don't save time by using the exception reports, there may be no value to this benefit.

On the other hand, some benefits can be reasonably estimated. For instance, shortening the billing time from seven days to two days after shipping should reduce accounts receivable by five times the average daily billing amount. Then if the accounts receivable reduction is estimated at $100,000, some percent of this may be taken as the estimated value of the benefit. In figure 3-16, 10 percent is used, on the assumption that the company is in debt and pays about 10 percent for its loans. By reducing its loans by $100,000, it will save $10,000 per year.

Similarly, a better method of catching bad credit risks (before their orders are shipped) can be assigned some value. If, for example, the company lost $20,000 in uncollectable debts the preceding year, the credit manager may estimate that this can be reduced by 20 percent by the new system. Thus the credit authorization system might contribute $4000 per year to corporate profits.

This brings us to the user's role in assigning values. In many cases, the user department is able to assign benefit values better than the system analyst is. After all, the users should know to what extent the benefits of a new system should improve their effectiveness. In any event, the users should be consulted for whatever insight they are able to provide. They may be overly enthusiastic about the new system and overestimate its values. They may be unenthusiastic about the system and refuse to accept values assigned by the analyst. But they are going to use the system, so their opinions must be given heavy consideration.

Because of the difficulty in assigning values to benefits, analysts may bracket values just as they do costs. Thus a low, middle, and high estimate may be given for each benefit. This practice can give greater perspective to the potential of a benefit and to its risks as well.

In some cases, if the project involves large development costs, a *pilot system* may be run to aid in estimating the values of one or more benefits. For instance, if modern management techniques are proposed for inventory control, a pilot application system may be run on a small percentage of the company's items—say 200 items selected at random out of the company's 10,000 total items. Then after several months, the analyst will have data on how much the inventory investment has been reduced and how much the service level has been increased. Using the results of this pilot system, the analyst can better estimate the results of the proposed system.

THE PROCESS OF ANALYSIS

Once the costs and benefits of a system have been determined, it is relatively straightforward to evaluate the alternative systems. Four factors that should be considered are *payback period, return on investment, risk,* and *system life.*

The *payback period* is the time required to recover the development costs of the system. If, for example, a company spends $1,000,000 to develop a system and reduces operating costs by $300,000 per year after installation, the payback period will be three-and-one-third years.

Because the cost projections may vary by year, a table is often constructed showing the costs by year. Thus the table in figure 3-17 can be used to determine the payback period. Here benefit values, as well as operating costs, are shown by years. As you can see, if the development costs for this system are $35,000, the costs will be recovered in less than two years when benefits are considered. But it will take over three years to recover costs if they aren't considered.

Return on investment is an inexact measure that gives some idea of a

Year	Present system costs	Alternative system			
		Projected operating costs	Projected benefits	Projected profit contribution	Cumulative contribution
1	$53,000.	$44,000.	$10,000.	$19,000.	$ 19,000.
2	$58,000.	$47,000.	$12,000.	$23,000.	$ 42,000.
3	$64,000.	$50,000.	$15,000.	$29,000.	$ 71,000.
4	$70,000.	$54,000.	$18,000.	$34,000.	$105,000.

FIGURE 3-17   Payback analysis

project's contribution to profits in relation to its development cost. As a rough measure, you can calculate return on investment by dividing profit contribution by investment and multiplying by 100. Thus, a system that reduces costs by $300,000 per year but costs $1,000,000 to develop has a return on investment of 30 percent:

$$\frac{\$300,000}{\$1,000,000} \times 100 = 30\%$$

If, as in figure 3-17, the projected profit contribution varies from year to year, various averaging techniques can be used. As a rough measure, you can divide the total profit contribution by the number of years and use this average in your return on investment calculation. Thus the average profit contribution in figure 3-17 is $105,000 divided by four, or $26,250. Then, if the development cost is $35,000, the return on investment can be stated as 75 percent. Bear in mind, however, that there are far more sophisticated techniques that can be used to derive return on investment.

Whether rough or precise, return on investment is a useful measure for determining which of several projects should be given the highest priority. Thus an inventory-control project with a high return on investment may be much more desirable to pursue than a billing project with a low return on investment. Because payback period is closely related to return on investment, many analysts use only one of these measures during cost/benefit analysis.

Another factor to consider is risk. If the low, middle, and high estimates for costs and benefits have a wide variance, there is obviously more risk in the decision-making process than if they are closely bracketed. Similarly, if the project is complex, there is greater risk that something will go wrong than there is if the project is a simple one. And if the project hasn't been done by other companies, this too implies a greater risk that all will not go well. In any event, if the risks are large, the project is going to seem less desirable, regardless of its projected return on investment— and rightfully so.

Finally, the life of the system should be considered. If it is likely that the system will be used for many years, this is a factor in its favor. On the other hand, if the company is growing rapidly and may outgrow the system in a short period, this may mean the project should be delayed until it can be done thoroughly.

When all four factors are considered, it is likely that one of the proposed alternatives will stand out from all the rest. Or it may be that none of the alternatives has clearcut advantages over the existing system, so the existing system is retained. Remember, however, that the analysis can only be as good as the cost-and-benefit projections. If gross errors are made in estimating development costs, operating costs, or value of benefits, the analysis is doomed.

DISCUSSION

Although this topic centers on cost/benefit analysis, you should realize that there are other sides to the feasibility decision. In brief, there are three types of feasibility: technical feasibility (Is the equipment capable of performing as specified? Is our staff capable of installing the equipment properly?); operational feasibility (Will our people use the system as intended? Will they cooperate in getting the full benefit from the new system?); and economic feasibility (Will the system contribute to profits?). Although cost/benefit analysis focuses on economic feasibility, both technical and operational feasibility should be given their proper weight.

In any event, I hope you can see by now how absolutely critical cost/benefit analysis is to effective systems development. If it isn't done well, a company is likely to install systems that do not make significant profit contributions. The systems are likely to cost more to develop and operate than expected—and they may not provide the expected benefits. Judging by the experience of many computer users, cost/benefit analysis has been a major area of failure in the process of systems development.

SUMMARY

1. Cost/benefit analysis focuses on the economic feasibility of proposed systems. To a large measure, it determines which of the system alternatives will be implemented so it is critical to effective systems development.

2. For proper analysis, both development costs and operating costs must be estimated as precisely as possible. Because it isn't easy to be precise, three estimates (low, middle, and high) are often given.

3. Although many systems have been installed based on cost reductions, other benefits are often of greater value to a company. For effective analysis, the analyst must assign proper dollar values to these benefits.

4. During analysis, payback period, return on investment, risk, and system life should be considered. Since payback period and return on investment are related values, it is common to use only one of these measures.

TERMINOLOGY

cost/benefit analysis
development costs
operating costs
management-by-exception
exception reporting

intangible benefit
pilot system
payback period
return on investment

1. In studies of systems projects, these are some common complaints made by management:

   a. "We selected the wrong system in the first place."
   b. "The implementation phase took longer and cost more than we expected."
   c. "We never did realize the expected reduction in operating costs."
   d. "Our managers don't use the information the new system provides."
   e. "The new system has never worked properly."
   f. "The new system works okay, but it really hasn't contributed anything to our overall operation. I wish we had implemented some other application instead."

   Which of these complaints are related to cost/benefit analysis?

2. In question 1, try to pinpoint the cause of the problem mentioned. Where exactly did the systems project go wrong?

3. Based on figure 3-15, what would you say about the risk related to the expected reduction in operating costs? If the development costs are bracketed at $100,000, $125,000 and $150,000, what are your feeling about feasibility (disregard any other benefits?)

4. Explain how each benefit listed in figure 3-16 might improve a company's operations. If possible, explain how a dollar value might be assigned to each benefit (what additional information would you need? what pilot system might be run?).

5. Suppose the operational costs are actually 20 percent higher than those projected in figure 3-17 and the benefits are 25 percent lower. If the development cost is $35,000, how does this affect the payback period and return on investment?

4 AN INTRODUCTION TO PROGRAMMING AND SOFTWARE

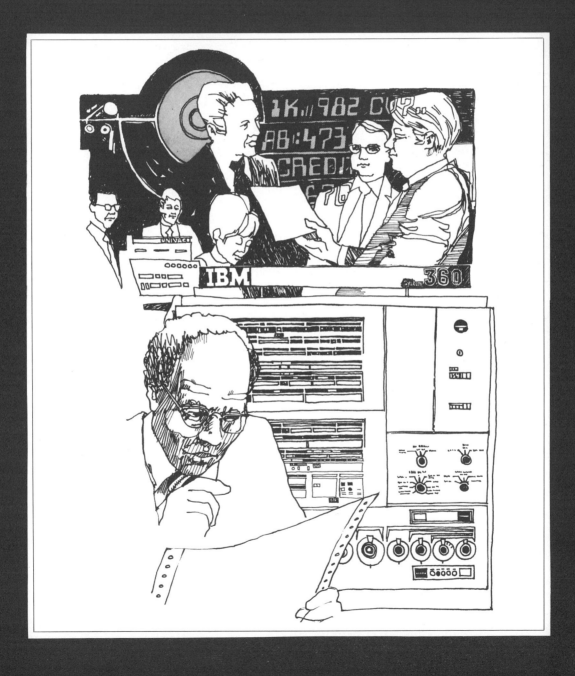

This chapter is divided into three topics. The first describes the process of program development. It tells you how a programmer creates a program. The second topic introduces you to operating systems. An operating system is a collection of programs that is supplied with the computer system. To a large extent, the operating system controls the operation of the computer system. Finally, topic 3 describes how a program relates to the computer system; it gives you good perspective about the capabilities of any program.

TOPIC 1
WRITING A PROGRAM

When a programmer writes a program, he or she uses a specific programming language. For instance, a programmer may write a program using the COBOL, FORTRAN, or BASIC language. In other words, COBOL, FORTRAN, and BASIC are the names of three common programming languages. (There are many programming languages, and each is designed for a certain purpose.)

Regardless of the programming language used, a programmer goes through five phases when he or she writes a program: (1) defines the problem to be programmed; (2) plans a solution to the problem; (3) codes the solution using one of the available programming languages; (4) tests the program to be sure that it does what is intended; and (5) documents the program. These five steps are explained in this topic.

DEFINING THE PROBLEM

Defining the problem is simply making sure that you know what the program you are going to write is supposed to do. You must understand what the input is going to be, what the output of the program must be, and what calculations or other procedures must be followed in deriving the output from the input.

When a program is assigned to a programmer, complete specifications may be passed on to him or her from the systems staff. For instance, the programmer may receive record layouts for all input and output records and a print chart for each printed output document. He or she may also receive a system flowchart, indicating where the program fits into the entire system as well as what the inputs and outputs of the program are to be. If the processing logic is complex, the programmer may also receive decision tables or grid charts. In addition, he or she may receive written instructions in narrative form.

On the other hand, programmers may receive specifications that are sketchy. In this case, they may create their own record layouts and print charts based on written or spoken instructions. They may also create decision tables or grid charts to summarize processing requirements.

Whether the program specifications are complete or not, certain aspects of the programming problem are likely to need clarification. That's why a programmer will usually question the person who assigns the program. For instance, supposed you are asked to write a program that prepares a report, like the one charted in figure 4-1, from a file of inventory records with the format given by the record layout form in figure 4-2. What additional information would you need? Here are some ideas:

1. How is the amount invested calculated? Is it the on-hand balance multiplied by unit cost, or is it on-hand balance multiplied by unit price?
2. Should the input deck be checked to be sure it is in numerical sequence by item number? (This is a common programming practice.)
3. Is one line supposed to be printed for each card in the input deck or would it be better to print a line for only certain items—say those items with an inventory investment over $10,000?

The point is that you must know exactly what the program is supposed to do before you can write it. Often, an error in testing a program stems from not completely understanding what the program is supposed to do.

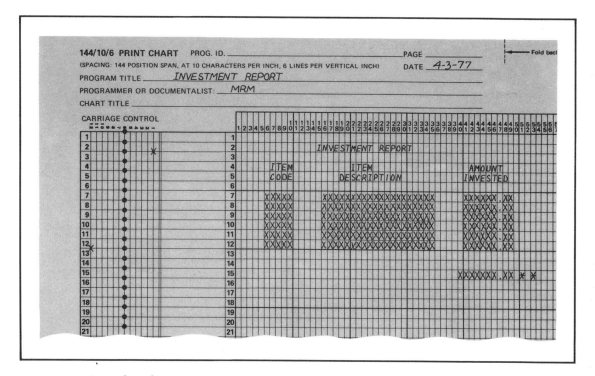

FIGURE 4-1   Print chart for investment report

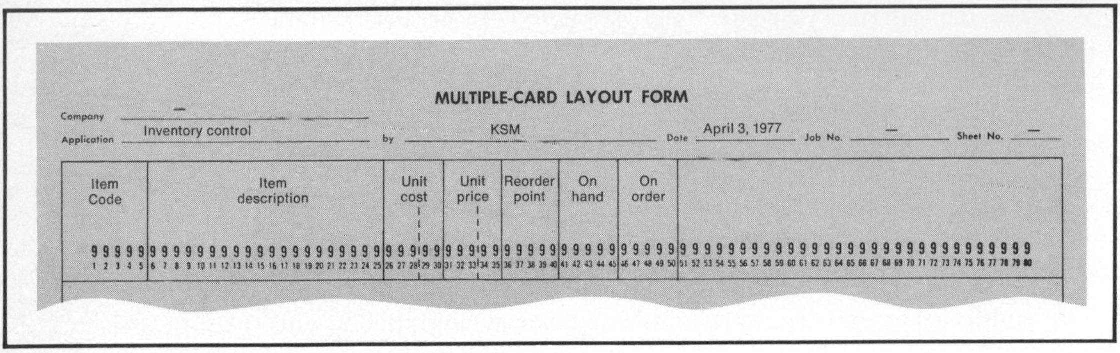
MULTIPLE-CARD LAYOUT FORM

Company —
Application Inventory control by KSM Date April 3, 1977 Job No. — Sheet No. —

Item Code	Item description	Unit cost	Unit price	Reorder point	On hand	On order	
1–5	6–25	26–30	31–35	36–40	41–45	46–50	51–80

FIGURE 4-2 Record layout for inventory master record

PLANNING THE SOLUTION

Planning the solution to a programming problem means deciding what must be done to solve the problem. This normally concerns itself with the sequences of instructions to be used and the logic required to derive the output from the input. It may also concern itself with deciding what parts a program should be divided into to help simplify it.

When planning a solution, a programmer often draws a *program flowchart* of the planned solution—something like the flowchart shown in figure 4-3. The flowchart can then be used as a guideline for coding the program. Basically, there are two levels at which a program flowchart can be drawn: general and detailed. A *general* flowchart (sometimes called a *macro* flowchart) gives the major functional requirements of the program. It is often prepared by the systems staff and is too general to be used as a guideline for coding. On the other hand, the *detailed* flowchart (sometimes called a *micro* flowchart) is intended to be a guide for coding. As a result, it directly corresponds to the logic of the eventual program. In this book, only detailed flowcharts are used.

Figure 4-3 is a detailed flowchart for an inventory program that prepares a report like the one specified by the print chart in figure 4-1 from a deck of balance-forward cards with the format given in figure 4-2. When the last card is read, the program is supposed to print the total amount invested for all input cards.

The flowchart uses the symbols shown in figure 4-4. These symbols conform to the flowcharting standards approved by the American National Standards Institute (ANSI) and will be used throughout this book. Although many companies have not yet converted to these standards, almost all use symbols that vary in only a minor way from the standard ones.

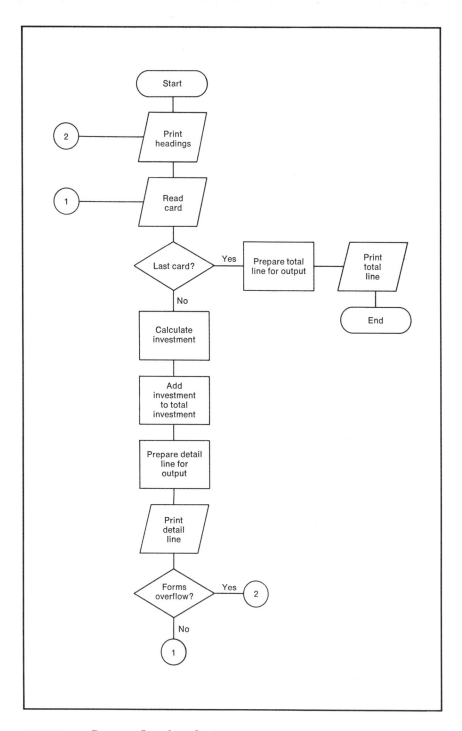

FIGURE 4-3   Program flowchart for investment report program

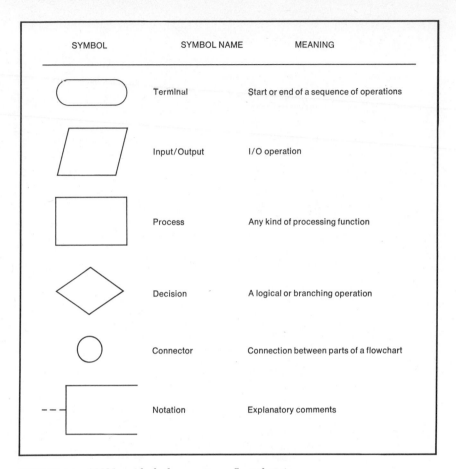

SYMBOL	SYMBOL NAME	MEANING
	Terminal	Start or end of a sequence of operations
	Input/Output	I/O operation
	Process	Any kind of processing function
	Decision	A logical or branching operation
	Connector	Connection between parts of a flowchart
	Notation	Explanatory comments

FIGURE 4-4   ANSI symbols for program flowcharting

To follow a flowchart like the one in figure 4-3, you start at the top and read down and to the right unless arrows indicate otherwise. When you come to a connector circle with a number in it, you continue at a connector circle containing the same number. For example, after printing a detail line (a line representing one input record), the program reaches a connector circle with a 2 in it if forms overflow is to take place (that is, the maximum number of lines per page has been printed). This means that the flow of the program continues at the connector circle leading into the PRINT HEADINGS symbol. If forms overflow is not to take place, the program reaches the connector circle containing a 1, so the program continues with the block containing READ CARD.

When drawing flowcharts, the main concern is that all processing and all branches required by the program are indicated. In this respect, if words used in the symbols clearly indicate what operations are to take place, they serve their purpose. When drawing a flowchart for a specific language, though, the programmer normally uses words or code that corresponds to the language to be used.

As an aid in drawing the symbols, a programmer uses a plastic flowcharting template such as the one shown in chapter 3, figure 3-11. By placing a pencil or pen in the symbol to be drawn, the programmer is able to draw a more exact symbol than can be done freehand. Because using the template is somewhat slower than drawing freehand, a programmer is likely to make one or more freehand sketches of a flowchart before using the template to draw the final version.

In the last several years, there has been a great emphasis in the data-processing industry on new methods of designing and writing programs. Some of the names for these methods are *structured programming*, *top-down design*, and *HIPO* (Hierarchical Input, Processing, and Output). To some extent, these techniques reduce or eliminate the need for flowcharts. Nevertheless, flowcharting is a common technique, one that can be useful, and one that you should be familiar with.

CODING

Coding a program involves writing the code that eventually is translated into a machine-language program—that is, a program that can be run by the computer. In general, special coding sheets are used, and, when the program is finished, one card is keypunched for each coding line. The resulting deck of cards is called the *source deck*.

Because the source deck may contain keypunching or programming errors, programmers *desk check* the source deck after it is keypunched. They usually do this by studying a listing of the contents of the source cards, but they can also do it by studying the printing at the top of the source cards done by the keypunch. Figure 4-5 illustrates these two alternatives. Since the listing simply prints the contents of the cards in the source deck, it is often referred to as an *80-80 listing*: the contents of the 80 card columns are printed in the first 80 print positions of the printed form. If the programmer finds any errors, he or she makes the appropriate corrections to the source deck. When the programmer is sure that the source deck is as accurate as he or she can make it, it is ready to be *compiled*.

Compiling a source deck means converting the source code of the source deck into an *object program*. The object program may be punched into cards, called an *object deck*, or stored on magnetic tape or disk. In any case, the object program, which is in machine language, can be *loaded* into the storage of the computer and then executed. In other words, the object program is ready to run.

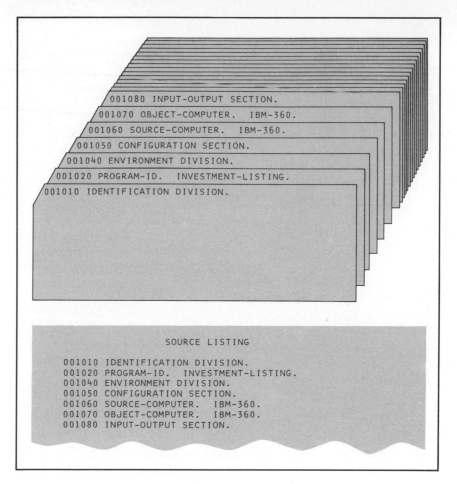

FIGURE 4-5   Source deck and source listing

The translation of a source deck into an object program is called a *compilation* and is done by the computer itself under control of a translator program called a *compiler*. A typical compilation is illustrated in figure 4-6. This compilation takes place in two steps:

1. The compiler, which is stored on magnetic disk as an object program, is loaded into the computer.
2. The computer executes the compiler, thus processing the source deck and creating the object program, which is written on a disk ready to be loaded and executed. During the compilation, a *source listing* is printed by the computer.

Although the object program can be punched into cards (an object

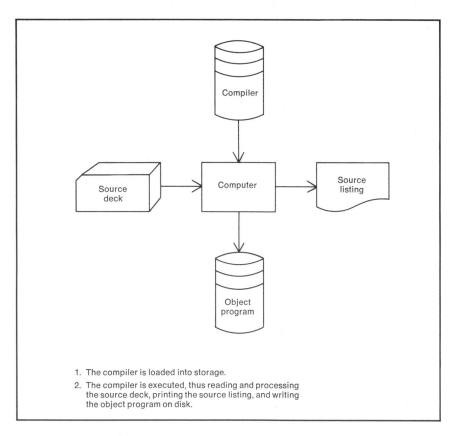

FIGURE 4-6   Compilation

deck), in most cases it is stored on a disk as shown in this illustration. Since card punching and reading is very slow in comparison to disk operations, this increases the speed with which object programs can be stored and loaded.

The source listing is a listing of the source deck as well as a listing of various reference tables. If any errors are caught by the compiler during the compilation (as is usually the case), one or more *diagnostic messages* (or just *diagnostics*) are printed as part of the source listing and the object program is not created. Each diagnostic calls attention to one source-deck error.

If there are diagnostics, the programmer makes the necessary corrections to the source deck and the deck is recompiled. The process is repeated until there are no more diagnostics in the source listing. At this stage, the program is ready to be tested.

TESTING

To test a program, the programmer tries the object program on some *test data*. This test data is intended to simulate all of the conditions that may occur when the program is actually used. For card-to-printer programs, the test data is punched into cards; but for more complex programs, the test data may include card decks, tapes, disks, and any other form of input used. When the program is executed, the programmer compares the actual output with the expected output. If they agree, the programmer can assume that the program does what it is intended to do.

More likely, however, the actual output and the intended output will not agree. Programmers must then *debug* the program. They must find the errors (bugs), make the necessary corrections to the source deck, re-compile the source program, and make another *test run*. This process is continued until the program executes as intended.

Although debugging techniques vary depending on the language used, testing is often the most difficult phase of programming. In a program consisting of thousands of instructions, the original deck may have dozens of bugs, require dozens of recompilations, and take weeks to debug.

In actual practice, a series of test runs is made using different sets of test data. The test data for the first test run is usually low in volume—perhaps only a dozen input records—and may be designed to test only the main processing functions of the program. After the program is debugged using this data, it may be tested using data that tries all conditions that may possibly occur during the execution of the program. This set of test data is usually much greater in volume than the first one. After the program executes correctly with this data, a test run may be made using actual, or "live," test data. Then, an entire group of programs may be tested together to be sure that the output from one program is valid input to the next. Only after a program has proved itself under conditions that are as close to real as possible is the program considered ready for use.

DOCUMENTATION

In data-processing terminology, *documentation* refers to the collection of records that specifies what is being done and what is going to be done within a data-processing system. For each program in an installation, there is a collection of records referred to as *program documentation*. One of the jobs of a programmer is to provide this documentation.

Why is programming documentation necessary? Data-processing re-quirements change. For example, tax laws change: the percent used to calculate social security tax has increased periodically over the last several years as has the maximum amount of social security tax that must be paid in any one year. Company policies also change: discounts may vary from year to year, production departments may switch to new forecasting techniques, and accounting practices may change. For each change, all affected programs must be modified.

Change is so common, in fact, that large companies have special maintenance programmers whose entire job is to modify existing programs. This frees other programmers to work on new programs without interruption. Without adequate documentation, however, maintenance programmers could not make changes within a reasonable period of time. Even when programmers modify their own programs, documentation is valuable. Three months after writing a program, it is difficult to remember specific details about it.

Some of the more important documents likely to be required by a company's documentation standards are the following:

1. Specifications that give the detailed requirements of the program
2. Layouts of all input and output records on special layout forms
3. A flowchart of the entire program
4. The source listing created during the last compilation
5. Listings of the input data used for testing and listings of the output results of the test runs

Most of these documents, of course, are prepared and used as the program is developed. The flowchart, for instance, is both an aid for coding the program and a record of the completed program. Nevertheless, programmers normally spend considerable time refining and finishing documentation when they complete a program. As a result, a company tries to reach a balance between too much and too little documentation. With few exceptions, however, they have too little rather than too much.

There are five phases to program development. The programmer must define the problem and then plan, code, test, and document the solution.

SUMMARY

TERMINOLOGY

program flowchart	loading a program
general flowchart	compilation
macro flowchart	compiler
detailed flowchart	source listing
micro flowchart	diagnostic message
source deck	diagnostic
desk checking	test data
80-80 listing	debugging
compile	test run
object program	documentation
object deck	program documentation

QUESTIONS

1. As mentioned earlier, programming can be one of the causes of errors within a data-processing system. If programming errors are discovered after a system is in operation, which phases of programming development would you blame?

2. Sometimes a programmer writes and tests a program and feels that it has tested out perfectly. Then when the program is tested in conjunction with the others in the system (called a systems test), his or her program blows up (fails). Again, which programming phase or phases would you say were done inadequately?

3. Based on the flowchart in figure 4-3, would headings print on every page of the investment report?

TOPIC 2
INTRODUCTION TO
OPERATING SYSTEMS

At one time, computer manufacturers first designed a computer and then decided what programming support, such as assemblers or compilers, should be supplied with it. About the mid-1960s, however, the manufacturers realized that the programming support, or software, was almost as important as the equipment, or hardware. They then began to design software in conjunction with the hardware. One result was the development of operating systems, which today are supplied along with tape or direct-access computer systems.

An *operating system* is a collection of programs designed to improve the efficiency of a computer installation. It does this in two ways. First, an operating system decreases the amount of time a computer system is idle by using *stacked-job processing*. Second, an operating system increases programming efficiency by providing various processing and service programs that eliminate or reduce the programming efforts required of a computer user. (This topic will introduce some of the programs of an operating system; chapter 10 will introduce you to the others.)

STACKED JOB PROCESSING

Before stacked-job processing was developed, a computer system stopped when it finished executing a program. The operator removed the program output, such as card decks or magnetic tapes, and made ready the I/O units for the next program. He or she then loaded the program— usually in the form of an object deck—and placed any cards to be processed in the card reader. The program was then ready to be executed.

The trouble with this intervention by the operator between programs is that it wastes computer time. If a company runs 120 programs a day and the operator takes thirty seconds to set up each program, one hour of computer time is lost. With computer time on a medium-sized system costing $100 or more per hour, that lost time can be very costly.

When stacked-job processing is used, the computer rather than the computer operator loads programs. To make this possible, all of a company's programs are stored in *libraries* on a *system-residence device*, which is usually a disk device (although it can be a tape on a tape system). As a result, programs can be directly accessed from the system-residence device and loaded into storage at a high rate of speed.

At the start of a day's computer operations, then, the computer operator loads a *supervisor program* (or just *supervisor*) into storage, and control of the computer is transferred to this program. The supervisor program, which is one of the programs of the operating system, is responsible for loading all of the other programs to be executed from the system-residence device. The supervisor program, which may require

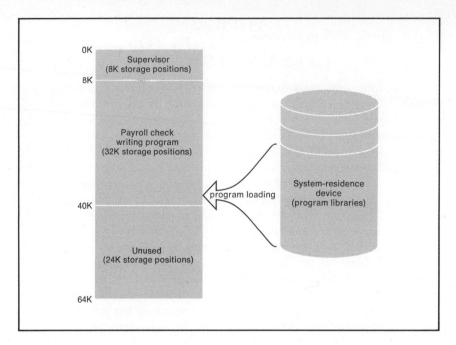

FIGURE 4-7   Internal storage during execution of an application program

6000 storage positions or more, remains in storage during the execution of all other programs.

Figure 4-7 illustrates the storage of a typical computer while a payroll program is being executed. In this case, total storage consists of 64,000 storage positions with the supervisor occupying 8000 positions and the payroll program occupying 32,000 positions; 24,000 positions aren't used while this program is being executed. When the payroll program finishes its execution, it passes control to the supervisor program so the next program can be loaded.

To tell the supervisor which programs are supposed to be executed, the operator places a stack of *job-control cards,* such as the stack in figure 4-8, in the card reader. These cards give the names of the programs to be executed, along with information such as which tape should be mounted on which tape drive. There are usually several job-control cards for each program to be executed, and, if a program requires card input, the data deck follows the job-control cards. In the illustration, programs 2 and 3 require card input, while programs 1, 4, and 5 do not. The stack of job-control cards is commonly referred to as a *job deck.*

When the computer finishes executing one program, loading and executing the next one typically takes place in four steps as illustrated in figure 4-9. First, control of the computer passes from the completed program to one of the instructions of the supervisor program. Second, the

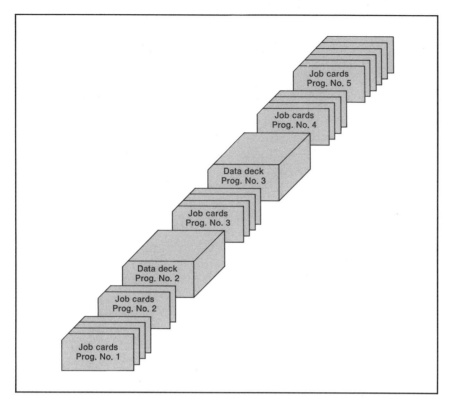

FIGURE 4-8   A job deck

supervisor loads a program called the *job-control program* from the system-residence device and passes control to it. This job-control program is one of the programs of the operating system. Third, the job-control program reads and processes the job-control cards for the next program. If there are any errors in the job-control cards or if any necessary information is omitted, the job-control program prints a message on the console typewriter. When all job cards for the next program are processed, control passes back to the supervisor. Finally, the supervisor loads the next program from the system-residence device and passes control to its first instruction.

THE PROGRAMS OF AN
OPERATING SYSTEM

As stated earlier, an operating system is simply a collection of programs stored in library files on a disk pack. These programs are designed to improve operating and programming efficiency. A description of some of the basic programs of an operating system follows.

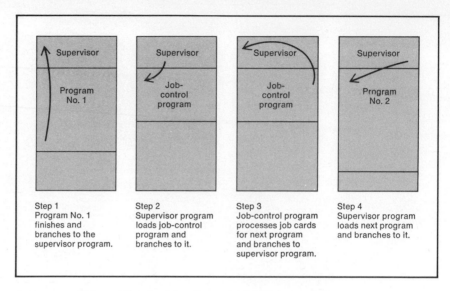

FIGURE 4-9   Job-to-job transition in stacked-job processing

Supervisor

The most heavily used program of an operating system is the *supervisor program,* or just *supervisor.* It is loaded into storage at the start of a day's operations, remains in storage throughout the day, and controls the overall operation of the computer system. Although the duties of a supervisor vary from system to system, two of its common functions are (1) loading all other programs and (2) starting all I/O operations.

Job-Control Program

Job-to-job transition begins when the supervisor loads the *job-control program,* or a program like it, into storage. This program processes all the job-control statements used to request the execution of a program and checks the availability of the required input and output devices. If a job-control statement is invalid or a specified device isn't available, the job-control program will print an error message on the console typewriter so that the operator can correct the job deck or make the device available. When all the job-control statements have been processed with no errors found, control returns to the supervisor so the requested program can be loaded and executed.

Language Translators

Language translators are the compilers supplied with an operating system. For example, an operating system might include a COBOL

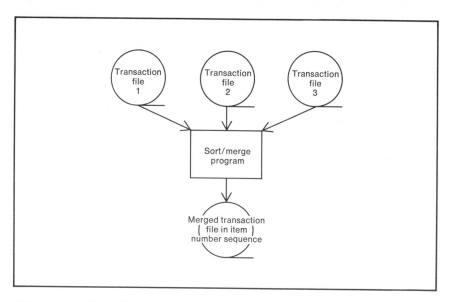

FIGURE 4-10   Typical function of a sort/merge program

compiler plus FORTRAN, PL/I, and RPG compilers. One goal of a translator is to reduce the programming time required to prepare a working object program. As a result, all of the translators print diagnostic listings to aid in correcting clerical errors in the source deck and often provide debugging statements to aid in testing the object program.

Sort/Merge Programs

In any computer installation, much of the processing requires that records be in certain sequences. As a result, two or more tape or direct-access files often have to be merged into one file, or one tape or direct-access file has to be sorted. For example, figure 4-10 is a systems chart for a sort/merge run that combines the transactions from three input tapes into one sorted output tape.

Although sorting and merging may take up a large portion of the total running time of a computer system, the programs themselves are very much the same. They differ primarily in the number of files to be merged, the length of the records in the files, the length and location of the field on which the file is to be sequenced, and the number of I/O devices to be used.

Typically, an operating system provides one or more *sort/merge programs*, depending on the I/O devices of the system. These are generalized programs that can be used for many different jobs. The user simply supplies coded specifications and the sort/merge program adjusts accordingly, thus eliminating the need for sort programs to be written.

Utility Programs

Many of the programs of a typical computer installation are relatively simple ones that convert data from one I/O form to another; for example, printing the contents of a file of tape records or converting a disk file to a tape file. To eliminate the need for a computer user to write such programs, an operating system provides *utility programs,* in which the user need only specify in coded form the characteristics of the files involved. The utility programs then adjust accordingly and do the desired processing. Thus, routine programs such as card-to-printer, card-to-tape, card-to-disk, tape-to-printer, tape-to-tape, and many others are supplied with an operating system.

Library-Maintenance Programs

As explained earlier, the programs executed by a tape or direct-access system are usually stored in libraries on the system-residence device. As a result, other programs must be available to add, change, or delete the programs in the libraries. These programs are called *library-maintenance programs.* In other words, a library-maintenance program is first loaded from the system-residence device. Then, during its execution, it will add new programs to the library, delete old programs from the library, or replace old programs with modified ones.

DISCUSSION

We can now make the distinction between systems and applications programs and programmers. An *applications program* is one that performs a function related to a business application. An *applications programmer* is a person who writes this type of program. In contrast, a *systems program* is one that relates to the operation of the system, such as any of the programs in an operating system. A *systems programmer* is a person who writes, modifies, or maintains this type of program. In general, systems programs are far more complex than application programs.

Traditionally, systems programs were supplied by computer manufacturers. For instance, IBM provides operating systems with all of its tape and direct-access systems. In the last several years, however, many software companies have successfully competed with the manufacturers in developing systems software. As an example, one software company sells sort/merge programs that are reported to outperform those sold by the computer manufacturer. In general, the software companies concentrate on a specific function of an operating system; they do not provide entire operating systems.

In closing, you should know that operating-system terminology varies depending on the computer being used. Up to this point, we have used IBM System/360-370 terminology. In contrast, some manufacturers refer to supervisor programs as monitors, some as executives, and some as MCPs (Master Control Programs). Similarly, IBM refers to the job-control language for its System/3 as operations-control language. You should be aware of these variations when you come in contact with other computer systems.

SUMMARY

1. An operating system increases productivity in two ways: (1) by reducing idle time between programs and (2) by eliminating the duplication of programming effort.

2. When stacked-job processing is used, a job deck containing job-control cards for each job to be run is placed in the card reader. When one program finishes, the supervisor program loads the next program to be executed from the system residence device.

3. In addition to control programs, an operating system contains language translators, sort/merge programs, utility programs, and library-maintenance programs.

TERMINOLOGY

operating system
stacked-job processing
library
system-residence device
supervisor program
supervisor
job-control card
job deck
job-control program

language translator
sort/merge program
utility program
library-maintenance program
applications program
applications programmer
systems program
systems programmer

QUESTIONS

1. Suppose a job-control card has a keypunching error. A program named PRO46 is supposed to be run, but PF046 is punched in the card. Do you think the error will be detected by the operating system and, if so, when?

2. Suppose a job-control card has this error—instead of EXEC PRO46, the card contains EXXEC PRO46. (EXEC tells the operating system to execute the program name that follows.) Which of the programs of the operating system will detect this type of error?

3. Suppose a payroll program uses all four tape drives for various I/O files. Then, the next program to be executed requires all four tape drives for inventory files. If stacked-job processing is used, will there be a delay for operator intervention between the execution of these two programs? If so, why?

TOPIC 3
THE STORED
PROGRAM

This topic gives a conceptual description of the stored program. It tries to give you an idea of what an object program is like and what instructions a computer can actually execute. When you complete this topic, you should have a much better idea of what a computer can do and what its logical capabilities are.

INTERNAL STORAGE

When a program is loaded into a computer, it is placed in the storage of the CPU. That's why a computer program is often referred to as a stored program. Small computers may have only a limited amount of storage—say 8000 *storage positions*—while some of the largest computers have over 1 million storage positions. Because the word *kilo* refers to 1000, K is often used to refer to 1000 storage positions: a 16K computer has approximately 16,000 storage positions. (I say approximately, because 1K is actually 1024 storage positions, so 16K is 16,384 storage positions. In normal conversation, however, the excess storage positions are dropped.)

Associated with each of the storage positions of a computer is a number that identifies it, called the *address* of the storage position. A 16K computer, for instance, has addresses ranging from 0000 to 16,383. You can therefore talk about the contents of the storage position with address 180 or the contents of storage position 14,482.

Contents: G E O R G E 3 4 3 9 9 8 2 ⁎ 1 1 2 1 4
Addresses: 480 ... 485 ... 490 ... 495

You can then say that storage position 480 contains the letter G, storage position 487 contains the number 4, position 494 contains an asterisk, and position 493 contains a blank. Or you can say that there is a 2 at address 497 and the number 343 is stored in positions 486 through 488. This is simply the way data-processing people talk about storage and its contents.

Several storage positions in a row that contain one item of data such as an item number or unit price are commonly referred to as a *field*. For instance, in the above example, storage positions 486–490 (which is read as 486 through 490) might represent an on-hand balance field, while positions 495–499 represent an item-number field. To address a field, a typical instruction specifies the address of the leftmost storage position as well as the number of storage positions in the field. Thus, address 486 with a length of five would address the field in positions 486–490, while address 1024 with a length of twenty would address the field in positions 1024–1043.

Of course, a storage position isn't really a small box with a character of data in it. Instead, each storage position consists of a number of electronic components called *binary components,* because they can be switched to either of two conditions, commonly referred to as "on" and "off."

In most computer systems, the binary component used is the *magnetic core.* These tiny, doughnut-shaped components can be magnetized in either of two directions: clockwise and counterclockwise. When magnetized in one direction, a core is said to be *on;* when magnetized in the other direction, a core is said to be *off.* A string of cores makes up one storage position in a computer, and thousands of cores in planes make up a computer's storage. Because most storage consists of magnetic cores, you will often hear storage referred to as *core storage.*

In order to represent data, the cores at a storage position are turned on or off in selected combinations by wires that run through the center of the cores. Each combination of on and off cores represents a digit or digits, a letter, or a special character. Figure 4-11, for example, might represent three storage positions. By decoding the combinations at each storage position, it can be determined that the characters B, 2, and 9 are stored. (The shaded cores are "on"; the white cores are "off.")

Figure 4-11 is a simplification, because actual core storage has more than two wires through each core. These wires are used to sense whether the core is "off" or "on." However, this electronic detail is unrelated to data processing. The important notion for the student of data processing is that data is represented internally by off-on combinations of binary components.

On some of the more recent computer systems, magnetic cores are *not* used for storage. Instead, transistor-like solid materials are used as the binary components. Furthermore, the number of binary components per storage position and the codes used for representing data vary from computer to computer. Regardless of these variations, however, the principles are the same: a fixed number of binary components make up one storage position and one or more storage positions represent a field in storage.

In chapter 14, CPU Concepts, some of the codes used in storing data, as well as some of the other forms of data representation, are described in detail. On the System/360-370, for example, there are four different forms in which numeric data can be stored, three of which are covered in chapter 14.

INSTRUCTIONS

While a program is being executed, both the instructions of the program and the data being processed are contained in storage. The

FIGURE 4-11   Core storage

instructions, in coded form, indicate the operations that are to be performed and give the addresses of the storage positions that hold the data to be operated upon. The number of storage positions required to store an instruction varies from computer to computer and from instruction to instruction. In System/360-370, instructions are two, four, or six storage positions in length, depending on the function of the instruction.

Although a program may consist of thousands of instructions, there are basically only four types that a computer can execute, plus some miscellaneous ones. As a result, a program with 6000 instructions consists of the same types of instructions being executed over and over again.

These basic types are (1) input and output (I/O), (2) data-movement, (3) arithmetic, and (4) logic (or program-control) instructions.

I/O Instructions

An I/O instruction specifies the type of input or output operation to be performed and the storage positions to be used in performing the operation. For example, an input instruction such as a card reading instruction might specify that a card is to be read and its data is to be stored in the eighty storage positions beginning with address 5501. In this case, storage positions 5501–5580 are called the *card input area,* or just the *input area,* of storage. When the read instruction is executed, the data that is read from a card replaces the data that the card input area originally contained. The data from card column 1 is stored in storage position 5501, the data from card column 2 is stored in storage position 5502, and so on, until the data from card column 80 is stored in storage position 5580.

Similarly, an output instruction such as a printing instruction specifies the storage positions from which the output line is to be printed (called the *printer output area,* or just *output area,* of storage). If a print instruction specifies that a line should be printed from locations 5601 through 5700, the content of storage position 5601 is printed in print position 1 on the printer, the content of storage position 5602 is printed in print position 2, and so on. Since a typical printer may have up to 144 print positions between the left and right margins, the printer output area may require up to 144 storage positions.

Depending on the computer, the print instruction may also contain a code for spacing or skipping the continuous form. For example, one print instruction may indicate one space after printing, another print instruction may indicate a skip to a 1-punch in the carriage-control tape after printing, a third may indicate two spaces after printing. On other computers, spacing and skipping may be controlled by I/O instructions separate from the print instruction.

Other I/O instructions enable a computer to make use of the other I/O capabilities of the system. For example, a read instruction for the card reader may cause a card to be stacked in an alternative output stacker. Instructions for card punches cause cards to be punched from output areas, while instructions for tape units cause tape records to be read into input areas or written from output areas.

Data-Movement Instructions

Data-movement instructions allow a computer to move data from one field in storage to another. The basic data-movement instruction, commonly called the move instruction, causes the data from one field to be moved unchanged to another field. If, for example, a move instruction specifies that the contents of storage positions 541–545 should be moved to storage positions 701–705, the execution of the instruction can be shown as follows:

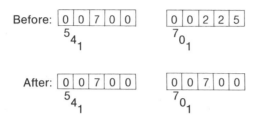

The effect is that the data in the first field is duplicated in the second field.

Other data-movement instructions may refine data for printing or convert data from one storage form to another. For instance, the edit instruction on the System/360 will refine data by removing lead zeros from a field, inserting commas and decimal points, and so on. Then, when the data is printed, it is more readable (1.23 is more readable than 00123).

Arithmetic Instructions

In general, there are two different ways in which arithmetic instructions operate within a computer. In one way, the instruction specifies the arithmetic operation and the two fields to be operated upon. The result of the arithmetic operation replaces the second field specified, while the first field remains unchanged. This type of instruction is illustrated below.

Typical arithmetic instructions are the add, subtract, multiply, and divide instructions. To illustrate the add, suppose the contents of storage positions 546–550 are to be added to the contents of storage positions 701–705. Then, the execution takes place as follows:

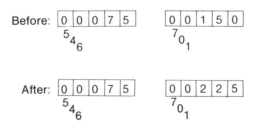

In actuality, another form of data representation is usually used for data involved in arithmetic operations, but conceptually this is what happens.

Because the result of a multiplication or addition may be larger than either field operated upon—555 plus 500 equals 1055—one of the fields is usually moved to a larger field before the calculation takes place. Similarly, because the result of a division has a remainder, the number that is divided must be placed in a larger field, part of which becomes the quotient and part of which becomes the remainder.

Logic Instructions

The basic logic instruction and the basis of logic in the computer is the branch instruction. When a program is initially loaded into storage, the object deck specifies in which storage positions the instructions are to be stored and at which storage position the computer is to begin executing the program. When the computer finishes executing one instruction, it continues with the next instruction in storage. After executing the instruction in positions 1000–1005, for example, the computer executes the instruction starting with address 1006. The only exception to this sequence results from use of the branch instruction. When the branch instruction is executed, it can cause the computer to break the sequence and jump to the instruction beginning at the address specified in the branch instruction.

For instance, one type of branch instruction tells the computer to branch whenever it is executed. This is called an *unconditional branch*. Suppose then that an unconditional branch instruction, which is stored in positions 4032–4035, specifies a branch to address 801. When it is executed, the computer will continue with the instruction starting in storage position 801.

Conditional branch instructions cause branching only when specified conditions are met. For example, one type of conditional branch instruction specifies a branch if the result of an arithmetic instruction is negative. Suppose this instruction occupies storage positions 2044–2047 and specifies that the computer should branch to address 1000 if the result of the preceding arithmetic instruction is negative. If the result is zero or positive, the computer continues with the instruction starting at address 2048, the next instruction in storage. If the result is negative, however, the computer continues by executing the instruction starting at address 1000.

Other branch instructions specify that a branch should take place when the result of an arithmetic calculation is zero, when the result of an arithmetic calculation is larger than the result field, or when an I/O device isn't working. Perhaps the most used branch instruction, however, specifies a branch based on the results of a comparison between two fields in storage. This branch instruction is used in conjunction with the other type of logic instruction, the compare instruction.

The compare instruction specifies that two fields are to be compared. When it is executed, the computer determines the relationship between the two fields: Are they equal? Is the first field greater in value than the second? Is the first field less than the second? The branch instruction then specifies a branch based on any of these three conditions. If, for example, the compare instruction compares two fields representing ages, the branch instruction can specify that a branch should take place if the first age is less than the second.

A compare instruction can operate on alphanumeric as well as numeric fields. For example, if two fields containing alphabetic names are compared, the branch instruction can specify that a branch take place when the second name is higher in alphabetic sequence than the first name. Or, if a one-position alphanumeric code is compared with a storage position containing the code *M*, the branch instruction can specify that a branch take place when the codes are equal.

DISCUSSION

Although this has been a simplified explanation of how the instructions of a computer operate, it is a good analogy of the actual operation of a computer. There are two concepts that you should now understand. The first concerns input/output areas in storage. Quite simply, when an input record is read from a card reader, tape drive, or direct-access device, it is read into an input area. Similarly, before a record is written out on a printer, tape, or direct-access device, it must be arranged properly in the output area for that device. Although this is a simple idea, it is referenced in other chapters in this book and has application in several different programming languages.

The second concept is that a program flowchart can adequately represent the instructions of a program. The I/O symbol represents input and output operations, the process symbol represents arithmetic and data-movement instructions, and the decision symbol represents logic instructions. The flowlines of a flowchart represent the consecutive execution of a stored program's instructions as well as the various branching instructions within the program.

With this introduction as background, you can now reflect upon two types of computer programs. The first type performs the same sequence of operations for each input record or set of input records. The investment-listing program charted in figure 4-3, for example, will process as many inventory cards as the input deck contains. Because a program like this can be used over and over again, it relieves people of many routine and monotonous duties.

The second type of program repeatedly performs a series of calculations in an effort to derive an answer to a problem or to derive a result that is a reasonably close approximation to an answer. To illustrate this type of program, consider a somewhat trivial problem. In 1627, Manhattan Island was purchased from the Indians for $24. If the Indians had put the $24 in a savings account at $4\frac{1}{2}$ percent interest compounded annually, how much would they have in their savings account today?

The flowchart in figure 4-12 represents a program that could be used for solving this problem. Briefly, the interest is calculated each year and added to the principal; then 1 is added to the year field, which started at 1627. This sequence of instructions is repeated until the year field is equal to the present year. Then, the total in the principal field is printed.

Although the method of solving this problem is simple, it would take a human many hours to perform the series of calculations, even with a

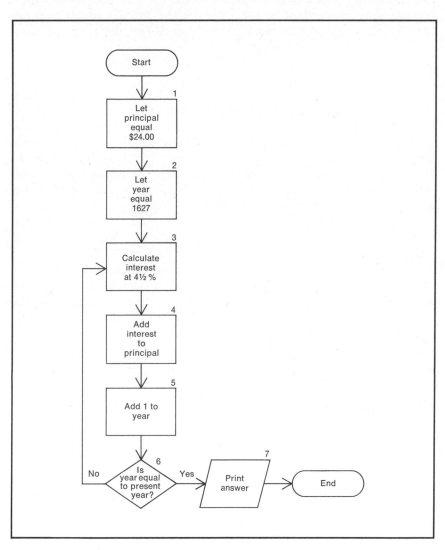

FIGURE 4-12   Flowchart for solution of the Manhattan problem

calculator. If you don't think so, do the calculations for about ten years. When this program is executed by a computer, however, the result is calculated in a matter of seconds.

This type of program illustrates how the computer can extend human capabilities. No longer do we have to actually solve a problem. With the computer, we need only to conceive the series of steps that will lead to a solution. Because the computer's electronic circuits operate several million times faster than human nerve cells, the computer can perform in minutes calculations that would take man a lifetime to perform. It is in this respect that the computer has been credited with solving problems that were considered unsolvable. It is also in this respect that the computer has been advertised as capable of doing the work of 100,000 mathematicians.

Although there are many variations of these two types of programs—the two techniques are often used within the same program—they do typify the power of the computer. On the one hand, the computer can relieve us of the tedious aspects of our occupations; on the other hand, the computer can extend our problem-solving capabilities.

SUMMARY

1. The storage of a computer is made up of a number of storage positions—usually 4000 (4K) or more—each having a unique storage address. In one common form of data representation, one character is stored in each storage position. However, there are several other storage forms, some of which are described later in this book.

2. In general, there are four types of instructions that can be executed by a computer: I/O, data movement, arithmetic, and logic. Though these may seem limited, they are capable of directing extensive processing sequences when they are combined in a program.

3. Input areas are areas in storage into which data records are read. Output areas are areas from which output records are written.

4. The power of a computer becomes evident when you consider the two types of programs it performs. In the first, the same sequence of instructions is repeated for many different sets of input data. In the second, generally involving mathematical procedures, a sequence of instructions is repeated many times for a single set of input data.

TERMINOLOGY

storage address
field in storage
binary component
magnetic core
core storage
card input area

input area
printer output area
output area
unconditional branch
conditional branch

QUESTIONS

1. During the execution of a program, the program's instructions reside in the storage unit of the CPU. What else does internal storage contain?

2. Pretend you're a computer. Do the processing described in the flowchart in figure 4-12 for five executions of the loop (blocks 3, 4, 5, and 6). After each execution of the loop, show what the year and principal fields contain.

SECTION TWO

CARD, TAPE, AND DIRECT-ACCESS CONCEPTS

This section shows you how a few basic applications are done on card, tape, and direct access systems. Once you complete it, you should have a good understanding of what a computer system is and what makes it work. This is the most important section in the book, so you should give it special attention.

5 CARD SYSTEMS

Before you can appreciate how a card computer system is used for a business application, you need to know more about punched cards and the machines that process them. As a result, topic 1 of this chapter describes the 80-column and the 96-column punched card in detail. Then topic 2 presents machines that are used to sort cards, and topic 3 presents a special card I/O unit that is used on many small computer systems. Finally, topic 4 will show you how a card system is used for billing, accounts receivable, and inventory control.

TOPIC 1
THE PUNCHED CARD

At one time or another, you have probably come into contact with a standard punched card—perhaps in the form of a payroll check, a utility bill, or a student registration card. The question is: Can you decode the data that is punched in a card?

Figure 5-1 presents the basic characteristics of a standard punched card, the 80-column card. This card has 80 vertical *columns,* numbered from left to right. A hole can be punched in twelve different positions in each card column. For the purpose of illustration, each of these punching positions is punched in column 2 of the card. From bottom to top, these punches are called the 9-punch, 8-, 7-, 6-, 5-, 4-, 3-, 2-, 1-, 0- (zero), 11-, and 12-punch. Because an 11-punch is often used to distinguish one type of card from another, it is also referred to as an X-*punch.* (For example, an 11-punch in column 1 of a card may indicate that it is a payroll card.)

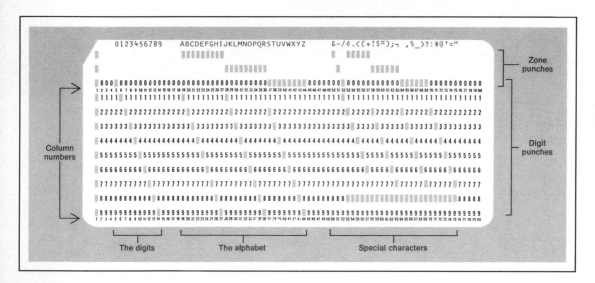

FIGURE 5-1 The standard 80-column punched card

As you can see at the right edge of the card, the 0- through 9-punches are called *digit punches;* and the 12-, 11- and 0-punches are called *zone punches.* The 0-punch, therefore, can be either a zone or a digit punch. It is a digit punch when no other punch is recorded in the column; but it is a zone punch if a digit punch is recorded below it.

Each column of a punched card can contain one character of data; namely, a number (0 through 9), a letter (A through Z), or a *special character* (such as an asterisk, a dollar sign, or a decimal point). In the illustration, the numbers are punched in columns 5 through 14, the letters in columns 19 through 44, and twenty-seven special characters in columns 50 through 76. The character punched in each column is printed at the top of the card directly over the column.

The combinations of punches used to represent charcters in a punched card make up a code called *Hollerith code,* named after Herman Hollerith, inventor of the punched card. As you can see in the illustration, the numbers 0 through 9 are represented by the corresponding digit punch; and the letters by the combination of a zone and a digit punch. The special characters are represented by one, two, or three punches in a single card column. For example, a decimal point consists of a 12-, 3-, and 8-punch, while a hyphen (-) consists of an 11-punch only.

When a punched card is used to represent business data, groups of adjacent columns, called *fields,* represent specific data items. For instance, columns 21–40 (21 through 40) may be used for the description of a product, while columns 76–80 are used for the number of the customer that bought the product. In the card in figure 5-2, there are ten fields in columns 1–60. From left to right, they are the card-code field, the salesman-number field, the customer-number field, the order-number field, the transaction-date field, and so on. If an item is back-ordered, column 61 is supposed to contain an X-punch. Because a card like this contains information relating to a single business record—in this case, one line item of billing—punched cards are sometimes referred to as *unit-record cards.*

If you study the fields in figure 5-2, you can see that they are punched differently, depending on whether they are numeric or *alphanumeric.* (An alphanumeric field may contain letters, numbers, or special characters.) For an alphanumeric field, the data begins in the leftmost column of the field and continues to the right. When there are no more characters to be punched, the remainder of the field is left blank. Thus, the item-description field contains 1/2 INCH ADJ WRENCH in columns 32–50 and blanks in columns 51–55.

In contrast, numeric fields are punched to correspond with an assumed decimal point—the decimal point itself isn't punched. For example, the unit-price field in figure 5-2 assumes two decimal places, as indicated by the dotted line. Thus, the unit price of $2.75 is punched as the number 275 in columns 58–60. Since all columns of a numeric field should be

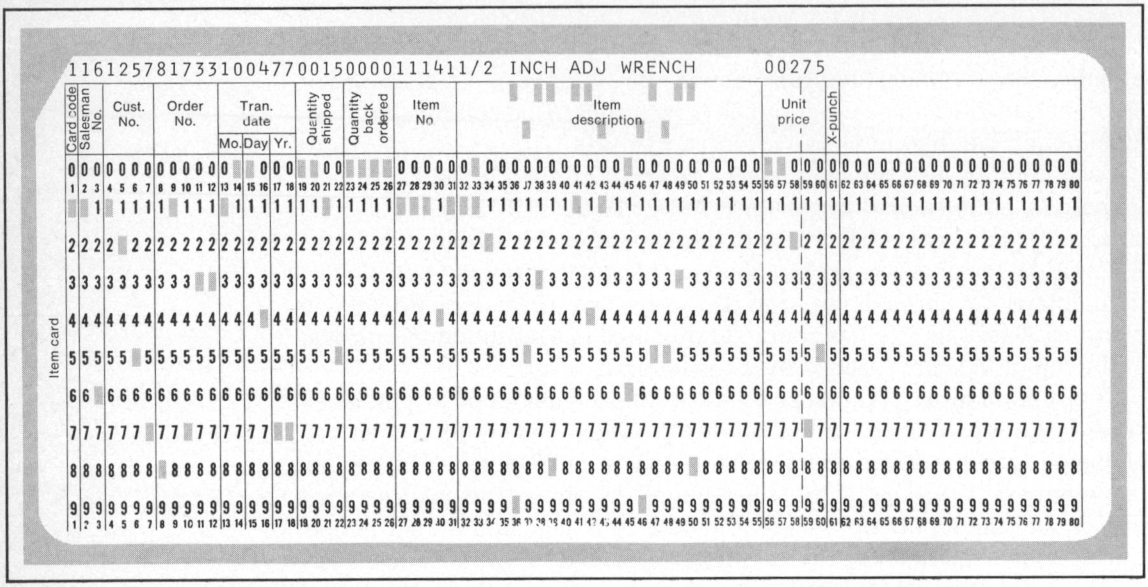

116125781733100477001500001114 11/2 INCH ADJ WRENCH   00275

FIGURE 5-2   A unit-record card

punched with a digit, zeros are punched in columns 56 and 57 to fill the unit-price field.

In some cases, a numeric field in a card may contain a negative number. This is normally indicated by an X-punch in the rightmost column of the field. For example, a customer may have a credit balance of $12.85 in his or her accounts receivable record with a company. If the balance field is in columns 51–56, the field would contain 00128N. Since N is the combination of an X-punch and a 5-punch and two decimal places are assumed, it would indicate a negative 12.85.

Incidentally, although the punched card is a standard size, it can be printed or colored in any way. Thus, a typical computer installation will have cards of several different colors. For example, green cards may be used in the payroll application, while yellow cards may represent the line items in a billing application. Similarly, punched cards can be printed to indicate the location of fields (as in figure 5-2) or to represent a check or a utility bill. Since machines read only the holes punched in the card, both color coding and printing are for the convenience of those working with the punched cards.

A corner cut, as illustrated in figure 5-2, is used to be sure that all cards in a deck are facing the same way. For example, if a card is turned upside down in a deck with right corner cuts, that card will stick out at the right corner. The corner cut can be on either the left or the right, but all corner cuts should be on the same side for any one deck of cards.

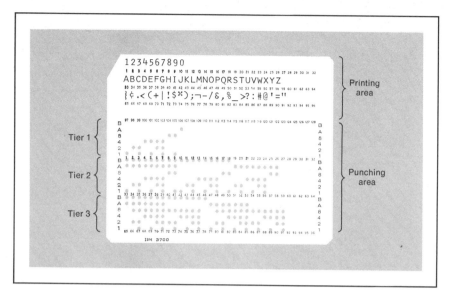

FIGURE 5-3 The 96-column card

The 96-Column Card

In 1969 IBM announced a new card computer system, called the System/3, that was designed for small companies who until then had not been able to afford a computer system. The unique feature of the System/3 is that it does not use the standard 80-column punched card. Instead, it uses a 96-column card that is less than half the size of the standard card. Because the card is smaller, the card-handling components of the system are also reduced in size, thus cutting the manufacturing costs of the components. And, because each card can store 96 characters of data, fewer cards are likely to be needed for any one application. Since the introduction of this new card, 96-column card-reading devices have also been developed by other manufacturers.

The 96-column card is illustrated in figure 5-3. As you can see, 96 columns are stacked in three *tiers,* each consisting of thirty-two columns of data. The first tier contains columns 1–32, the second tier columns 33–64, the third tier columns 65–96. At the top of the card, there is space for four lines, or 128 characters, of printing. The keypunch can print in the first three rows of the card; the multifunction card unit used by the System/3 (described in topic 3) can print in all four printing rows. In the illustration, the digits 1–9 and 0 are punched and printed in columns 1–10, the letters in columns 33–58, and twenty-seven special characters in columns 65–91.

For each card column, there are six punching positions referred to, from top to bottom, as the B-, A-, 8-, 4-, 2-, and 1-positions. These punching positions correspond to standard punched-card code in that the B- and A-punches are *zone punches*, the 8-, 4-, 2-, and 1-punches are *digit punches*. With one exception, a digit is represented by one or more digit punches, a letter by a combination of zone and digit punches, and special characters by digit punches, zone punches, or both zone and digit punches.

The codes for the digits 0–9 are as follows:

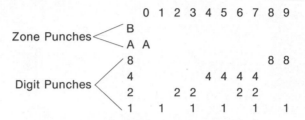

The zero consists of an A-punch only, while the digits 1–9 are made up of one or more digit punches. To convert the code to the digit, you add the values of the digit punches. Thus, a 1- and a 2-punch represent the digit 3 ($1 + 2 = 3$); a 4-, 2-, and 1-punch represent the digit 7.

By referring to figure 5-3 again, you can see that both the A- and B-punches are used for the letters A–I, the B-punch for the letters J–R, and the A-punch for the letters S–Z. These zone punches are combined with digit punches in order to represent all twenty-six letters.

SUMMARY

The standard punched card is an 80-column card that can store up to 80 characters of data, one character per column. The 96-column card can store up to 96 characters of data. By assigning groups of adjacent card columns to various items of data, a card is divided into fields.

TERMINOLOGY

column
X-punch
digit punch
zone punch
special character

Hollerith code
field
unit-record card
alphanumeric
tier

QUESTIONS

1. Suppose a deck of cards was going to be used for printing three-line mailing labels. What fields would it require? Approximately how many card columns do you think each of these fields should consist of?

2. Suppose a −21 is punched in columns 3-4 of a 96-column card. What punches would column 4 contain, and what letter does this combination of punches represent?

TOPIC 2
CARD SORTING

Before a card computer system can process punched cards, the cards must be sorted into acceptable sequences. For instance, a deck of sales cards must be sorted into customer-number sequence before preparing invoices. This sorting is often done by a machine called a sorter. There is one version that is used for 80-column cards, another for use with 96-column cards.

THE 80-COLUMN CARD SORTER

The 80-column sorter, as shown in figure 5-4, has one input hopper and thirteen output pockets. From left to right, these pockets are called the 9-, 8-, 7-, 6-, 5-, 4-, 3-, 2-, 1-, 0-, 11-, and R- (reject) pockets. On the right side of the machine is the input hopper and a reading mechanism, which is a metal reading brush that can be set over any of the 80 card columns but can read only one column at a time. As the cards pass through the sorter, they are directed to the pocket corresponding to the data punched in the

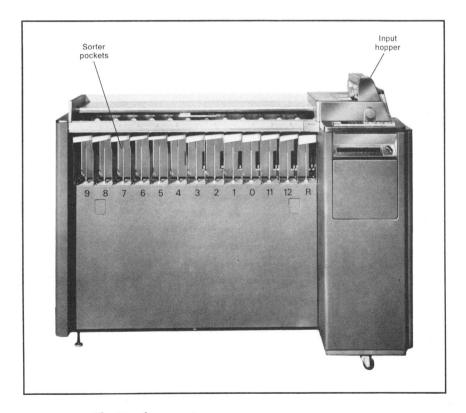

FIGURE 5-4   The 80-column sorter

card column that is being read. If a column contains more than one punch, the card is sent to the pocket corresponding to the first punch that is read, starting with the 9-edge of the card.

The most common use of the sorter is to sort a deck of cards based on the data in a numeric field—for example, customer number. To do this, the sorter operator passes the cards through the sorter once for each column in the field, from the righthand column to the left. If the customer is punched in columns 61–65, the operator sets the sorting brush on column 65, places the deck in the input hopper, and starts the machine. After the cards have passed through the machine—at perhaps 1000 cards per minute—the operator collects the cards from the pockets, places the deck in the input hopper, sets the sorting brush to the next column in the field (column 64), and starts the machine again. The operator continues in this way until the deck is sorted by the leftmost column of the field, column 61. At this time, the deck is in customer-number order.

Figure 5-5 schematically illustrates the sorting of a two-column numeric field. The numbers on each card represent the contents of the field that is being sorted. In the first pass, the cards are sorted on the rightmost column of the field; in the second pass, on the leftmost. Although this is a simplified example, requiring only four sorter pockets, it does illustrate numeric sorting.

By adjusting its switches, a sorter can also be used to sort a deck on an alphabetic field. The procedure is basically the same—sorting proceeds from the righthand column of the field to the left—but two passes are required for each column. The operator adjusts the switches so that each column is first sorted by digit punch and then by zone punch. Because of the extra time required for sorting on alphabetic fields—two passes for each column instead of one—it is avoided whenever possible.

THE 96-COLUMN SORTER

The 96-column card sorter, shown in figure 5-6, has only six pockets. Thus, sorting a deck of cards on a numeric field requires two phases for each card column in the sort field. To illustrate, suppose a deck of cards is being sorted into numeric sequence based on columns 21 and 22. This procedure is illustrated in figure 5-7.

Because sorting proceeds from right to left, the column selector is first set to column 22. In the first phase for this column, the cards containing even digits are stacked in their respective pockets, while cards containing odd digits are stacked in the reject pocket. For example, a column containing the code for the digit 4 is stacked in the 4-pocket; a card containing the code for a 7 is stacked in the reject pocket. In the second phase, the cards are taken from the reject pocket and sorted again. This time the odd-digit cards are stacked on top of the even-digit cards. When the cards are removed from the sorter pockets from right to left, the deck

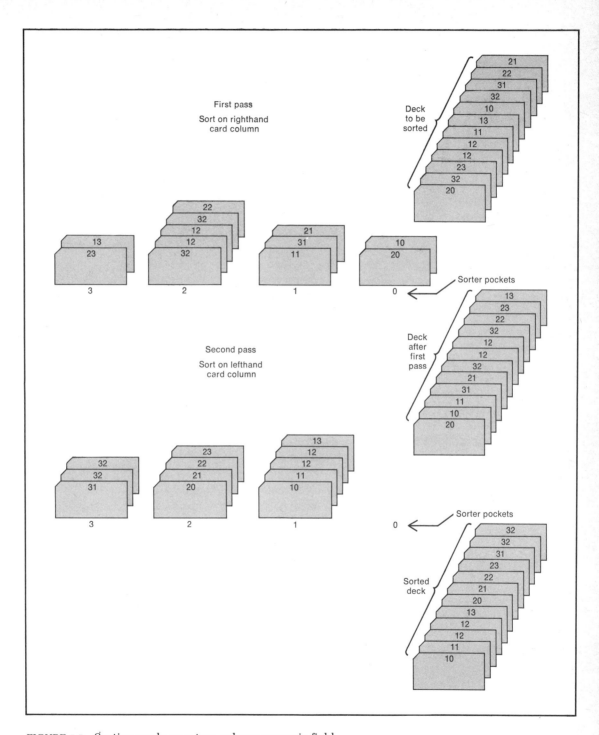

FIGURE 5-5 Sorting cards on a two-column numeric field

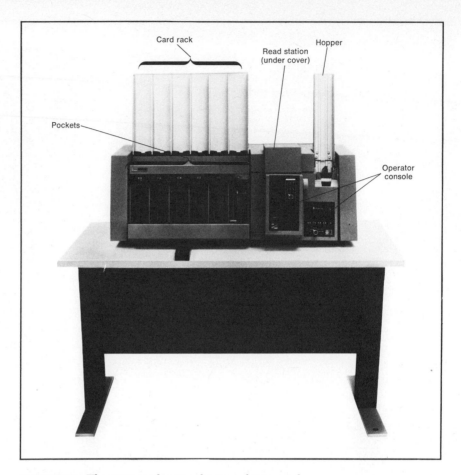

FIGURE 5-6   The 5486 card sorter for 96-column cards

is in sequence based on column 22. By repeating this procedure for column 21, the deck will be arranged in the desired sequence.

To sort a deck on an alphabetic field, three phases are required for each card column. After the digit sort (phases 1 and 2) for each card column, a third phase, which sorts by zone punches, is required. Because of the extra time required, alphabetic sorting is generally avoided when designing a system.

SUMMARY   The sorter is used to arrange card decks into sequence suitable for processing by a computer. Although a deck can be sorted on either an alphabetic or numeric field, numeric sorting is much more common.

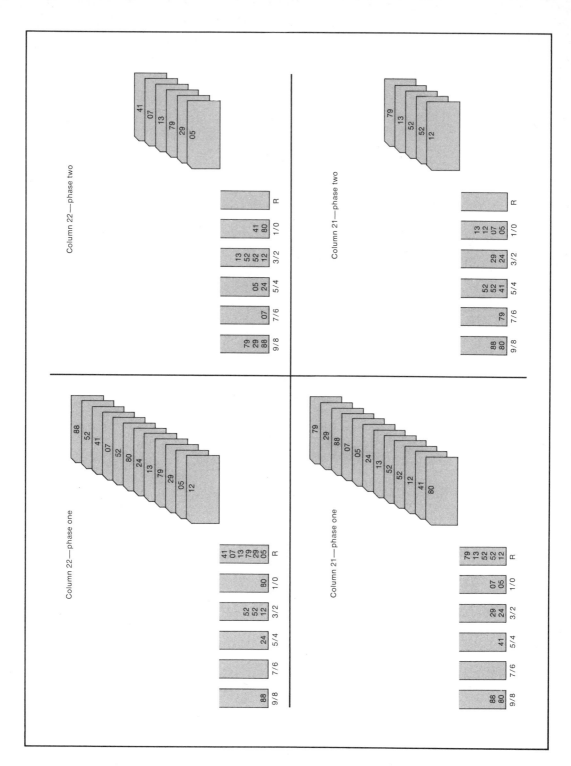

FIGURE 5-7 Sorting with the 5486 card sorter (columns 21 and 22)

TERMINOLOGY
sorter
numeric sorting
alphabetic sorting

QUESTIONS

1. Suppose you had a deck of item cards with item number in columns 7–11. With which card column would you begin sorting? Also, how many times would the cards have to be passed through to complete the sort using 80-column cards? Using 96-column cards?

2. Suppose you had a deck of customer cards and a deck of transaction cards with customer number punched in columns 12–15 in each card. Suppose also that you put the customer deck in the machine first with the transaction deck on top of it. If the decks are sorted together on columns 12–15, which type of card will be first for any specific customer number?

TOPIC 3
MULTIFUNCTION
CARD MACHINES

Until the mid-sixties, a card computer system was usually made up of printer, card reader, card punch, and CPU. To supplement the computer system, one or more auxiliary machines were also used. For instance, a sorter was commonly used to arrange card decks into acceptable sequences for processing. In addition, a typical system made use of machines like the collator, interpreter, and reproducer.

One of the functions of the collator was to merge two decks of sequenced cards into one sequenced deck. The interpreter printed the data punched in cards on the face of the cards (this is called *interpreting*). And the reproducer punched data from one deck of cards into another.

One of the limitations of these early card systems was the amount of card handling required. For each computer run, there was likely to be one or more auxiliary runs. For instance, a sort run and a collate (merge) run often preceded a computer run. And an interpreting run often followed a computer run when new cards were punched.

THE MFCM

To reduce card handling, the *multifunction card machine (MFCM)* was developed for the IBM System/360 Model 20. The MFCM, shown in figure 5-8, has two input hoppers and five output stackers. As cards pass through the machine from either hopper, they can be read, punched, or both read and punched, and they can be stacked in any of the five stackers. An optional feature allows the MFCM to print on cards from either hopper as they pass through the machine.

In figure 5-9, the schematic drawing of the card path of the MFCM shows that cards from either hopper pass through read, punch, and print stations. Hopper 1 of the MFCM is usually referred to as the *primary hopper* and hopper 2 as the *secondary hopper*.

The advantage of the MFCM is that it can reduce the number of steps required to do a job on a computer system. To illustrate, compare a Model 20 card system that has a card reader and a card punch with a Model 20 system that has an MFCM. Figure 5-10, then, presents two system flow-charts showing how a sales-by-customer report can be prepared from customer master cards and daily transaction cards.

System A of figure 5-10 represents the preparation of the sales report with a card reader. In the first step, the customer master cards and the transaction cards, both in customer-number sequence, are merged using the collator. The merged deck is then placed in the input hopper of the card reader, and the computer system prepares the sales report (step 2). In the third step, the merged deck is separated by sorting the cards again.

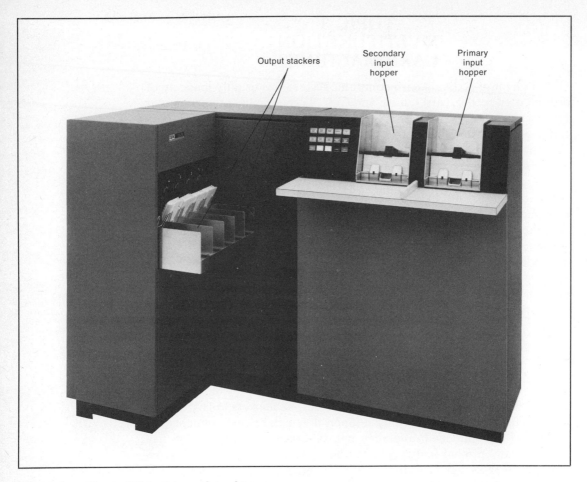

FIGURE 5-8   The multifunction card machine

Normally, the master cards are distinguished from the transaction cards by some control punch so that in one pass of the cards through the sorter, all master cards are stacked in one pocket and all transaction cards in another.

In contrast to system A, system B, which uses the MFCM, requires only one step. The master cards are placed in hopper 1 of the MFCM, the transaction cards are placed in hopper 2, and the program is executed. As the cards pass through the MFCM, they are stacked in separate stackers.

One particular advantage of the card-printing feature of the MFCM is its ability to prepare a punched-card bill, statement, or check. Because the MFCM can print in sixty-four printing positions on twenty-five different lines on the face of a card, it can be used to prepare a document such as the monthly statement in figure 5-11. Notice that starting in column

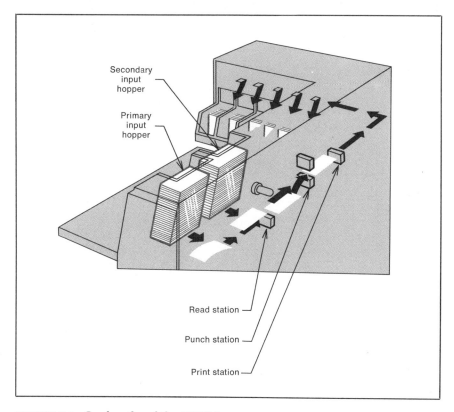

FIGURE 5-9 Card paths of the MFCM

1, customer number, statement date, and balance owed are also punched in the card. If the card is returned with the payment of $33.15, the statement itself can be used as a transaction card when updating the customer's accounts receivable balance. This, of course, eliminates the need for keypunching a transaction card. A card like this, which is both output from a computer system (the statement) and input to a computer system (the transaction card), is often referred to as a *turnaround document.*

THE MFCU

The IBM System/3, which uses 96-column cards, has a multifunction card unit (MFCU) available with it. In contrast to the MFCM, the MFCU has only four output stackers and can print on only four lines at the top of the card. Otherwise, it functions much the same as the MFCM. As cards pass through the MFCU from either of its two input hoppers, they can be

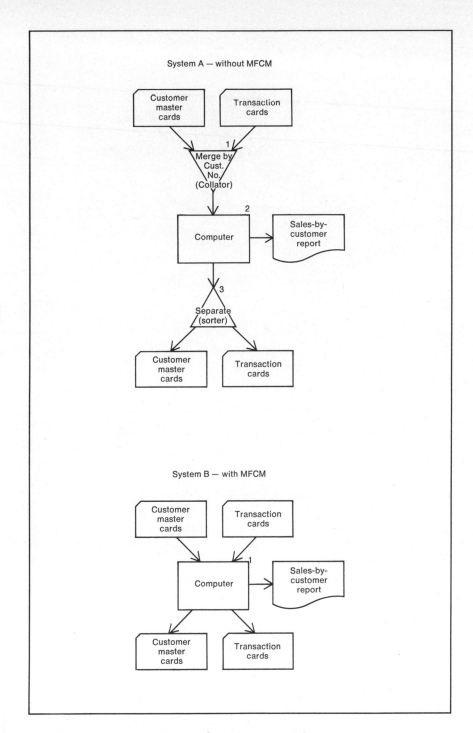

FIGURE 5-10 Comparing two card systems—example 1

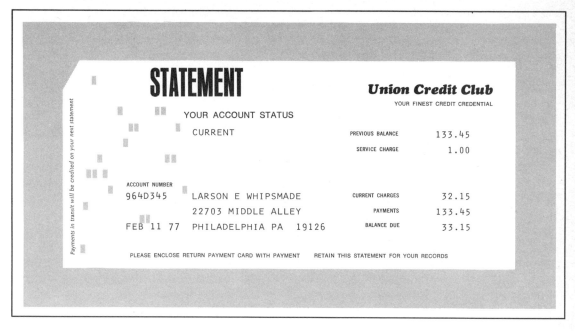

FIGURE 5-11   A turnaround document printed by the MFCM

read, punched, and printed, and then stacked in any of the four output stackers. Figure 5-12 illustrates the System/3 and the MFCU.

The MFCM and the MFCU were hardware breakthroughs for card systems, because they reduced card handling significantly. In addition, since they can perform all of the functions of collator, interpreter, and reproducer, the auxiliary machines traditionally found with card systems were no longer needed. As a result, a modern card system is likely to consist of a computer with MFCM or MFCU plus one sorter plus one or more keypunches and verifiers.

SUMMARY

A multifunction card device is an I/O unit that can read, punch, or print on cards fed from either of its two input hoppers. It can also stack the cards from either hopper into any of its several output stackers. As a result, it can significantly reduce the card handling required by earlier card systems.

TERMINOLOGY

multifunction card machine	turnaround document
MFCM	multifunction card unit
primary hopper	MFCU
secondary hopper	

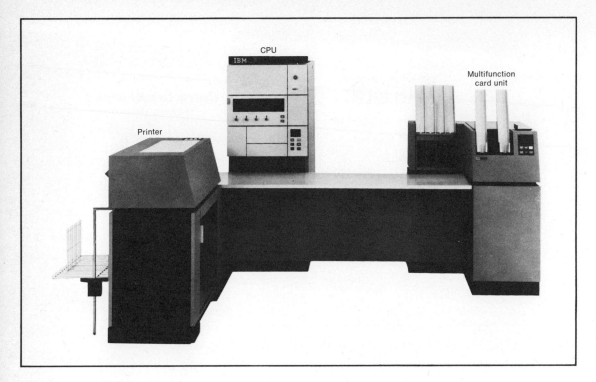

FIGURE 5-12   A System/3 card system

QUESTIONS

1. Suppose you want to merge two decks of cards that are already sorted in customer-number sequence. Do you think it could be done using an MFCM or MFCU? If so, how?

2. Suppose you want to duplicate a deck of cards; that is, punch the data from the first deck into a blank deck so you have two decks exactly alike. Do you think it could be done using an MFCM or MFCU? If so, how?

TOPIC 4
CARD SYSTEM DESIGN

In chapter 2 you were introduced to billing and accounts receivable as done by a small disk system. In this topic you will see how these applications are done by a small card system. You will also be introduced to sales analysis and inventory control as done by a card system.

Throughout this topic assume that the processing is done by a card system consisting of a CPU, printer, and MFCM. The only auxiliary machines this system needs, then, are keypunches, verifiers, and a sorter. Although many card systems do not have multifunction card devices, most of them do. And the concepts are the same whether or not a multifunction card device is used.

A POSTBILLING SYSTEM

Figure 5-13 is a systems flowchart for the billing application. Here the input document is the shipping order after it has been returned from the shipping department. As a result, it indicates whether or not any items have been backordered. The output of the system is the invoice. This is referred to as a *postbilling system* because the bills are prepared after the items are shipped.

The formats for the cards used in this system are given in figure 5-14. The transaction cards indicate which items have been shipped and backordered. The name-and-address (N/A) card gives the customer's name and address. And the accounts-receivable (A/R) card summarizes the data for each invoice prepared by the system. The date card is used as the first card of the billing deck processed in step 6 of the system—it gives the billing date and the invoice number for the first invoice to be printed.

In step 1 of figure 5-13, the transaction cards are keypunched and verified, one card for each line item of billing. Then these cards are sorted into customer-number sequence by the sorter in step 2. Why customer-number sequence? Because the name-and-address file is in customer-number sequence, and invoices naturally require the data for each customer to be grouped.

In step 3, the name-and-address cards are merged with the transaction cards. After this step, the merged deck is in customer-number sequence and each name-and-address card is followed by the transaction cards for that customer (if any).

In step 4, the control totals accumulated during merging are compared with those created during keypunching, and the necessary adjustments are made. Similarly, if there are any unmatched transaction cards, it indicates a keypunching error or a missing name-and-address card, so these errors must be corrected (step 5). (An *unmatched transaction* is one that doesn't match up with a name-and-address card that has the same

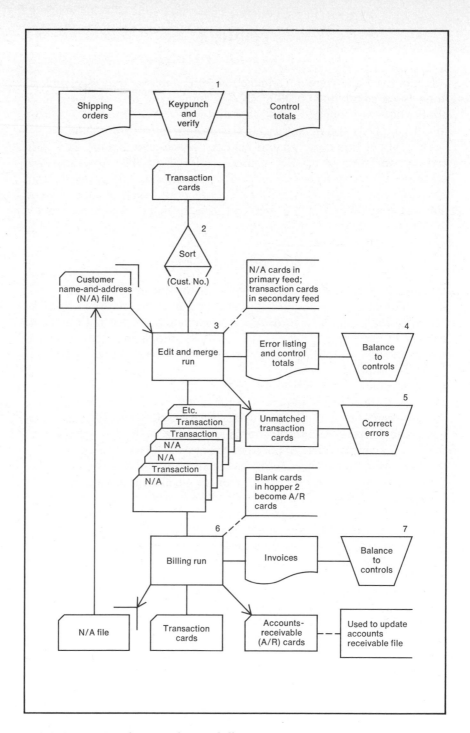

FIGURE 5-13   A card system for postbilling

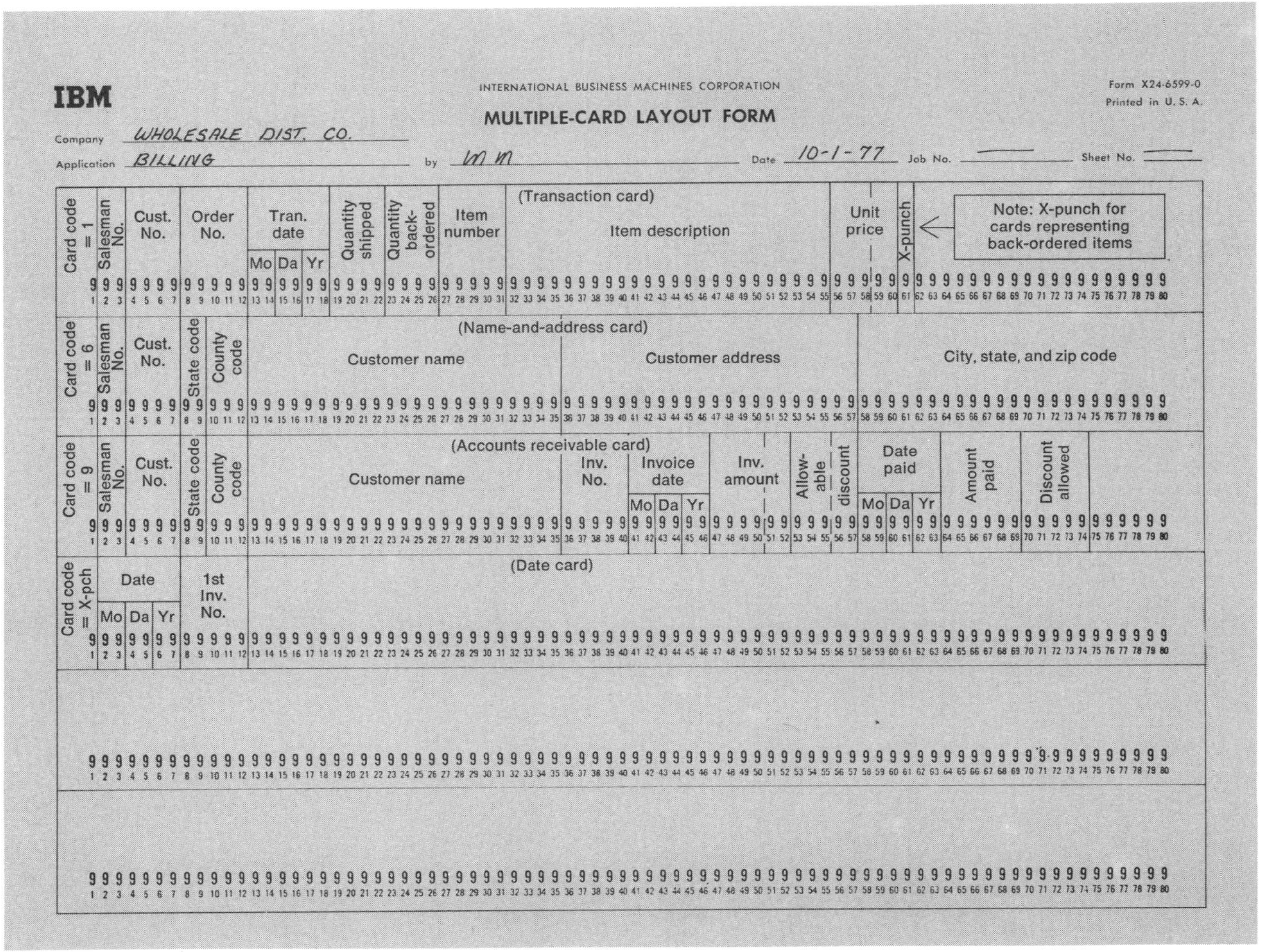
IBM
INTERNATIONAL BUSINESS MACHINES CORPORATION
MULTIPLE-CARD LAYOUT FORM
Form X24-6599-0
Printed in U. S. A.
Company WHOLESALE DIST. CO.
Application BILLING by mm Date 10-1-77 Job No. ____ Sheet No. ____

(Transaction card)

Card code = 1	Salesman No.	Cust. No.	Order No.	Tran. date (Mo / Da / Yr)	Quantity shipped	Quantity back-ordered	Item number	Item description	Unit price	X-punch	
1	2–3	4–7	8–12	13–14 / 15–16 / 17–18	19–22	23–26	27–31	32–55	56–60	61	62–80

Note: X-punch for cards representing back-ordered items

(Name-and-address card)

Card code = 6	Salesman No.	Cust. No.	State code	County code	Customer name	Customer address	City, state, and zip code
1	2–3	4–7	8–9	10–12	13–35	36–57	58–80

(Accounts receivable card)

Card code = 9	Salesman No.	Cust. No.	State code	County code	Customer name	Inv. No.	Invoice date (Mo / Da / Yr)	Inv. amount	Allow-able discount	Date paid (Mo / Da / Yr)	Amount paid	Discount allowed	
1	2–3	4–7	8–9	10–12	13–35	36–40	41–42 / 43–44 / 45–46	47–52	53–57	58–59 / 60–61 / 62–63	64–69	70–74	75–80

(Date card)

Card code = X-pch	Date (Mo / Da / Yr)	1st Inv. No.	
1	2–3 / 4–5 / 6–7	8–12	13–80

FIGURE 5-14 Card formats for billing

customer number.) After all adjustments are made to the billing deck, it is ready for the billing run.

Figure 5-15 is a schematic illustration of what happens during the billing run (step 6). Here the invoice number and invoice date are taken from the date card (the first card in the billing deck). After each invoice is printed, one is added to the invoice number, so it can be used for the next invoice. The rest of the heading data is taken from the name-and-address card, and the line-item data is taken from the transaction cards. Because the transaction cards don't contain the extension, the computer calculates the extension for each line item (quantity shipped times unit price) and accumulates the invoice total.

As the total line for each invoice is printed, one summary accounts-receivable card is punched by the MFCM. This card, shown in figure 5-15, can be used in the accounts-receivable application. Because the data it contains is printed on the top of the card, it can be read by clerks and is a permanent record of each invoice.

After the billing run, the transaction cards can be held in a temporary file, possibly for additional processing in a sales-analysis application. The name-and-address cards can be returned to their permanent storage file since they are reused for each billing run. And the accounts-receivable cards can be processed in the accounts-receivable application.

AN OPEN-ITEM
ACCOUNTS-RECEIVABLE
SYSTEM

Most manufacturers and wholesale distributors are paid by the invoice. In other words, when they receive a payment from a customer, it is for one or more specific invoices. For instance, a customer's check may indicate that it is for invoice numbers 4201, 5299, and 5479. As a result, *open-item accounts-receivable systems* are common in these businesses. Here, each unpaid invoice is called an *open item*. As each open item is paid, it is removed from the open-item file.

When a card system is used, the open-item file is a deck of cards. For example, the card file shown in figure 5-16 might represent an open-item file for a wholesale distributor. This file is made up of the accounts-receivable cards punched by the billing system in figure 5-13. As new invoices are printed, open-item cards are added to the file. As open items are paid, they are removed from the file. In general, a file like this is kept in sequence by invoice date within customer number. So the oldest invoice card is the first for each customer; the newest is the last.

To add open-item cards to the file, procedures such as those charted in figure 5-17 are commonly used. After billing, the accounts-receivable cards are printed, one line for each card, in an invoice *register*. A register

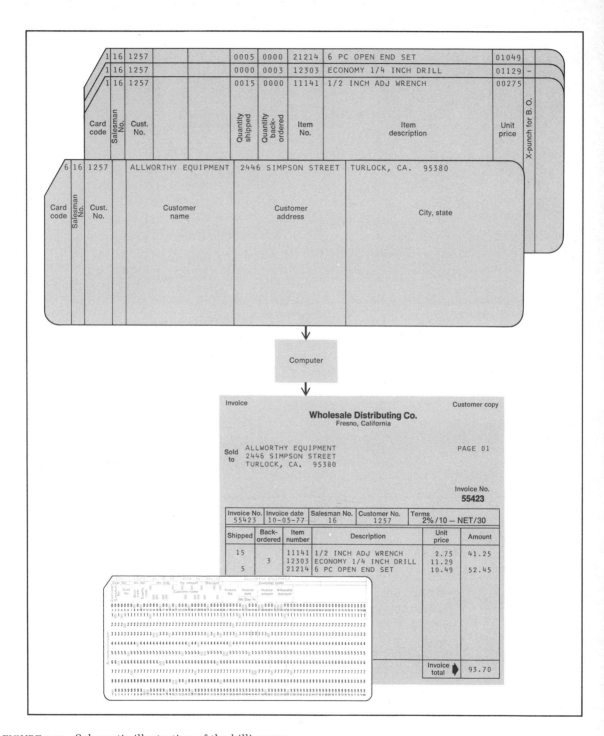

FIGURE 5-15 Schematic illustration of the billing run

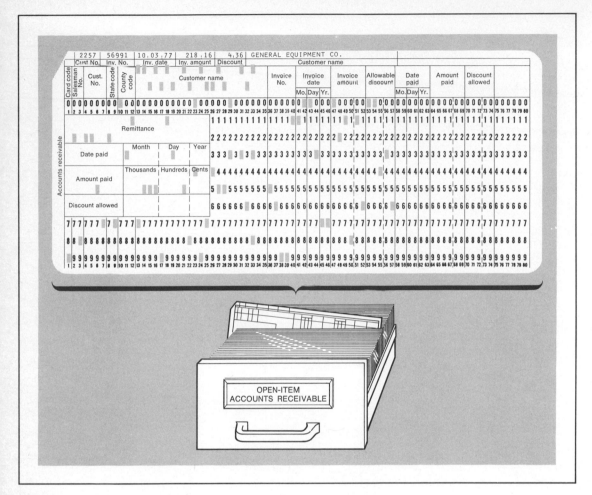

FIGURE 5-16   An open-item accounts-receivable file

is simply a listing of data punched in transaction cards of one kind or another. Because a register can help locate a missing card or an erroneous transaction, it is common to print a register immediately after punched cards are created. The invoice register is a permanent record of the invoices printed each day.

In step 3 of the chart in figure 5-17, the new accounts-receivable cards are merged into the open-item file. After this, the master file should represent the total amount owed the company. During the merging run, the computer can add all the invoice totals and derive the accounts-receivable total. Notice that steps 2 and 4 are balancing steps to assure the accuracy of the accounts-receivable system.

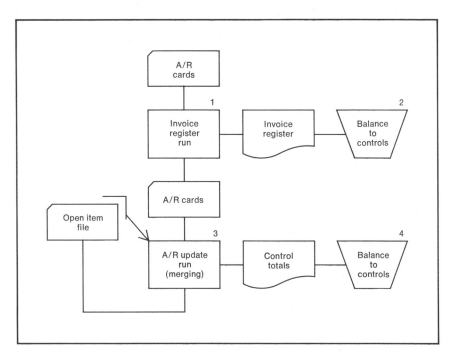

FIGURE 5-17   Processing charges in an open-item system

Processing Cash Receipts

The flowchart in figure 5-18 represents the daily procedures for processing payments to the accounts-receivable file. The basic idea is to remove accounts-receivable cards from the file as they are paid by the customer. Then the file will always represent only those amounts still owed. Although an actual cash-receipts procedure would have to provide for partial payments, the procedure illustrated assumes that all payments cover one or more complete invoices.

In steps 1–3, the checks and remittance advices from customers are sorted into alphabetic sequence (which is also customer-number sequence), and the check amount is recorded on the remittance advice. (The remittance advice indicates which invoices are being paid.) Then a bank deposit is made, and totals are taken and recorded on control sheets.

In step 4, clerks pull from the invoice file the accounts-receivable cards that have been paid. On the face of each card (see figure 5-16), the clerk writes the amount actually paid, the date paid, and the discount allowed. Then, in step 5, these fields are keypunched into the cards and verified. In this case, the keypunch and verifier operators read the source data from the face of the card as it passes through the machines.

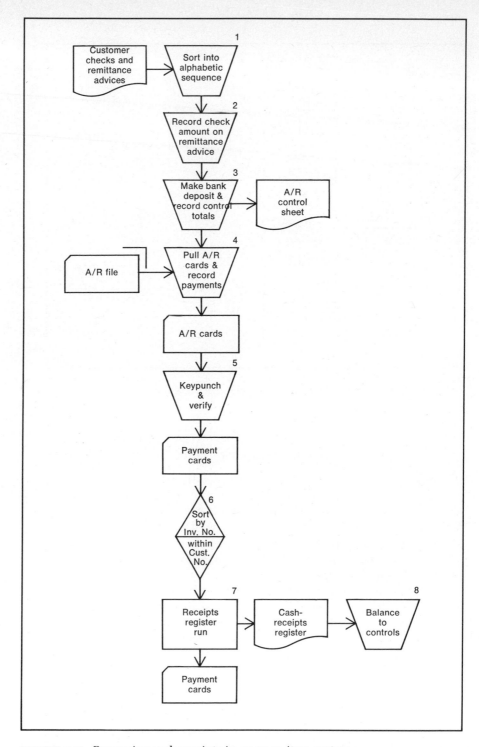

FIGURE 5-18 Processing cash receipts in an open-item system

In step 6, the payment cards are sorted into sequence by invoice number within customer number. This means that the cards are first sorted by invoice number, and then by customer number. After being listed in a cash-receipts register in step 7 and balanced to controls in step 8, the cards are filed in a paid file, to be used later for preparing accounts-receivable reports.

Month-End Procedures

Because the open-item file is updated daily, it is a simple matter to prepare such monthly documents as an aged trial balance and customer statements. Figure 5-19, for example, charts one way of preparing them.

To prepare an aged trial balance, the accounts-receivable file is processed by the computer (step 1). Since each accounts-receivable card contains the date and amount owed, the computer can determine whether the charge is current, over thirty, over sixty, or over ninety days, provided the present date is read into storage from a date card at the start of the program. Since the accounts receivable file is updated daily, the aged trial balance can be prepared at any time.

To prepared monthly statements, the name-and-address cards are placed in one hopper of the MFCM and the accounts-receivable file is placed in the other. For each customer, the name and address, the

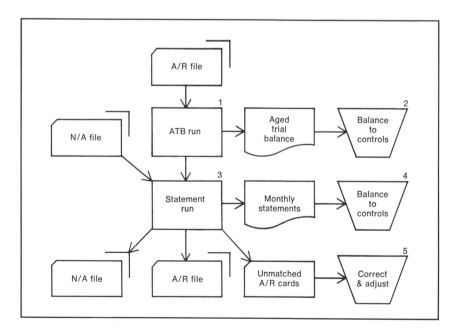

FIGURE 5-19   Monthly accounts-receivable procedures

amounts owed, and the total owed is printed on the statement. If desired, aging can also be shown on the statement.

FILE MAINTENANCE

By now you can see that a card system, like any other DP system, relies heavily on maintaining accurate master files. In the billing and accounts-receivable system just described, two master files were used: a customer name-and-address file and an open-item accounts-receivable file. In other applications, files would be kept for inventory items, employee payroll data, and so on. *File maintenance* means adding, deleting, changing, and updating the records in these files.

In a card system, of course, the master files are simply decks of cards. As a result, adding, deleting, or changing a record in a file is usually a manual operation. To change the address in a name-and-address card, for example, a new card is keypunched with the new address, the old card is removed from the master file, and the new card is added to the file. If the number of additions or changes is large, a computer with a multifunction card device can be used to merge the new cards into and to remove the old cards from the file. Because the accuracy of a file is so critical to the processing of the system, controls must be carefully planned for the file-maintenance procedures.

Updating generally refers to changing the data in a record as a result of one or more transactions pertaining to the master data. In the disk system described in chapter 2, for example, the inventory master records were updated by changing the on-hand field based on shipments to customers. Since the fields in a card cannot be changed, however, file updating on a card system means creating new master cards and discarding the old.

The flowchart in figure 5-20 illustrates this process of updating a master file on a card system with an MFCM. Here an inventory master file is updated based on issues from inventory (sales), receipts to inventory (purchases), returns from customers, and items ordered by the purchasing department. The format of the master item card is given at the bottom of the figure.

In steps 1–6, the data is punched into transaction cards and arranged into an inventory deck consisting of old master cards followed by issue, receipt, return, and order cards. To do this, one sort and two merge steps are required. Then, in step 7, new master cards are punched with the on-hand field calculated based on this formula:

New On Hand = Old On Hand + Receipts + Returns − Issues

Similarly, the on-order field is calculated based on this formula:

New On Order = Old On Order − Receipts + Orders

At the end of this step, the new master cards replace the old master cards and the file is up-to-date.

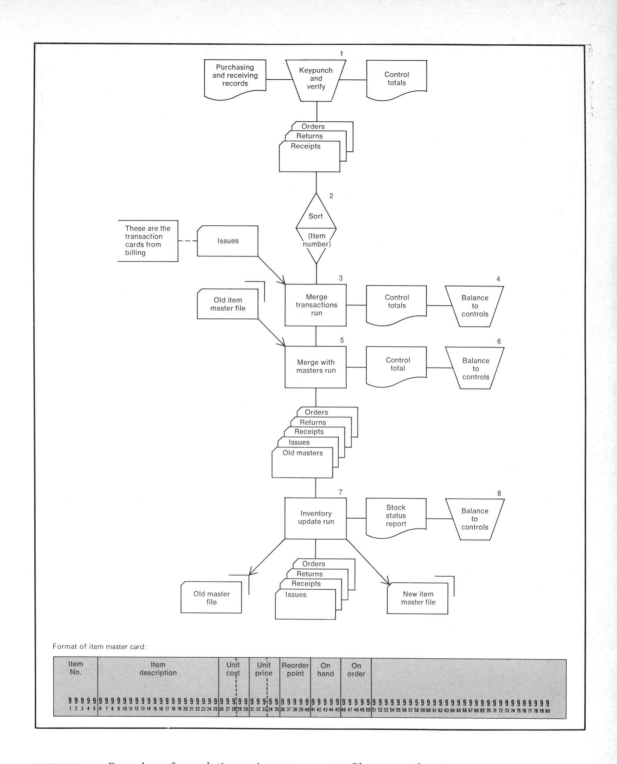

FIGURE 5-20   Procedures for updating an inventory master file on a card system

This then is the general method of updating a card master file. First, transaction cards are keypunched. Second, they are sorted into the sequence of the master file and merged with the old master records. Finally, the computer calculates the new balances, punches new master records, and the old master records are no longer needed.

MANAGEMENT INFORMATION

One of the primary advantages of an EDP system—whether card, tape, or direct-access—is that management information is an automatic by-product of the routine applications. If, for example, a card system is used for billing, the item cards can also be used to prepare sales reports. Similarly, cards used to prepare payroll checks can also be used to prepare cost-accounting reports.

To illustrate the ease of report preparation in a card system, consider the flowchart in figure 5-21. This system will prepare sales-by-item and sales-by-customer reports. The card formats used in this system are given in figure 5-22. To prepare the first report, the item cards for the month are sorted into item-number sequence in step 1. Then, in step 2, the cards are processed by the computer, and the report is printed. After this run, you would balance to controls to make sure that no cards were lost.

To prepare the second report, the item cards are first sorted into customer-number sequence. Then, the item cards are merged with customer year-to-date (YTD) cards. Finally, the computer processes the merged deck, the report is printed, and new YTD cards are punched. The new YTD cards are used for preparing the next month's report. The preparation of this report is shown schematically in figure 5-23.

Incidentally, there are two types of reports commonly printed by a computer system. In the first type, called a *listing,* or *detail-printed report,* one line is printed for each input record. Interspersed among the detail lines, there may be summary lines giving accumulated totals for a group of records. In the second type of report, called a *group-printed,* or *summary, report,* one line is printed for each group of cards. Since the report in figure 5-23 shows only one line for each customer-number group, it is a group-printed report.

To prepare management information on a card system, either transaction or master files can be used. In general, the transaction cards are sorted into the sequence required by the report, merged with master or summary cards (if required), and the report is printed.

Because punched cards can be processed at machine speeds and with machine accuracy, the cost of management information on a card system is usually low in comparison with less-automated systems. Because a card system has the logic ability to prepare exception reports of considerable complexity, the quality of the management information is

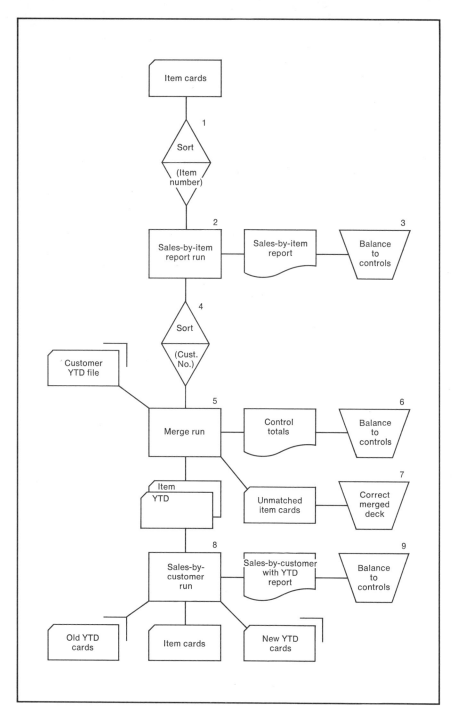

FIGURE 5-21   Preparing two sales reports

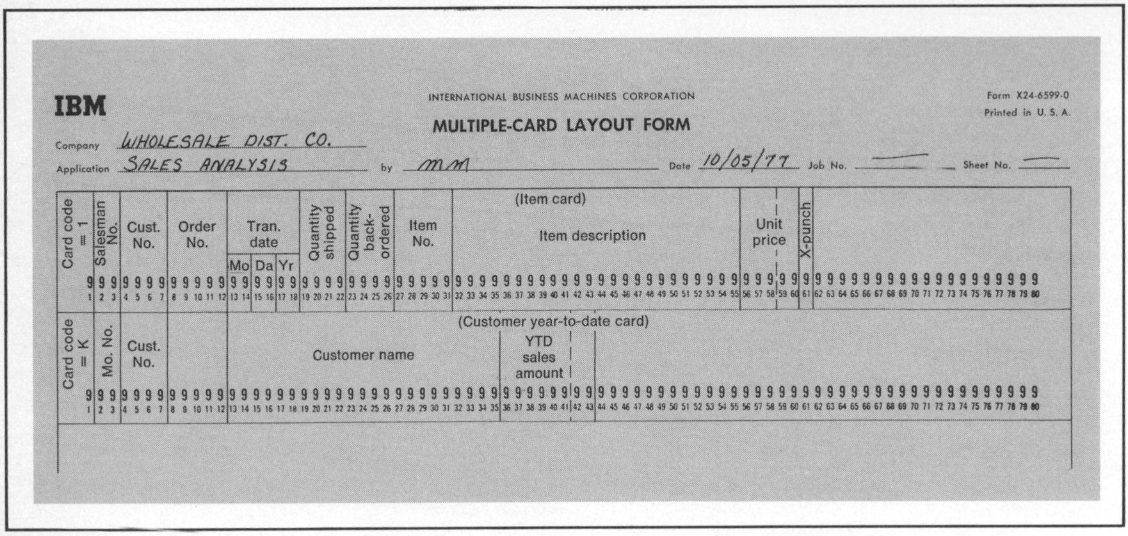

FIGURE 5-22   Card formats for sales-analysis system

generally high in comparison to that prepared by less-automated systems. Although a card system may be limited in comparison to a tape or direct-access system, it is nonetheless capable of producing low-cost, high-quality, management information.

A PREBILLING SYSTEM

In contrast to a postbilling system, a *prebilling system* is one that prepares invoices before actually shipping the items. When prebilling is used, it is important to keep absolutely accurate inventory records. Otherwise, items may be listed on the invoice as shipped when they are actually out of stock and listed as backordered when they are available.

In a prebilling system, the inventory records must be checked before billing to make sure that the order can be filled (not back ordered). There must also be a procedure for filling back orders as soon as the company receives new stock. Although this can be done with relative ease on a tape or disk system, it can be cumbersome on a card system.

For instance, figure 5-24 presents a card system for updating inventory records and filling back orders as receipts come in. Five types of cards are used in this system, as shown by the formats in figure 5-25. The balance-forward cards represent the current stock status of an inventory item, while the item, receipt, return, and adjustment cards represent transactions affecting inventory balance. If an item is back-ordered, the item card receives an X-punch in column 79 (X79). An X-punch in column 80 (X80) indicates that the back order is filled, and an X-punch in column

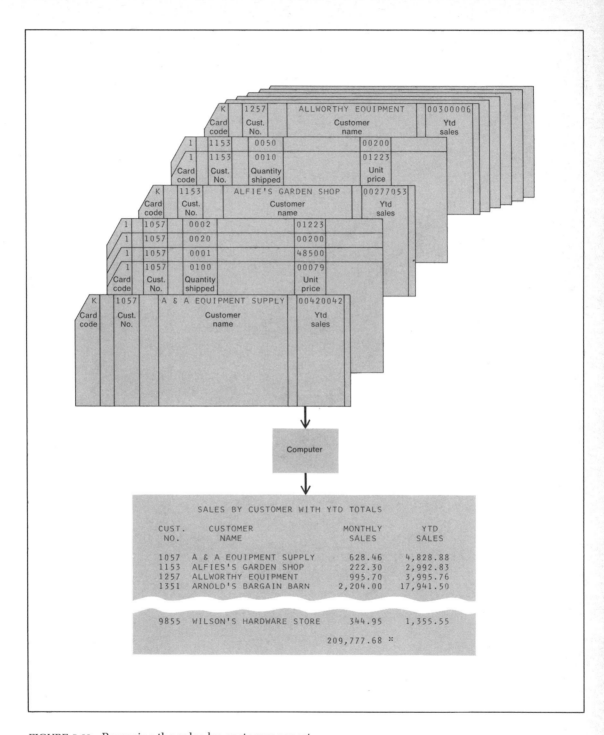

FIGURE 5-23 Preparing the sales-by-customer report

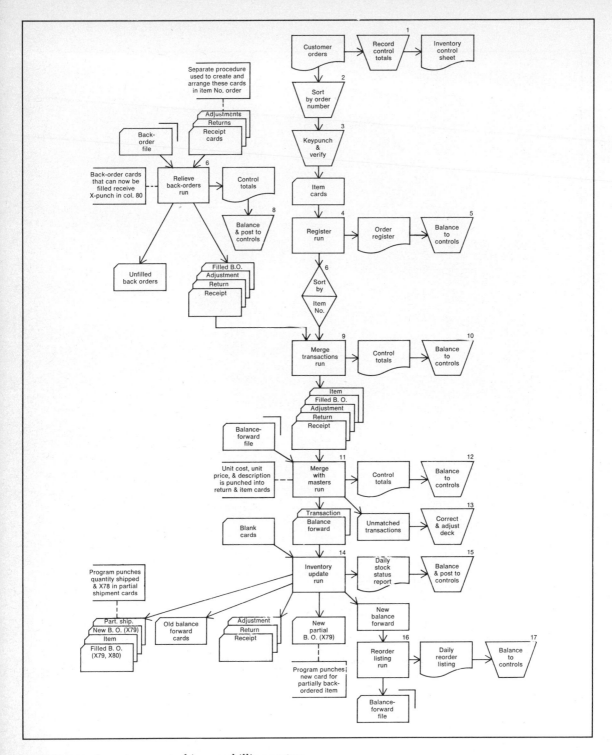

FIGURE 5-24 Inventory control in a prebilling system

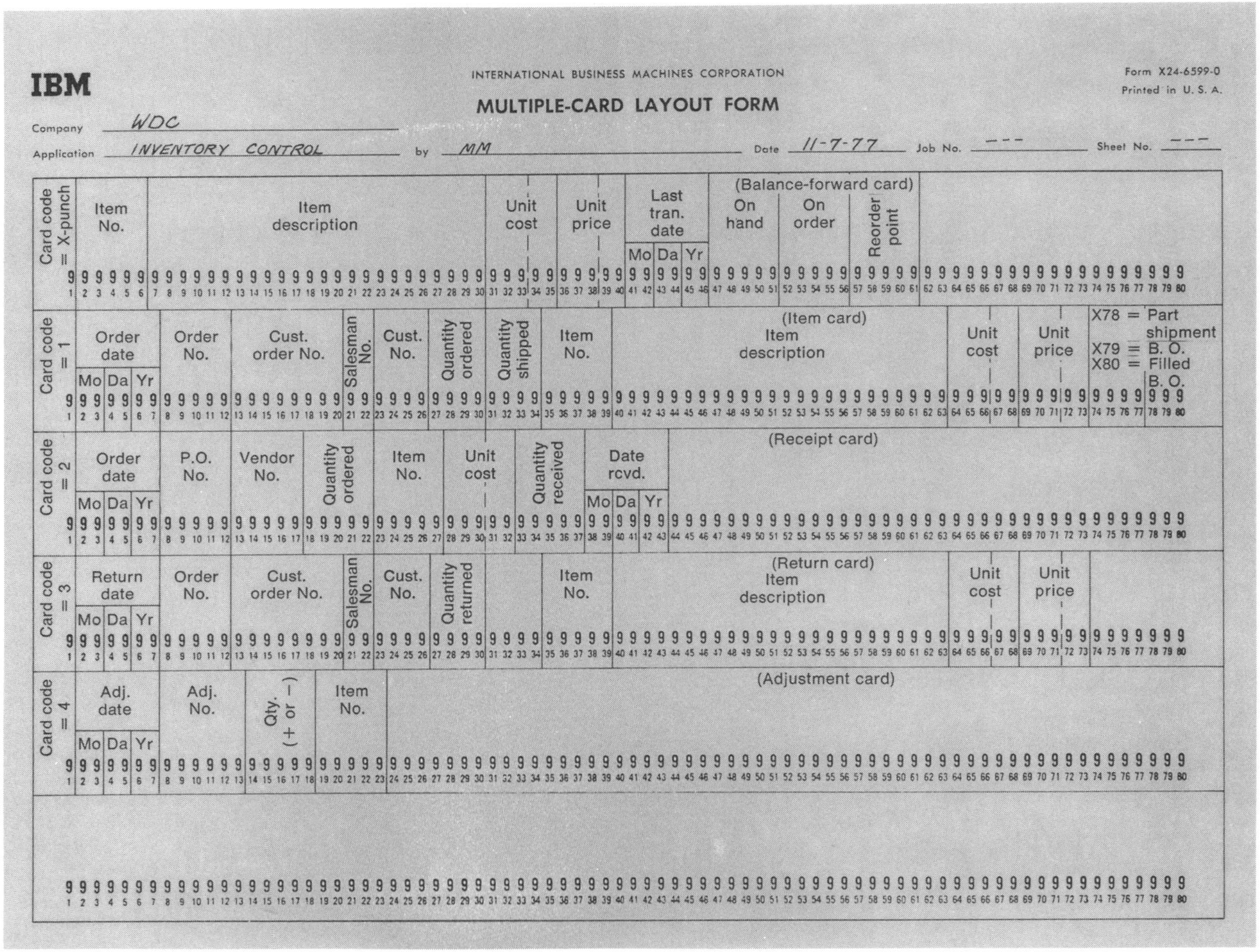

FIGURE 5-25 Card formats for inventory control

78 (X78) indicates a partial shipment of the total amount ordered (say 12 items instead of 25).

Although you should be able to make some sense out of this system, it's not really necessary to go through it in detail. In steps 1–5 the item cards are created from the customer orders, a register is printed, and the cards are sorted into item-number sequence. In steps 7 and 8, old back orders are processed against the receipt and return transactions to see if any of these orders can now be filled. In steps 9 and 11 the transaction cards, the filled back-order cards, and the old item master cards are merged before the update run. Then, in step 14, new master cards are punched. At this point, the filled back-order cards, item cards, new back order cards, and partial-shipment cards are ready for processing in a billing application.

Because a system like this requires many steps and many different types of cards, it is usually difficult to control. As a result, it is common to use manual procedures in various phases of a card prebilling system. For instance, a manual procedure may be used for filling back orders as inventory items are received. This can reduce the amount of card handling and simplify the system.

Because of the difficulty in automating a prebilling application on a card system, postbilling is more common. In general, when a company decides it is ready for a prebilling system, it also decides that it is ready for a tape or direct-access system. As you will see in the next two chapters, prebilling is more in tune with the capabilities of tape and direct-access systems.

DISCUSSION

If you compare the card systems described in this chapter with the disk systems of chapter 2, what would you say are the primary differences? I would say the main difference is in the card handling. On a disk system, cards are usually used only one time, for transaction data, while a card system relies on cards throughout. Master files, transaction files, even object programs all take the form of decks of cards when a card system is used. As a result, the operator has to keep track of many different decks, and there is considerable possibility for operator error.

To illustrate, consider the operator's procedures for running a billing program on a card system with reader and punch (not an MFCM). This is shown schematically in figure 5-26. Here, the operator puts the continuous-form invoices in the printer and pushes its start button. Then she puts the object deck for the billing program in the card reader and puts the data deck (name-and-address and transaction cards) on top of it. After she pushes the start button on the card reader, she puts blank cards in the card punch and pushes its start button. Finally, she pushes the load button on the computer; then the object deck is loaded and executed, thus processing the data deck.

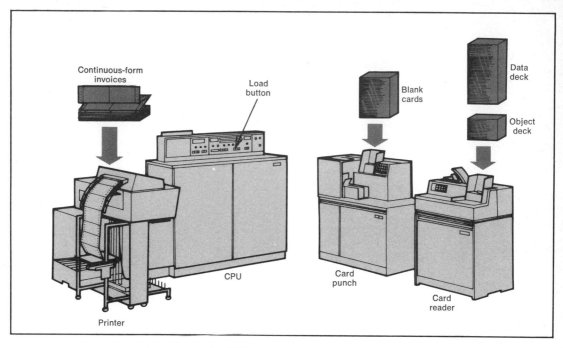

FIGURE 5-26   Loading and executing the billing program

What if the operator puts the data deck in the card reader before the object deck? The computer will be unable to load the program, error lights will go on, and the operator will have to start over. What if the operator puts a data deck in the card punch instead of blank cards? The deck may be punched with new data and thus ruined. What if an operator drops a deck or loses a card? Problems.

Because of the card handling, control balancing takes on added importance in a card system. Because cards can be lost, there must be some assurance in each run that all cards have been processed. As a result, control balancing is usually done after each computer run.

Card handling can also affect the speed of a system. Because the transition from one run to another depends upon the operator, it is common for the computer system to be idle while waiting for the operator. This affects the overall productivity of the system.

Furthermore, the elapsed time required to prepare any document depends to a large extent on how little delay there is between steps in a system. If, for example, the delays between billing steps are lengthy, it will mean that bill preparation is delayed. In contrast, once card data is entered into a tape or direct-access system, processing takes place with little operator intervention and few delays between processing steps.

In summary, a card system is the first stage of EDP complexity and capability. When compared to less-automated systems, a card system is likely to be faster and more accurate and is almost certain to have better information capabilities. On the other hand, when compared to tape or direct-access systems, a card system has shortcomings. The number of steps required for an application, the amount of operator intervention, the amount of card handling: these are limitations not found on more sophisticated systems.

SUMMARY

1. Four phases commonly take place within a card system: (1) source data is recorded in punched cards; (2) the decks are sorted and merged into sequences acceptable for processing by the computer; (3) the computer reads the input cards, processes the data, and gives output; and (4) the cards are returned to their various files.

2. A large part of any system concerns itself with file maintenance. Adding, deleting, and changing records in a card file is often done manually. Updating records usually involves the creation of new master cards while discarding the old.

3. In general, a card system can provide low-cost, high-quality management information that pinpoints exceptional conditions. This is perhaps its principal advantage over less-automated systems.

4. A prebilling system prepares bills before the inventory items are actually shipped. Thus this type of system depends heavily on the accuracy of inventory records and on an effective subsystem for handling back orders. Because it is difficult to implement on a card system, postbilling card systems are more common than prebilling ones.

TERMINOLOGY

postbilling system
unmatched transaction
open item
open-item accounts-receivable system
register

file maintenance
listing
detail-printed report
summary report
prebilling system

QUESTIONS

1. In the flowchart in figure 5-13, why do customer N/A and transaction cards need to be merged in step 3? In other words, why couldn't the N/A cards be placed in hopper 1 and the transaction cards in hopper 2 in step 6 of the system?

2. Consider the flowchart in figure 5-18. What if a clerk pulled the wrong A/R card from the file in step 4? If this card has the right amount but the wrong customer number, when and how will the mistake be caught?

3. In the flowchart in figure 5-19, suppose an unmatched A/R card turns up in step 3. What is the likely cause of this problem?

4. Suppose you want to prepare a daily exception report showing the items that need to be reordered (on hand plus on order is less than reorder point). How could this be done using the master file with format given in figure 5-20? (Flowchart it.)

5. Suppose you want to prepare a sales-by-salesperson report from the cards with format given in figure 5-14. Could it be done? If so, how? (Flowchart it.)

6. Why is the information prepared by a card system likely to be less expensive than that provided by a noncomputerized system? Why is it likely to be of higher quality?

6 TAPE SYSTEMS

This chapter is divided into three topics. In the first, the characteristics of the magnetic tape and its associated I/O devices, the tape drives, are described. In the second topic, the use of magnetic tape within a data-processing system is discussed. Then the programming and system complications peculiar to systems that use tape are covered in the last topic.

TOPIC 1
TAPE
CHARACTERISTICS

A magnetic tape is a continuous strip of plastic wound on a reel, as shown in figure 6-1. Although a typical tape is 2400 feet long and 1/2 inch wide, there are other widths and lengths, in particular, 2400-, 1200-, 600-, and 250-foot reels. Data is recorded on the surface of the tape as patterns of magnetized spots on a magnetic surface coating. Between the individual data records on the tape are spaces—often 0.6 or 0.75 inch—with no data recorded on them. These spaces are called *inter-record gaps,* or *IRGs.* Although there are some limitations, for most uses a data record can be as short or as long as necessary.

Figure 6-2 illustrates one type of coding used on tape. In this code, there are nine vertical positions in which a magnetized spot, called a *bit,* may

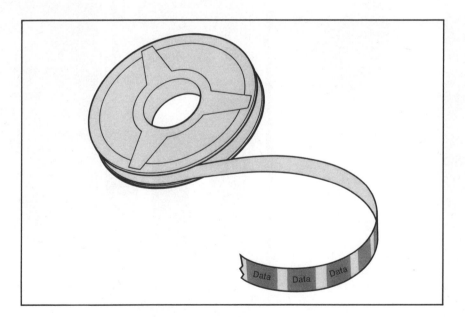

FIGURE 6-1   A magnetic tape

or may not be recorded. The letters, numbers, and special characters are represented by combinations of these "on" or "off" bits. In figure 6-2, the on-bits are indicated by a line in a bit position, the off-bits by a space. Because the human eye is unable to see the bits recorded on a tape, there is no point in describing the actual codes used. You only need to know that each letter, number, or special character is represented by a unique combination of bits.

Because each of the nine vertical bit positions in figure 6-2 forms a horizontal track, a tape such as this is called a nine-track tape. Although these tapes are the most common right now, seven-track tapes are still used by many companies.

Actually, only eight of the nine bit positions are used in the code for each character. The ninth bit, called a *check bit,* or *parity bit,* is used as a check on the accuracy of tape operations. The idea is to make the number of on-bits in the individual codes either all odd or all even. Because the parity bits are adjusted accordingly, all of the codes in figure 6-2 contain an odd number of on-bits—the letter A has three, the letter B has three, the letter C has five, and so on. Then, if a character is read that consists of an even number of on-bits, the computer system has detected an input error.

Parity checking of the code for a single character—which may be called *vertical parity checking*—is only one of the checks done in tape operations. At the end of each tape record is a *longitudinal check character*—the last character before the interrecord gap. This character consists of off-on bits that make the sum of the on-bits in each horizontal track either odd or even, depending on the computer. Then, if a computer that uses even parity finds an odd number of bits in a track, it has detected an input error. With the combination of vertical and *horizontal parity checking,* most tape input errors can be caught. Incidentally, from the point of view of programming or system design, it isn't necessary to

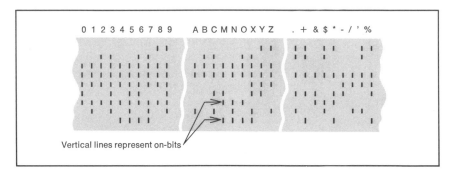

FIGURE 6-2   Coding on tape

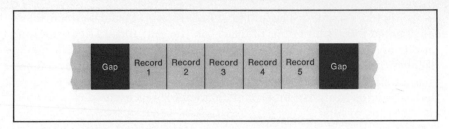

FIGURE 6-3   Blocked records

understand parity checking. You should, however, realize that all input and output operations on tape are checked.

In many cases, more than one data record is recorded between two inter-record gaps. This is called *blocking* records, and the group of records between gaps is called a *block* of records. The *blocking factor* of a file of records is the number of records stored in one block. In figure 6-3, for example, the blocking factor is 5. In other words, five records are stored between the gaps. Because blocking is such a common practice when using tape files, the IRG is often referred to as the *interblock gap,* or *IBG.* The advantage of blocking is that it increases the storage capacity of a reel of tape as well as the speed at which the records on the tape can be read or written.

THE TAPE DRIVE

The *tape drive,* shown in figure 6-4, is used to write records on tape and read records from tape. To mount a tape on the tape drive, the computer operator threads the tape through a read/write mechanism in the center of the unit and then onto an empty take-up reel, as shown in figure 6-5. This process is similar to mounting a tape on a tape recorder.

Once the tape is mounted, the operator pushes the start button; the tape drive locates the first record on the file by searching for a *loadpoint marker,* which is a reflective spot on the surface of the tape. Tape records can then be read or written under control of a stored program.

When data is read from a tape, the data on it remains unaltered; thus it can be read many times. When data is written on a tape, it replaces [and thus destroys] the data that was on the tape. Before removing a tape from the tape drive, the tape is rewound onto the original reel, ready to be read or written again.

Although the basic programmable functions of a tape drive are reading and writing records, there are a number of others. For example, most tape drives can be programmed to rewind a tape, to backspace a tape one block of records, and to skip over faulty sections of tape. In addition,

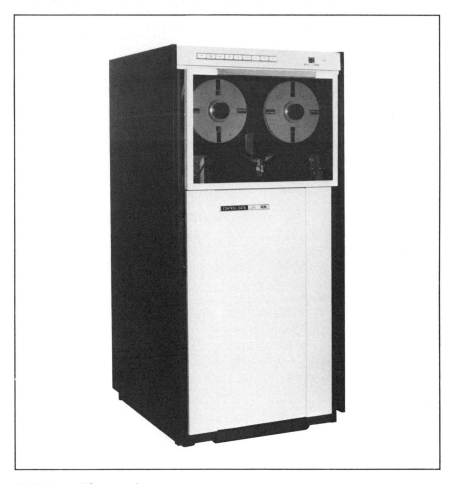

FIGURE 6-4   The tape drive

some tape drives can be programmed to read tapes backwards, which in some applications can increase the speed of tape operations.

During reading operations, input records are checked for vertical and horizontal parity. In writing operations, output records can be checked immediately after being written since the reading mechanism is located just after the writing mechanism. As soon as a character or block of records is written, it is checked for vertical and horizontal parity by the reading mechanism.

A computer system may have one or many tape drives attached to it. A medium-sized direct-access system, for example, may consist of a card reader, a card punch, a printer, a CPU, four disk units, and two tape drives. A tape system, however, usually consists of a card reader, a card punch, a printer, a CPU, and four or more tape drives.

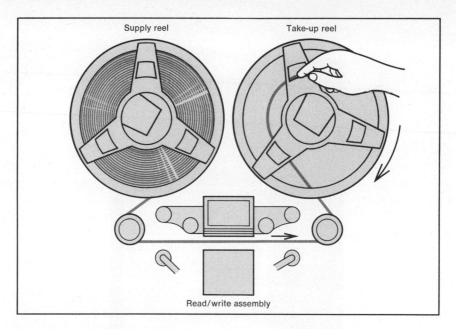

Supply reel   Take-up reel

Read/write assembly

FIGURE 6-5   Mounting a tape

TAPE SPEED AND CAPACITY

One measure of the speed of tape operations is the *transfer rate,* or *transfer speed,* of a tape drive. It is measured in characters or *bytes* per second and measures how long it takes to transfer data from the tape drive to storage, or vice versa. For example, one common tape drive has a transfer rate of 60,000 bytes per second. [Chapter 14, CPU Concepts, explains the nature of the byte, but for now think of it as the equivalent of a character—most of the time, it is.] Other tape drives have speeds that range from about 5000 bytes per second all the way up to 400,000 bytes per second. To appreciate tape speeds, consider that a transfer rate of 80,000 bytes per second is the equivalent of reading 1000 eighty-column cards per second, or 60,000 cards—a stack thirty-five feet high—in a minute.

Transfer rate is misleading because a tape drive actually stops and starts every time that it comes to an IBG—yet transfer rate does not reflect this *start/stop time.* To appreciate this, suppose that a file of 6000 records, each consisting of 100 bytes of data, were stored on a tape with a blocking factor of 1. At 60,000 bytes per second, it would take 10 seconds [600,000 bytes divided by 60,000] to read the data in the file. However, the tape would also have to stop and start 6000 times. Since the start/stop time of a typical tape drive is 8/1000 second [8 milliseconds], the time required for stopping and starting would be 48 seconds [0.008 times 6000]. In other words, the tape drive spends 10 seconds reading data and 48 seconds starting and stopping. The effective transfer rate, therefore, is much less than 60,000 bytes per second.

Now suppose the records are blocked with a blocking factor of 10. Ten seconds are still required for reading the 600,000 bytes of data, but only 4.8 seconds are required for starting and stopping. Since the total time for reading the file is reduced from 58 seconds to 14.8 seconds, you can see the effect of blocking in the speed of tape operations.

The capacity of a reel of tape depends on the length of the tape, the length of the IBGs, and the *density* of the tape. Density measures the number of characters or bytes of data that can be recorded on an inch of tape. For example, one model tape drive records data at a density of 800 bytes per inch and has an IBG that is 0.6 inch. Common densities are 200, 556, 800, and 1600 bytes per inch; common lengths are 0.6 and 0.75 inch.

To appreciate the effect of blocking on the capacity of a tape, consider how much tape is required to store 8000 records, 100 bytes each, with a blocking factor of 1. Here, the data requires 1000 inches of tape [800,000 bytes divided by 800], and the IBGs require 4800 inches of tape [8000 times 0.6 inch]. If the blocking factor is increased to 10, however, only 480 inches of tape are required for IBGs and the entire file is reduced from 5800 to 1480 inches.

How large can a blocking factor be? It depends on the storage capacity of the computer. When a block of records is read, all of the data between the two IBGs is transferred into storage. As a result, if a block of records consists of 4000 bytes of data, 4000 storage positions must be available for the input block.

On medium- to large-size systems, where internal storage is generally available, the blocking factor is often selected so the block will be around 4000 bytes long. Based on past experience, this block size has proven to be an efficient one. Any increase in block size contributes little to I/O speed, even though it increases the requirements for internal storage.

On smaller systems, the blocking factor often depends on the amount of storage available for running the programs that use a file. To illustrate, suppose a tape file is going to be used by three programs and 16,000 storage positions are available for the programs. Not including the input area for the tape file, program A requires 12,000 storage positions, program B 7500 storage positions, and program C 14,500 storage positions. The maximum block length is therefore 1500 bytes. This concept is illustrated in figure 6-6.

SUMMARY

1. The magnetic tape is a compact storage medium that can be read or written at high speed by I/O units called tape drives.

2. To increase the storage capacity of a reel of tape and to increase the speed at which the reel can be read or written, tape records are normally blocked. In general, the blocking factor is chosen so the block will be

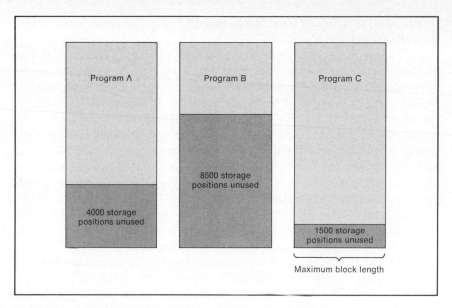

FIGURE 6-6   Determining the blocking factor on a small system

around 4000 bytes, provided that core storage isn't exceeded during the execution of any of the programs using the tape.

TERMINOLOGY

interrecord gap	blocking factor
IRG	interblock gap
bit	IBG
check bit	tape drive
parity bit	load-point marker
vertical parity checking	transfer rate
longitudinal check character	transfer speed
horizontal parity checking	byte
blocking records	start/stop time
block of records	density

QUESTIONS

1. Assume a transfer rate of 80,000 bytes per second and a start/stop time of .008 seconds. How long would it take the tape drive to read 10,000 40-byte records blocked 10 per block? Blocked 100 per block? Blocked 1000 per block?

2. What is the transfer rate per second of a 600 card-per-minute card reader? Of a 1200 line-per-minute printer with a 132 character print line?

3. Suppose a bit is dropped in the third byte of a record in a tape reading operation. Will vertical or horizontal parity checking catch the error? What if two bits are dropped in the third byte?

TOPIC 2
TAPE SYSTEM DESIGN

In any data-processing installation, much of the processing time is devoted to maintaining files. For example, inventory records, accounts receivable records, sales-analysis records, and payroll records must be continually updated. Periodically, reports and other documents are printed from these files.

Figure 6-7 shows a system flowchart that represents the four steps usually involved in updating a file on a tape system. The first step is keypunching and verifying data. The procedure is much the same as that for a card system; for example, the keypunch operator punches the data from source documents. Depending on the file being updated, the transactions may represent orders, inventory receipts, hours worked, and so on.

The second step, called a *card-to-tape run,* converts the card data into tape records. This requires a relatively simply program that reads a card, processes it, and writes a tape record. However, the program should also *edit* the input data. *Editing* refers to programmed testing for valid input data. Editing routines may include tests to make sure that alphabetic fields contain alphabetic data, that numeric fields contain numeric data, that numeric fields do not contain blanks, that transaction codes are valid, and that the contents of a field are within reasonable limits. As output, an editing run provides a printed listing of all invalid transactions in order that they may be corrected. These invalid transactions are not included on the output tape file so that processing can continue without them.

The third step is to sort the transaction records on tape into the sequence of the master file that is going to be updated. For example, if an inventory master file is in item-number order, the inventory transaction records should be sorted into item-number order.

When records are sorted on a tape system, three or more tape drives are used—even though the system flowchart shows only one input tape and one output tape. During execution each of the tapes used will be read and written several times. A *sort program* is a very complex program that is usually written and supplied by the computer manufacturer. To use the program, a computer user need only supply the sort specifications—such as the location of the field on which the records are going to be sorted. Since sorting may account for a large percentage of the processing done on a tape system, the efficiency of a sort program can significantly affect the efficiency of the tape system.

The fourth step is the *update run.* In an update program, the master records and the transaction records are read into storage. If one or more transaction records apply to a master record, the affected fields in the

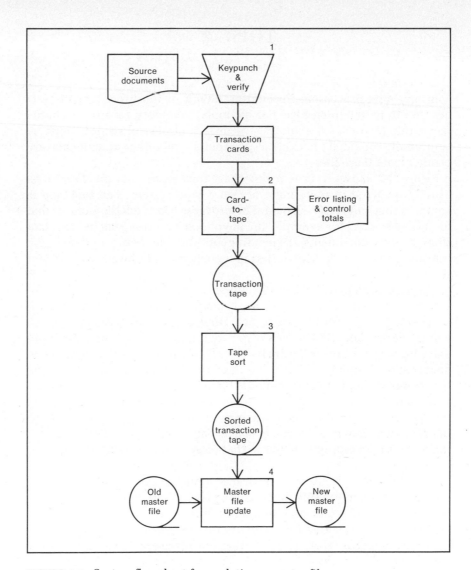

FIGURE 6-7   System flowchart for updating a master file

master record are changed accordingly. If a master record has no transactions that apply to it, the master record remains unchanged. The output tape—the updated or new master tape—consists of all the master records, both those that were changed and those that were not changed.

To illustrate, consider the example shown schematically in figure 6-8. Suppose the first ten master records of an inventory file have these item numbers: 01, 03, 04, 06, 09, 12, 13, 17, 18, and 19. The first three transaction

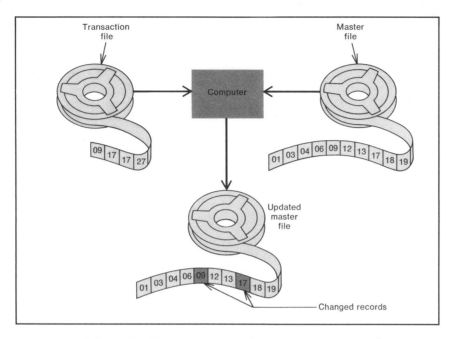

FIGURE 6-8 Schematic of the master-file update

records have these item numbers: 09, 17, and 17. The update program starts by reading one master record and one transaction record. Since the first transaction—item number 09—doesn't match the first master record—item number 01—the master record is written unchanged on the new master tape. Then, the next master record—03—is read. Since it too is unmatched, it is written unchanged. The same is true for master records 04 and 06.

The first master record to be matched is item number 09. The transaction for this item number is processed against the master, the master is updated, and another transaction is read. Since the next transaction record applies to master record 17, master record 09 is written on the new tape and another master is read. After master records 12 and 13 are written unchanged, the two transaction records for master 17 are processed. The program continues in this way until all of the master and transaction records have been read. If there are 5000 master records in the file, 5000 master records will be written—regardless of the number that are actually affected by transactions.

Of course, a report is often printed during an update program. For example, during an inventory update, a listing of items to be reordered could be printed. This is shown on a system flowchart as follows:

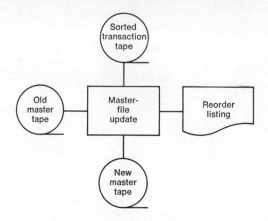

Otherwise, reports can be printed at any time from master files, using *tape-to-printer programs*. For example, a sales report could be printed from a sales master file, as follows:

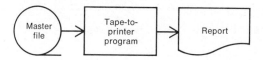

A tape-to-printer program is a relatively simple program that reads a tape record, converts the data to a readable form, and prints the data.

To delete, change, or add records to a master file, a procedure like the update procedure in figure 6-8 is normally followed. First, the deletion, change, and addition cards are keypunched and verified. Second, the cards are edited and written on tape. Third, the maintenance records are sorted into the sequence of the master file. Fourth, a file-maintenance program is run with the old master file as input and an updated master file as output. To ensure accuracy, a list of all changes to the master file is printed along with control totals. Regardless of the number of changes, all the records must be read from the old master file and written on the new one.

TAPE APPLICATIONS

With this background, you are ready for a description of a group of applications. Figure 6-9 shows a system flowchart of the daily procedures for the order-writing, billing, inventory, and accounts receivable applications. In the eleven steps shown, inventory records and accounts receivable records are updated, and shipping orders and invoices are printed. Since this application allows back orders, procedures are included for maintaining a back-order file and for filling back orders

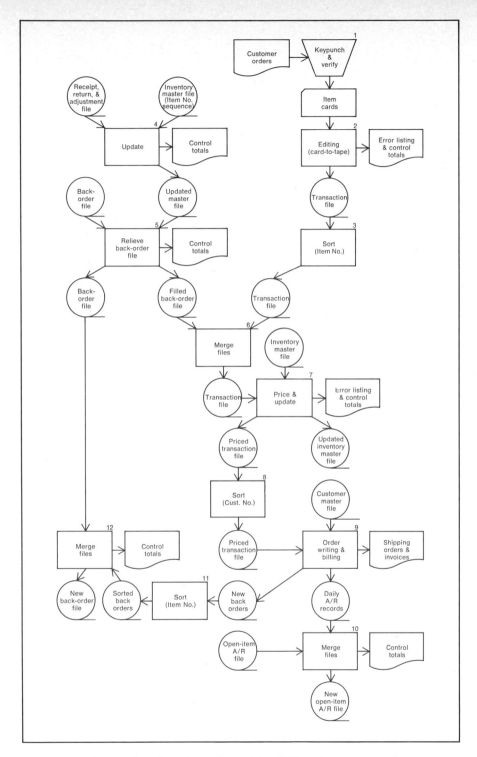

FIGURE 6-9   System flowchart for order writing, billing, inventory, and accounts receivable

when inventory items are received. Because invoices are printed before items are shipped, this is a prebilling system. Although control posting and balancing steps would normally be shown on a flowchart such as this, they are omitted here in order to emphasize processing.

Figure 6-10 is a record layout form that shows the layouts of the card and tape records used in the system. Eight record formats are given—the first is for the item card, the other seven for tape records. Since 100 positions can be laid out on each line of the form, a tape record of over 100 positions requires more than one line. In this example, all records are less than 100 positions long. The small black triangles, called carets, indicate the location of a decimal point in a field.

The system used in this application consists of a CPU, a combined card reader and punch, a printer, and four tape drives. Auxiliary equipment required consists of keypunches and verifiers. If additional tape drives were available on the system, the procedures would be much the same, although in some cases two steps could be combined into one.

In steps 1–3, item cards are keypunched and verified, converted to tape records, and sorted into item-number sequence in preparation for an inventory-update run. During step 2, editing routines are performed and a listing of invalid cards is printed. As you can see from the record layouts for the item card and the transaction record on tape, none of the data fields are changed during the conversion from card to tape, although the record size is reduced from eighty to thirty-five characters. The blocking factor for the transaction file and all other files indicated in this flowchart would be as large as the available core storage would permit.

In step 4, daily receipts, returns, and adjustments are processed against the inventory master file, thus providing an updated master file. The back-order file and the inventory master file are then processed together to detemine if any back orders can now be filled. If so, those back orders that can be filled are written on a separate tape to be used in subsequent processing steps. The still unfilled back orders are written on another tape to represent the new back-order file.

In step 6, the filled back-order tape and the transaction tape are merged in preparation for an inventory-update run and for order writing and billing. The output tape consists of new orders and filled back orders in item-number sequence.

Step 7 is an inventory-update run. In addition, a priced transaction tape is created during this step. As you can see from the record layout in figure 6-10, the priced transaction records have the same fields as the transaction records, plus some additional ones. By comparing quantity ordered with the on-hand balance of the inventory master record, quantity shipped and quantity back-ordered are derived. Item description, unit cost, and unit price are taken from the inventory master record. Sales amount is calculated by multiplying quantity shipped by unit price. The priced transaction records are thus ready to be used to print the lines on an invoice or to prepare sales reports.

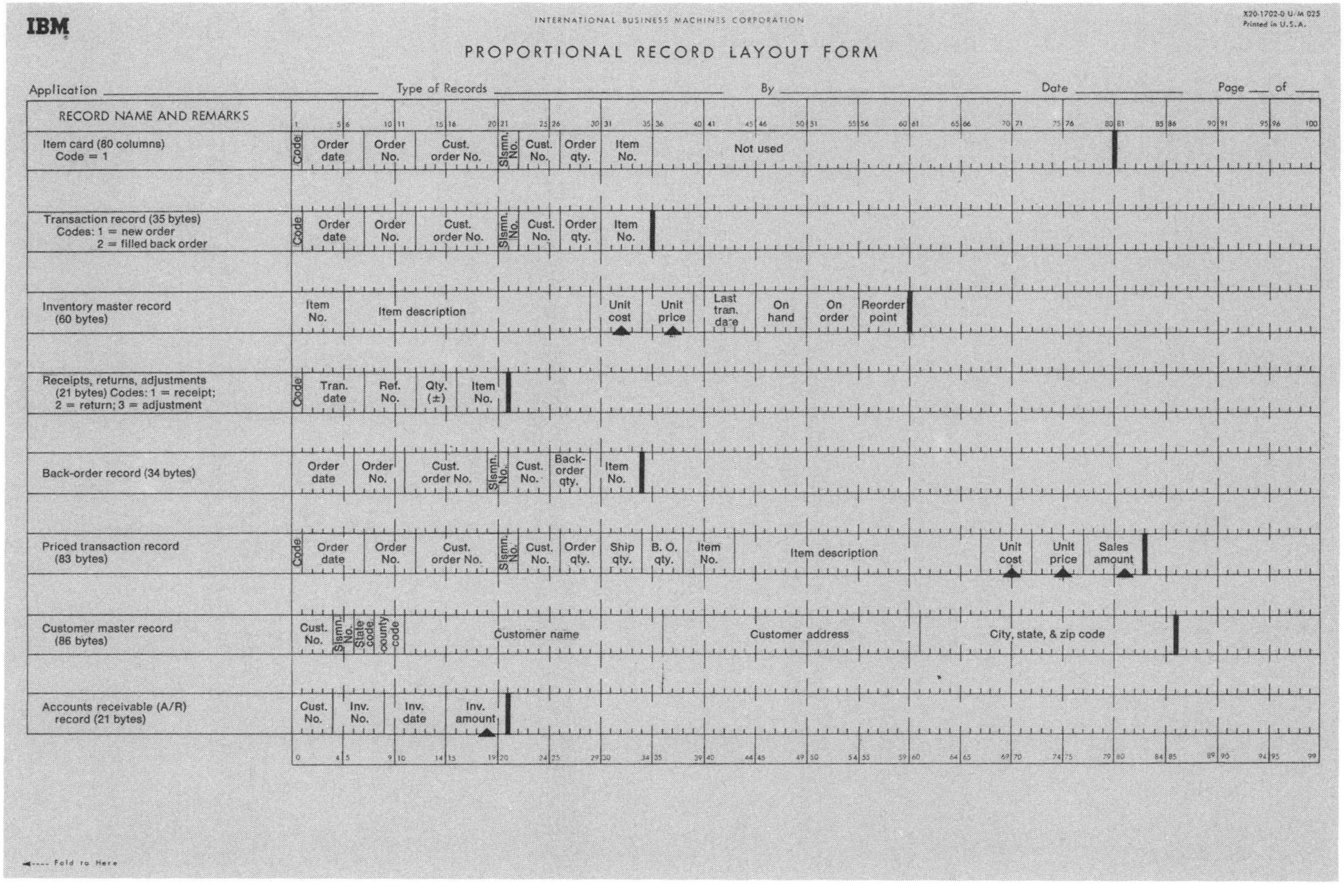

FIGURE 6-10 Formats for the tape applications

In steps 8 and 9, the priced transaction records are sorted into customer-number sequence, and the shipping orders and invoices are printed. Two additional tapes are created during the billing run. One consists of new back-order records; the other consists of accounts receivable records, one record for each invoice.

In step 10, the new accounts receivable records are merged into the open-item file of accounts receivable records. This file represents the unpaid invoices for all customers. It can be used to prepare monthly statements or an aged trial balance at the end of the month.

In step 11, the new back orders are sorted into item-number sequence, and in step 12, they are merged with the old back orders to create an up-to-date back-order file. This file is checked daily (step 5) to determine if any of the back orders can be filled.

In summary, although these procedures are typical, they are intended to show only the processing that takes place within the order-writing, billing, inventory and accounts receivable applications. Thus, they do not necessarily demonstrate the full processing capabilities of a tape system. For example, the inventory master records could be expanded to include fields for monthly and year-to-date sales. During the update run, step 7, these fields could be updated. At the end of the month, then, an up-to-date sales report could be printed from the inventory master file in a tape-to-printer run. By using techniques such as this, the number of steps required to prepare sales, inventory, or accounts receivable reports can be reduced.

DISCUSSION

When you compare card and tape systems, you will find several advantages in tape systems. First, because of the difference between card and tape I/O speeds, a tape system can handle much larger volumes of data than a card system.

Second, a tape system generally requires fewer steps for comparable processing results. For example, the tape flowchart in figure 6-9 requires fewer steps than a comparable card system using an MFCM. When you compare a tape system with a traditional card system, the difference is even more pronounced.

Third, because data on tape is easier to handle than data in cards, a tape system is likely to spend more time executing programs and less time waiting for an operator to get the system ready to load and execute a program. For instance, imagine the difference between stacking 10,000 cards in a card reader and mounting one tape on a tape drive. A good operator can mount a tape in less than fifteen seconds. In addition, programs in a tape system are loaded from an object tape. This is considerably more efficient than using an object deck for each program.

Finally, there is little chance of a record being lost when tapes are used. Thus, in control procedures, less emphasis needs to be placed on determining if all records in a file have been processed. In fact, as you will see in the next topic, control totals of the number of records in a file can be kept on the tape itself, and when reading a file, the computer can check to be sure that all records have been processed. If not, the computer prints a message on the console typewriter or printer to alert the computer operator in regard to the error.

On the negative side, tape systems—as you would expect—cost more than card systems. For example, a typical card system might rent for $2000 per month, whereas a small tape system using the same CPU and four tape drives might cost $3000 per month. The idea, of course, is that the increased processing capabilities of the tape system more than make up the difference in cost.

Regardless of its features, a tape system comes out far less favorably when compared with a direct-access system. Because a direct-access device can read any record in a file without reading the preceding records, it can perform file-maintenance routines in ways that are impossible on a tape system. As a result, the concept of direct-access processing has pervaded the computer industry to such a degree that today there are relatively few pure tape systems. Instead, tape devices are normally used in conjunction with direct-access systems. For example, a small direct-access system is likely to consist of a CPU, a card reader and punch, a printer, four disk drives, and two tape drives.

Tape is valuable on a direct-access system for two reasons. First, it is much less expensive to store data on a tape than on a direct-access storage device. For example, a magnetic tape costs about $30, while a comparable amount of storage on a direct-access storage device is likely to cost over $500. When you consider that a large company may have over 10,000 tapes in its storage files, you can appreciate the tremendous difference in costs.

Second, tape is the most efficient way of transferring data from one computer system to another. Although direct-access devices often cannot be transferred from one type of computer system to another, tapes are somewhat standard. As a general rule, tape from one computer system can be read on a comparable system, even that of another manufacturer.

In summary, the place of tape in the computer industry is changing. Where once a computer user moved from a card system to a tape system when his processing volumes grew, today he is likely to move to a direct-access system. As a result, the use of magnetic tape is still growing but at a slower rate than the rest of the computer industry. Nevertheless, magnetic tape will continue to play an important role, first as a storage medium and second as a medium for transferring data from system to system.

SUMMARY

1. One of the basic procedures in a tape system is updating a master file. After transactions are converted into tape records, they are sorted into master-file sequence and processed against the master file. The result is a new (updated) master file.

2. A tape system has several advantages over a card system, including faster I/O speeds, fewer procedural steps, ease in handling data and programs, and greater accuracy due to less chance of losing records.

3. Because of the merits of direct-access devices, the use of tape is growing more slowly than the rest of the computer industry. Nevertheless, tape continues to be important (1) as an inexpensive storage medium and (2) as a medium for transferring data between systems.

TERMINOLOGY

card-to-tape run
editing
sort program
update run
tape-to-printer program

QUESTIONS

1. How do procedures for updating a master file on a tape system and a card system differ?

2. How do file-maintenance procedures differ as you move from a card to a tape system?

3. In figure 6-9, why do you think the transaction file and the filled back-order file have to be merged in step 6? In other words, why couldn't they be separate input files to the update run in step 7?

4. In figure 6-9, how many tape drives are used in step 8? Explain.

5. Based on the data given in the record layouts in figure 6-10, how would you prepare an aged trial balance report? Flowchart it.

6. In your opinion, what is the primary reason a tape system is more efficient than a card system?

TOPIC 3
PROGRAMMING AND
SYSTEM
CONSIDERATIONS

When computer users move from one system to a larger or more sophisticated system, they usually encounter increased programming and system complexity. This topic presents some of the considerations peculiar to tape-system users.

PROGRAMMING
CONSIDERATIONS

A certain portion of any object program using tape input and output is taken up by input and output routines. Some of the most important of these are error-recovery, blocking and deblocking, and label-checking routines. Although a programmer today doesn't actually have to write these routines, he or she must understand what they do and be able to state related specifications.

Error-Recovery Routines

When an error is detected during a card-reading operation, the program has no alternative but to ignore the card or halt processing. When a tape-reading error is detected, however, the error may often be recovered. If, for example, a piece of dust or dirt on the surface of the tape caused an error, it may be brushed off as the tape passes through the reading mechanism. If the tape is backspaced and the record is reread, the data can then be transferred to storage without error. In a typical tape routine, such as the one represented by the program flowchart in figure 6-11, a tape is backspaced and reread 99 times before the program stops trying to recover the error. If the error still exists, a message is printed on the console typewriter and the program is terminated.

The same type of programming routine is used for a writing operation. If a writing error is detected, a program backspaces and tries again. After a number of attempts, the program may skip a certain amount of tape—the equivalent of a long IRG—and try again. If errors still persist, the programming routine ends the job.

Blocking and Deblocking Routines

When a tape drive is given a read command, it reads an entire block of records into storage. However, a program usually processes only one record of a block at a time. As a result, *deblocking routines* are needed to keep track of which record in storage is being processed and which

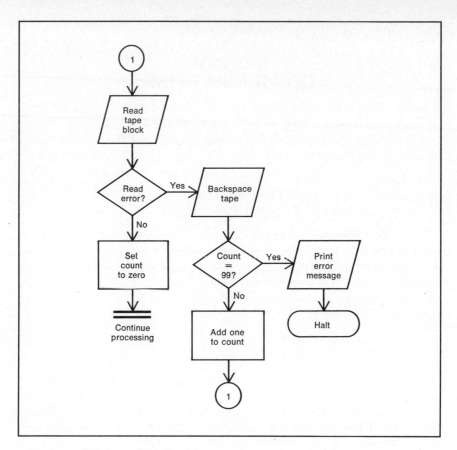

FIGURE 6-11 Program flowchart for an error-recovery routine

record is to be processed next. When writing a block of records, *blocking routines* must move the individual records into the output area of storage before the entire block is written.

Label-Checking Routines

The instructions given to a computer operator for running a job tell which reel of tape to mount on which tape drive. The reels of tape are identified by external labels on the outside of the reels. Suppose, however, that the operator makes a mistake and mounts a tape containing current accounts receivable records on a tape drive that is going to write a file of updated inventory records. If this mistake isn't caught, the accounts receivable records will be replaced by inventory records.

To prevent this type of error, *internal labels*—labels that are actually records on the tape itself—are used. For example, a typical tape file

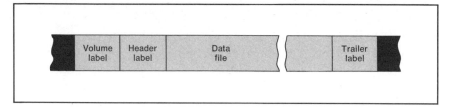

FIGURE 6-12 Labels for a tape file

consists of the three label records shown in figure 6-12. (IBGs aren't shown in this illustration.) The *volume label,* which is immediately after the load-point marker, identifies the reel of tape. The *header label,* which contains information such as the file name, the date the file was created, and the date after which it can be destroyed, identifies the file. The *trailer label,* found after the data records of the file, contains the same data as the header label, plus a block count indicating the number of blocks of data the file contains.

On a typical system, these labels are processed by comparing the data that the labels contain with data supplied by *job-control cards* at the time the object program is run. The job-control cards indicate which program should be loaded and executed, as well as which file should be mounted on which tape drive and what the volume and header labels should contain.

To appreciate the value of label checking, consider how a typical program checks header labels before writing an output file. After the operator mounts a tape on a tape drive, the reading mechanism is positioned just before the volume and header labels. The first thing the program does is to read these labels and analyze the volume number of the volume label and the expiration date in the header label. If the volume number agrees with the volume number given in the job-control cards and if the expiration date has passed (that is, the file can be destroyed), the program backspaces the tape, writes a header label for the output file, and then begins processing. Otherwise, a message to the operator is printed, indicating that he has mounted the wrong file; thus a costly error is avoided.

For input files, the header labels are checked to make sure that the identifying information agrees with the information given in the job-control cards. At the end of the file, the block count given in the trailer label is compared with a block count accumulated by the program. This is a type of automatic balancing to controls. If the block count in the trailer label and the block count accumulated during program execution are the same, all blocks on the tape have been read. If they aren't the same, the computer prints a message on the console typewriter to alert the operator to the error.

What the Programmer Must Know

If the programmer had to write these I/O routines for each program, programming for tape systems would be an extremely tedious and repetitive job. Fortunately, however, modern programming languages automatically compile the coding for tape I/O routines. The programmer need only know how to specify characteristics such as the record length and block length. Once these specifications are given, the programmer uses simple macro instructions that cause the appropriate I/O routines to be executed.

SYSTEM CONSIDERATIONS

Even with label-checking procedures, it is possible to destroy a current file of records by writing other records on the same tape. One way that this can happen is to disregard the error message printed by the computer, indicating an unexpired file. For example, if the computer operator keys a code on the console that indicates it is okay to write on the unexpired file, the file can be destroyed.

To decrease the likelihood of this type of error, *file-protection rings* must be mounted with a tape before a tape drive can write on the tape. The file-protection ring, illustrated in figure 6-13, pushes in a pin that is part of the tape drive, thus allowing writing operations to take place. The operator's instructions for a computer run indicate which tapes are to be mounted on which drives and which tapes should be mounted with file-protection rings. If the ring is not present, the file cannot be written on, and thus destroyed, no matter what other errors take place.

Even with the precautions of label-checking and file-protection rings, however, a system designer must provide for *backup*. Backup refers to the ability of a system to recreate tape files should they become lost or destroyed. For example, if the surface of a portion of a tape becomes damaged, the system must be able to recreate the lost records. Similarly, in case of fire or theft, the system must provide for backup.

On a tape system, backup is provided by saving the old master file and the transaction tape whenever a file is updated. Then, if the new master file is destroyed, it can be recreated by repeating the processing of the transactions against the old master file. In case both new and old master file are destroyed, the master file from which the old master was created is also saved, along with the transactions used to update it. This method of backup is referred to as the *grandfather-father-son method* since, for every current file (the son), two previous files (the grandfather and father) are kept. To insure that all three generations of tapes aren't destroyed by some disaster, the backup master files and transaction tapes are kept either in a separate building or in a fireproof vault.

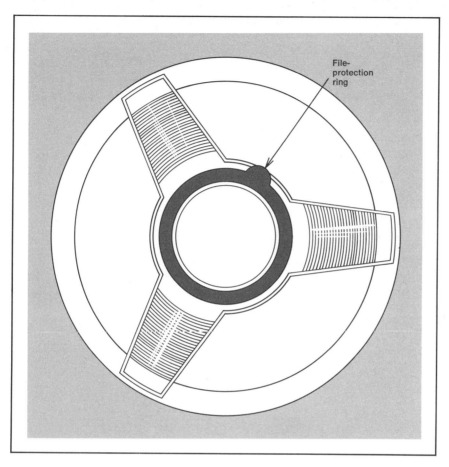

FIGURE 6-13   The file-protection ring

SUMMARY

1. I/O routines for tape files must provide for error recovery, blocking and deblocking, and label checking. Fortunately, modern programming languages provide these routines automatically when specifications are given by the programmer.

2. Even with label checking and file-protection rings, the system designer must provide for backup on a tape system. Normally, the grandfather-father-son method is used.

TERMINOLOGY

error-recovery method routine
deblocking routine
blocking routine

label-checking routine
internal label
volume label

header label   file-protection ring
trailer label   backup
job control card   grandfather-father-son method

QUESTIONS

1. Which do you think is more important—an input label-checking routine or an output label-checking routine? Why?

2. In figure 6-9, suppose the new master file created in step 7 is destroyed by fire. When the backup procedures are followed, the operator discovers that the old transaction tape has also been destroyed in the fire. How could the current master file be recreated?

7 DIRECT-ACCESS SYSTEMS

This chapter is divided into four topics. The hardware characteristics of some typical direct-access devices are described in the first topic, while several ways in which records can be stored on and accessed from direct-access devices are discussed in the second topic. After topic 3 covers the use of direct-access devices in a data-processing system—in particular, in an order-writing, billing, inventory, and accounts receivable system—topic 4 presents some programming and system considerations peculiar to direct-access systems.

TOPIC 1
DIRECT-ACCESS
DEVICES

Unlike tape devices, direct-access devices vary considerably in physical characterstics. For example, *disks* record data on platters that are somewhat analogous to phonograph records in a stack; *drums* record data on the outside of cylindrical (drum-like) surfaces; and *data cells* record data on plastic strips that are kept in bins. For each type of device, there are further variations depending on manufacturer and model. For instance, some disks have eight, some ten, and some twenty recording surfaces. Because of the variations, it is impractical to describe all of the direct-access devices in detail.

One of the most widely used direct-access devices is the disk—in particular, the IBM 2314 disk that is used on the System/360-370. With regard to system design and programming, the 2314 disk is also one of the most complex of the direct-access devices. By learning the concepts that apply to it, you will learn not only most of the concepts that apply to other disk models, but also most of those that apply to all direct-access devices.

Although the 2314 is used on the System/360 as well as on the System/370, the 3330 disk facility is the predominant device on the System/370. It is very similar to the 2314, but it offers greater storage capacity and faster access. It is described after the 2314.

Finally, the Burroughs B9372 disk is covered. This device illustrates many of the direct-access concepts not illustrated by the 2314. On the theory that it is better to learn about a few devices in depth than to learn about many devices superficially, the 2314, the 3330, and the B9372 are the only direct-access devices described in detail in this book.

THE IBM 2314 DISK DRIVE
AND DISK PACK

The *disk pack* is the device on which data is recorded; the *disk drive* is the input/output unit that writes data on and reads data from a disk pack.

The disk pack used with the 2314 disk drive, called the 2316 pack, is schematically illustrated in figure 7-1. It consists of eleven metal disks— fourteen inches in diameter—permanently stacked on a central spindle. When the disk pack is mounted on the 2314 disk drive, it rotates at a constant speed of forty revolutions per second while data is read from or written on it. When the disk pack is removed from the disk drive, a protective plastic cover is placed over it for storage.

Except for the top surface of the top disk and the bottom surface of the bottom disk, data can be recorded on both sides of the eleven disks that make up the 2316 pack; this is similar to sound being recorded on both sides of a phonograph record. Thus, this disk pack has a total of twenty recording surfaces, each of which has a magnetic surface coating on which data can be recorded.

On each of the twenty recording surfaces are 200 concentric circles called *tracks,* as illustrated in figure 7-2. These tracks are numbered from 000 through 199. Since there are twenty surfaces and 200 tracks per surface, the 2316 pack has a total of 4000 tracks on which data can be recorded. Although these tracks get smaller toward the center of the disk, each of the tracks can hold the same amount of data, a maximum of 7294 characters, or *bytes.*

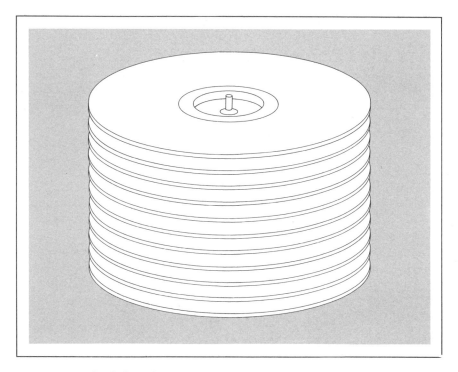

FIGURE 7-1   The disk pack

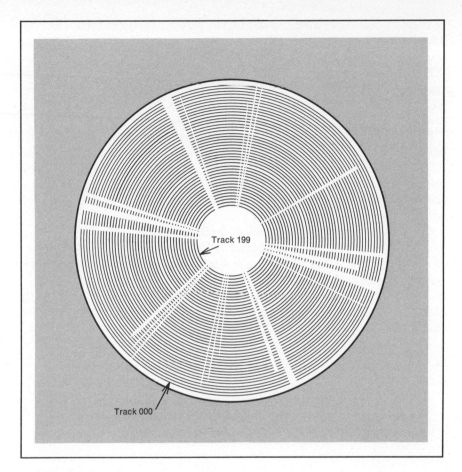

FIGURE 7-2   Tracks on a disk surface

Data is recorded on a track in the form of magnetized spots, called *bits*. These bits, which can be either "on" or "off," are strung together on a track so that eight bits make up one byte of data. To illustrate, suppose that figure 7-3 represents a portion of one track on one recording surface. If 0 represents an off-bit and 1 represents an on-bit, this portion of track contains three bytes of data. In System/360 code, the first byte, 11000001, represents the letter A; the second byte, 11110010, represents the digit 2; and the third byte, 01011011, represents the special character $. Other bit combinations are used to represent the remaining letters, numbers, and special characters.

The actual number of records on any track of a disk pack for the 2314 varies depending on the size of the records being stored. For example, one track can hold one 7294-byte record, two 3520-byte records, or three 2298-byte records. You can see that the capacity of a track decreases as

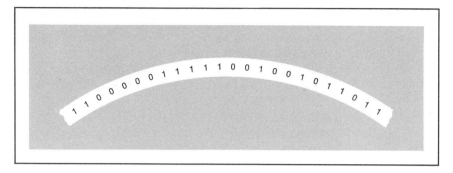

FIGURE 7-3   Coding on one section of a track

the number of records on the track increases. If records are stored one per track, the track capacity is 7294 bytes; if two per track, the capacity is 7040 bytes (2 times 3520); if three per track, the capacity is 6894 bytes; and so on. By the time you get to records that are 100 bytes long, the track capacity is only thirty-six records, or 3600 bytes.

When records are stored on a disk pack, they can be stored in either of two track formats. The first, called the *count-data format,* is illustrated in figure 7-4. In this format, each record (*data area*) on a track is preceded by a *count area.* Since the illustration, which represents only one track, has four data areas, there are four count areas on the track. Each count area contains the *disk address* of the record following it. Just as a storage address identifies one and only one storage position, a disk address identifies one and only one data area on a disk pack. By using the count area, each of the records on a disk pack can be directly accessed and read.

In addition to count areas and data areas, each track in the count-data format has a *home address.* The home address, which is located immediately before the first count area on a track, uniquely identifies each of the tracks on a disk pack. On the 2316 disk pack, there are 4000 different home addresses, one for each of the 4000 tracks.

The second track format that can be used is called the *count-key-data format.* As in the count-data format, there is a home address at the start of each track. However, unlike the count-data format, there is a key area between each count and data area, as shown in figure 7-5. This *key area,* which can be from 1 through 255 bytes in length, contains control data that uniquely identifies a record in a file. For example, in a file of inventory master records, the part number would logically be recorded in the key area. In a file of master payroll records, the employee number would be recorded in the key area. The difference, then, between count and key areas is that the count area contains a disk address that uniquely identifies a record location on the disk pack, and the key area contains a control field that uniquely identifies a record in a file. As you will see

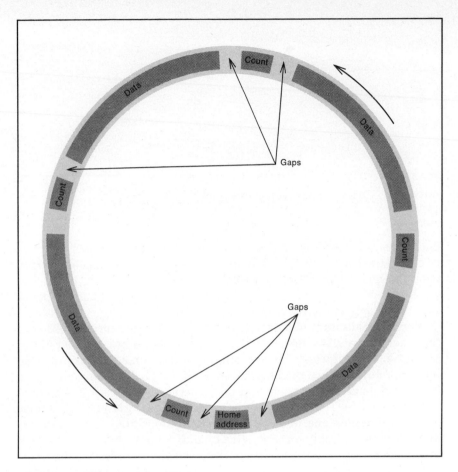

FIGURE 7-4 The count-data format

later, both count and key areas can be used to locate records when directly addressing them.

Because the count-key-data format has gaps separating the key from the count and data areas, the track capacity of this format is less than that of the count-data format. For example, with one record per track (one home address, one count, one key, and one data area), the track capacity for the count-key-data format is 7249 bytes. This includes both key and data areas—say a 10-byte key and a 7239-byte data area. In contrast, the capacity of the track in count-data format is 7294 bytes. Similarly, with a 5-byte key and a 95-byte data area (a total of 100 bytes of data), only twenty-nine records can be recorded per track in contrast to thirty-six records with the count-data format.

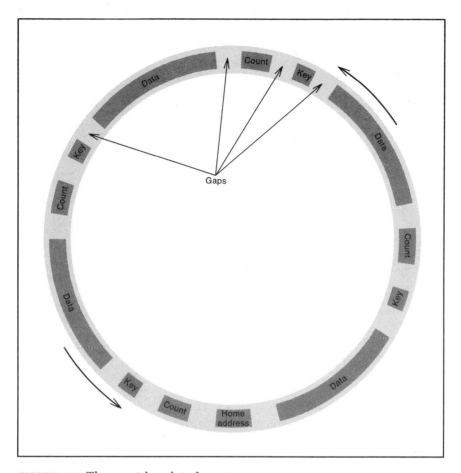

FIGURE 7-5   The count-key data format

The Disk Drive

The IBM 2314 Direct-Access Storage Facility contains from one to nine independent disk drives. In figure 7-6, for example, a facility with five disk drives is shown. To mount a disk pack on one of the five drives, the operator pulls out the selected disk drive, places the disk pack on the drive's spindle, and pushes the compartment back into the facility. In a multidrive device such as this, a drive is often referred to as a *spindle*. Thus, the device in figure 7-6 can be called a 2314 with five spindles.

When the operator pushes the start button of the unit, the disk pack begins rotating until it reaches a speed of forty revolutions per second. At this speed, the drive can read data from or write data on the recording

FIGURE 7-6   The 2314 direct-access storage facility

surfaces. When it reads data, the data on the disk pack remains unchanged; when it writes data, the data that is written replaces the data that was previously in that location on the disk.

The *access mechanism,* which is illustrated in side view in figure 7-7, is used to read and write data on the 2314. It consists of twenty *read/write heads,* one for each of the twenty recording surfaces. These heads are numbered from 0 through 19. Only one of the twenty heads can be turned on at any one time; thus, only one track can be operated upon at a time. Each of the heads can both read and write data but can do only one operation at a time.

In order to operate on all 200 tracks of each recording surface, the access mechanism moves to the track that is to be operated upon. When the access mechanism moves, all twenty heads move in unison so that 20 tracks can be operated upon in any one setting of the access mechanism. These 20 tracks are said to make up one *cylinder* of data. In other words, if the access mechanism is positioned at the seventy-fifth cylinder, the seventy-fifth track on each recording surface can be read or written. Since there are 200 tracks on each surface of the 2316 pack, there are 200 different settings of the access mechanism—and 200 cylinders. In figure 7-7, the access mechanism is positioned at approximately the sixty-fifth cylinder.

Any programming references to data records on disk are eventually reduced to cylinder number, head (track) number, and either record

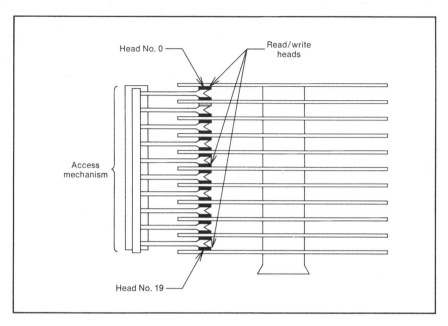

FIGURE 7-7   Side view of the access mechanism

number or key. The cylinders are numbered 0 through 199, the heads 0 through 19, and record number starts at 0 and continues through the maximum number of records that can be stored on the track. Because record number 0 is used by the operating system, data records always begin with record number 1.

When directly accessing and reading a record on a disk, there are four phases that the disk drive goes through. During the first phase, called *access-mechanism movement,* the access mechanism moves to the cylinder that is going to be operated upon. The time required for this movement depends on the number of cylinders moved. If it is just one cylinder—for instance, a move from the twenty-fifth to the twenty-sixth cylinder—it takes 25 milliseconds (25/1000 second). On the other hand, if the movement is 180 cylinders—say from the tenth to the one-hundred-ninetieth cylinder—the time required is 115 to 120 milliseconds, depending on the model used. In any event, the more cylinders moved, the more time required for access-mechanism movement. The average access-mechanism movement when processing a file that uses all 200 cylinders of the disk pack is 75 milliseconds on one model of the 2314, 60 milliseconds on another.

Once the heads are moved to the correct cylinder, the appropriate head must be turned on. This is called *head switching.* If the track on the third recording surface is supposed to be read, head number 2 is turned on. In figure 7-7, head number 2, which is on, is shaded, while the others are dark. Since head switching takes place at electronic speeds, it has a negligible effect on the total amount of time required to read or write a record.

After the head is turned on, there is a delay while the appropriate record rotates around to the head. This phase is called *rotational delay* (or *latency*). Since one complete rotation on the 2314 takes 25 milliseconds, the maximum time that rotational delay could be is 25 milliseconds. On the other hand, the appropriate record might just be reaching the head as the head is switched on. In this case, rotational delay would be 0 milliseconds. Since rotational delay will vary between 0 and 25 milliseconds, the average delay is about 12.5 milliseconds.

The last phase in the process of accessing and reading a record is called *data transfer*. Here, data is transferred from the disk to storage in the CPU. On the 2314, data transfer takes place at a rate of 312,000 bytes per second. At this speed, a 312-byte record requires 1 millisecond for data transfer.

When accessing and writing a record, the same four phases are completed. First, the access mechanism is moved; second, the appropriate head is turned on; third, rotational delay takes place; and, fourth, the data is transferred from storage to the disk. In either a reading or a writing operation, access-mechanism movement and rotational delay are by far the most time-consuming phases.

Like other I/O devices on a computer system, the disk drive checks to make sure that reading and writing take place without error. Although I didn't mention it before, there are actually two *cyclic check characters* at the end of each count, key, and data area that are used as a check on accuracy. During a writing operation, these characters are calculated based on the combinations of bits used in the count, key, or data area. Then, when a record is read, the cyclic check characters are recalculated and compared with those that are read. If they don't agree, an input error is indicated.

A writing operation may be checked by using the Write-Verify instruction. When this instruction is executed following a Write instruction, the data that has just been written is read and the cyclic check characters are checked as in a read operation. If there is a discrepancy, it indicates that the writing operation did not take place correctly. The Write-Verify, however, is time consuming since the disk must make one complete rotation before the record that has been written can be read. Nevertheless, Write-Verification is commonly used when recording permanent files.

The actual *commands* (I/O instructions on System/360 are called commands) that a 2314 disk drive can be programmed to execute are many. These commands can be broken down into five types: Seek, Search, Read, Write, and Write-Verify.

The Seek command causes the access mechanism to be moved to the specified cylinder and the specified head to be turned on. A typical

Search command searches a track until it finds a count or key equal to the one specified in the command. Rotational delay takes place during a Search. If the specified key or count isn't found, the search may be continued on successive tracks in the cylinder.

Once the Seek and Search have been executed, a Read or Write can take place. This is the data-transfer phase of the operation. In a typical business program, data only or data plus key is transferred during a Read or Write command. Following the Write command, a Write-Verify can be executed.

To illustrate the use of the commands, suppose that the fifth record on the seventh track of the one-hundred-twentieth cylinder must be accessed and read. The Seek command would specify that the access mechanism be moved to the one-hundred-twentieth cylinder and the seventh head (head number 6) be turned on. Next, a Search command would compare the counts on the track with the count specified in the command. Since the count for a record indicates the cylinder number, head number, and record number on the track, the count for this record would indicate that it is the fifth record on the track. When the count in the command and the count on the track are equal, the Read command would be issued, thus causing the data area following the count to be read.

When using the count-key-data format, a slightly different set of instructions can be used. First, the Seek finds the selected cylinder and turns on the selected head. Second, the Search looks for a key on the track that is equal to the one specified in the command. When they match, a Read command is issued, thus transferring the data area following the selected key into storage.

THE 3330 DIRECT-ACCESS
STORAGE FACILITY

The physical characteristics of the 3330 Direct-Access Storage Facility are very similar to those of the 2314. Like the 2316 pack, the 3336 disk pack has eleven disks with twenty recording surfaces. The 3330, which consists of up to nine modules, also spins this removable pack and reads or writes data through an access mechanism that carries the twenty read/write heads to the same position on each recording surface.

The 3330, however, offers significantly faster access-mechanism movement, faster data-transfer rate, and nearly four times the storage capacity of the 2314. Part of the increase in storage capacity is due to the number of cylinders being doubled. Each recording surface on the 3330 is divided into 400 tracks instead of 200 as on the 2314. The increased storage capacity is also due to the nearly doubled capacity of each data track—13,030 bytes on a fully used 3330 track as compared to 7294 bytes on a 2314 track. However, on the 3330, only nineteen of the twenty tracks in each cylinder are used for storing data. The twentieth track is used as a synchronizing track to help guide the twenty read/write heads.

Because the pack on the 3330 spins at sixty revolutions per second instead of forty as on the 2314, its rotational delay averages only 8.4 milliseconds as compared to 12.5 milliseconds on the 2314. Since the 3330 access mechanism also moves faster, the average time for access-mechanism movement is only 30 milliseconds versus 60 or 75 milliseconds on the 2314. Finally, since more data is passing under the heads at a faster rotational speed, the data-transfer rate is increased to 806,000 bytes per second, or 806 KB.

A second model of the 3330 has twice as many cylinders as the basic model. This, of course, means the storage capacity of each pack is doubled. The operational features of the device are otherwise the same as the basic model 3330.

THE BURROUGHS B9372
DISK DRIVE

The Burroughs B9372 Disk File consists of one to five disk drives. Instead of a removable pack, each drive consists of nonremovable disks that are referred to as a disk module. Each module has four disk platters and eight surfaces on which data can be recorded. Disk files with two modules are shown in figure 7-8. There are several models of the B9372; the description that follows applies to the Model 1 unit.

Like the 2316 pack, there are circular tracks on each recording surface of the B9372. Data is recorded on these tracks as strings of bits, eight of which make up one character or byte of data. Unlike the format of the 2316 disk pack, however, each track of the B9372 consists of fixed-length 100-byte *segments*. Since 12,500 segments can be recorded on each surface, the storage capacity of each storage module is 10 million bytes (8 surfaces × 12,500 segments × 100 bytes).

One of the outstanding features of the B9372 drive is that there is one read/write head for each track of the storage module. As a result, there is no access mechanism and no access-mechanism movement. To access a record, the appropriate read/write head is switched on, the selected record rotates to the head (rotational delay), and the data is transferred. Since one rotation of the disk takes 40 milliseconds, the average rotational delay is 20 milliseconds. Because the time for head switching is negligible and there is no access-mechanism movement, the total access time for each record averages 20 milliseconds.

One of the other features of the B9372 is the way in which records are addressed. Since there is no access mechanism, the concept of cylinders does not apply to this type of disk storage. Instead, the 100,000 segments in each storage module are numbered consecutively, starting with zero. The first module contains segments 0000000 to 0099999, the second

FIGURE 7-8   The Burroughs B9372 disk file

module (if there is one) contains segments 0100000 to 0199999, and so on. You can therefore think of storage on the B9372 as consecutively addressed 100-byte storage areas. Unlike the 2314, each record can be accessed in approximately the same amount of time (20 milliseconds), no matter where it is located on the disk.

Besides these major variations, the 2314 and B9372 differ in some other ways. The B9372 has a transfer rate of 208,000 bytes per second, as compared to 312,000 bytes per second for the 2314. However, the B9372 doesn't require a Seek command, because it doesn't have access-mechanism movement. In contrast to the 2314, which uses cyclic check characters for checking the accuracy of input operations, the B9372 uses vertical and longitudinal parity checking, much like a tape drive does.

OTHER DIRECT-ACCESS DEVICES

Besides the 2314 and the B9372, there are many other disk models made up of various combinations of the characteristics illustrated thus far. Disk models vary as to number of recording surfaces, number of tracks,

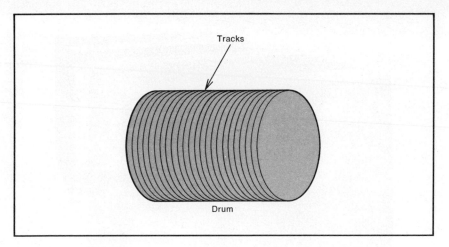

FIGURE 7-9   The drum

byte capacity per track, rotation speed, and so on. This results in a choice of devices with varying storage capacities, transfer rates, and access speeds.

Although the disk is by far the most common direct-access device, another that you might come in contact with is the *drum*. It is illustrated in figure 7-9. The drum is a cylindrical device with data recorded in tracks on the outside of the device. Because there is one read/write head for each track, the average access time is equal to the rotational delay, often less than 10 milliseconds per record. The two outstanding features of this device are (1) access speed and (2) transfer speed. One model drum, for example, has a transfer speed of over 1 million bytes per second—more than three times as fast as the 2314.

Regardless of the device, there are two basic record formats—variable format as with the 2314 and fixed format as with the B9372. When a device has a fixed format, each addressable portion of a track is called a segment or *sector*, depending on the terminology used by the manufacturer. While many devices follow the idea of cylinder, track, and record or sector when addressing a record, other devices consecutively number the sectors and address them by sector number.

SUMMARY

1. The 2314 and 3330 are disk devices consisting of one to nine spindles. They use removable disk packs that have a variable track format. To read or write a record on the 2314 or 3330 requires four phases: access-mechanism movement, head switching, rotational delay, and data transfer.

2. The B9372 consists of one to five modules with nonremovable disks and features one read/write head per track. It has a fixed track format—100 bytes per segment—and addresses records by segment number. To read or write a record on the B9372 requires three phases: head switching, rotational delay, and data transfer.

3. The drum is another type of direct-access device. It is noted for fast access and transfer speed.

TERMINOLOGY

disk	key area
drum	spindle
data cell	access mechanism
disk pack	read/write head
disk drive	cylinder
track	access-mechanism movement
byte	head switching
bit	rotational delay
count-data format	latency
data area	data transfer
count area	cyclic check character
disk address	command
home address	segment
count-key-data format	sector

QUESTIONS

1. List the commands that must be executed in order to access and write a record in count-key-data format on the 3330; in order to access and read a record on the B9372.

2. Why do you think the transfer rate of a drum is usually faster than that of a disk?

TOPIC 2
FILE ORGANIZATION

For a device such as a tape drive or a card reader, the records in the file may be organized in only one way: sequentially. On a direct-access device, however, there are a number of possible file organizations. Three of the most common are: (1) sequential, (2) direct, and (3) indexed sequential.

SEQUENTIAL FILE
ORGANIZATION

Although direct-access devices were designed for directly accessing records, they may also store and process records sequentially. In fact, sequential organization is the most efficient method for some files. When writing records sequentially on a 2314 disk device, the first record of the file is stored in the first record position on the first track of the first cylinder of the file, the second record is stored in the second record position on the first track of the first cylinder of the file, and so on. Sequential records on the B9372 are stored in consecutively numbered segments.

When reading the records in a sequential file, they are read beginning with the first physical location of the file and continuing consecutively until an end-of-file record is reached. Because the records in a sequential file are almost always processed sequentially, keys aren't needed on the 2314 and the count-data format is used.

To make efficient use of direct-access storage, the records in a sequentially organized file are usually *blocked*. This means that more than one record is read or written in a single Read or Write command. To illustrate, suppose a block consists of five 120-byte records. On the 2314, there will be 600 bytes in the data area following each count and five records will be read by one Read command. On the B9372, six segments containing five records will be read or written by a single I/O command.

Blocking is important because it reduces the time required to read or write a sequential file. With unblocked records, one Search and, therefore, one rotational delay is required for each record that is accessed. If the records are blocked, however, only one Search (rotational delay) is required for each block of records. When one Read command is executed, an entire block of records is read into storage. By eliminating rotational delay, blocking can significantly reduce the time required to read the records in a sequential file.

Blocking also affects the storage capacity of a direct-access device. On the 2314, for example, 7200 100-byte records will take 200 tracks, or ten cylinders, if the records are unblocked. If they are blocked nine to a block, however, seven such blocks may be recorded on each track—a total of 63 records per track. Then, the entire file requires only 115 tracks, or less than six cylinders.

On a device with segments or sectors, blocking helps to make full use of storage by eliminating wasted bytes within a sector. If 120-byte records are to be stored on the B9372, for example, each unblocked record will require two segments since a Read or Write command can only operate on complete segments. Thus 80 bytes of storage are wasted for each record stored. If the records are blocked with a blocking factor of 5, however, no storage space is wasted. Then, five records are stored in six segments.

DIRECT FILE ORGANIZATION

In direct file organization, the records on the direct-access device are in no particular sequence. When a program is ready to read or write a record using this organization, it must supply the information required to locate the record in the device. On the B9372, for example, the program must supply the segment number of the desired record before the Search command can be executed. On the 2314, the program must supply the cylinder and head number of the desired record before the Seek command can be executed. And before the Search can be executed, either the record location on the track or the key of the desired record must be supplied. The trick in processing records in direct file organization, then, is determining the direct-access address for each record that is to be processed. This information is normally developed in a programming routine called a *randomizing routine*.

To illustrate the use of randomizing routines, suppose that 9600 inventory master records are to be stored on a 2314. These records are going to be in the count-key-data format with a key length of 7 bytes and a data area of 149 bytes. As you would guess, the key area for each record will contain the part number of the master inventory item.

Since twenty-four 149-byte records with 7-byte keys can be stored on one 2314 track, this file requires 400 tracks (9600 ÷ 24), or twenty cylinders. However, because of the difficulty of assigning these records to a specific track and because additional master records may be added to the file later, twenty-five cylinders, or 500 tracks, are allotted for the file. These cylinders are numbered from 060 through 084.

For this file, the problem of the randomizing routine is to convert a record's part number, which may range from 100,000 through 9,000,000, to a specific cylinder and head number somewhere within cylinders 060–084. This data will be used in the Seek command when accessing a record. After the access mechanism has been moved to the selected cylinder and the selected head is turned on, the Search command will locate the record on the track by searching for a key equal to the record's part number.

One common method used in randomizing routines is called the *division/remainder method*. In this method, the part number is first divided by the prime number closest to, and less than, the number of tracks allotted to the file. (A prime number can be divided evenly by only 1 and itself; for example, 1, 2, 3, 7, 11, and so forth.) Since there are 500 tracks assigned to the file, the prime number is 499. If the part number is 254932, then, the quotient is 510 with a remainder of 442. In the division/remainder method, though, only the remainder of this first division is significant. This number, 442, gives the relative location of the track on which the record should be stored. Because the divisor is always 499 for this file, the remainder will always be from 000 through 498.

Once the relative track location is determined, the randomizing routine must convert it to a cylinder and head number. In the example, if the relative track, 442, is divided by 20 (the number of tracks in a cylinder), the remainder is a head number between 0 and 19. Then, if 60 is added to the quotient, the result is a cylinder number between 060 and 084. For the part number 254932, the cylinder number becomes 82 (442 ÷ 20 = 22; 22 + 60 = 82) and the head number becomes 2 (442 ÷ 20 = 22 with a remainder of 2). Figure 7-10 summarizes the characteristics of the file and the randomizing routine used in this example.

When initially loading the inventory records on the 2314, each master part number is converted to a cylinder and head number as described. Then, the record is written in the first available location on the track indicated. If the track is filled (it already has twenty-four records), additional programming routines are required. Two of the most widely used alternatives are (1) to write the record on the next track in the cylinder, assuming that it has an available record location, or (2) to write the record in an *overflow area* somewhere else on the disk.

An overflow area is simply an area that is used for records that cannot be stored in the locations assigned to them by the randomizing routine. In the example of the inventory file, cylinder 085 could be used as an overflow area. Then, if there is no room for record number 254932 on cylinder 82, head 2, the record could be written in the first available location in cylinder 085.

When accessing and reading an inventory record from a 2314 file, the part number of the desired record is first converted to cylinder and head number by the randomizing routine. Then, after the Seek locates the selected cylinder and head, the Search looks for a record with a key equal to the part number of the desired record. If it finds the selected key, the record is read into storage. If it does not find the key, programming routines are required that correspond to the routines used in loading the file. For example, if an overflow area is used, the program must seek the overflow cylinder and search for the selected record there.

Although the randomizing routine summarized in figure 7-10 creates a valid cylinder and head number for each record in the master file, it may

A DIRECT-ACCESS FILE ON THE 2314

Characteristics of the file:
1. A file of 9600 inventory records is to be stored in cylinders 060 through 084.
2. Each track can hold a total of 24 inventory records, which consist of 149-byte data areas and 7-byte keys.
3. The part numbers, which are the keys, range from 100,000 to 9,000,000.

Problem of randomizing routine:
To convert the part numbers of the 9600 master records to cylinder and head numbers that are within the 25 cylinders assigned to the file.

The division/remainder method:
1. Divide part number by 499 — the remainder is the relative track, which will always be between 0 and 498.
2. Divide the remainder by 20 — the remainder is the head number.
3. Add 60 to the quotient of the second division to obtain the cylinder number.

Examples of randomizing:

Part No.	Cylinder No.	Head No.
100,000	70	0
254,932	82	2
794,210	75	1
1,048,342	82	2
9,000,000	61	16

Loading the records on the 2314:
1. Convert the part number to cylinder and head number.
2. Seek cylinder and head number.
3. Search for next available location on the track.
4. Write the record in the first available location.
(If entire track is filled, the record must be written in successive tracks of the cylinder or in an overflow area of the disk.)

FIGURE 7-10   Direct file organization

not be the best randomizing method available. One major problem is that 17,835 other part numbers between 100,000 and 9,000,000 will randomize to the same cylinder and track as part number 254932—but only 24 records can be stored per track and only 480 per cylinder. As a result, some other randomizing method may be more suitable for the file—the division/remainder method is only used as an example. In actual practice, a programmer or a system designer considers several different randomizing methods and sometimes actually tries one or more of the methods before making a final decision.

On the B9372, or any device that addresses records by sector number, the randomizing routine must convert the control number in a record to a segment or sector number. To illustrate, suppose 800 customer master records, 100 bytes long, are to be stored on the B9372. To give the randomizing routine some leeway, 1000 segments are assigned to the file—segments 8000—8999. The customer numbers are five-digit numbers ranging from 10000—99999.

Using the division/remainder method, the customer number is divided first by the prime number nearest but less than the total number of segments assigned to the file—in this case, 997 is used. The remainder of this division gives the relative segment number within the file. For example, if the customer number is 34405, the relative segment number is 507. Then, by adding 8000 to this number, a segment number between 8000 and 8999 is derived.

When initially loading a file on the disk, a problem arises when two or more records randomize to the same segment. When a record is already stored in a segment, the other records assigned to that address—called *synonyms*—must be assigned to unfilled segments. Customer number 34405, for example, has eighty-nine possible synonyms—eighty-nine other customer numbers that randomize to segment 8507. As a result, additional programming routines must be available to store synonyms in other segments.

There are several methods for handling synonyms on a fixed segment or sector device; one of these is to write the synonyms in the next available direct-access location. For example, if customer number 38393 randomizes to segment 8507 but record number 34405 is already stored in this segment, the randomizing routine tries to write record number 38393 in segment 8508. If this segment already contains a master record, segment 8509 is tried, and so on.

To help locate a synonym when accessing a record, a *chaining* technique is commonly used. This means that each record stored in the file contains a field, called a *chaining field,* that gives the segment or sector number of the first synonym that was not stored at its randomized address. This process is illustrated in figure 7-11. If you go through the sequence of records to be stored you will find that the first synonym is record number 41383, which randomizes to segment 8506. Since record number 11473 is already stored in this segment, record 41383—the synonym—is stored in the next available segment, segment 8508. As a result, segment number 8508 is stored in the chaining field of the record located in segment 8506. To access a record when chaining is used, a program first determines the direct-access address by a randomizing routine. It then reads the record at this address and checks to see if the control field is the desired one. If not, it reads the segment address given by the chaining field. If this segment does not contain the correct record, the next segment in the chain is read. The program continues in this way until the desired record is found or no further chaining address is given. In the latter case, the program assumes that the record is not stored on the file.

When records in a direct file are blocked, additional programming routines are required. When loading a file, the records have to be randomized to a block of records rather than to an individual storage location. Overflow records for each block can be stored in the next

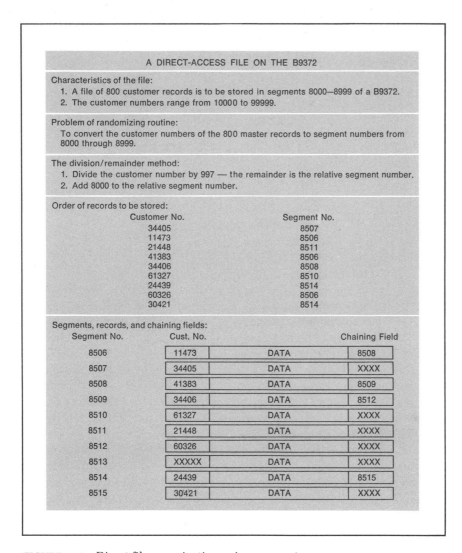

A DIRECT-ACCESS FILE ON THE B9372

Characteristics of the file:
1. A file of 800 customer records is to be stored in segments 8000—8999 of a B9372.
2. The customer numbers range from 10000 to 99999.

Problem of randomizing routine:
To convert the customer numbers of the 800 master records to segment numbers from 8000 through 8999.

The division/remainder method:
1. Divide the customer number by 997 — the remainder is the relative segment number.
2. Add 8000 to the relative segment number.

Order of records to be stored:

Customer No.	Segment No.
34405	8507
11473	8506
21448	8511
41383	8506
34406	8508
61327	8510
24439	8514
60326	8506
30421	8514

Segments, records, and chaining fields:

Segment No.	Cust. No.		Chaining Field
8506	11473	DATA	8508
8507	34405	DATA	XXXX
8508	41383	DATA	8509
8509	34406	DATA	8512
8510	61327	DATA	XXXX
8511	21448	DATA	XXXX
8512	60326	DATA	XXXX
8513	XXXXX	DATA	XXXX
8514	24439	DATA	8515
8515	30421	DATA	XXXX

FIGURE 7-11   Direct file organization using segments

available block or in overflow areas; and a chaining technique, with one chaining field for each block of records, may be used. Blocking is likely to improve the use of the available disk storage, but it will probably decrease the speed at which records are accessed and read. Thus, the use of blocking depends on considerations such as the addressing characteristics of the device used, the access speeds required, and the available storage capacity.

In actual practice, direct files aren't commonly used for two reasons. First, it is usually difficult to develop an efficient randomizing routine. Second, the programmer must code file-maintenance routines that keep track of available record spaces as records are added to and deleted from a file. These routines can be very complex. Together these two problems make direct files very difficult to use.

INDEXED SEQUENTIAL
FILE ORGANIZATION

Although sequential and direct file organizations have their advantages, they also have their limitations. For example, while a blocked sequential file may make maximum use of the storage capacity of a direct-access device, it has many of the limitations of a tape file. To update a sequential file, all of the records in the file are read instead of just those affected by transactions, and the entire file has to be rewritten in order to add a record to the file. On the other hand, while direct file organization allows a record to be accessed rapidly, it wastes storage capacity. (Remember the example where twenty-five cylinders are assigned to a file consisting of twenty cylinders of data.) In addition, a direct file must usually be sorted into sequential order before a sequential report can be prepared from it.

Indexed sequential file organization is designed to allow both sequential and direct (or random) processing. (Random means that records are not processed in any particular sequence.) Using indexed sequential organization, the records of a file are stored on the direct-access device so that they can be read sequentially, but indexes are kept so that any record can be read randomly by looking up its location in the indexes. If records are added to the file, an additional file area called an overflow area is used, thus making it unnecessary to rewrite the entire file as done in sequential organization. When a record is stored in the overflow area, the indexes are changed so that the records can still be processed in sequence.

In a typical indexed sequential file on a 2314, two indexes are kept: a *cylinder index* and a *track index*. The cylinder index is used to find the cylinder in which a record is located. To illustrate, suppose a file of master customer records is stored in cylinders 11-15 of a disk pack and the cylinder index is kept on the first track of cylinder 16. Since five cylinders are used in the file, there will be five records in the cylinder index, always in the count-key-data format. The key in each index record contains the highest customer number stored in each cylinder of the file and the data area indicates in which cylinder the records are located. For example, the cylinder index might contain the following data:

Key	Data
1949	C11
3241	C12
5972	C13
7566	C14
9840	C15

By searching this index, a program can determine that the record for customer 6500 is stored in cylinder 14. (C is used to indicate that the number in the data area is a cylinder number.)

The same idea is used when searching track indexes. These indexes, which are found on the first track of each cylinder in the file, indicate the key of the highest customer number on each track of the cylinder. For example, the track index for the fourteenth cylinder might contain the following data:

Key	Data	Key	Data
6198	T2	6893	T11
6258	T3	6979	T12
6322	T4	7053	T13
6398	T5	7119	T14
6449	T6	7200	T15
6570	T7	7303	T16
6609	T8	7471	T17
6701	T9	7566	T18
6813	T10		

By searching this index, a program can determine that record 6500 is on the seventh track of the cylinder. (T is used to indicate that the number in the data area is a track number.)

Once the program has determined the track number, it can find a record by searching for a key equal to the control number in the record—in this case, customer number 6500. Because the search is always for key rather than count, indexed sequential files must always be in the count-key-data format.

If you wonder why the track index in the above example indicates only seventeen tracks (tracks 2-18), remember that the first track is used for records that make up the track index. If there is space left over on this first track, it can be used for storing data records, in which case, there will be an index for track number 1 also. In the example, it is assumed that the index uses the entire first track.

The nineteenth and twentieth tracks of the cylinder are used when records are added to the file. These tracks make up the *cylinder overflow area*. They contrast tracks 2-18, which make up the *prime data area* of the cylinder. The number of tracks assigned to the overflow area is based on the number of records likely to be added to a cylinder.

When an indexed sequential file is created, the records are written in sequence in the prime data area. As the records are written, the cylinder and track indexes are created so the records in the file can be directly accessed. When all of the records are stored on the file, an end-of-file record is written just as if the file had sequential organization. After the file is loaded, track 1 of each cylinder contains the track index records, tracks 2-18 contain the records of the file in sequence, and tracks 19-20, the cylinder overflow area, contain no data at all.

When a record is added to an indexed sequential file, it is placed in its sequential location in the prime data area. All records on the track with higher keys are moved up one record location and the record that is moved off the track is placed in the cylinder overflow area. To allow records in this overflow area to be processed sequentially as well as directly, overflow index records are kept in the track index along with the normal index records. When a record is placed in the overflow area, the overflow index is changed so that it locates the next record in sequence following the records on the normal track in the prime data area. If more than one record is moved from one normal track to the cylinder overflow area, a chaining field in each overflow record is used to point to the direct-access address of the next record in sequence. Thus a chain of sequential records is maintained.

To illustrate the use of a cylinder overflow area, overflow index records, and chaining, consider the example in figure 7-12. It illustrates the normal and overflow index records in the track index of one cylinder, cylinder 11, as well as nine overflow records in the overflow area, cylinders 19 and 20. C, T, and R are used to indicate cylinder, track, and record numbers. Since the keys in the normal and overflow index records for track 2 are the same, it means that there are no overflow records for this track. The same is true with track 3. For track 4, however, the key of the normal index entry is 322, whereas the key of the overflow index record is 339. This means that there are one or more overflow records from this track. Both the normal and overflow records can be read sequentially, however, in this manner:

1. Read the records on the normal track in sequence. (These records are always in sequence.)
2. Read the overflow record indicated in the overflow index; namely, record 4 on track 19. This is the next record in sequence.
3. Read the record indicated in the chaining field of the overflow record. Since this field points to the second record on track 20, that record is next in sequence.
4. Continue reading the chain of records until the chaining field indicates record number 255; then continue with the first record on the next normal track—in this case, track 5.

The same logic holds for processing the other overflow records in sequence. As a result, the next records in sequence would be those from track 5, then those from track 6, then record 3 on track 20, then record 3 on track 19, then the records from track 7, and so forth. If you wonder why the records in the overflow area aren't in sequence, it is because the records are placed there in the order in which additions are made to the file. The only sequential linkage between these records comes from the chaining fields.

To directly access records when there are overflow records, a somewhat different logic is used. First, the track indexes are searched as usual—the order of these indexes is track 1 normal index, track 1 overflow index, track 2 normal index, track 2 overflow index, and so on. If the desired record is in the prime data area, the track is searched for the selected key as if there were no overflow records. If the desired key falls in the overflow area, however, the record indicated by the overflow index is searched for and read. If this isn't the desired record, the record indicated in the chaining field is searched and read. This search is continued until the desired record is found or the end of the chain is reached.

To illustrate, consider a search for record number 555 in figure 7-12. Since 555 is greater than 513 but less than 580, the track indexes indicate that the record is in the cylinder overflow area. As a result, the search begins with the record indicated in the overflow index record, record 3 of track 20. Since this record is the desired record, the search ends. However, if it were not record 555, the search would continue with the record indicated in the chaining field. Because of the extra searching (rotational delay) required for records in the overflow area, indexed sequential files should be reorganized periodically so that all records are returned to the prime data area.

On a device such as the B9372, the concept of indexed sequential is similar, although the details are different. Rather than loading the file sequentially, the file can be loaded in any order; chaining fields are used in all records so that the file can be accessed sequentially. Since the B9372 doesn't have cylinders, the terms cylinder index and track index don't apply. Instead, a *coarse index* and a *fine index* are used. The coarse index gives the location of the fine index to be used; the fine index gives the location of individual records to be accessed. Thus the coarse index may indicate that the location of record number 73349 can be determined from the fine index starting in segment 10025. Then the fine index may indicate that the record is located in segment 12104. When records are added to a file, a chaining technique is used so that the records in the overflow area can be accessed in both sequential and random order.

In addition to the concepts described, there may be many other variations in the organization and handling of indexed sequential files. Nevertheless, any indexed sequential file can be processed in sequential or random order with relative ease—the major feature of this method of file organization. When processing sequentially, however, an indexed sequential file is likely to be slower than a sequential file. (Consider the extra searches for records in the overflow areas.) Similarly, when processed randomly, an indexed sequential file is likely to be slower than a direct file. (Consider the seeks and searches required for finding a record in the indexes used.) Because each type of file organization has its advantages and limitations, you can decide which type of organization to use only after considering a file's characteristics, as well as all of the uses to which a file will be put.

TRACK 1	TRACK INDEX RECORDS		
NORMAL		OVERFLOW	
Key	Data	Key	Data
187	T2	187	T2
284	T3	284	T3
322	T4	339	T19, R4
397	T5	397	T5
513	T6	580	T20, R3
641	T7	641	T7
787	T8	787	T8
940	T9	949	T20, R1
991	T10	991	T10
1205	T11	1205	T11
1297	T12	1297	T12
1391	T13	1404	T19, R2
1522	T14	1522	T14
1639	T15	1639	T15
1740	T16	1742	T19, R5
1833	T17	1833	T17
1949	T18	1949	T18

TRACKS 2–18	THE PRIME DATA AREA					
Track	Keys on Track					
2	012	041	049	094	101	187
3	188	210	218	247	250	284
4	287	291	294	301	307	322
5	341	348	354	363	370	397
6	410	415	420	434	470	513
7	585	592	601	615	621	641
8	660	680	685	710	740	787
9	812	819	901	914	927	940
10	951	957	967	984	985	991
11	1032	1105	1117	1121	1187	1205
12	1207	1208	1231	1239	1250	1297
13	1330	1337	1341	1355	1366	1391
14	1410	1415	1423	1480	1481	1522
15	1523	1530	1537	1539	1599	1639
16	1641	1645	1691	1701	1703	1740
17	1748	1780	1788	1790	1805	1833
18	1838	1847	1897	1901	1930	1949

TRACKS 19–20	THE CYLINDER OVERFLOW AREA		
Count	Key	Chaining Field	Data Record
C11, T19, R1	339	R255	DATA
C11, T19, R2	1397	T19, R6	DATA
C11, T19, R3	580	R255	DATA
C11, T19, R4	331	T20, R2	DATA
C11, T19, R5	1742	R255	DATA
C11, T19, R6	1404	R255	DATA
C11, T20, R1	949	R255	DATA
C11, T20, R2	333	T19, R1	DATA
C11, T20, R3	555	T19, R3	DATA

FIGURE 7-12 Indexed sequential file organization

SUMMARY

1. Sequential files on direct-access devices are comparable to tape files. They can be read only in the sequence in which the records are located on the direct-access device. To maximize I/O speed and storage use, sequential files are normally blocked.

2. In direct files, the records are loaded based on a randomizing routine. The control number in the record to be stored must be converted to a direct-access address such as cylinder and track number or sector number. Additional routines must be available to handle overflow records or synonyms.

3. Indexed sequential file organization is designed to allow records to be processed on either a sequential or a random basis. Two or more indexes are kept to locate records on a random basis, and overflow areas are used for additions to the file. So that records in the overflow area can be processed in sequence, chaining is used.

TERMINOLOGY

sequential file organization	random
blocking	index
direct file organization	cylinder index
randomizing routine	track index
division/remainder method	cylinder overflow area
overflow area	prime data area
synonym	coarse index
chaining	fine index
chaining field	
indexed sequential file organization	

QUESTIONS

1. If unblocked records are stored on a disk, how many Seeks and Reads are required to read 10 records? If the records are blocked 10 per block, how many Seeks and Reads are required?

2. How many access mechanism movements are required to read a sequential file stored in 21 cylinders on a 3330?

3. Refer to figure 7-10. If you assume that track 2 on cylinder 82 is filled when the load program tries to load record number 1,048,342, where will this record be written? Also, what I/O commands have to be executed in order to access and read this record in subsequent programs?

4. Refer to figure 7-11. What I/O commands must be executed to access and read record number 41383? Record 24439?

5. Refer to figure 7-12. List the steps required to directly access and read record 1341; record 1397.

TOPIC 3
SYSTEM DESIGN

One of the basic procedures in any system is the procedure for updating a master file. For example, inventory records, accounts receivable records, sales records, and payroll records must be continually updated. In figure 7-13, a system flowchart for one method of updating direct-access files is illustrated.

In step 1, transaction data from source documents is keypunched and verified. This is similar to the first step when processing data on a card or tape system.

The second and last step in the system is the *update run* on the computer. To illustrate what takes place here, assume that a master file of inventory records is stored with indexed sequential or direct file organization and that it is processed on a random basis. The first four transactions to be processed have item numbers 217, 109, 217, and 540. When the update program reads the first transaction, item number 217, it searches for master record 217, processes the record, and writes the updated master record in the same location from which it was read. When the program reads the second transaction, it searches for master record 109, updates the record, and writes it on the disk in its original location. The program continues in this way with records 217 and 540. During the program, various checks on the validity of input data may be performed and a list of error transactions may be printed. Invalid transactions are ignored, so they do not affect the master file.

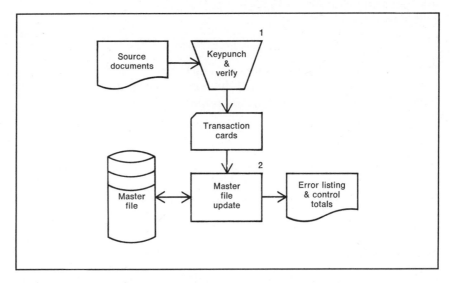

FIGURE 7-13   System flowchart for a master-file update

Although transaction records for random updates do not have to be in sequential order, it is often more efficient if they are. In the previous example, because the transactions weren't in order, master record 217 had to be read and written twice, once for each transaction. In contrast, if the input records had been in sequence—109, 217, 217, and 540—master record 217 would have been read and written only once. For this reason, transaction records are often sorted before processing, even though they are processed on a random basis.

Unlike tape processing, there is no old master file when a direct-access file is updated. Because the updated record replaces the old record, the old record is destroyed. As a result, it is extremely important that no mistakes are made during an update program. Consequently, an editing program for transaction data is usually run before the update actually takes place. This program checks to be sure that all fields in the transaction records contain valid data by testing that numeric fields contain numeric data, that transaction codes are valid, that the contents of a field are within acceptable limits, and so on.

Figure 7-14, then, presents another procedure for updating a master file. In step 1, the transactions are keypunched and verified. In step 2, the card transactions are edited and converted into a sequential disk file by a *card-to-disk* program that includes editing routines.

Step 3 is a sort step in which the sequential transaction file is sorted into master-file order. Although a *sort program* will use several different areas of the disk or several different disks, only one input and one output file is shown on a flowchart. A disk sort program is complex and usually supplied by the computer manufacturer. To use the program, the user supplies only the specifications of the sort to be run; the sort program does the rest. Because of the unique capabilities of a direct-access device, a disk sort program is likely to take considerably less time to execute than a comparable tape sort program.

In step 4, the update program is executed as previously described. Because the transactions are in master-file order, however, each affected master record is read and written only once.

If you compare the flowchart in figure 7-14 with the flowchart for a tape update (figure 6-7), you will find them very similar. In fact, if the master file in figure 7-14 has sequential or indexed sequential organization, it could be processed sequentially. The update would then be the same as tape processing with these exceptions: (1) the updated master record is written in its original location on a direct-access device, and (2) it is not necessary to rewrite a master record on the device if it has not been affected by transactions.

The decision as to whether sequential or random processing is used depends on how many of the records in a master file are affected during a typical day's processing. If 80 percent of the records are affected, sequential processing will likely be more efficient. If only 10 percent of

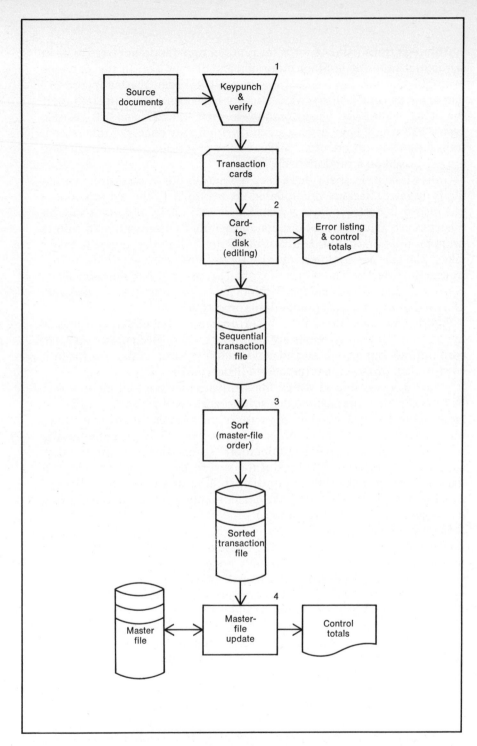

FIGURE 7-14 System flowchart for the refined master-file update

the records are affected, random processing will probably be more efficient. The important feature of a direct-access device is that it allows the computer user to choose whichever method is better.

To add, change, or delete records on a master file, a procedure such as the one in figure 7-13 can be used. Records that are added to an indexed sequential file make use of the overflow area of the file; records that are added to a direct file are stored using the logic of the file-creation program. Normally, deleted records are not removed from the file. Instead, a code is placed in the deleted record indicating that it is no longer active. For example, an asterisk in the first byte of a record can indicate that it has been deleted. Because additions, changes, and deletions are commonly handled on a random basis, only the affected master records are read or written.

If records are processed on a random basis, more than one master file can be updated by the same set of transactions during the same update run. For example, both inventory and salesman records can be updated by transaction records that indicate which items have been sold to which customers by which salesman. The multiple update can be shown as follows:

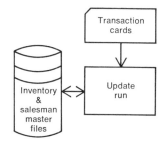

Here, the files could be on the same or separate disk drives. For each transaction card, two master records—the inventory and salesman records—are updated.

Using *disk-to-printer programs,* reports may be printed at any time from up-to-date master files. For example, a sales-by-salesman report could be printed from a file of salesman master records as follows:

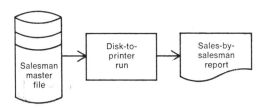

A disk-to-printer program normally processes records in sequential order; it simply reads a record, converts the data to a readable form, and prints the data. If the file is stored in direct organization, the records are sorted into sequential order by a sort program before the disk-to-printer program is executed.

DISK APPLICATIONS

Because of the direct-access capabilities of a disk, a disk system can eliminate many of the steps common to sequential systems. Sorting and merging can be eliminated and more than one file can be updated by a single program. In a simple billing, inventory, and accounts receivable application, for example, two files can be updated and invoices can be printed in just a few steps. This is illustrated in the flowchart in figure 7-15. Because invoices are printed after the items are shipped, this is a

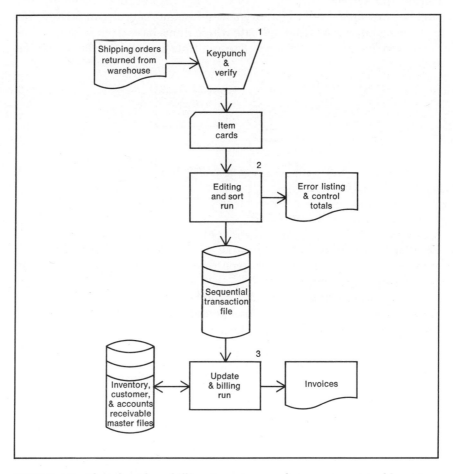

FIGURE 7-15   Flowchart for a billing, inventory, and accounts-receivable system

postbilling system. In step 1, the transaction records are keypunched and verified. In step 2, the input data is edited, sorted, and converted to disk. In step 3, the invoices are printed, and the inventory and accounts receivable files are updated. This is like the system described in chapter 2.

This procedure of course does not provide for the handling of back orders or the processing of receipt, return, and adjustment records against the inventory file. Figure 7-16, then, presents a more complete system. In the eight steps shown, inventory, accounts receivable, and back-order files are updated; back orders are relieved; and shipping orders and invoices are printed. Since invoices are printed before items are actually shipped, this is a prebilling system. Although control posting and balancing steps would normally be shown, they are omitted here to emphasize processing.

Figure 7-17 is a record layout form that gives the layouts of the card and disk records used in this system. Seven record formats are shown—the first two for the item and receipt, return, and adjustment cards, the other five for disk records. Notice that the inventory and customer master records have indexed sequential file organization so they can be processed on either a sequential or random basis. The back-order and accounts-receivable files are kept in sequential organization. The system used consists of a CPU, a combined card reader and punch, a printer, and a direct-access device with four spindles. Auxiliary equipment consists of keypunches and verifiers.

In steps 1 and 2, the item records are keypunched and verified, edited, and converted into a sequential disk file. This file is then ready to be processed in the order-writing and invoicing run (step 5).

In step 3, receipts, returns, and adjustments in item-number order are processed to update the inventory master file. At the same time, the back-order file, also in item-number order, is processed to determine whether any of the back orders can now be filled. If so, the filled back-order record is written on a new disk file, the filled back-order file. To delete filled back orders from the back-order master file, an asterisk is placed in the first byte of the deleted record. Remember that although three separate disk symbols are shown on the flowchart, all three disk files could be stored in separate areas of the same disk drive.

In step 4, the filled back-order file is sorted into customer-number order in preparation for the billing run of step 5. Here again, several areas of one or more disk drives are used during the sort, although they are not shown on the flowchart.

In step 5, inventory master records are updated and the shipping orders and invoices are printed. For each new customer number, the corresponding customer master record is read and used to print the heading of the invoice. Then, as each transaction record or filled back-order record is read, the corresponding inventory master record is read to determine

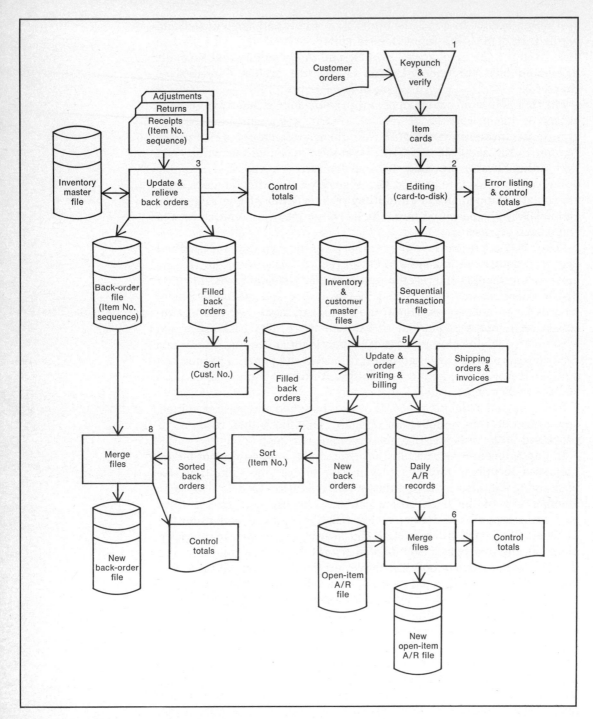

FIGURE 7-16   Direct-access applications

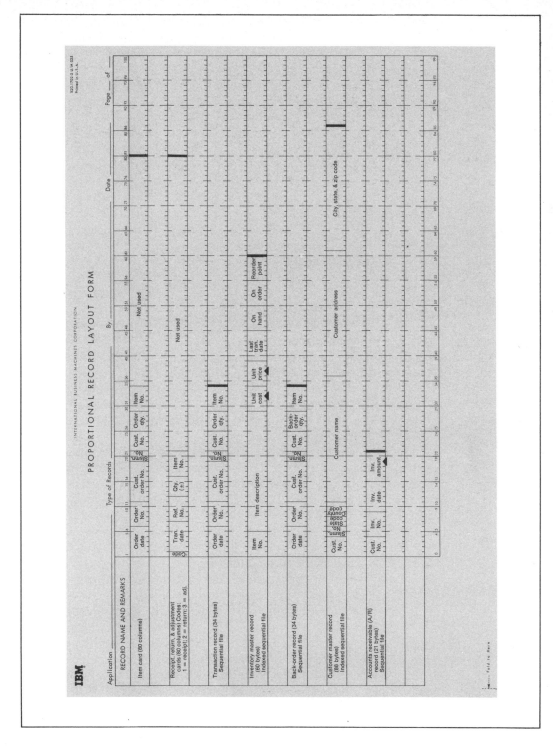

FIGURE 7-17 Formats for the direct-access applications

whether the item ordered can be filled. If so, item description and unit price are taken from the master record to print the line item on the invoice. If the item can't be filled, a back-order record is written on the new back-order file. After all transactions and filled back orders for one customer have been processed, the total line of the invoice is printed and an accounts receivable record is written on the daily accounts receivable file.

In steps 6, 7, and 8, the open-item accounts receivable file and the back-order file, both with sequential organization, are updated by merging the new records into the files. This is comparable to what takes place on a tape system. Two input files are merged together, resulting in one output file.

In summary, both sequential and random processing techniques can be used, and are likely to be used, within the procedures of a direct-access system. The system designer must consider both possibilities and choose the one that leads to the most efficient system.

DISCUSSION

In comparison to a tape system, a disk system has several advantages. The primary one is that a disk system generally requires fewer steps than a tape system. For example, the tape system in figure 6-10 requires twelve steps, while the comparable disk system in figure 7-16 requires only eight. As a result, the disk system should take less time for processing even if individual runs take longer than comparable tape runs. By eliminating a step, operator setup time is eliminated as well as the time required to load and execute the program.

A second advantage is that file-maintenance programs are likely to be executed faster on disk than on tape—particularly, if the percent of affected master records is low. To illustrate, suppose a file of 5000 master records is being maintained, but only 50 master records are affected. On a tape system, all 5000 records will be read and written during the file-maintenance run. In contrast, if the records are stored on a disk and processed on a random basis, only 50 master records will be processed.

A third advantage is that programs stored on disk can be accessed and loaded faster than programs on tape. Rather than searching sequentially for the selected program, the computer directly accesses the program, which is then loaded into storage at the relatively high transfer rate of disk.

One final advantage of a disk system is its inquiry capability. Because records on disk can be accessed in milliseconds, it is practical for a clerk or manager to inquire into the contents of a disk record. For example, an inventory-control clerk can inquire into the contents of an inventory master record by keying the item number on a typewriter-like device attached to the computer. This device can be in the same room as the computer or many miles away, attached via telephone lines. Under program control, the selected record is accessed, read, and printed on the typewriter device. Because a master inventory tape would have to be searched sequentially, this type of inquiry is time consuming, and thus impractical, on a tape system. Although the inquiry capability is not used on many of the smaller direct-access systems, it is this capability that makes possible many types of data-communication systems, as described in chapter 16. As a result, it is used heavily on the more sophisticated computer systems.

Regardless of the advantages of direct-access devices, tape drives are likely to be found on direct-access systems. For example, a typical direct-access system might consists of a CPU, a printer, a card reader and punch, a five-drive 2314, and two tape drives. Because tape storage is far less expensive than disk storage, the use of tape can reduce storage costs considerably.

On a disk system with nonremovable disks, tape drives are essential. To provide for backup, a disk file is copied onto tape by a disk-to-tape program. The tape can then be used to recreate the master file if it is destroyed or becomes unreadable. If the capacity of a fixed-disk system isn't large enough to store all of the files at once, tape must also be used as temporary storage of master files. For example, after updating a disk file, the file would be copied onto tape. The disk can then be used for some other file. Prior to the next update run, the tape is copied back onto the disk and the update program is executed.

Because of the features of direct-access processing, direct-access systems account for much of the growth in the computer industry. At present, the growth rate for direct-access devices is 25 percent in contrast to a rate of 6 or 7 percent for tape devices.

SUMMARY

1. A direct-access master file can be updated on a sequential or a random basis. The choice depends on the characteristics of the file and the device used. In a random update, only the affected master records are read and written. In a sequential update, all master records are read, but only the affected records are written.

2. A major advantage of a disk system is that it allows a job to be done in fewer steps than a sequential system. In addition, a disk system makes it possible (1) to process only the affected records in a file-maintenance program, (2) to rapidly access and load object programs stored on disk, and (3) to inquire into master files on a random basis. The inquiry ability is the primary reason why more sophisticated systems depend heavily on direct-access devices.

TERMINOLOGY

update run
card-to-disk program
sort program
disk-to-printer program

QUESTIONS

1. In figure 7-13, if 700 master records in a file of 5000 are updated by 1300 transaction records, how many master records must be read and written? How many in figure 7-14 using the same numbers of records?

2. How does file maintenance on a disk system differ from that on a tape system?

3. Assume four disk drives are available for the system shown in figure 7-15. Should the customer, inventory, and accounts-receivable master files be on the same or separate disk drives? Explain.

4. In step 5 of figure 7-16, is the inventory file being read on a sequential or random basis? How can you tell?

5. In step 6 of figure 7-16, is the open-item accounts-receivable file being rewritten in its entirety? If so, why?

6. Based on the record form given in figure 7-17, how would you prepare an aged trial balance report from the available master files? Flowchart it.

7. Why is tape required on a system with nonremovable disk modules?

8. Why are direct-access devices essential to the more sophisticated communication systems such as an airlines reservation system?

TOPIC 4
PROGRAMMING AND
SYSTEM
CONSIDERATIONS

When computer users move from a card or tape system to a disk system, they normally increase their processing capabilities considerably. However, they also increase the complexity of their systems. In comparison to a sequential system, a disk system generally demands much more from operators, programmers, and system designers. Some of the programming and system complications common to direct-access systems are described in this topic.

PROGRAMMING
CONSIDERATIONS

In a direct-access program, a certain portion of the object code is taken up by input and output routines. One immediate complication is that a program can't just read or write a record on a direct-access device. Instead, the program must use the proper combination of Seeks, Searches, Reads, and Writes. Beyond this, direct-access programs always require error-recovery and label-checking routines, and, depending on file organization, may require blocking, deblocking, and file-handling routines.

Error-Recovery Routines

When a record on a direct-access device is read, parity or the cyclic check characters are checked to be sure that the read operation has taken place without error. If an error is detected, however, it may be recovered. Sometimes, for example, a piece of dust that caused an error can be brushed off as the recording surface passes under the read/write head. If the program rereads the record by waiting one complete revolution while the record rotates under the read/write head again, the record may be read without error. In a typical error-recovery routine for a sequentially organized file, the record is reread ten times. If the error still exists, a message is printed on the console typewriter and the system is halted.

If an error is detected during a writing operation, it too may be corrected. In a typical routine, the record is written on an alternate track, and, if this attempt to write the record takes place without error, the program continues. A direct-access device commonly has several cylinders or tracks that can be used for alternate tracks in the event of writing errors. For example, the 2314 actually has 203 cylinders—the first 200 are used for normal processing and the last 3 are used for alternate tracks.

Label-Checking Routines

When using direct-access files, one danger is the possiblity of destroying current records by mistakenly writing other records over them. For example, suppose that an operator mounts a disk pack containing current accounts receivable records on a disk drive that is going to be used for writing payroll records. If the mistake isn't caught, the accounts receivable records will be destroyed when the payroll records are written.

Records can also be destroyed by programming error. If one disk pack contains two or more files—say accounts receivable records in cylinders 2–50 and inventory records in cylinders 51–200—a Seek to the wrong cylinders could mean disaster. If the inventory program mistakenly writes records in cylinders 2–50, the accounts receivable records would be destroyed.

To prevent this type of error, internal labels are used for each file that is stored on a disk. These labels are actually records on the device itself. On the 2314, for example, the entire label area is called the *Volume Table of Contents,* or *VTOC* (pronounced vee-tock); it is usually found in cylinder 0. The first record in the VTOC is a *volume label* containing a six-character serial number assigned to the pack. Then, for each file on the disk, there are one or more records called *file labels.* These labels give the name of the file, its organization, its location on the disk, and its expiration date. The expiration date indicates when a file is no longer needed so that its area can be assigned to another file. If a file is to be found in more than one area of the disk—cylinders 11–20 and 41–49, for example—this information is also given in the file label. Each area of a file is referred to as an *extent* of the file; it is expressed as lower and upper limits of the area in terms of cylinder and head numbers.

System/370 labels are processed by comparing the data in the labels with data supplied in *job-control cards* at the time the program is executed. These job-control cards indicate which program should be run, as well as which pack should be mounted on which disk drive and what information the volume and file labels should contain. They also indicate the extents of each file that is going to be processed.

To appreciate the value of label checking, consider how System/370 programs check labels before writing an output file on a 2314. After the operator mounts the disk pack and starts the drive, the program reads the volume label and compares it with information in the job-control cards. If the correct disk pack (volume) has been mounted on the correct drive, the program checks each label in the VTOC to make sure that the output file that is going to be written will not overlap the extents of any other file on the device. In other words, if the job-control cards indicate the output file will be written in cylinders 31–50, the label-checking routines make sure that all files in those cylinders have reached their expiration date. If cylinders 31–50 are clear or contain only expired files, the program continues by writing the file label of the output file in the label area and then executing the program. Otherwise, a message is printed to the operator and processing is stopped, thus avoiding a costly error.

For input files, the file labels are checked to be sure that the identifying data agrees with that given in the job-control cards. Also, the extents given in the file label are checked against the extents given in the job-control cards. If any discrepancy is detected, the operator is alerted.

Although System/370 label information is given in job-control cards at the time a program is executed, some manufacturers provide for certain label information to be supplied as part of the program itself. Thus, in the program the programmer specifies the name of the file and its expiration date.

Blocking and Deblocking Routines

If blocked records are used, all of the records in the block are read or written when a Read or a Write command is executed. As a result, when a program reads a block of five records, five records are placed in the input area of storage. *Deblocking routines* must then be used to keep track of which record in the block is being processed and which record is next to be processed. Similarly, before a block can be written, *blocking routines* must assemble the individual records in the output area of storage.

File-Handling Routines

Both direct and indexed sequential files require certain file-handling routines that aren't required by sequential files. For example, randomizing routines are needed for direct files. For indexed sequential files, special routines are needed to keep indexes up to date, to locate records by using the indexes, to add records to the overflow areas, and to search the chain of records in the overflow area. Such routines may require dozens of machine-language instructions.

What the Programmer Must Know

Because of the many I/O routines needed for direct-access files, it is fortunate that programming languages automatically assemble or compile most of the required routines. In general, programmers need never worry about error-recovery, label-checking, blocking, or deblocking routines. Also, they need not think about the individual Seek, Search, Read, Write, or Write-Verify commands or about the file-handling routines for indexed sequential files.

What then must programmers know? They must be able to specify the blocking characteristics of the file—what the length of each record is and how many records are in each block. They must know which track format is being used, and, if keys are used, what the key length is. They must be able to specify the exact file organization being used, including such details as how overflow records or synonyms are to be handled; and they must know whether the records are to be procesed in sequential or random order. Once these specifications are given, the programmer uses simple macro instructions that automatically generate the required I/O routines. When writing programs for direct files, however, the programmer is completely responsible for the logic of the randomizing routine.

SYSTEM CONSIDERATIONS

With regard to system design, a direct-access system is considerably more complicated than a tape system. Because of the flexibility of direct-access devices, there are many different ways that a system can be designed and still provide the desired results. Before deciding on a system, the designer must consider all of the alternatives, and then can choose the one that meets the requirements of speed and accuracy, but still minimizes cost. Because the difference between a well-designed and poorly designed system is significant, the design will in large part determine whether or not a system is effective. Two problems of particular significance to the design of a direct-access system are (1) file organization and (2) backup.

File Organization

The choice of file organization is of course closely tied in with the system flow. If a random file update is planned, the master file must have direct or indexed sequential file organization. If a sequential update is planned, the file must have sequential or indexed sequential organization. Remember, however, that a direct file can be converted into a sequential file by sorting prior to processing.

To illustrate the problem of determining file organization, consider the three flowcharts in figure 7-18. Although they are different, all three accomplish the same things—updating a master file and printing a sequential exception report from the master file. The first system, using a sequential file, prints the exception report when the master file is being updated. The second system, using an indexed sequential file, updates the master file on a random basis, then prints the sequential exception report. The third system, using a direct file, updates on a random basis, sorts the master file into sequence, and then prints the sequential exception report.

The question is: Which of these systems is most efficient? To decide, the system designer must estimate the time required for all the steps within each system in order to determine which system requires the least time. Because each estimate depends on factors such as the number of

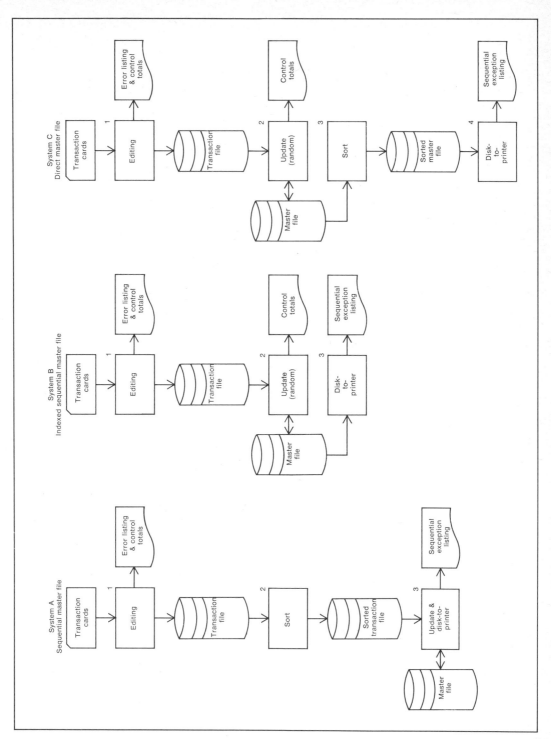

FIGURE 7-18 Determining file organization

records in the file, the exact characteristics of the method of file organization, and the percent of master records affected during an update, the decision depends on a complicated, time-consuming analysis. In actual practice, a master file is used in several (rather than only two) different processing runs, plus file-maintenance runs; thus, the decision is all the more complicated.

Once a general plan for file organization is chosen, there are many questions on a more detailed level yet to be answered. For an indexed sequential file, how many tracks per cylinder should be assigned for file additions; how often should the file be reorganized so all records are returned to the prime data area; should an independent overflow area be assigned in case a cylinder overflow area becomes filled? For a direct file, how many extra tracks should be assigned to the file to reduce synonyms; what randomizing technique should be used; how should synonyms be handled? In making decisions such as these, the system designer tries to keep the number of Seeks and Searches required to read or write a file as low as possible, thus reducing the processing times.

Although these questions are often very technical, they can have a significant effect on the run times for all programs that involve the file. For example, one company reports that it reduced run times 55 percent by changing a master file from one type of indexed sequential organization to another. In other words, a master-file update program that took two hours was reduced to less than an hour.

Backup

Although label-checking routines greatly reduce the chance that a direct-access file can be destroyed accidentally, they are not foolproof. In addition, there is a chance that direct-access records can be damaged by mechanical failure or destroyed by fire or theft. As a result, the designer of a direct-access system must provide for *backup*. Because the old master record is normally replaced by the new record in a direct-access update run, the grandfather-father-son method of backup cannot be used. However, there are several different methods of backup used on direct-access systems, all of which require extra computer time.

With removable disk packs, one method of providing backup is to copy the old master file onto a second disk pack after each update run; this is done by using a disk-to-disk program. Then, if the master file is destroyed, a backup file is available. This, of course, is comparable to the grandfather-father-son method of backup on tape. If tape is available on the direct-access system, a master file can be copied onto tape after each update run by using a disk-to-tape program. Since a reel of tape is considerably less expensive than a disk pack, this is a less costly way of providing backup.

Because copying a file after an update run requires that all the records in the file be read and written, much of the advantage of a random update is negated. As a result, system designers have developed less time-consuming methods of providing backup. For example, instead of copying the entire master file after each update run, the entire file can be copied only once a week. Then, during the daily update runs, only the updated records are copied onto tape. If a master file has to be recreated, the weekly tape, the daily tapes, and the transactions that have occurred since the last daily tape was written are processed to recreate the current master file. This significantly reduces the amount of time required for copying master records even though it makes reconstruction of a master file more difficult.

SUMMARY

1. Programming considerations for direct-access systems include error-recovery, label-checking, blocking, deblocking, and file-handling routines. Although a programmer doesn't have to write these routines, he must be able to give specifications relating to them.

2. The choice of file organization is one of the critical decisions in designing a direct-access system. File organization is closely tied to system flow and, on a detailed level, affects the run times of individual programs.

3. Backup on a direct-access system involves copying master files onto disk packs or tapes. Since this requires computer time, an attempt is made to keep copying for backup to a minimum; otherwise, many of the advantages of direct access are lost.

TERMINOLOGY

Volume Table of Contents
VTOC
file label
volume label
extent

job-control cards
blocking routine
deblocking routine
backup

QUESTIONS

1. An accounts-receivable file is stored in cylinders 100–150 of a 3330 pack. For a card-to-disk editing run, the extents given in the job-control cards assign cylinders 120–140 of the same disk pack to the new transaction file. How would label-checking routines prevent the accounts-receivable file from being destroyed?

2. Indexed sequential and sequential file organizations are far more commonly used than direct organization. Why?

3. Refer to figure 7-18. During the update run in each system, assume 1000 transactions are processed, and 500 master records in a file of 10,000 are updated. Which of the three update runs (not systems) would you expect to execute fastest? Slowest? Discuss.

4. Repeat question 3 assuming 5000 transactions affecting 1000 master records in the 10,000 record file. Which update run would you expect to be fastest and slowest? Then explain how you could improve the speed of update run B by modifying the system?

5. How could you provide backup in each of the systems charted in figure 7-18?

PROGRAMMING
AND SOFTWARE
CONCEPTS

This section surveys the common programming languages, introduces you to the important notion of structured program design, and describes some of the facilities of a typical operating system. The chapters within this section are independent, so they may be read in any sequence you choose.

8 A SURVEY OF PROGRAMMING LANGUAGES

There are many different programming languages. Perhaps the most widely used are assembler language, COBOL, FORTRAN, RPG, PL/I, and BASIC. This chapter introduces you to each of these languages.

In general, programming languages can be classified as *machine-oriented* or *problem-oriented languages*. A machine-oriented language is one that corresponds to the instructions of the computer. In contrast, problem-oriented languages are designed to express solutions for various types of programming problems. For instance, COBOL was designed for business problems; FORTRAN was designed for mathematical computations.

After a programmer codes a program in whatever language he or she is using, it must be translated into the object code of the computer before the program can be executed. If the language used is machine oriented, this translation process is called an *assembly*. It is done by the computer under control of a language-translator program called an *assembler*. On the other hand, if the language used is problem-oriented, the translation process is called a *compilation*. It is done by the computer under control of a translator program called a *compiler*.

From an operator's point of view, assembly and compilation are much the same as summarized in figure 8-1. After the source code of the language is punched into cards, the cards are processed by the computer. On a typical system, the assembler or compiler is loaded into storage from a disk library, at which time the translator is executed. During execution, it converts the source code into object code and stores the object code on disk ready for testing. If any errors are detected during assembly or compilation, the errors are printed in a diagnostic listing, along with the assembly or compiler listing. Because of the similarity between assembly and compilation, it is common to refer to *any* language translation as a compilation.

In the rest of this chapter, six common languages are described. When complete program examples are used, they are solutions for the problem shown in figure 8-2. The problem here is to prepare a reorder-listing report from a deck of inventory master cards. The logic of the program is shown by the flowchart in figure 8-3. Quite simply, one line is printed on the report whenever on-hand plus on-order is less than the reorder point for an item. To keep it simple, no headings or total lines are required on the reorder listing. Now, on to the languages.

Assembler Language

Theoretically at least, it is possible for a programmer to write a program in *machine language*; that is, object code. These machine-language instructions can then be punched into an object deck that can be loaded and executed by the computer. In the early days of computing, before language translators were developed, all programming was done in machine language.

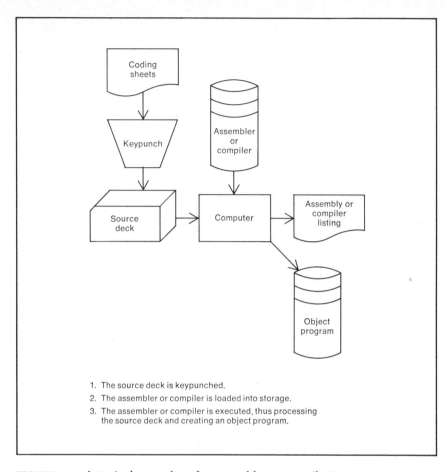

1. The source deck is keypunched.
2. The assembler or compiler is loaded into storage.
3. The assembler or compiler is executed, thus processing the source deck and creating an object program.

FIGURE 8-1   A typical procedure for assembly or compilation

In actual practice, however, nobody writes a program in machine language because it would be an extremely tedious job. The machine-language programmer would have to know the machine codes for all of the instructions that can be executed by a computer (often over 100) and would have to keep track of the actual machine addresses used for all storage fields of the program. In addition, the programmer would need detailed knowledge of what takes place when each type of instruction is executed.

To compound the difficulty, the codes and addresses of machine language usually are not represented by our regular alphabet and decimal number system. Instead, some other system of representation, such as the hexadecimal number system, is used. As a result, a simple System/360 instruction that moves data from one storage field to another

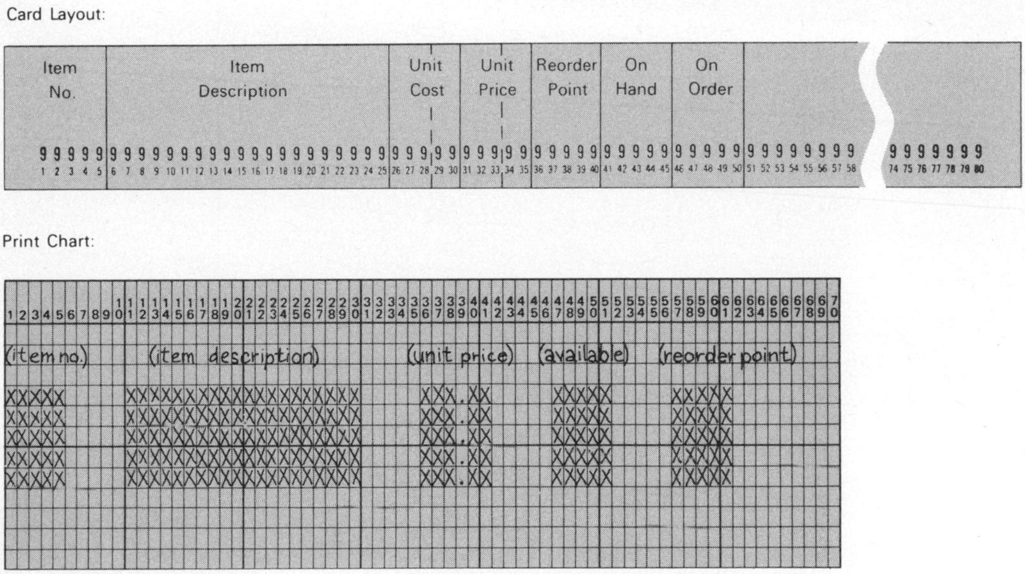

Card Layout:

Print Chart:

Processing Specifications:

1. Add on-hand to on-order to derive available.
2. Print a line on the reorder listing only when available is less than the reorder point.

FIGURE 8-2   The reorder-listing problem

might be written as

D204F080F068

Because of the difficulties in using machine language, various language translators were developed. The first of these was an *assembler* and the resulting language was called *assembler language*. By using easily remembered symbols for instruction codes and storage addresses, the programmer was relieved of much of the detail required by machine language. For example, a Move instruction in System/360 assembler language might be

MVC FIELD2,FIELD1

Here, MVC stands for Move Characters, FIELD2 is the symbolic name for the receiving field, and FIELD1 is the symbolic name of the field being moved.

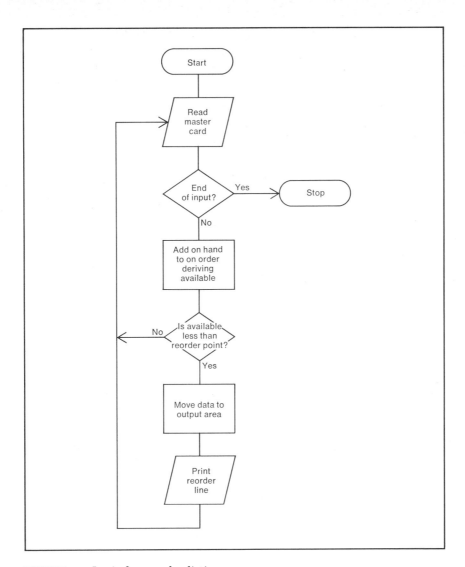

FIGURE 8-3   Logic for reorder-listing program

Originally, the distinguishing feature of an assembler language was that one machine-language instruction was assembled for each symbolic instruction. As assembler languages developed, however, *macro instructions* were added. When a macro instruction is translated, more than one machine-language instruction is assembled. In fact, in some cases, dozens of machine-language instructions are assembled from a single macro instruction. This means less coding for the programmer. Nevertheless, an assembler language is still primarily translated on a one-for-one basis: one machine-language instruction for each symbolic instruction.

In general, each computer has its own assembler, and hence, its own assembler language. For instance, the Univac 9200 and the IBM System/360 both have an assembler language. Because they correspond to machine capabilities, assembler languages for two different types of computers are not the same—and indeed may not be alike at all.

Figure 8-4 illustrates System/360 assembler language. This is an 80-80 listing for the solution to the reorder-listing problem that was described earlier. The first 27 cards represent the instructions of the program, most of which will be assembled into only one machine-language instruction. All I/O instructions on the System/360 are macro instructions, however, so they will be assembled into more than one machine instruction. The main reason for showing you this listing is so you realize that an assembler language conforms to the machine and not to any particular type of problem. As a result, the listing shouldn't make any sense to you unless you know how the instructions of the System/360 work.

Although an assembler language, in comparison to machine language, greatly reduces the time required for preparing programs, it has limitations. Perhaps most limiting is the fact that assembler-language programmers still must write detailed instructions that correspond to the instructions of the computer itself. Thus, they still must have detailed knowledge of the way a computer's instructions are executed. How much better it would be if a programmer could write a program in terms of the type of problem he or she is trying to solve!

COBOL

The other languages described in this chapter are all problem-oriented ones. COBOL, which stands for COmmon Business Oriented Language, was first introduced in 1960 and is one of the oldest problem-oriented languages. As its name implies, it was designed for business data processing, and it is currently the most widely used business language. In general, COBOL compilers are available for all major business computer systems.

One of the objectives of the designers of the COBOL language was to make it easy to read and understand. As a result, COBOL approximates English perhaps more closely than any other programming language. To illustrate this, consider the reorder-listing program written in COBOL as listed in figure 8-5. Here, the Procedure Division represents the instructions and logic of the program. If you compare the paragraphs named BEGIN and PRINT-LINE with the flowchart in figure 8-3, you'll probably be able to follow the COBOL code even if you have never seen a COBOL program before.

```
REORDLST  START  0                                                        ORDR0010
BEGIN     BALR   3,0                                                      ORDR0020
          USING  *,3                                                      ORDR0030
          OPEN   CARDIN,PRTOUT                                            ORDR0040
READCARD  GET    CARDIN                                                   ORDR0050
          PACK   WRKAVAIL,CRDONHND                                        ORDR0060
          PACK   WRKONORD,CRDONORD                                        ORDR0070
          AP     WRKAVAIL,WRKONORD                                        ORDR0080
          PACK   WRKORDPT,CRDORDPT                                        ORDR0090
          CP     WRKAVAIL,WRKORDPT                                        ORDR0100
          BNL    READCARD                                                 ORDR0110
          PACK   PACKAREA,CRDITNBR                                        ORDR0120
          MVC    PRTITNBR,PATTERN1                                        ORDR0130
          ED     PRTITNBR,PACKAREA                                        ORDP0140
          MVC    PRTITDES,CRDITDES                                        ORDR0150
          PACK   PACKAREA,CRDPRICE                                        ORDR0160
          MVC    PRTPRICE,PATTERN2                                        ORDR0170
          ED     PRTPRICE,PACKAREA                                        ORDR0180
          MVC    PRTAVAIL,PATTERN1                                        ORDR0190
          ED     PRTAVAIL,WRKAVAIL                                        ORDR0200
          MVC    PRTORDPT,PATTERN1                                        ORDR0210
          ED     PRTORDPT,WRKORDPT                                        ORDR0220
          PUT    PRTOUT,PRTDETL                                           ORDR0230
          PRTOV  PRTOUT,12                                                ORDR0240
          B      READCARD                                                 ORDR0250
CRDEOF    CLOSE  CARDIN,PRTOUT                                            ORDR0260
          EOJ                                                             ORDR0270
* THE CARD FILE DEFINITION FOLLOWS                                       ORDR0280
CARDIN    DTFCD  DEVADDR=SYSIPT,IOAREA1=CRDINPA,EOFADDR=CRDEOF           ORDR0290
* THE PRINTER FILE DEFINITION FOLLOWS                                    ORDR0300
PRTOUT    DTFPR  DEVADDR=SYSLST,IOAREA1=PRTOUTA,BLKSIZE=132,PRINTOV=YES, XORDR0310
                 WORKA=YES                                                ORDR0320
* THE DATA DEFINITIONS FOR THE CARD INPUT AREA FOLLOW                    ORDR0330
CRDINPA   DS     0CL80                                                    ORDR0340
CRDITNBR  DS     CL5                                                      ORDR0350
CRDITDES  DS     CL20                                                     ORDR0360
          DS     CL5                                                      ORDR0370
CRDPRICE  DS     CL5                                                      ORDR0380
CRDORDPT  DS     CL5                                                      ORDR0390
CRDONHND  DS     CL5                                                      ORDR0400
CRDONORD  DS     CL5                                                      ORDR0410
          DS     CL30                                                     ORDR0420
* THE DATA DEFINITION OF THE PRINTER OUTPUT AREA FOLLOWS                 ORDR0430
PRTOUTA   DS     CL132                                                    ORDR0440
* THE DATA DEFINITIONS FOR THE PRINTER WORK AREA FOLLOW                  ORDR0450
PRTDETL   DS     0CL132                                                   ORDR0460
PRTITNBR  DS     CL6                                                      ORDR0470
          DC     5C' '                                                    ORDR0480
PRTITDES  DS     CL20                                                     ORDR0490
          DC     4C' '                                                    ORDR0500
PRTPRICE  DS     CL7                                                      ORDR0510
          DC     4C' '                                                    ORDR0520
PRTAVAIL  DS     CL6                                                      ORDR0530
          DC     4C' '                                                    ORDR0540
PRTORDPT  DS     CL6                                                      ORDR0550
          DC     70C' '                                                   ORDR0560
* THE DATA DEFINITIONS THAT FOLLOW DEFINE OTHER WORK AREAS NEEDED        ORDR0570
* BY THE PROGRAM                                                         ORDR0580
PATTERN1  DC     X'402020202020'                                         ORDR0590
PATTERN2  DC     X'40202021482020'                                       ORDR0600
WRKAVAIL  DS     PL3                                                      ORDR0610
WRKONORD  DS     PL3                                                      ORDR0620
WRKORDPT  DS     PL3                                                      ORDR0630
PACKAREA  DS     PL3                                                      ORDR0640
          END    BEGIN                                                    ORDR0650
```

Instructions

File definitions

Data Definitions

FIGURE 8-4   The reorder-listing program in System/360 assembler language

```
     Column 8 ─┐      ┌─ Column 12
               │      │
               IDENTIFICATION DIVISION.
               PROGRAM-ID. INVENTORY-REORDER-LISTING.

               ENVIRONMENT DIVISION.
               CONFIGURATION SECTION.
               SOURCE-COMPUTER.  IBM-360.
               OBJECT-COMPUTER.  IBM-360.
               INPUT-OUTPUT SECTION.
               FILE-CONTROL.
                   SELECT BAL-FWD-FILE ASSIGN TO SYS005-UR-2540R-S.
                   SELECT REORDER-LISTING ASSIGN TO SYS006-UR-1403-S.

               DATA DIVISION.
               FILE SECTION.
               FD  BAL-FWD-FILE
                   LABEL RECORDS ARE OMITTED
                   DATA RECORD IS BAL-FWD-CARD.
               01  BAL-FWD-CARD.
                   02   BF-ITEM-CODE           PICTURE IS 9(5).
                   02   BF-ITEM-DESC           PICTURE IS A(20).
                   02   FILLER                 PICTURE IS X(5).
                   02   BF-UNIT-PRICE          PICTURE IS 999V99.
                   02   BF-REORDER-POINT       PICTURE IS 9(5).
                   02   BF-ON-HAND             PICTURE IS 9(5).
                   02   BF-ON-ORDER            PICTURE IS 9(5).
                   02   FILLER                 PICTURE IS X(30).
               FD  REORDER-LISTING
                   LABEL RECORDS ARE OMITTED
                   DATA RECORD IS REORDER-LINE.
               01  REORDER-LINE.
                   02   RL-ITEM-CODE           PICTURE IS Z(5).
                   02   FILLER                 PICTURE IS X(5).
                   02   RL-ITEM-DESC           PICTURE IS A(20).
                   02   FILLER                 PICTURE IS X(5).
                   02   RL-UNIT-PRICE          PICTURE IS ZZZ.99.
                   02   FILLER                 PICTURE IS X(5).
                   02   RL-AVAILABLE           PICTURE IS Z(5).
                   02   FILLER                 PICTURE IS X(5).
                   02   RL-REORDER-POINT       PICTURE IS Z(5).
                   02   FILLER                 PICTURE IS X(71).
               WORKING-STORAGE SECTION.
               77  WS-AVAILABLE                PICTURE IS 9(5).

               PROCEDURE DIVISION.
               SET-UP.
                   OPEN INPUT BAL-FWD-FILE.
                   OPEN OUTPUT REORDER-LISTING.
               BEGIN.
                   READ BAL-FWD-FILE RECORD AT END GO TO END-OF-JOB.
                   ADD BF-ON-HAND BF-ON-ORDER GIVING WS-AVAILABLE.
                   IF WS-AVAILABLE IS LESS THAN BF-REORDER-POINT
                       GO TO PRINT-LINE,
                   ELSE GO TO BEGIN.
               PRINT-LINE.
                   MOVE SPACES TO REORDER-LINE.
                   MOVE BF-ITEM-CODE TO RL-ITEM-CODE.
                   MOVE BF-ITEM-DESC TO RL-ITEM-DESC.
                   MOVE BF-UNIT-PRICE TO RL-UNIT-PRICE.
                   MOVE WS-AVAILABLE TO RL-AVAILABLE.
                   MOVE BF-REORDER-POINT TO RL-REORDER-POINT.
                   WRITE REORDER-LINE.
                   GO TO BEGIN.
               END-OF-JOB.
                   CLOSE BAL-FWD-FILE.
                   CLOSE REORDER-LISTING.
                   STOP RUN.
```

FIGURE 8-5   The reorder-listing program in COBOL

In an attempt to make COBOL a standard language, the American National Standards Institute published specifications for standard COBOL in 1968. Theoretically, if all COBOL compilers conformed to these specifications, it would be possible to take a program written for one computer, make a few modifications to its Environment Division, and recompile it so that it would run on another computer. This would make it easier for a computer user to transfer programs from one system to another. In 1974, a revised version of the standards was published to get closer to this goal of program transferability.

In actual practice, however, there is no such thing as a transferable COBOL language. Since each manufacturer has added its own refinements to the COBOL standards, converting COBOL programs from one system to another is usually a major task. Nevertheless, the standards have set some important guidelines for building COBOL compilers.

FORTRAN

FORTRAN, which stands for *FOR*mula *TRAN*slator, was designed to express any problem involving numerical computation. Thus its language corresponds to mathematical or algebraic notation. For example, the equation

$$X = \frac{(A + B)(A - C)}{(B + D)}$$

can be expressed in FORTRAN as

$$X = (A + B) * (A - C) / (B + D)$$

Here, * represents multiplication and / represents division. Because of its mathematical orientation, FORTRAN is easily *learned* by scientists, engineers, and mathematicians.

Because of its design, FORTRAN is somewhat limited in scope. For example, it is difficult to edit output data in FORTRAN so that it is easy to read. Thus it is easy to convert 0123456 to $1234.56 in COBOL, while it is very difficult to do in FORTRAN. Similarly, FORTRAN has limited capabilities for handling alphanumeric data or direct-access files.

Figure 8-6 shows the reorder-listing program in FORTRAN. As you can see, it is much shorter than the assembler language or COBOL programs because only two lines are required for describing the input and output formats (lines 101 and 201). In contrast, COBOL requires a formal description of the input and output records. Because of the difficulty of processing alphabetic data in FORTRAN, the item-description field isn't printed in the reorder-listing by this program.

FORTRAN is available on computer systems of all sizes, ranging from minicomputers to the very largest systems. In 1966, the American

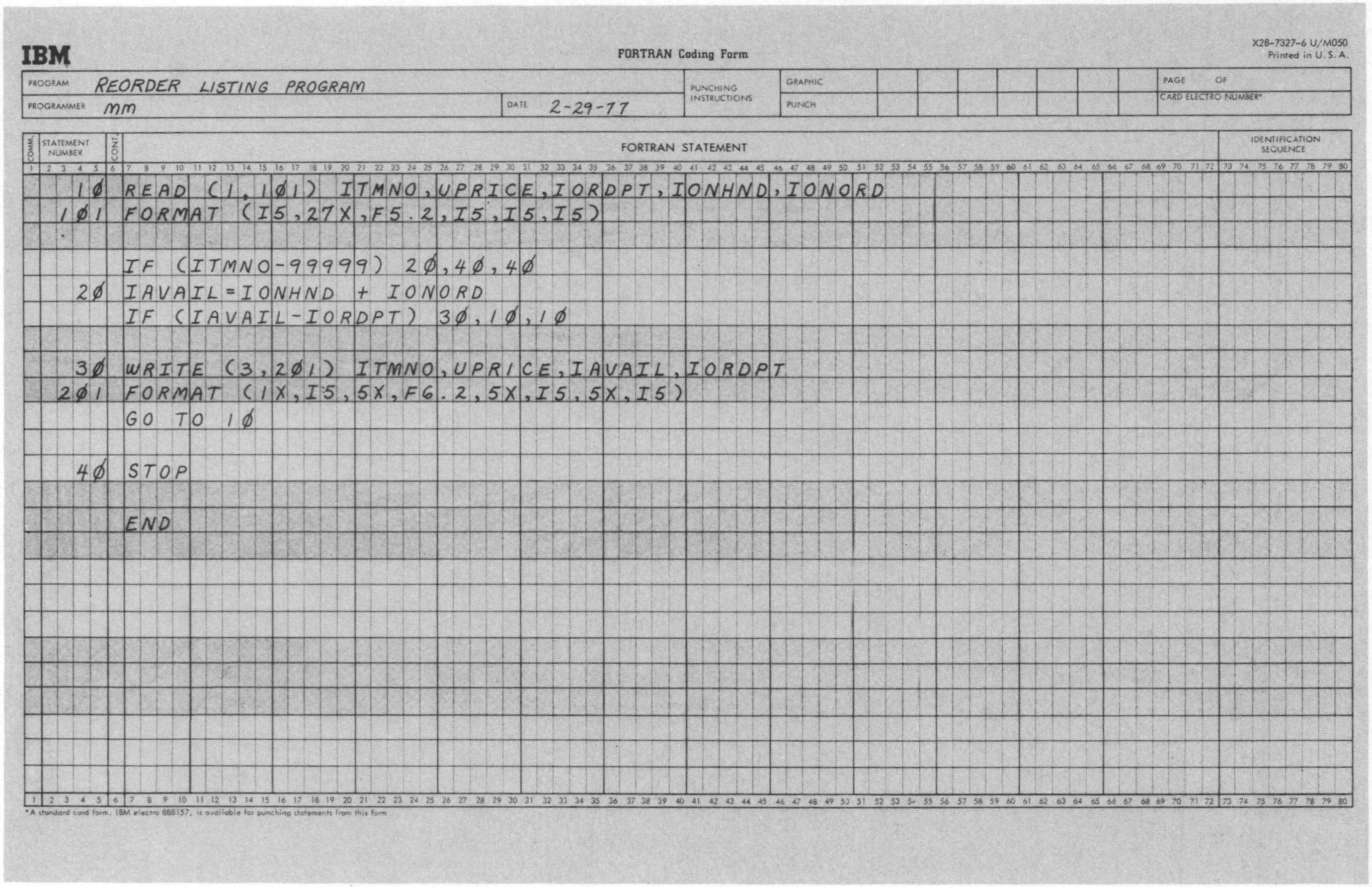

IBM — FORTRAN Coding Form — X28-7327-6 U/M050 Printed in U.S.A.

PROGRAM: REORDER LISTING PROGRAM
PROGRAMMER: mm — DATE: 2-29-77

```
   10 READ (1,101) ITMNO,UPRICE,IORDPT,IONHND,IONORD
  101 FORMAT (I5,27X,F5.2,I5,I5,I5)

      IF (ITMNO-99999) 20,40,40
   20 IAVAIL=IONHND + IONORD
      IF (IAVAIL-IORDPT) 30,10,10

   30 WRITE (3,201) ITMNO,UPRICE,IAVAIL,IORDPT
  201 FORMAT (1X,I5,5X,F6.2,5X,I5,5X,I5)
      GO TO 10

   40 STOP

      END
```

*A standard card form, IBM electro 888157, is available for punching statements from this form

FIGURE 8-6 The reorder-listing program in FORTRAN

National Standards Institute published FORTRAN standards, so there is little variation in FORTRAN as you move from one system to another.

RPG

RPG, which stands for Report Program Generator, was initially designed to make it easy to create programs that print reports. As the language developed, however, it was given many other capabilities. In 1969, an advanced version of RPG was announced (called RPG II) that extended the RPG capabilities once more. Today, RPG can be used for a wide range of business applications.

Unlike COBOL, FORTRAN, and the other problem-oriented languages, RPG doesn't require the programmer to code instructions that give the logic of the program. In fact, a program flowchart is useless when coding in RPG. Instead of instructions, the programmer gives specifications that indicate what the input and output is, and what calculations must be done to derive the output from the input. When the RPG code is compiled by the RPG compiler, the specifications are converted into machine language instructions.

Figure 8-7 illustrates the RPG code for the reorder-listing program. As you can see, the programmer has used four different coding sheets for this program. If the program requires table handling or certain types of file manipulations, a fifth type of coding form may be required.

Each of the coding forms indicates where certain specifications should be placed. On the input specification form, for example, columns 44–51 indicate where each input field is located, and column 52 indicates how many decimal positions each input field has. Thus the field named ITMCDE is located in columns 1–5 of the input card and has zero decimal positions; the field named UPRICE is located in columns 31–35 of the input card and has two decimal positions.

Logic is achieved in the RPG program through the use of indicators. For instance, the indicator 70 is turned on in the calculation specifications in figure 8-7 if AVAIL is less than REORDP. Then, in the output specifications, a reorder line is printed if indicator 70 is turned on. By using up to 99 different indicators, complex logic requirements can be achieved in the RPG program.

Because it is a relatively straightforward language, RPG can be learned quickly. Furthermore, coding can be done much more quickly in RPG than in a language like COBOL (as you might guess by comparing figure 8-7 with 8-5). On the other hand, the use of indicators for logic capabilities can become overwhelming if the programming problem is complex. And some business tasks just cannot be done in RPG. As a result, you will find RPG widely used on small systems like IBM's System/3; you will find it infrequently used on medium-and large-sized systems.

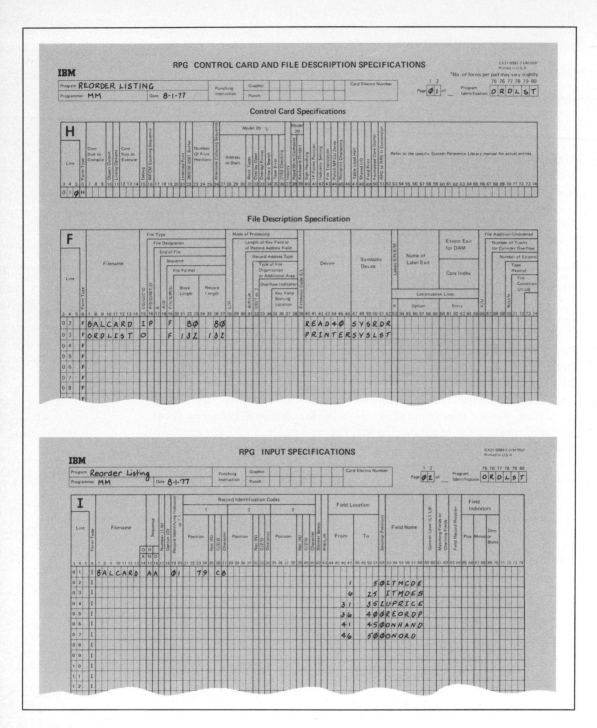

FIGURE 8-7   The reorder-listing program in RPG

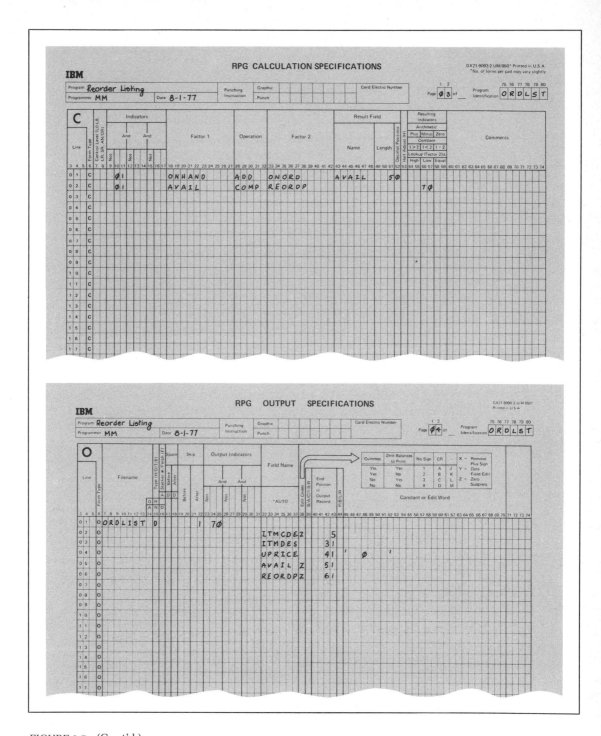

FIGURE 8-7 (Cont'd.)

RPG is available on most IBM systems and with variations on some non-IBM systems. With minor modifications, an RPG program written for a small IBM system like the System/3 can be upgraded to a larger system like the System/360 by recompiling.

PL/I

In 1966 IBM developed a new programming language called PL/I, which many interpret as Programming Language I. This language was intended to combine the business capabilities of a language like COBOL with the numerical capabilities of a language like FORTRAN. In addition, it had other capabilities not offered by COBOL or FORTRAN. At the time of its announcement, many predicted that all computer manufacturers would develop PL/I compilers. In addition, many people felt that PL/I would pass COBOL and FORTRAN as the primary business and scientific language. Now, ten years later, only a few other manufacturers have developed PL/I compilers, and PL/I is used far less than either COBOL or FORTRAN.

In the last couple of years, however, interest in PL/I has been renewed partly because of the emphasis on structured programming (see chapter 9). Unlike COBOL or FORTRAN, PL/I has the language capabilities needed to implement the structured concepts. The primary advantage of PL/I is its broad range of capabilities. However, this range also makes the language complex and relatively difficult to learn. As a result, tangible benefits are required to cause a COBOL or FORTRAN user to switch to PL/I. Maybe structured programming will highlight these benefits.

BASIC

BASIC, which stands for Beginners's All-purpose Symbolic Instruction Code, was developed at Dartmouth College for the GE 235 computer system. It is available today on a wide range of computer systems. BASIC is primarily a *time-sharing language*. This means that more than one BASIC user is connected to a central computer system at the same time via remote terminals. The terminals are either typewriter-like devices or visual-display units with television-like output and keyboard input. The programmer enters BASIC code through the keyboard of the typewriter or visual-display unit, and the program is compiled and executed. The output from the BASIC program is either printed by the typewriter terminal or displayed on the visual-display unit. Because one computer can handle many terminals, it appears to each terminal user as if he has complete control of the computer system.

BASIC was designed for the beginner who has little computer knowledge but wants to use the computer for solving problems. As a result, the language is easy to learn but it is extremely limited. It is an algebraic language like FORTRAN, and because of its simplicity is growing in popularity—even in the scientific and engineering community.

DISCUSSION

There are many other languages besides those described in this chapter. Some are special-purpose languages like COGO, which is designed to help solve civil engineering problems (COordinate GeOmetry). Some languages are attempts to improve on existing ones. As the years progress, I'm sure many new languages will be developed.

If you look at figures 8-5 through 8-7, perhaps you can see what any language must provide for. In simplest terms, a language must provide for describing (1) the input characteristics and formats, (2) the output characteristics and formats, and (3) the processing requirements. In the COBOL program in figure 8-5, for example, the input and output records and files are described in the Data Division, and the processing statements are given in the Procedure Division. In the FORTRAN program, the FORMAT statements give the input and output characteristics; the other statements give the processing sequence. And in the RPG program, there is one form for input specifications, another for output specifications, and a third for calculations.

One question you might have at this point is: how does a company decide which language to use? This is usually determined by (1) the languages available on the company's computer system, (2) the capabilities of these languages, and (3) the language skills of the programming staff.

For instance, a Burroughs' B2500 offers COBOL, FORTRAN, and a version of RPG. That limits the choices. Of these languages, COBOL is designed for business problems and has the widest range of business capabilities. Furthermore, because COBOL is a standard language, it is easier to hire COBOL programmers than those skilled in any other language. As a result, most B2500 shops write their programs in COBOL.

On a System/360, a user has a slightly wider range of choices. In addition to COBOL and FORTRAN, an assembler language (called Basic Assembler Language, or BAL), RPG, and PL/I are available. Here again, most System/360 users do most of their programming in COBOL, because of the language capabilities and the availability of COBOL programmers. In general, they only use PL/I or BAL as their primary programming language if they have special processing or management requirements.

Take one more example. COBOL, FORTRAN, and RPG II are available on the System/3. In general, System/3 users are small shops with little experience in programming so training is often required. Furthermore, processing requirements in System/3 installations are likely to be relatively straightforward. As a result, RPG is widely used on these systems, because the language is easy to learn and it can greatly reduce programming time when the programs are limited in complexity.

In summary then, language choices are made based on the practical considerations of language availability and programmer skills. As a result, the vast majority of medium- and large-sized business installations are *COBOL* shops. That means they use COBOL as their primary language with other languages used for special programming requirements. Similarly, the vast majority of small business installations are *RPG* shops.

SUMMARY

1. Assembler language is symbolic machine language. Because it is a machine-oriented language, it can be used to represent all of a computer's functions, but its use requires detailed machine knowledge.

2. The problem-oriented languages are designed to express programming problems in the language of the problem. COBOL, FORTRAN, RPG, PL/I, and BASIC are all problem-oriented languages.

3. The choice of a programming language is usually done on a practical basis, considering language availability, language capabilities, and programmer capabilities.

TERMINOLOGY

machine-oriented language
problem-oriented language
assembly
assembler
compilation
compiler

machine language
macro instruction
time-sharing language
COBOL shop
RPG shop

QUESTIONS

1. Which do you think would compile faster: a source program from a machine-oriented language or a source program from a problem-oriented language? Why?

2. Which do you think would require more storage: the object program from an assembler language source program or the object program from a COBOL or FORTRAN source program? Why?

3. Which do you think would execute faster: the object program from an assembler language source program or the object program from a COBOL or FORTRAN source program? Explain.

4. Which language do you think is most efficient from the programmer's point of view: assembler language or COBOL?

5. What does the basic choice between a machine-oriented language and a problem-oriented language get down to in terms of money? If personnel costs are twice as much as hardware costs in a typical installation, how does this affect the choice?

9 PROGRAM DESIGN AND STRUCTURED PROGRAMMING

One of the main differences between an effective and ineffective programmer is program design. As you will see in this chapter, there are ways of designing programs so that they are relatively easy to code, debug, and maintain. Since program flowcharting is basic to the understanding of program design, this chapter begins by providing additional information about flowcharting.

To some extent, chapter 9 takes a historical approach to the subject of program design. Modular program design, which began as far back as the 1950s, is described in topic 1. Then, top-down program design and structured programming, more recent developments, are described in topics 2 and 3.

TOPIC 1
FLOWCHARTING AND
MODULAR PROGRAM
DESIGN

In chapter 4 you were introduced to the basic flowcharting symbols and concepts. One purpose of this topic is to broaden that base of knowledge. After flowcharting is described in more detail, you will be introduced to the concepts of modular program design.

PROGRAM FLOWCHARTING

To begin with, a flowcharting form such as the one illustrated in figure 9-1 is often used when drawing flowcharts. This form consists of fifty boxes that are numbered so each block can be identified. For example, box D1 refers to the I/O symbol containing the words READ CARD; J5 refers to the terminal symbol containing the word STOP. By using these letter/number combinations in connector symbols, it becomes easy to follow connections within a flowchart. For instance, the connector symbol in box H4 indicates a branch to connector symbol E1, which is to the left of box E1.

If the connector symbol is used to connect a flowline on one page to a flowline on another page, the number of the page to be branched to should be written to the upper left of the connector symbol. Thus

indicates that the program continues at box A4 on page 4. Similarly,

P.1

J2

indicates a return to box J2 on page 1.

The flowchart in figure 9-1 presents the logic for a program that reads a deck of employee job cards and prints a report like the sample in figure 9-2. This report includes the amount earned on each job, the total amount of pay for each employee, and the grand total for all employees. The input cards are in sequence by employee number, one report line is printed for each input card, and a group total line is printed after all the cards for one employee have been processed. If an out-of-sequence card is detected, an error message is printed and another card is read.

This flowchart introduces the predefined process and preparation symbols. Like the other symbols used in this book, these symbols conform to the standards set by the American National Standards Institute. Figure 9-3 summarizes all of the ANSI symbols you are likely to use for program flowcharting.

The predefined process symbol is used in box G1 of figure 9-1. A predefined process consists of one or more program steps that are defined in another set of flowcharts. Often, the predefined process, which may have been programmed by someone else, is used in two or more different programs. For example, the pay-rate lookup routine of figure 9-1 might be used in other payroll programs as well as in the wage-report program.

The preparation symbol represents the modification of an instruction or a constant that in some way affects the flow of a program. In figure 9-1, for example, the preparation symbol is used in box C1 to set the field named END-SWITCH to N and in box A4 to set END-SWITCH to Y. Then, in box G4, the flow of the program depends on the contents of END-SWITCH: if N, the program continues with box E1; if Y, the program continues with box G5. By using the preparation symbol, the programmer can more easily locate the points in the program at which the contents of the END-SWITCH data field are changed. Incidentally, modifying the concepts of a field in this way to determine which of two paths a program should take is often referred to as *setting a switch*.

The key point of this flowchart is the decision symbol in block B3. Here, the *control field* (employee number) of the card just read (the new card) is compared with the control field of the previous card (the old card). If the employee numbers are equal (O = N), the new card is processed. If the new employee number is greater than the old one (O<N), a group total line for the previous employee is printed, the group totals are set to zeros, and the new card is processed for the next employee. If the old employee number is greater than the new one (O>N), an out-of-sequence error message is printed.

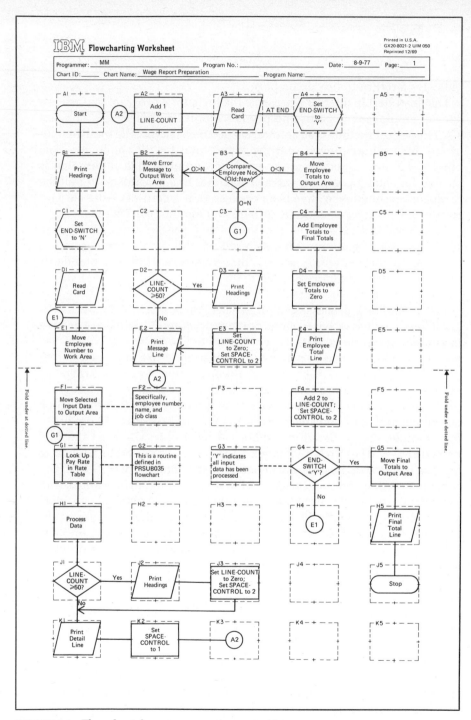

FIGURE 9-1 Flowchart for wage-report preparation

```
                    EMPLOYEE WAGE REPORT

     EMP.         EMPLOYEE              JOB     EMP.
     NO.            NAME                CODE    WAGES

      767      NORMART, L. O.            2      12.85
      767      NORMART, L. O.            7      69.21
      767      NORMART, L, O.           11      35.80
                                               117.86 *

     1045      MATHIESEN, MICHAEL        1      14.00
     1045      MATHIESEN, MICHAEL        4      72.50
     1045      MATHIESEN, MICHAEL       13      25.20
     1045      MATHIESEN, MICHAEL       13      12.50
                                               124.20 *

     1320      MC KEIGHAN, GARY          7     145.00
                                               145.00 *

                                               387.06 * *
```

FIGURE 9-2   A sample employee wage report

MODULAR PROGRAM DESIGN

Although the program presented in figure 9-1 is relatively simple, the flowchart is relatively difficult to follow. Imagine then what a flowchart for a large file-maintenance program might look like. With its multiple input and output files and processing routines, it might require a dozen or more flowcharting pages with branches from one page to another. And preparing and reading the chart might be difficult indeed.

To reduce the complexity of flowcharts, program design is important. In particular, the concept of *modular program design* can improve flowchart clarity. The idea is to break a program into a number of separate *modules*—one *mainline module* and one or more *subroutine modules*. As much as possible, each module should be independent of the other modules.

The advantage of modularity is that the logic of the total program becomes more manageable. Instead of one extensive program, it becomes a group of small, understandable programming segments. Thus, it is easier to code the program, and, if a problem occurs during testing, it is easier to locate the routine (module) that is causing the error. Similarly, if the program needs to be modified later because of a change in processing requirements, locating, modifying, and testing the routine that needs to be changed can be done more efficiently.

SYMBOL	SYMBOL NAME	MEANING
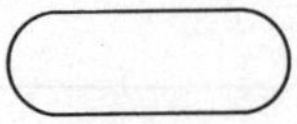	Terminal	Start or end of a sequence of operations
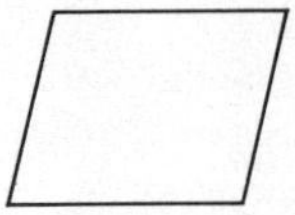	Input/Output	I/O operation
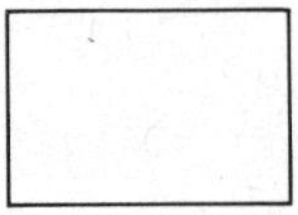	Process	Any kind of processing function
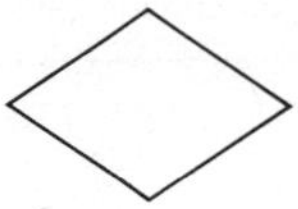	Decision	A logical or branching operation
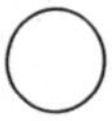	Connector	Connection between parts of a flowchart
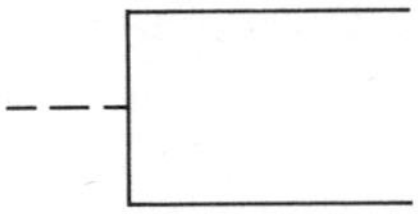	Annotation	Explanatory comments
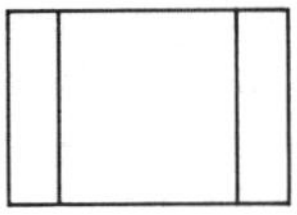	Predefined Process	A routine or function described in another set of flowcharts
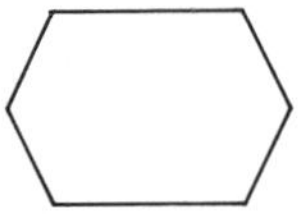	Preparation	Modification of a field or instruction that changes the sequence of processing in the program itself.

FIGURE 9-3 ANSI symbols for program flowcharting

To achieve modularity, the mainline module should indicate all of the major processing routines as well as the logical decisions required to direct the program to these routines. For instance, figure 9-4 represents the mainline module of the wage-report program originally flowcharted in figure 9-1. Each symbol that represents a subroutine module uses *striping* at the top of the symbol to indicate the name of the module. As a result, the wage-report program consists of the mainline module plus seven other modules, named HOUSEKEEPING, READ-RECORD, PRO-CESS, DETAIL-LINE, MESSAGE-LINE, TOTAL-LINE, and EOJ. In addition, the predefined process in block E2 is a subroutine named RATE-LOOKUP.

Although this mainline module consists of only thirteen blocks, it could well be the mainline for a program requiring hundreds of instructions; it depends upon the complexity of the subroutine modules. As a general rule, even in complex programs, the mainline module shouldn't require more than two dozen flowcharting blocks. In fact, because the primary purpose of the mainline module is to direct the flow of processing to the other modules, it may well be the shortest module of the program.

After the mainline module is flowcharted, each of the subroutines can be flowcharted. To continue the concept of modularity, each subroutine module may be broken into additional, more specific modules, depend-ing of course on the length and complexity of the module. Since the idea is to make each programming segment manageable, each module should be kept to between 50 and 200 statements in length.

To easily relate subroutine flowcharts to a higher level flowchart such as the mainline flowchart, cross-references are used as shown in the mainline flowchart of figure 9-4 and the subroutine flowcharts of figure 9-5. In block J1 of the mainline flowchart, for example, the stripe gives the name MESSAGE-LINE to a subroutine. Page 3 (P.3), which is written to the upper left of the flowcharting symbol, indicates that the flowchart for the MESSAGE-LINE subroutine can be found on page 3 of this set of flowcharts. (Page 3 is shown in figure 9-5.) To complete the cross-referencing, MESSAGE-LINE is written in the terminal symbol at the start of the subroutine flowchart on page 3, and page 1—a reference back to the mainline flowchart—is written to the upper left of this terminal symbol. Similarly, flowchart page numbers and module names are used to cross-reference the other module flowcharts and the mainline flowchart.

Within the MESSAGE-LINE subroutine module, another subroutine module, named HEADING, is indicated. This subroutine contains the code for a line counting and printing routine. The page number above the symbol indicates that the flowchart for the HEADING subroutine can be found on page 5. This flowchart will in turn refer back to page 3.

One of the critical points in developing a modular program is to keep each module independent of the other modules. In other words, each subroutine should branch back to only the next block in the mainline

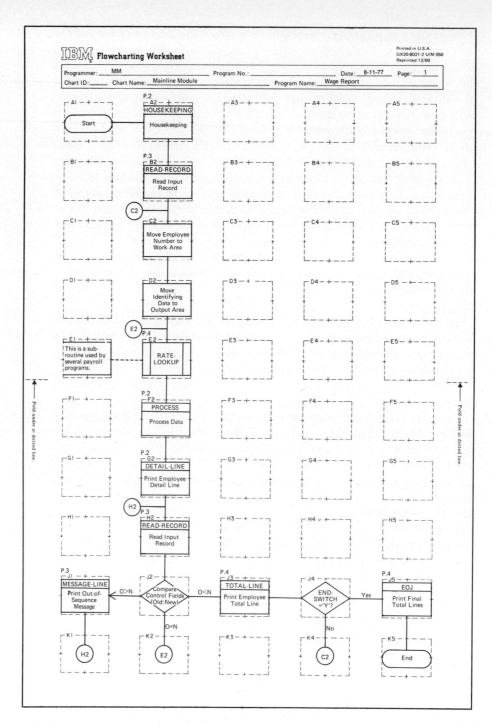

FIGURE 9-4   Flowchart for the mainline module of the wage-report program

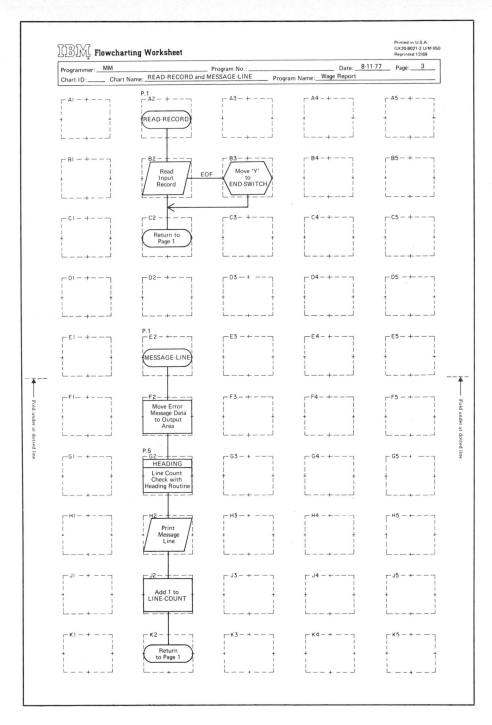

FIGURE 9-5   Flowcharts for the READ-RECORD and MESSAGE-LINE subroutines of the wage-report program

routine, not to other subroutines. Furthermore, no subroutine module should contain any processing that affects the flow of any other subroutine. For example, no subroutine should set a switch that will be tested in another subroutine. Note that the switch named END-SWITCH, which is set in the READ-RECORD subroutine in figure 9-5, is tested in the mainline routine only, not in a subroutine.

Although the logic of the wage-report program is simple enough so as not to require modular program design, you can probably see the value of modularity. If you experiment with modular design, you will discover how it can simplify programming logic. You may even find that simple programs are more manageable when broken into at least five modules: (1) a mainline module, (2) a housekeeping module, (3) at least one input module, (4) at least one output module, and (5) an end-of-job module.

A Tape Update Program

To illustrate modular program design once more and also to illustrate some typical programming logic, consider the sequential update program described by the system flowchart in figure 9-6. Here, an old master file and a transaction file are the input files; a new master file with updated master records is the output. If any unmatched transaction records are detected during the update run, they are listed on the printer so the errors can be corrected.

Figure 9-7 is a flowchart for the mainline module of the tape update program. This flowchart, which uses modular program design, controls

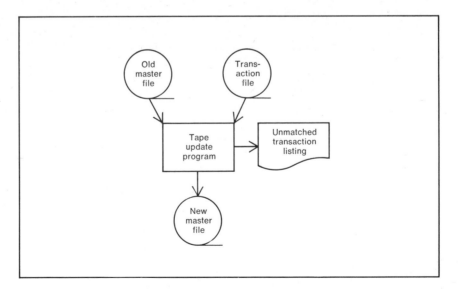

FIGURE 9-6   System flowchart for a master file update

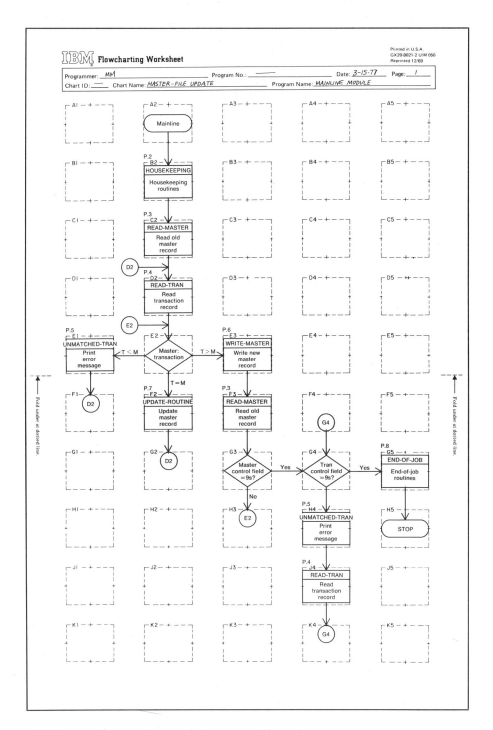

FIGURE 9-7　The mainline module—master-file update program

the use of eight subroutine modules. It is typical of the processing required in most sequential update programs. Perhaps the key to the mainline flowchart in figure 9-7 is the decision in box E2. When the control field of the master record is compared with the control field of the transaction record, there are three conditions that can occur. If the control fields are equal (T = M), the transaction is used to update the old master record. If the transaction is greater than the master (T>M), the master record is written in the new file and another master record is read. If the transaction is less than the master (T<M), an unmatched transaction is indicated.

When there are no more records in an input file, the READ-MASTER and READ-TRAN subroutines move 9's into the control fields of the last record. As a result, box G3 tests to see whether the last record in the old master file has been read; box G4 tests to see whether the last record in the transaction file has been read. If all master records have been read but transactions remain, it indicates that there are one or more unmatched transactions. As a result, the program lists the unmatched transaction, reads another transaction record, and tests again to see if the control field equals nines. If not, the program loops again; if so, the program ends.

DISCUSSION

Although some companies put considerable emphasis on flowcharting and program design, you should not be misled. In most companies, you would have a difficult time finding an up-to-date flowchart for a program, let alone a modularly designed system of flowcharts. In real life, many programming departments are poorly managed, many programmers have never used modular design, and, because of the time involved in flowcharting, many programs are never flowcharted.

Furthermore, there is a definite movement away from flowcharting. The general feeling in industry seems to be that there has to be a better way to design programs than through flowcharts, because flowcharts just haven't been effective. The question is, what should be used? Top-down design and structured programming, as described in the next two topics, try to give some answers.

SUMMARY   1. Although from company to company there are variations in the use of flowcharting rules and symbols, the standards set by the American National Standards Institute are widely accepted. These standards give specifications concerning the use of symbols, flowlines, and methods of cross-referencing between flowcharts within a set of flowcharts.

2. Modular program design refers to dividing a program into independent modules, each consisting of 50 to 200 statements. By keeping each module independent of the others and by designing a mainline module to direct the flow to the subroutine modules, coding and testing a large program becomes more manageable.

TERMINOLOGY

setting a switch
control field
modular program design
mainline module
subroutine module
striping

QUESTIONS

1. Draw a flowchart for the READ-MASTER module in figure 9-7. Include proper cross references.

2. Draw a flowchart for the UNMATCHED-TRAN module of figure 9-7. Include proper cross references.

3. Can you draw a flowchart for the UPDATE-ROUTINE module in figure 9-7? If so, do it. If not, why not?

TOPIC 2
TOP-DOWN
PROGRAM DESIGN

Modular program design is useful, because it can divide a large or complex problem into a series of smaller, more manageable programming modules. However, it is a rather general theory of program design. As a result, its effectiveness depends to a large extent on who is doing the program design.

Traditionally, for example, a modular program has been defined as a program that consists of modules made up of from 50 to 200 program instructions. But this says nothing about the independence or cohesiveness of the modules; it says nothing about how the modules are linked through program code. As a result, it is possible for a modular program to be a collection of interdependent modules that are themselves logical nightmares. In this case, the modular program can be just as difficult to code, debug, and maintain as the nonmodular program.

Then in the mid-1960s, efforts began to develop a more rigorous method of designing programs. Two results of these efforts were (1) top-down program design and (2) structured programming. Although these techniques are presented in separate topics in this chapter, they are usually combined in practice, since one technique seems to enhance the other. As a result, top-down program design is often considered to be one of the techniques of structured programming.

The Theory of Top-Down Design

Top-down program design tries to change the traditional process of program design. Instead of worrying about details through flowcharting, top-down design tries to focus first on the major functional modules of a program. After these major modules have been planned, the programmer can decide on the next level of modules, and so on. When this theory of design is used, details can be put off until the lowest-level modules are implemented.

When top-down design is used, the program flowchart is replaced by some sort of *structure chart* or *structure diagram*. These diagrams, unlike the flowchart, are designed to show the program modules and the relative importance of each of these modules. For instance, figure 9-8 shows a structure diagram for the tape update program described in topic 1. Here, the program designer has created a driver module and three first-level modules. In addition, the designer has divided the update-master-records module into three second-level modules: one module for changing master record fields, one for listing unmatched transaction records, and one for writing new master records.

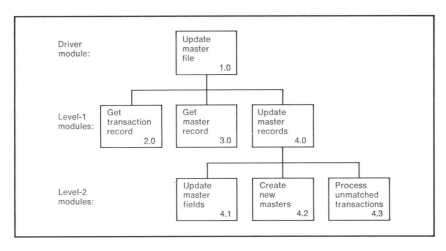

FIGURE 9-8 Structure chart for a tape-update program showing two levels
of subroutine modules

If necessary, the designer can further subdivide, thus creating additional subroutine levels. For example, the chart in figure 9-9 takes the update program down one more level. Here the three modules that make up the update-master-records module are broken down into their component parts. (You might notice that the get-master and get-transaction modules are used at level 1 as well as at level 3.)

One of the principles of effective top-down design is keeping the modules functional. In other words, each module should represent one program function. This can be done by making sure that each module can be described by a single imperative sentence, such as "update the records in the master file." On the structure diagram itself, the programmer tries to describe each module by one imperative verb, one adjective, and one noun like "update master records."

In contrast to top-down design, modular flowcharting techniques often lead to modules that aren't functional. For instance, housekeeping and end-of-job modules aren't functional. The elements within them are related only in that they are done at the start or end of a program. Similarly, modules created through flowcharting techniques are often procedural rather than functional; that is, they are related because they are part of the same procedure.

Another principle of top-down design is that each module must be independent of all others except for the module above it. In other words, a module should only communicate with the one above it. And a module will begin execution only when control is passed to it from the module above it. In contrast, flowcharting, with its emphasis on procedures, tends to develop modules that aren't completely independent.

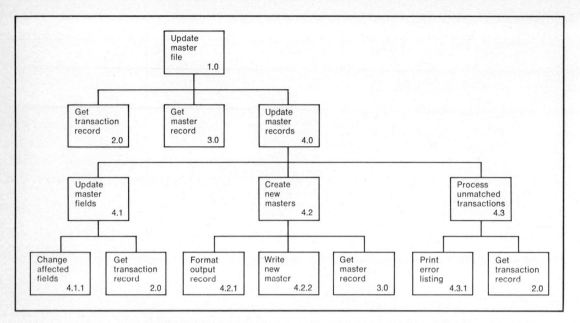

FIGURE 9-9 Structure chart for tape-update program showing three levels of subroutine modules

Because good program design tries to divide a problem into modules of manageable size, top-down design has its own rules for determining module size. In general, the program designer tries to make modules that are no longer than 50 program statements, the number that can be printed on a single computer page. Experience has shown that programs that consist of modules of from 30 to 50 statements can be tested and debugged more efficiently than programs made up of smaller or larger modules.

Two notions associated with top-down program design are *top-down coding* and *top-down testing*. The idea here is to code and test each module independently of the rest, starting with the highest-level modules and working down. In other words, the update-master-file module (the driver or control module) in figure 9-8 would be coded and tested first. This can be done by using *program stubs,* or *dummy modules,* for each of the three modules it controls. These stubs would be programmed so that they would simply receive control from the driver module, perhaps print a message that they have received control, and return to the driver module. In the case of an input module, the program stub might pass some dummy data back to the driver module. After the driver module has been tested, coding and testing can proceed by combining one of the level 1 modules with the driver module.

The advantage of top-down coding and testing is that testing proceeds in an orderly fashion. Modules are added to the driver module one at a time, so if a bug is detected during testing, it is easy to isolate the offending module. In contrast, the traditional method of testing a program in its entirety gave no clues to the location of a bug. When a large program was tested, perhaps containing hundreds of bugs, the programmer had to analyze the entire program to determine the cause of each bug—an inefficient process to say the least.

Program Documentation

Traditionally, the program flowchart has been one of the primary pieces of program documentation. When top-down design is used, however, there is a definite movement away from program flowcharting. Why? Because it just hasn't proved effective.

In general, programmers don't like to flowchart, because the flowchart doesn't really help them get their programs finished more quickly. As a result, they start programming before they have a complete set of flowcharts. Then when they finish testing, they rush to complete the flowcharts so they can show their documentation to management and get on to their next assignment. In the rush, they are likely to omit details, so their flowcharts don't actually correspond to their programs. Thus the flowchart isn't effective as an aid to coding and is usually inaccurate as documentation.

When top-down design is used, the structure chart is the overall guide to design and documentation. After the structure chart is prepared, however, each of the modules must be further documented before actually coding. Although the program flowchart can be used for this purpose, several new documentation techniques are being tried because of the flowchart's shortcomings.

One of these documentation techniques is illustrated in figure 9-10. It is a HIPO diagram for the update-master-records module in figure 9-9. As you can see, it shows the inputs to this module as well as the outputs from it. In addition, it gives a general description of the processing required in the module.

When *HIPO (Hierarchy plus Input-Process-Output)* is used, the structure diagram like the one in figure 9-8 is called a *visual table of contents*. After it is prepared, overview HIPO diagrams like the one in figure 9-10 are created for each module. Then, if necessary, detailed HIPO diagrams are created to describe the module more specifically. Once HIPO diagrams are prepared for a module, the programmer can begin to code it. In other words, the flowchart is eliminated completely from the design and implementation process.

Although HIPO is one of the more popular replacements for traditional design and flowcharting techniques, there are others. No doubt there will

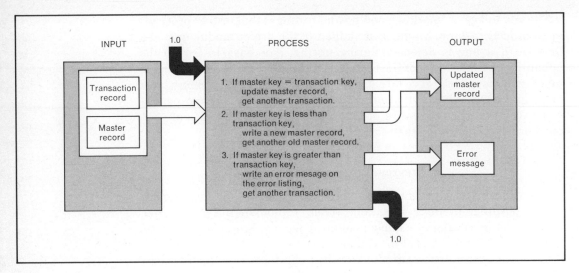

FIGURE 9-10   An overview HIPO diagram for the update-master-records module
of the tape-update program

be more to come. The intent here is simply to describe the movement
away from flowcharting, not to describe all of the alternative techniques.

DISCUSSION

Top-down design is here to stay because it works. In contrast to
traditional methods, top-down design allows a programmer to concentrate on the major functions of a program before he or she starts to worry
about trivial details. It also allows a programmer to code and test a
program from the top down, a significant improvement over traditional
bottom-up techniques.

On the other hand, top-down techniques are by no means uniform.
Although the theory is relatively clear, the actual charting and documentation techniques are still evolving. As a result, structure charts are done
in a variety of ways throughout the industry, and module documentation
is done in several different forms. At present, top-down design is used in
about one-fourth of the computer installations, but I would predict that it
will be several years at least before its techniques become standardized.

SUMMARY   1. Top-down design attempts to change the traditional focus of programming. The programmer plans modules, one level at a time, until the
modules are down to 50 statements or less. In contrast to modular

program design, top-down design tends to create completely independent, functional modules of manageable size.

2. HIPO is one of the documentation techniques used with top-down design. There are others, and at present there are no standard industry practices.

top-down program design
structure chart
structure diagram
top-down coding
top-down testing

program stub
dummy module
HIPO
visual table of contents

1. How are modular and top-down program designs alike?

2. What does top-down design do that modular program design doesn't?

3. Suppose the get-transaction module in figure 9-9 involved several tests to determine whether or not the input fields contain valid data. If any fields are invalid, an error message should be printed on the error list, and the record should be ignored. How might this change the chart in figure 9-8?

4. Consider the wage-report program described in topic 1 and flow-charted in figure 9-4. Create a structure chart for this program, showing the driver module and at least the level-1 modules below it.

TOPIC 3
STRUCTURED
PROGRAMMING

Traditionally, professional programmers have created their programs using their own logical structures. In the mid-1960s, however, various computer scientists began to give rigid definitions for the structure of a *proper* program. These efforts led to *structured programming,* which is intended to improve program clarity, increase programmer productivity, and decrease debugging problems.

The basic notion of structured programming is that any program can be written using only three logical structures. These structures are summarized in figure 9-11. They are called the sequence, selection, and iteration structures.

The *sequence structure* is simply the idea that program statements are executed in sequence. As a result, a sequence box can consist of one statement or many. And two sequence boxes can be combined into one without changing the basic sequential structure.

The *selection structure* is a choice between two and only two actions based on a condition. If the condition is true, one function is done; if false, the other is done. This structure is often referred to as IF-THEN-ELSE, and many programming languages have code that closely approximates it.

The *iteration structure* provides for doing a function as long as a statement is true. It is often called the DO-WHILE structure. When the condition is no longer true, the program continues with the next structure.

A fourth structure shown in figure 9-11 is the DO-UNTIL. It is logically related to the DO-WHILE and is a common alternate structure for iteration. For instance, COBOL has a DO-UNTIL structure, but it doesn't have a DO-WHILE structure. The DO-UNTIL performs a function until a condition becomes true.

Notice that all of the structures in figure 9-11 have only one entry and one exit point. As a result, a program made up of these statements can have only one entry and one exit. The program will also be executed in a controlled way from the first statement to the last. These characteristics make up a proper program.

One of the principles of structured programming is that any of the three basic structures can be substituted for a function box in any of the other structures. The result will still be a proper program. This means that structures of great complexity can be created with the assurance that they will only have one entry and one exit, and that they will be executed in a controlled manner from start to finish.

Structured programming has contributed to programmer productivity, because it has placed necessary restrictions on program structure. If you are familiar with the GO TO statement that is common to most

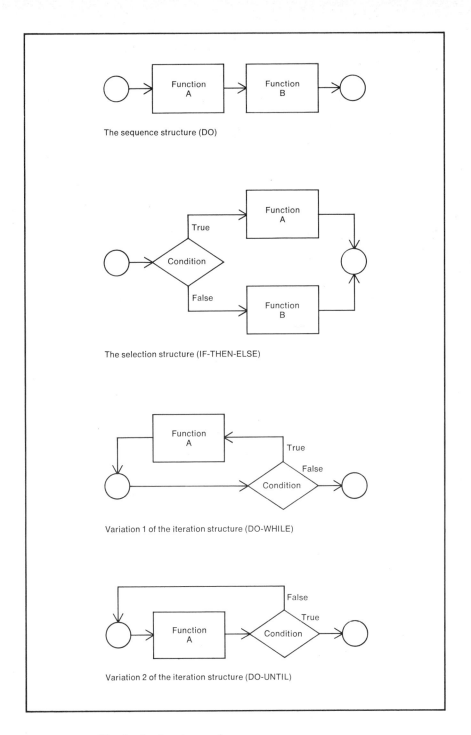

The sequence structure (DO)

The selection structure (IF-THEN-ELSE)

Variation 1 of the iteration structure (DO-WHILE)

Variation 2 of the iteration structure (DO-UNTIL)

FIGURE 9-11   The basic structures of a proper program

DO 2.0 (get transaction record)
DO 3.0 (get master record)
DO 4.0 (update master records)
UNTIL there are no more
records in both the master
and transaction file.

FIGURE 9-12   Pseudocode for the driver module of the tape-update program

programming languages, you should realize now that it is "illegal" in structured programming. As a result, uncontrolled branching is impossible. This in turn reduces the likelihood of program bugs and increases productivity. In addition, handled correctly, the structured program should be easier to read and understand than the unstructured program.

PSEUDOCODE

Although it is possible to draw flowcharts for structured programs, new documentation techniques have been developed in conjunction with structured programming. One of these is called *pseudocode*. The idea here is to use a language that represents the logical structures of structured programming but to avoid the details of actual programming languages. As a result, the programmer uses formal language for the structures, but everything else is at his or her own discretion.

To illustrate, consider figure 9-12, which gives the pseudocode for the driver module of the update program of figure 9-8. Here the structure words are capitalized and the functions are described by the programmer in lower-case letters. Quite simply, the driver module executes module 2.0, then 3.0, then does module 4.0 until there aren't any more records in the master or transaction file.

The pseudocode for the update-records module (4.0) is given in figure 9-13. Here, one selection structure is contained within another. Again, the structure words are capitalized, whereas the program words are in lower case. Pseudocode is useful because it can describe the processing within a module at least as well as a flowchart, even though it can be created more quickly than a flowchart. Also, the pseudocode can be easily converted to actual program code since it closely corresponds to actual code. In comparison, coding from a flowchart is a time-consuming job.

```
IF master key equals transaction key
        THEN 4.1 (update master fields)
ELSE
        IF master key is greater than transaction key
                THEN 4.2 (create new masters)
                ELSE 4.3 (process unmatched transactions)
```

FIGURE 9-13   Pseudocode for the update-master-records module (4.0) of the tape update program

DISCUSSION

Structured programming is related to the theory of top-down program design, because it is difficult to create structured code without first planning the modules. If, for example, you try to convert an unstructured program into a structured one, it generally forces you to redesign the program, using top-down techniques. Looking at it another way, structured programming is important to top-down design because it creates modules that are properly independent—with only one entry and one exit point. In practice then, top-down design is commonly used in conjunction with structured programming.

In fact, the term *structured programming* has come to mean far more than its theory implies. In the data-processing industry today, structured programming refers to a whole range of techniques for increasing programmer productivity. These include top-down design, top-down coding, top-down testing, the use of pseudocode for documentation, and structured coding.

SUMMARY

1. Structured programming was initially a theory for creating proper programs using only three program structures: sequence, selection, and iteration. Today, structured programming is used to refer to a whole range of techniques for increasing programmer productivity.

2. Pseudocode is an alternative to flowcharting. It specifies the logical structure of a module as well as its general functions.

TERMINOLOGY

proper program
structured programming
sequence structure

selection structure
iteration structure
pseudocode

QUESTIONS

1. Refer to figure 9-1. What portions of this flowchart violate the principles of structured programming?

2. Refer to figure 9-4. What portions of this flowchart violate the principles of structured programming?

3. Using the techniques of top-down design and structured programming, convert the program represented by the flowchart in figure 9-4 to a proper program. Show your solution in pseudocode.

4. How does setting a switch tend to violate the principles of top-down design and structured programming?

10 THE FACILITIES OF AN OPERATING SYSTEM

In chapter 4 you were introduced to stacked job processing and some basic programs of an operating system. The supervisor, the job-control program, language translators, sort/merge programs, utilities, library-maintenance programs are programs that all operating systems offer in one form or another.

This chapter introduces you to some additional facilities of an operating system: linkage editing, multiprogramming, spooling, and virtual storage. Although linkage editing and multiprogramming are found in all major operating systems, spooling and virtual storage are offered only by the more sophisticated operating systems.

LINKAGE EDITING

Linkage editing refers to the process of combining two or more segments of object code (called *object modules*) to form one object program. To illustrate, suppose a programmer wants to use an object module for calculating square roots in conjunction with her inventory-control program. Because the square-root module is already written and tested, it can save her considerable programming time. However, the square-root module is programmed to occupy storage positions 4001 through 5000 and her program module is programmed to occupy positions 4001 through 12,000. Obviously, then, the addresses in one of the modules must be relocated so both modules can be combined.

But when a module is relocated, the addresses of the data fields upon which it operates also change. Since two object modules such as this operate on common data fields—for example, the square-root module determines the square root of one of the fields in the main program and returns the answer—changes must be made to both modules when one is relocated. If more than two object modules are linked, the problem becomes even more involved.

In any event, it is the *linkage editor* program that handles the relocation of the object modules and the eventual linking of them into a complete program. Besides making it possible for commonly used routines to be stored in an object library and combined before execution, the linkage editor also makes it possible to divide a large program into several segments, each of which can be assigned to a different programmer. Each segment can then be written in the most appropriate language, translated into an object module, and tested. When all object modules are ready, the linkage editor performs the necessary relocating and linking. Then the complete program can be tested. By dividing a programming task into segments, the total time for completing a program can be reduced and each segment can be assigned to the programmer best qualified for the job—the most difficult segment to the most experienced programmer, and so on.

If you read chapter 9 and understand the reasons for modular and structured program design, you can now see how linkage editing supports the notion of independent modules. If the modules are object modules rather than source modules, the linkage editor can combine them prior to program execution. And all major programming languages have specifications that provide for linking one program module with another after they have been compiled into object modules.

MULTIPROGRAMMING

Multiprogramming means the simultaneous execution of more than one program. Actually, this is misleading, because what really happens is that, simultaneously, multiple programs are present in separate parts of storage, but only one program executes at any given time. The others wait for input or output operations to be completed, or simply just wait to be given control by the supervisor.

Multiprogramming is valuable because it can increase the overall productivity of a computer system. As you learned earlier, internal operations such as data-movement and arithmetic operations can be executed thousands of times faster than input or output operations. Since it is the nature of business programs to have little internal processing between I/O operations, the CPU is normally idle a great percentage of the time with the program waiting for an I/O operation to be completed. In an effort to make use of this idle time, multiprogramming systems allow additional programs to be in storage so their instructions can be executed while the first program waits for its I/O operations to be completed.

In a simple system, for instance, up to three programs may be multiprogrammed at one time. Under supervisor control, the storage area above the supervisor is divided into three *partitions* called *background* (BG), *foreground 1* (F1), and *foreground 2* (F2). Although they can be altered by special operator commands, the sizes of these partitions are assigned standard values at the time the system is generated. Figure 10-1 shows the storage allocations for the three partitions in a typical multiprogramming system. The supervisor then has the added responsibility of deciding which partition will begin processing after the supervisor has started an I/O operation. To solve this problem, a priority system is used, with the supervisor always giving control to the F1 program first. If the F1 program is waiting for an I/O operation to finish, the supervisor then gives control to the F2 program. If F2 is also waiting, control is given to the BG program.

On more advanced operating systems, it is possible to multiprogram more than three programs. On these systems, the size and number of partitions allowed may be fixed, or the partition concept may not be used at all. On the most advanced systems, for instance, all storage other than that used by control programs is treated as an area that can be shared by

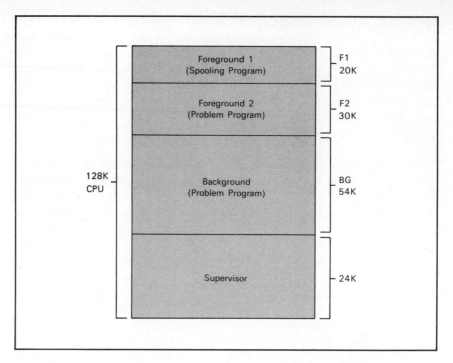

FIGURE 10-1 Storage allocation in a typical multiprogramming system

as many programs or parts of programs as will fit. In other words, the control programs of the operating system assign available storage to programs or parts of programs as the storage becomes available.

SPOOLING

Even with three programs running together, there is still usually more CPU time available than can be used because of the difference between internal processing speed and the speed of the I/O units. In a further effort to make better use of the available CPU time, *spooling programs* serve as an interface between the very slow I/O devices—the card readers, punches, and printers—and the processing programs. When the processing program attempts to print a line on the printer, for example, a spooling program causes the line to be written as a record on a tape or disk file instead. Since these devices are much faster than the printer, they allow the problem program to resume processing much sooner. Later, when little is being done by the computer, the spooling program prints out the lines that were temporarily stored on tape or disk.

The same spooling procedure is used in reverse for card input files. The spooling program first places the data in the cards on tape or disk. Then,

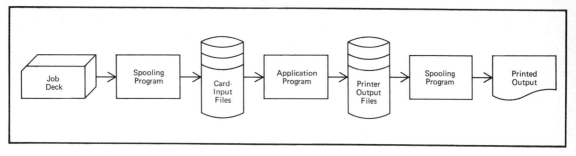

FIGURE 10-2   Spooling

when the processing program tries to read a card from the card reader, it is actually read from the tape or disk, and the program thus waits a much shorter time for I/O completion. A spooling program is usually run in the F1, or top priority, partition as shown in figure 10-1, so the I/O operations will keep running regardless of the other demands on CPU time.

Figure 10-2 is a schematic illustration of the concept of *spooling*. Quite simply, the job deck, which consists of job-control statements plus data decks, is read by the spooling program and converted to a number of disk files. These disk files can then be processed by the job-control program for the job-control statements and by the processing programs for the data files. When an application program is executed, it processes the appropriate disk file for the original card deck just as though it was the card deck itself. For output, the lines intended for the printer are written in a disk file area reserved for printer output. Later, when the spooling program processes the output disk file for this application program, the disk file is converted to printed output.

Incidentally, spooling takes place even though the programmer may be completely unaware of it. In fact, the processing programs are written as though they are using card input and printer output, even though they are actually using disk input and output. The operating system itself makes the necessary adjustments so that spooling takes place automatically.

VIRTUAL STORAGE

Virtual storage is another facility of advanced operating systems. It allows simulation of a very large CPU on a much smaller one by using disk storage as an extension of internal storage. In a typical virtual storage system, for example, a computer with 256K bytes of *real storage* might appear to the user to have 512K bytes; it is thus said to consist of 512K bytes of virtual storage.

During processing, only small portions of the programs being executed are present in real storage. The parts of the program that aren't currently being used are stored on disk. As additional portions of programs are required, parts that are no longer needed are written out on the disk and the new ones replace them in real storage.

Virtual storage is accomplished in different ways on different computer systems. Figure 10-3 illustrates the relationships and terms used for one version of an IBM system. Here, real storage consists of a supervisor area plus a *page pool*. The page pool area consists of portions of the programs currently being multiprogrammed. These portions are fixed-size blocks, usually 4K bytes long, called *pages,* and the 4K blocks of real storage they occupy are called *page frames*. As a program is executed, the required pages are brought into real storage from disk after the pages that are no longer needed are written back on the disk. This shuttling of pages back and forth from CPU storage to disk storage is called *paging* or *swapping*. The result of this paging is a system that appears to the user to have 512K bytes of storage that contains a supervisor and several complete programs being multprogrammed.

The advantage of virtual storage is that more programs can be multiprogrammed, thus increasing the efficiency of the computer system. Although the operating system itself is less efficient because of the additional control routines demanded of it and the need for page

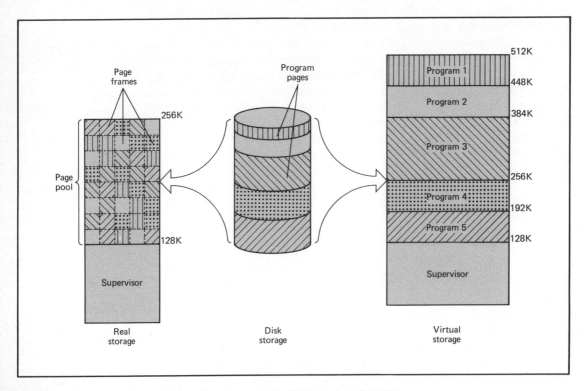

FIGURE 10-3   The concept of virtual storage on the IBM System/360-370

swapping or its equivalent, the overall productivity of the computer system is increased. From the programmer's point of view, the computer functions as though it were a traditional system without virtual storage.

DISCUSSION

The overall objective of any operating system is, of course, to maximize the total amount of productive work done by the computer system in a given period of time. This is often referred to as maximizing *throughput*. However, multiprogramming and virtual storage result in a supervisor that by itself requires a significant amount of the available CPU cycles of a system. This requirement of the supervisor or operating system is often referred to as its *overhead*. In other words, overhead is a negative factor when attempting to maximize throughput. Fortunately, the general experience of the data-processing industry is that the additional overhead of an advanced operating system is more than justified by the increase in system throughput.

There have been exceptions, though. In some cases, a user moves to a more sophisticated operating system only to find that his throughput decreases. This has happened, for example, when a user has moved from a system without virtual storage to one with virtual storage. In general, the decreased throughput in a case like this is caused by failure of the user to utilize all the facilities of the operating system. Then, the increased overhead of the operating system is not offset by increased work by the system.

To further illustrate this point, suppose a user moves from a simple multiprogramming system, such as the one in figure 10-1, to one that can multiprogram up to seven jobs at one time. Suppose also that under the old system an average of 2.1 programs were multiprogrammed throughout a sixteen-hour work day. To justify the increased overhead of the new operating system, then, the average number of jobs being run must be increased. However, if the new system isn't used efficiently or if the mix of jobs being run won't allow an increase in the multiprogramming average, decreased throughput is likely.

Because of this need to use an operating system efficiently, systems programmers usually spend a good deal of time "fine tuning" a system, particularly during the first months after installation. This involves experimenting with factors pertinent to the operating system as well as with factors pertinent to the jobs being run. In many cases, the results are dramatic.

For instance, one company did an experiment in which thirteen jobs were run by their operating system. Before tuning, the jobs took seventy-six minutes to complete. After tuning the operating system, however, the jobs took only sixty minutes to complete, a significant increase in throughput. Finally, using a tuned operating system as well as tuned jobs, the thirteen jobs required only fifty-one minutes of run time, an overall increase in throughput of about 35 percent. Meanwhile, CPU cycle utilization increased from 50 to 88 percent.

In actual practice, the average number of jobs run at any given time in a multiprogramming system is somewhere between two and three. This highlights the fact that the use of operating systems can be improved considerably. Not only can the operating systems and the jobs be fine tuned more effectively, but more efficient combinations of hardware and software can be developed and installed.

SUMMARY

1. Linkage editing is the process of combining two or more object modules into one complete object program.

2. Multiprogramming is the execution of more than one program at a time. It attempts to increase throughput by making use of CPU cycles that would otherwise be unused.

3. Spooling and virtual storage are facilities of an advanced operating system.

4. Whenever a move is made to a more advanced operating system, the increased overhead must be justified by increased throughput. To achieve this goal, an operating system must usually be fine tuned after installation.

TERMINOLOGY

linkage editing
object module
linkage editor
multiprogramming
partition
background
foreground 1
foreground 2
spooling program
spooling

virtual storage
real storage
page pool
page
page frame
paging
swapping
throughput
overhead

QUESTIONS

1. The supervisor for IBM's Disk Operating System (DOS) may require about 24K storage positions. As users move to IBM's full operating system (OS), they may find that the supervisor requires 140K or more. How do you explain this? What would you say about the overhead of each of these systems?

2. Suppose a system uses multiprogramming with an average of 2.6 programs in storage. By adding some main storage and some additional I/O devices, the average increases to 3.4 programs in storage at one time. How do you think the change would affect throughput? What about the cost per unit of production?

SECTION FOUR

AUXILIARY
SUBJECTS

This section consists of subjects related to hardware, software, applications, and systems analysis. Again, the chapters are independent, so they may be read in any sequence you choose.

11 COMPUTER APPLICATIONS

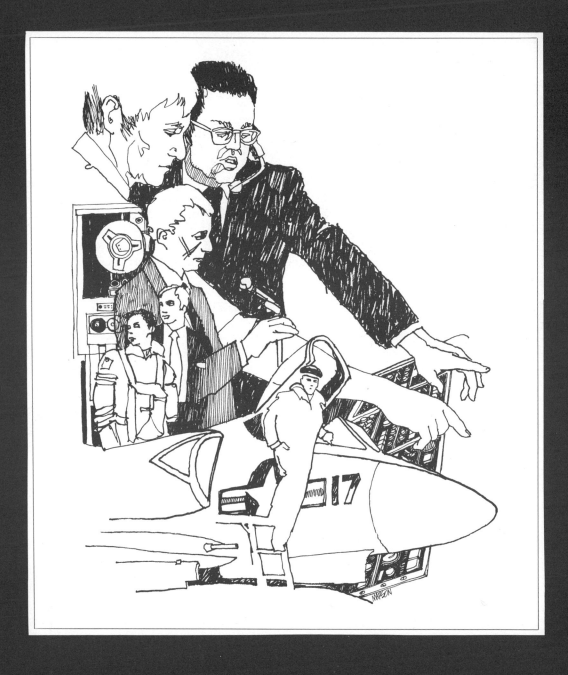

In chapter 2 you were introduced to five of the basic accounting applications: order writing, billing, accounts receivable, inventory control, and sales analysis. In this chapter (which is divided into two topics), you will be introduced to other applications. Topic 1 describes the other accounting applications; topic 2 presents a survey of business applications, including some of the more advanced applications.

TOPIC 1
THE ACCOUNTING APPLICATIONS

Accounting applications are concerned with recording and reporting costs and revenues (sales) within an organization. Thus accounts receivable and sales analysis are accounting applications. Because order writing, billing, and inventory control deal with basic accounting data, they too are commonly considered to be accounting applications. In brief, all of the applications described in chapter 2 can be called accounting applications. This topic describes three other accounting applications: payroll, accounts payable, and general ledger. As you read about each application, you should (1) try to become familiar with the documents used and (2) note how each application relates to profits.

PAYROLL

The primary goal of the *payroll* application is to prepare accurate payroll checks and to get them into the hands of the employees on payday. The input documents are attendance and time records in the form of time cards, time sheets, and job tickets indicating the amount of time an employee spends on a particular job. The output is the *payroll check* and *earnings statement*. The earnings statement, which is required by law, must show the amounts of federal tax and social security tax withheld. It also shows other deductions such as union dues, insurance premiums, and state and local taxes.

A payroll system must also provide several other types of output. First, up-to-date records of wages paid and deductions retained for each employee must be kept. In a small company, this information is often kept on ledger cards, one for each employee. Second, quarterly and annual reports to the government and to the employees indicating wages paid, taxes withheld, and unemployment tax contributions must be prepared. The W-2 form sent to each employee on or before January 31 of each year is an example of a form required by the government. Third, the system should provide management with information that will help to control labor costs. This information should answer questions such as: What departments have excessive absenteeism or labor turnover? What is the amount of overtime for each department? Is labor performing above or below efficiency standards?

Within a company there may be several different types of payrolls. For example, a manufacturer may have a monthly salaried payroll for office employees and a weekly incentive payroll for factory workers. The incentive wages are dependent on the employee's performance as compared to established standards. In addition, a company may have a sales staff that is paid on a commission or bonus basis.

Because of the amount of computation required for payroll, particularly in an incentive payroll plan, computers have long been used for this application. In fact, when a company first installs a computer system, payroll is commonly the first computer application. Because of its computational speeds, a computer can very often reduce the costs of the payroll application.

ACCOUNTS PAYABLE

Since accounts payable refers to the amounts owed to other companies, the *accounts payable* application involves keeping track of amounts owed and writing checks payable to suppliers *(vendors)*. The input documents are purchase orders, receiving records, and vendor invoices. The purchase order, normally issued by the purchasing department, indicates what was ordered; the receiving report indicates what has been received. By comparing purchase order, receiving report, and vendor invoice, a company can determine whether it has been billed correctly. If so, the bill is authorized for payment.

The primary outputs on an accounts payable system are (1) accounts payable records indicating charges and payments, and (2) *payables checks* and *remittance statements* as shown in figure 11-1. In a small company, as you might guess, accounts payable records are often kept on ledger cards. Because vendors are normally paid on an open-item basis, the remittance statement issued with the check indicates which invoices are being paid. Although it is primarily concerned with making payments to outside vendors, the accounts payable application also keeps records of and writes checks for internal expenses such as petty cash and salesman expense accounts.

To encourage early payment of bills, vendors often offer a cash discount for early payment—for example, a 2 percent discount if the bill is paid within ten days. This is usually indicated on the invoice in an abbreviated form such as 2%/10-NET/30. (NET/30 means the full amount should be paid within thirty days if the discount isn't taken.) Because 2 percent is a substantial discount, one of the objectives of the accounts payable application is to pay all checks on the last day of the discount period. That way the company's cash is retained for as long as possible, but all discounts are received.

The third output of an accounts payable system is management

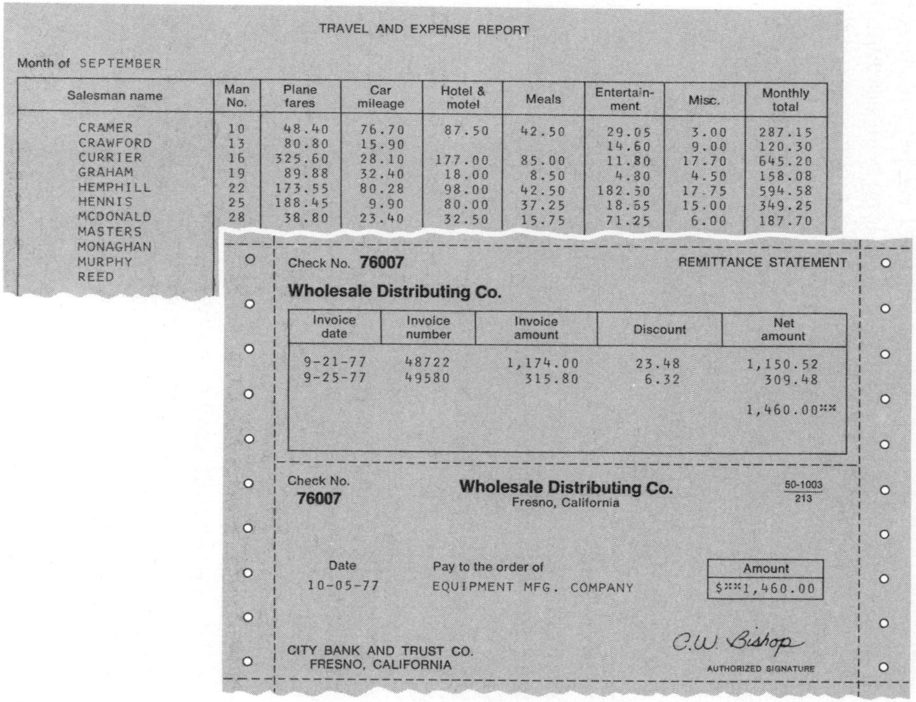

TRAVEL AND EXPENSE REPORT

Month of SEPTEMBER

Salesman name	Man No.	Plane fares	Car mileage	Hotel & motel	Meals	Entertainment	Misc.	Monthly total
CRAMER	10	48.40	76.70	87.50	42.50	29.05	3.00	287.15
CRAWFORD	13	80.80	15.90			14.60	9.00	120.30
CURRIER	16	325.60	28.10	177.00	85.00	11.80	17.70	645.20
GRAHAM	19	89.88	32.40	18.00	8.50	4.80	4.50	158.08
HEMPHILL	22	173.55	80.28	98.00	42.50	182.30	17.75	594.58
HENNIS	25	188.45	9.90	80.00	37.25	18.55	15.00	349.25
MCDONALD	28	38.80	23.40	32.50	15.75	71.25	6.00	187.70
MASTERS								
MONAGHAN								
REED								

REMITTANCE STATEMENT

Check No. 76007

Wholesale Distributing Co.

Invoice date	Invoice number	Invoice amount	Discount	Net amount
9-21-77	48722	1,174.00	23.48	1,150.52
9-25-77	49580	315.80	6.32	309.48
				1,460.00**

Check No. **76007**

Wholesale Distributing Co.
Fresno, California

Date 10-05-77

Pay to the order of EQUIPMENT MFG. COMPANY

50-1003/213

CITY BANK AND TRUST CO.
FRESNO, CALIFORNIA

Amount $***1,460.00

C.W. Bishop
AUTHORIZED SIGNATURE

FIGURE 11-1 Accounts-payable documents

information. Because the accounts payable application keeps track of all payments other than paychecks, it controls a vast amount of cost data. By having this data organized into various types of reports, management can use it to control costs more effectively. The travel and expense report in figure 11-1, for example, breaks down selling expenses by salesman. Other reports may answer questions such as who the largest suppliers are, which vendors have the most goods returned to them, what cash discounts have been lost, and what the daily cash requirements are.

GENERAL LEDGER

The term *general ledger,* as any accounting student knows, refers to the records of a company's revenues and expenses, assets and liabilities. The individual records within the general ledger are referred to as *accounts.* Accounts receivable and accounts payable, for example, are two of the general-ledger accounts. Other typical accounts are gross sales, merchandise purchases, and salaries and wages. Although a small company may keep account records in a single general-ledger book, these records are likely to be kept in punched cards, on magnetic tapes, or on direct-access devices when an automated general-ledger system is used.

The input documents for a general-ledger system are primarily records from the accounts receivable, inventory, accounts payable, payroll, and sales-analysis applications. In addition, some other accounting records are needed, such as those that give the present value of land, buildings, and equipment owned by the company.

The major output documents of a general-ledger system are the *balance sheet* and the *income statement* (also known as the *operating statement* or the *profit-and-loss statement*). These documents are illustrated in simplified form in figure 11-2. The balance sheet indicates a company's assets, liabilities, and net worth as of a certain date. Note that it does not show changes in assets, liabilities, or net worth; for this information, a current balance sheet must be compared with the balance sheet for a previous period. While totals for some of the accounts on the balance sheet are derived from the basic applications such as the accounts-receivable, inventory, and accounts-payable applications, totals for accounts such as cash, land, and buildings must be obtained from other accounting records. Note that total assets must equal total liabilities plus net worth; otherwise, there is an error in one or more of the general-ledger accounts.

The income statement shows the revenues and expenses of a company over a certain period of time, such as a month, a quarter, or a year. Most of the data for this report can be derived from the sales-analysis, accounts payable, and payroll applications. Quite simply, all expenses are subtracted from total revenue to derive the profit or the loss for a particular accounting period. The profit is carried over to the balance sheet as retained earnings.

```
                    BALANCE SHEET--DEC. 31, 1976

                ASSETS

CURRENT ASSETS
  CASH                                 19,200
  ACCOUNTS RECEIVABLE                 225,800
  MERCHANDISE INVENTORY               850,500
      TOTAL CURRENT ASSETS                       1,095,500 **

FIXED ASSETS
  LAND                                 90,000
  BUILDINGS AND FIXTURES              737,800
  EQUIPMENT                           148,000
      TOTAL FIXED ASSETS                           975,800 **

TOTAL ASSETS                                    $2,071,300 **


                LIABILITIES AND NET WORTH

CURRENT LIABILITIES
  ACCOUNTS PAYABLE                    122,800
  INCOME TAXES PAYABLE                 51,000
      TOTAL CURRENT LIABILITIES                    173,800 **

LONG-TERM LIABILITIES
  BONDS PAYABLE                       500,000
  CONTRACTS PAYABLE                    30,000
      TOTAL LONG-TERM LIABILITIES                  530,000 **

NET WORTH
  CAPITAL STOCK AND PAID-IN SURPLUS 1,130,000
  RETAINED EARNINGS                   237,500
      TOTAL NET WORTH                            1,367,500 **

TOTAL LIABILITIES AND NET WORTH                 $2,071,300 **
```

```
                    INCOME STATEMENT
                 YEAR ENDING DEC. 31, 1976

REVENUES
  SALES                              5,460,000
  LESS RETURNS                           4,300
      NET SALES                                  5,455,700 **

COST OF GOODS SOLD                               3,990,000 *

GROSS PROFIT                                     1,465,700 **

SELLING EXPENSES
  SALESMEN SALARIES                    205,800
  SALESMEN COMMISSIONS                 109,200
  SALES OFFICE SALARIES                 36,000
  SALES OFFICE MAINTENANCE              16,000
  MAINT. OF DELIVERY EQUIP.             26,000
  DEPRECIATION OF DEL. EQUIP.            7,200
      TOTAL SELLING EXPENSES                       400,200 **

GEN. AND ADM. EXPENSES
  OFFICERS' SALARIES                   360,000
  GEN. OFFICE SALARIES                 144,200
  PROPERTY TAX                          12,500
  INSURANCE                              8,400
  RENT                                  36,000
      TOTAL G & A EXPENSES                         560,900 **

TOTAL OPERATING EXPENSES                           961,100 **

NET OPERATING INCOME                               504,600 **

OTHER EXPENSES
  INTEREST PAID                         42,400
  CASH DISCOUNTS ALLOWED                22,700
      TOTAL OTHER EXPENSES                          65,100 **

NET INCOME BEFORE TAXES                            439,500 **

INCOME TAXES                                       202,000 *

PROFIT OR LOSS                                     237,500 **
```

FIGURE 11-2   General-ledger documents

Because financial data is critical to the management of a company, the general-ledger system should provide financial information beyond that given in the balance sheet and the income statement. Depending on the preferences of a company's financial officers, then, a general-ledger system may also provide reports similar to those in figure 11-3. The first report compares the present balance sheet with that of the previous period; the second shows the ratios of expenses to revenue. Other reports may break down expenses and revenues by branch offices or by departments, compare one branch office's income statement with those of other branches, or compare expenses with budgeted expenses. A general-ledger system should also be able to provide a detailed breakdown of expenses, thereby helping management to analyze those operations in which expenses are unusual or unexpected.

```
                    COMPARATIVE BALANCE SHEET

                            THIS      LAST    OVER (+) OR
         DESCRIPTION        YEAR      YEAR    UNDER (-)

CASH                        19,200    27,500     8,300 -
ACCOUNTS RECEIVABLE        225,800   175,220    50,580 +
MERCHANDISE INVENTORY      850,500   705,000   145,500 +

LAND                        90,000    90,000
BUILDINGS AND FIXTURES     737,800   558,500   179,300 +
EQUIPMENT                  148,000   163,500    15,500 -

ACCOUNTS PAYABLE
```

EXPENSE-TO-REVENUE STATEMENT		
DESCRIPTION	AMOUNT	% OF NET SALES
NET SALES	5,455,700	100.0
COST OF GOODS SOLD	3,990,000	73.1
GROSS PROFIT	1,465,700	26.9
SELLING EXPENSE	400,200	7.3
GEN. AND ADM. EXPENSES	560,900	10.3
NET OPERATING INCOME	504,600	9.3
OTHER EXPENSES	65,100	1.2
NET INCOME BEFORE TAXES	439,500	8.1

FIGURE 11-3 General-ledger reports

DISCUSSION

You have now been introduced to eight accounting applications: order writing, billing, accounts receivable, inventory control, sales analysis, payroll, accounts payable, and general ledger. Depending on the industry, however, there are many other types of accounting applications; for example, demand-deposit accounting and mortgage-loan accounting in banking, income tax and appropriation accounting in government, and premium and claim-payment accounting in insurance. As a class, accounting applications are likely to be the first applications computerized by an institution.

Because the computer has enabled accounting systems to more accurately represent the actual costs within an activity, some unexpected facts are often uncovered as a result of computerizing the accounting systems. For instance, supermarkets traditionally have not considered the cost of shelf space when determining the profits made by each product. Although the store costs, and therefore shelf costs, have been considered, actual shelf costs per product were too difficult to assign. When at last some stores calculated the shelf space and shelf cost for each product and combined this with product, packaging, and handling costs, there were some surprising results. One store, for example, discovered that it wasn't making a profit on beef and flour!

SUMMARY

1. The accounting applications are order writing, billing, accounts receivable, inventory control, sales analysis, payroll, accounts payable, and general ledger. Because they deal with basic accounting data, they are often crucial to the success of a company.

TERMINOLOGY

accounting application	remittance statement
payroll	account
payroll check	balance sheet
earnings statement	income statement
accounts payable	operating statement
vendor	profit-and-loss statement
payables check	

QUESTIONS

1. Traditionally, payroll has been one of the first applications that a company computerizes. Why do you think this is so?

2. Refer to figure 11-2. Which of the items shown on the balance sheet and income statement can be derived from data that is captured in each of the following applications: billing, accounts receivable, inventory control, payroll, and accounts payable?

TOPIC 2
A SURVEY OF
BUSINESS
APPLICATIONS

Although the accounting applications are basic to most businesses, they make up only a small portion of all computer applications. In fact, several thousand different computer applications have been identified, and more are being discovered every day. If you pick up a newspaper, you are likely to read about a computer controlling the operations of an oil refinery, predicting the outcome of an election, or helping to design a highway.

To give you some perspective on computer uses in business, five types of business applications are described in this topic. Included are operational control, management information systems, management science, process control, and scientific and engineering. These classifications, along with the accounting applications, do not encompass all computer applications. Furthermore, the distinction between classifications isn't always clearcut. Nevertheless, these groupings do illustrate the major computer activities in business.

OPERATIONAL CONTROL

During the last several years, many companies have discovered that a computer can be of more value when used to help control an operation than when used simply to account for an operation. In a typical manufacturing company, for example, improving production efficiency is likely to have a far greater effect on profits than improving the accounting system.

When a computer is used for *operational control,* it does more than merely record or report operations after they have occurred. In controlling operations, the computer is used to plan, schedule, and monitor the operations as they take place. In production control, for example, the computer can be used in all three phases. First, it can be used to forecast the demand for finished products and to plan material requirements based on these forecasts. Second, it can schedule machine operations, taking into consideration time requirements and machine capacities. Finally, it can monitor shop-floor operations as they occur and alert management to any deviations from the production schedule. As in a typical cost-accounting system, the computer can then be used to account for the material costs and labor involved in each product.

When computers are applied to production control, the improvements are often well worth the cost of the computer system. One company, for example, reduced the production time for its products from 8.2 weeks to 6.3 weeks while it increased production capacity by 36 percent. Another company reports production times dropped from 15 weeks down to 5 weeks and the service level of finished parts increased from 88 percent to a new level of 98 percent.

Operational-control systems can, of course, be applied to many operational areas within a business. Thus, there are systems for warehousing that determine the most efficient locations for items and the order in which items should be picked. There are customer-service systems in insurance companies that store all policyholder information on direct-access devices and retrieve the desired information upon request. When an inventory-control system forecasts demands, determines order quantities and reorder points, and prints purchase orders, it too becomes an operational-control system.

MANAGEMENT-INFORMATION SYSTEMS

Management information is an important aspect of many applications: accounts receivable, inventory control, sales analysis, payroll, accounts payable, and, of course, general ledger. A *management-information system* (MIS), however, implies more than just the traditional information. It is a system that (quite ambitiously) tries to provide all the information required by the managers of a company when they need it. As a result, even though the information is derived mainly from the files used in accounting and operational-control applications, an MIS is often treated as an application in itself.

An MIS is difficult to design because it must provide information at different levels. Within any company, for instance, there are several levels of management: top management; one or more levels of middle management; and operational, or lower, management. Because the information requirements differ for each level, the system must be able to arrange the same data into varying levels of information. Figure 11-4, for example, shows budget analysis reports for three levels of management. At the top level, the report indicates that selling expenses are over budget. At the next level, the four sales offices that are over budget are listed. At the third level, the over-budget selling expenses of the Denver sales offices are indicated. Needless to say, there can be levels below those shown, such as traveling and telephone expenses by salesperson.

One of the basic concepts of an MIS is management-by-exception. In designing a system, acceptable variances from standards are determined so that exceptional conditions can be indicated on all reports. Thus, the first level in figure 11-4 indicates items that have exceeded budget by more than 3 percent or items that are below budget by more than 5 percent—the others are labeled OK. At the second level, only the exceptional sales offices are listed; at the third level, only the exceptional budget items are listed.

```
                    TOP LEVEL
                 EARNINGS SUMMARY

4 WEEKS ENDING 9-29-77      DOLLARS IN THOUSANDS

                    PLANNED     ACTUAL     VARIANCE

SALES                4,800.0    4,750.0    OK
GROSS PROFIT         1,500.0    1,400.0    - 6.7%
SELLING EXPENSE        559.0      615.5    +10.1%
GEN. AND ADM. EXPENSE  450.0      449.3    OK
OPERATING PROFIT       490.0      335.2    -31.6%
```

```
                    SECOND LEVEL
             SELLING EXPENSE BY SALES OFFICE

                        4 WEEKS ENDING 9-29-77
                         DOLLARS IN THOUSANDS

                    PLANNED     ACTUAL     VARIANCE

      DENVER          40.0       43.3      + 8.3%
      MILWAUKEE       48.0       53.5      +11.5%
      OAKLAND         75.0       97.2      +29.6%
      SAN DIEGO       70.0       95.5      +36.4%
```

```
                    THIRD LEVEL
              DENVER SELLING EXPENSE

   4 WEEKS ENDING 9-29-77

                    PLANNED     ACTUAL     VARIANCE

   TELEPHONE          1,500      2,800     +86.7%
   TRAVELING EXPENSE  3,250      5,280     +62.5%
```

FIGURE 11-4 Levels of management information

Since a major goal of an MIS is to provide information when it is needed, data communications are normally involved. By keying an inquiry into a terminal, a manager can request the information he desires. The information is assembled by the computer and printed or displayed on the manager's terminal. If a manager requests successively lower levels of information—for example, the president may request both the first and second levels shown in figure 11-4—the system should be able to provide them.

Although there are many pros and cons, the concept of an MIS has great sales appeal. As a result, many MIS systems are being either developed or planned. One of the primary questions raised by objectors to MIS systems is whether the expense of such a system is justified by improved management. Here, it is a problem of comparing a measurable quantity—cost—with a quality that is difficult to measure.

MANAGEMENT SCIENCE

Management science refers to statistical and mathematical techniques and theories as they are applied to business problems. Although these techniques can be used in manual computation, the computer is often used for management-science applications because of its computational speeds. For example, a computation that takes twelve hours for a person working with pencil and paper might be done in less than a minute by a computer.

A typical management-science problem is to determine the shipping routes that will lead to the lowest total shipping costs. For example, suppose a company has five production plants and fifty warehouses located throughout the country. The sales of each warehouse are known and the production capacity of each plant is known. Also, the shipping cost between each plant and each warehouse is known. The problem is: Which warehouses should be supplied from which plants to minimize shipping costs? It is not just a matter of supplying each warehouse from the nearest plant because the requirements of the East Coast warehouses exceed the capacities of the East Coast plants.

By using mathematical techniques, the best solution can be determined. And by using a computer, the solution can be determined in a very short time and redetermined whenever the requirements of the warehouses change. To appreciate the complexity of the problems, consider that if there were only four plants and five warehouses, there would be 1024 possible solutions, with only one being lowest in cost.

Two techniques that are commonly used within the field of management science are *linear programming* and *simulation*. Linear programming is a mathematical technique that can be used to find an optimum solution when the relationships between the factors involved can be expressed in a series of linear equations. Thus, it is used to allocate resources in order to achieve the best (most profitable or lowest cost) balance between conflicting demands. For example, cattle companies use linear programming to determine the lowest-cost mix of grains that will meet certain nutritional requirements. The cost and nutritional makeup of the grains available for mixing and the nutritional requirements of the final product, the cattle feed, are the input data. The output is the best feed formula.

Simulation involves representing aspects of a business in terms of numbers or symbols that can be manipulated by a computer. By trying various alternatives on the simulation model, results in the real world can be more accurately predicted. For example, if a simulation model for investment practices has been developed, various investment strategies can be tried to determine which has the greatest likelihood of success.

In addition to linear programming and simulation, there are many other management-science techniques, all of which try to apply the techniques of science and mathematics to management problems. Although there have been many success stories so far, this area of applications is still in its infancy. Because of the expense of developing management-science solutions, most companies have yet to try them. Nevertheless, some management-science people claim that the best solution derived by management-science techniques is from 5 to 15 percent better than a typical manual solution. If so, many businesses could profit by more extensive use of management science.

PROCESS CONTROL

Process control refers to computer control of a production process. For example, paper production is a typical process-control application. As wood pulp is moved through a long series of operations, the computer receives test and measurement data such as rate of flow, temperature, pressure, and humidity. The computer processes this data and makes the appropriate adjustments to valves and other actuators that control the process. Thus, the process-control computer actually takes the place of the operator or operators who conventionally control the process.

The advantages of process control can be significant. Guaranteed uniformity, greater productivity, lower costs, reduced waste and scrap, better quality—all have been claimed in one process-control application or another. The overall claim of experts is that the best performance otherwise attainable (and then, only occasionally) is the average for a process-control system.

Because of its advantages, all leading companies in the processing industry use computers to control one or more processes. Some typical applications are oil refining, steel milling, and bakery blending. In all, more than 2500 different process-control applications have been installed or are being installed. In simple systems, input may come from a few or several dozen input sensors; in complex systems, the computer may monitor hundreds of input measurements and make appropriate adjustments.

To illustrate a simple process-control system, consider an application in the food-processing industry called *net-weight monitoring.* In accordance with government regulations, a food processor must print the net weight (product weight) on the outside of the container and fill it with at least as much product—such as processed cheese—as is specified. Because there are penalties for underweight packages, a food processor is likely to overfill rather than underfill. In a typical operation, the containers are weighed automatically after being filled by the machine. If they are underfilled or overfilled, they are pushed to the side. When too much product is being diverted from the filling line, the operator who watches this process makes an adjustment to the filling machine. Note, however, that the system measures gross weight—container weight plus product weight—so variations in container weight are not taken into consideration. Also, there is apt to be considerable delay in the adjustment process and much chance for error.

As an alternative, consider the system illustrated in figure 11-5. Here, a computer constantly monitors the process. Each container is automatically weighed both before and after it is filled. These measurements are

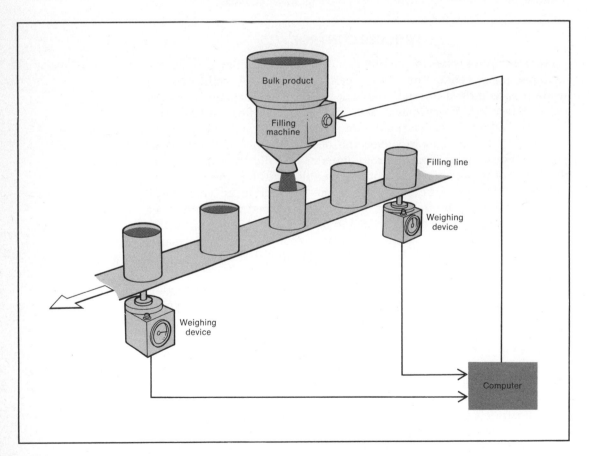

FIGURE 11-5 Net-weight monitoring—process control

input to the computer, which calculates the exact net weight (gross weight minus container weight) and, if necessary, makes immediate adjustments to the filling machine. If the density of the product changes during the process, the system will detect it, adjust the filling machine, and continue to fill the correct net weight.

The advantages of this second system should be obvious. Less product is given away because of overfills, and there is absolute assurance against underfills. Costs are usually reduced since filling-machine operators aren't needed and one computer can monitor several filling lines.

SCIENTIFIC AND ENGINEERING

Some of the first uses of computers were to solve scientific and engineering problems. By using the computer and its fantastic computational speeds, scientists and engineers were able to relieve themselves from the details of computation and spend more time on the problems themselves. Because the human mind is able to conceive solutions that it cannot carry out in a lifetime of manual calculations, the computer has actually solved problems that never would have been solved using other methods. With the development of the computer, we have only to state the steps required in a solution—we do not have to actually perform the computation.

To help the scientist and engineer communicate with the computer, a number of programming languages have been developed to allow problems to be expressed in mathematical or engineering notation. One of the oldest of these languages, FORTRAN, is designed to make it possible to express any mathematical computation in a type of mathematical notation. Similarly, there are languages to express various types of engineering problems, such as calculating the area of a triangular plot of ground when the lengths of two sides and the size of one angle are known. Thus, the scientist or engineer doesn't have to learn the computer's language but only a modification of a language with which he or she is familiar.

So that a number of engineers can make efficient use of a single computer, data-communication systems are often found in engineering departments. For example, if twelve typewriter terminals are located in an engineering department, twelve engineers can work on twelve different problems at one time. Because the computer works at speeds far beyond those of humans, each engineer feels that only he or she is working with the computer, even though the computer may be skipping from terminal to terminal many times a second. A system such as this, which may have dozens of terminals connected to a single computer, is referred to as a *time-sharing system*.

Besides doing computation, computers can assist engineers by storing and retrieving engineering designs. Using a visual-display terminal such as the one in figure 11-6, engineers can request a certain design and have it displayed before them. They can then make modifications to the design with a light pen. The light pen is input to the computer, and upon request, the computer stores these modifications. The engineer can thus experiment without making an extensive series of drawings. Because of the speed with which a computer can perform these visual-display operations, time sharing is also normally used for systems such as this.

Of course, to truly understand scientific and engineering applications, you have to be a scientist or an engineer. As a result, other than this superficial introduction, this book will not go into these applications.

FIGURE 11-6   Using a light pen and a visual-display terminal for engineering applications

DISCUSSION

As we said at the start of this topic, these five classifications of computer applications along with the accounting applications are not all-inclusive or clear-cut. For example, inventory control can be both an accounting and an operational-control application. Similarly, management-science techniques and theories are often used in operational-control applications—the economic-order-quantity formula, for instance, is an outgrowth of management science. Nevertheless, most computer activities fall into these classifications.

One distinction that is somewhat clear-cut, however, is that between *scientific* and *business applications*. The first is concerned with computation and problem solving; the second with the repetitive processing of business data. The computing requirements are so distinct, in fact, that computers were often designed for either scientific or business applications. In general, the scientific computer has rapid internal speeds; the business computer has rapid I/O speeds. But even this distinction is becoming less clear-cut. As scientific methods were applied to more and more business problems, computers that could handle both scientific and business applications were developed. Today, both scientific and business applications are often run on the same computer.

Within any one company, all types of applications plus the accounting applications might be found. For example, a company might have one computer that is used by the engineering and the research and development departments on a time-sharing basis. A second computer might be used to control a process on the factory floor. A third computer, located in the data-processing department, might be used for accounting, operational-control, management-information, and management-science applications. Although the trend is toward greater application in the process-control, management-information, and management-science areas, an overwhelming amount of the work done by computers can still be attributed to the accounting and operational-control applications.

SUMMARY

1. There are six major types of business applications. They can be referred to as accounting, operational control, management-information systems, management science, process control, and scientific and engineering.

TERMINOLOGY

operational-control application
management-information system
MIS
management science
linear programming
simulation

process control
net-weight monitoring
time-sharing system
scientific application
business application

QUESTIONS

1. Operational control systems are usually installed in areas where the potential benefits are large. In the area of production control, for example, what are the benefits of improved operational control, and how significant are they?

2. MIS feasibility studies are difficult, because most of the benefits are difficult to measure. How, for example, could you predict the value of an MIS system to corporate management? How could you determine the benefits once the system was installed?

3. Process control can lead to totally automated plants. One of the national bakery companies, for example, uses computers to mix ingredients, regulate ovens, and monitor packaging operations. In general, people are used only to feed conveyor belts and to remove packaged products for storage or shipping. Is this good or bad? Explain.

4. The idea in management science is to take a management scientist and a computer and derive better solutions for traditional business problems than those solutions derived by business managers. Is this good or bad? Why?

12 MANUAL AND MECHANICAL METHODS OF PROCESSING DATA

There are at least two reasons for learning about manual and mechanical methods of processing data. First, it gives you some perspective. To appreciate the speed, accuracy, and information capabilities of a computer system, you must learn what noncomputerized systems can provide. To appreciate why many people prefer noncomputerized billing to computerized billing, you must understand the nature of the noncomputerized system.

The second reason for studying noncomputerized methods is that they are common to all business systems, including EDP systems. No company can do all of its processing on computers alone. In fact, large companies are likely to have hundreds of office workers outside of the EDP department. Furthermore, the procedures used by these workers are likely to be critical to the efficiency of the EDP system.

To aid in the study and analysis of manual and mechanical procedures, *procedure charts* are used. These charts symbolically represent the operations within a system. The procedure chart in figure 12-1, for example, represents the operations within a manual order-writing and billing system. The symbols used are summarized in figure 12-2.

The purpose of the procedure chart is to show all operations that take place and to show the origin, flow, and final disposition of all documents used within a procedure. All the documents on the chart are numbered, and a document number placed on a flowline indicates the flow of the document. Thus

indicates that copies a and b of document number 3 are being moved from one operation to another. Arrowheads aren't necessary on a procedure chart since the direction of flow should be obvious.

The degree of detail shown in a procedure chart depends on the use of the chart. For an overall analysis of the flow of documents within a system, only the major processing operations need be shown. On the other hand, each step within an operation may be charted if the purpose of the chart is to determine ways of simplifying a procedure. In figure 12-3, for example, additional detail is given for steps 11 and 12 of figure 12-1.

In ths book, procedure charts are used to illustrate the characteristics of a system using manual and mechanical methods of processing data. By analyzing the accuracy, speed, and information capabilities of these systems, you are better prepared to evaluate the advantages and disadvantages of computer systems.

Accuracy

Have you ever added columns of thirty numbers or more, filed 250 folders into a filing cabinet, or typed a twelve-page sales summary? If you

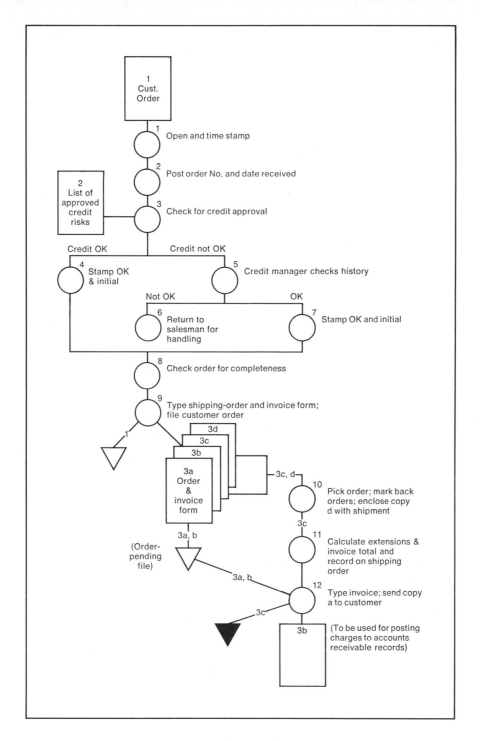

FIGURE 12-1 The order-writing and billing procedure

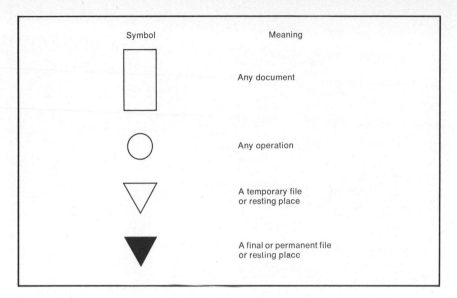

Symbol	Meaning
▯	Any document
◯	Any operation
▽	A temporary file or resting place
▼	A final or permanent file or resling placc

FIGURE 12-2   ANSI symbols for procedure charts

have, you know that manual procedures are prone to error. It is relatively easy to misfile, miscalculate, or hit the wrong typewriter key. And if you do these jobs for several hours at a time, boredom and fatigue increase the likelihood of error. When analyzing a manual procedure, the system analyst must remember that errors can occur in every operation in the procedure.

To increase the accuracy of manual procedures, checking operations normally follow arithmetic or recording operations. In the invoicing procedure in figure 12-3, for example, step 3 checks the calculations of step 2; step 6 checks the typing of step 5. It is common, in fact, for as much as 35 percent of a typical paperwork procedure to consist of checking operations. Because checking increases the cost as well as the accuracy of a procedure, a balance must be reached between the two. At some point, the cost of inaccuracy becomes less than the cost of increased checking.

Balancing to controls is commonly used in a paperwork procedure. To illustrate, consider the procedure shown in figure 12-4. Here, invoice amounts are added to accounts receivable ledger cards and monthly statements, and new accounts receivable balances are calculated. As illustrated in figure 12-5, when the clerk records the charge on the monthly statement, it is also recorded on the ledger card and accounts receivable *journal.* By using carbon-backed documents, a single recording by the clerk updates all three documents. The board that is used, called a *pegboard* or *writing board,* has pegs on the left side that are used to align the documents placed on the board.

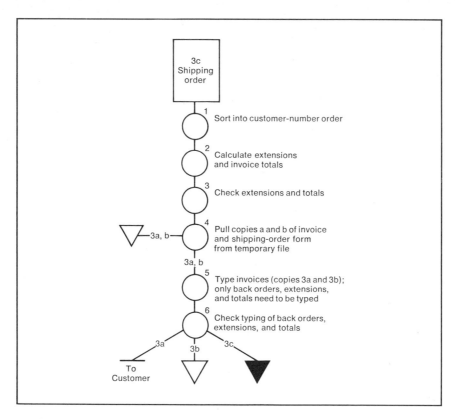

FIGURE 12-3   The billing procedure

After all charges have been posted to the accounts-receivable records, the journal becomes a record of transactions for the day. It can thus be used for balancing to controls. In step 5, the charges, old balances, and new balances are added and recorded on the journal. In step 6, these totals are compared with totals on the accounts receivable control sheet. If the totals agree, you can assume that the individual transactions have been posted correctly; if they don't agree, the errors must be found.

Note here the difficulty of correcting an error if the totals don't balance. If the charge total on the control sheet and the charge total on the journal are different, the charges may have been added incorrectly in either step 1 or step 5 of figure 12-4. If this addition proves correct, the clerk must compare the invoice amounts with the charge amounts on the journal. If there are many invoices, this can be a laborious job.

If the charges and old balances on the control sheet and journal are the same but the new balances differ, the addition on the control sheet and journal must be checked. If this is correct, an error was made in calculating the new balance on one or more individual records; thus, Old

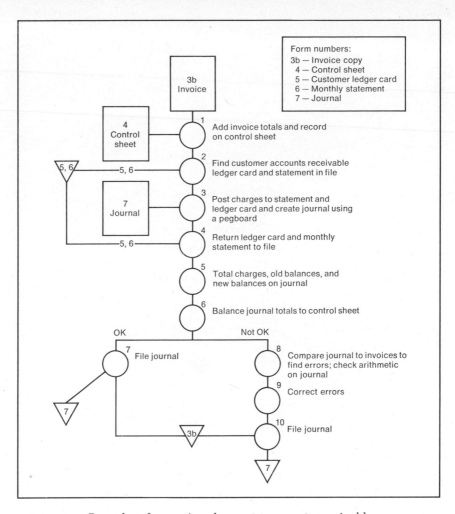

FIGURE 12-4   Procedure for posting charges to accounts receivable

Balance + Charge = New Balance must be recalculated for each line on the journal until the error is found.

In conclusion, it is possible to achieve a high degree of accuracy in a manual system when checking and control balancing are used. On the other hand, when only checking is used, the likelihood of error is relatively high. In some cases, the error rate for clerical procedures has been as high as 5 percent, even when checking all operations. For those procedures that do not use control balancing or have limited checking, the error rate can be overwhelming.

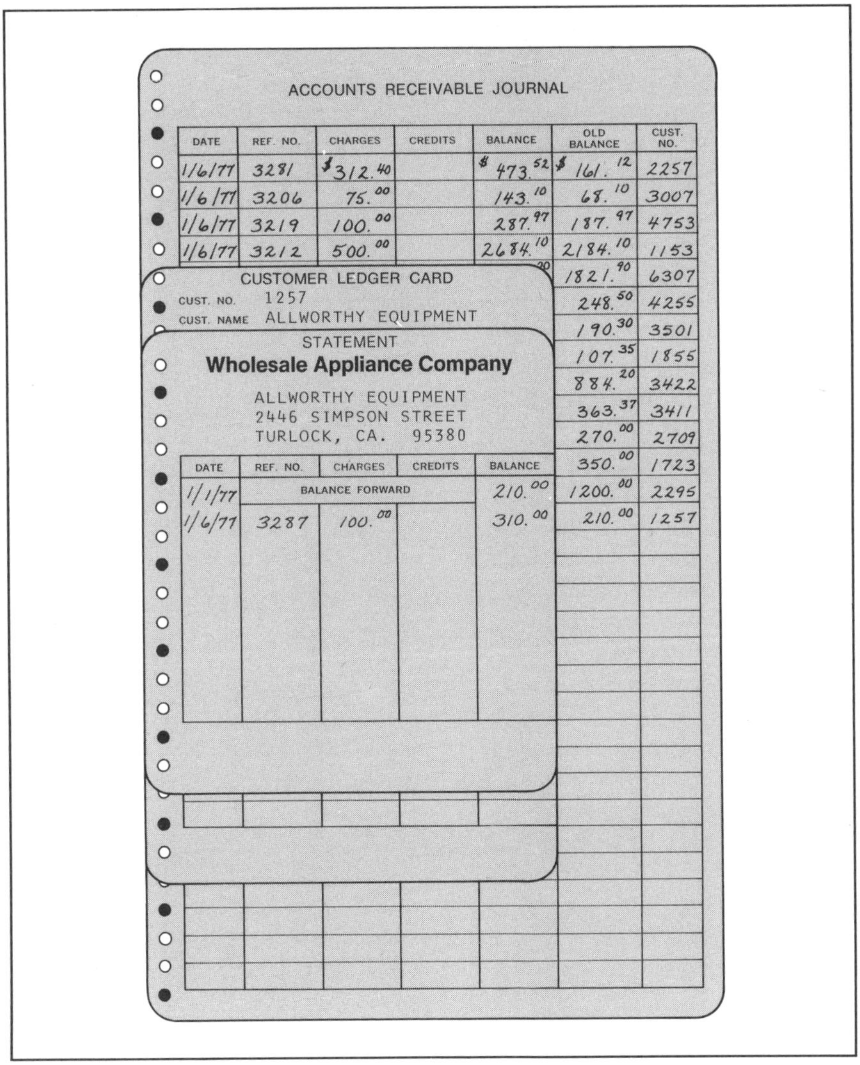

ACCOUNTS RECEIVABLE JOURNAL

DATE	REF. NO.	CHARGES	CREDITS	BALANCE	OLD BALANCE	CUST. NO.
1/6/77	3281	$312.40		$473.52	$161.12	2257
1/6/77	3206	75.00		143.10	68.10	3007
1/6/77	3219	100.00		287.97	187.97	4753
1/6/77	3212	500.00		2684.10	2184.10	1153
				.90	1821.90	6307
					248.50	4255
					190.30	3501
					107.35	1855
					884.20	3422
					363.37	3411
					270.00	2709
					350.00	1723
					1200.00	2295
					210.00	1257

CUSTOMER LEDGER CARD

CUST. NO. 1257
CUST. NAME ALLWORTHY EQUIPMENT

STATEMENT

Wholesale Appliance Company

ALLWORTHY EQUIPMENT
2446 SIMPSON STREET
TURLOCK, CA. 95380

DATE	REF. NO.	CHARGES	CREDITS	BALANCE
1/1/77		BALANCE FORWARD		210.00
1/6/77	3287	100.00		310.00

FIGURE 12-5   A pegboard application

Speed

The speed of a manual procedure is largely dependent on the delays within the procedure. For example, in the order-writing and billing procedure of figure 12-1, a delay is likely to take place after every operation as documents are moved from one clerk, desk, or department to another. Because a clerk normally performs several different operations a day, each clerk is likely to be working on one batch of documents when another batch for another operation is delivered. This second batch must wait to be processed until the clerk is finished with the first batch. If a clerk or department falls behind in work, several batches of documents may be waiting for a single clerk; thus, the delay between operations can extend to hours and even days.

Once a clerk or department falls behind in work, it is difficult to catch up. Unless the workload lightens or overtime hours are worked or additional people are hired, the group stays behind schedule and all documents involved continue to be delayed. In unexpected peak periods, a clerk or department may be overwhelmed by the volume of work. As incredible as it may sound, the author has seen entire departments so overloaded with paperwork that incoming mail hadn't been opened for over three weeks.

Of course, top priority operations can always be handled separately. For instance, a rush order can be processed by having a single clerk handle the order in steps 1–9 of figure 12-1, and then deliver the order to the shipping department. Special handling is expensive, however, because it does not make use of the efficiencies of batch processing. Whenever batch processing is interrupted in favor of a special job, all other jobs are delayed.

Although a manual system can be bogged down by the delays between operations, it is also possible to have a perfectly efficient manual system. If the workload is predictable, if batches are kept small, and if operations are carefully planned and scheduled, a manual procedure can provide all the speed that is required of it.

Information

One of the features of an EDP system is its ability to provide management information. Once data has been recorded in a machine-readable form, it can be repeatedly processed to provide a wide variety of reports. Because the cost of the EDP system is spread over several applications and many documents, the cost of any one report is relatively low.

In contrast, the manual system normally requires a separate procedure for each report that is prepared—reports are not by-products of other procedures. For instance, the procedure in figure 12-6, which prepares a monthly sales-by-salesman report, does not do any of the work needed to prepare a sales-by-customer or sales-by-item report. These reports would likely be prepared from accounts-receivable and inventory ledger cards. Because of this characteristic of a manual system, information is relatively expensive to obtain.

You might also consider the speed and error-correction cost of a procedure such as the one in figure 12-6. If the volume of documents to be processed for the month is large—say more than a thousand—preparing

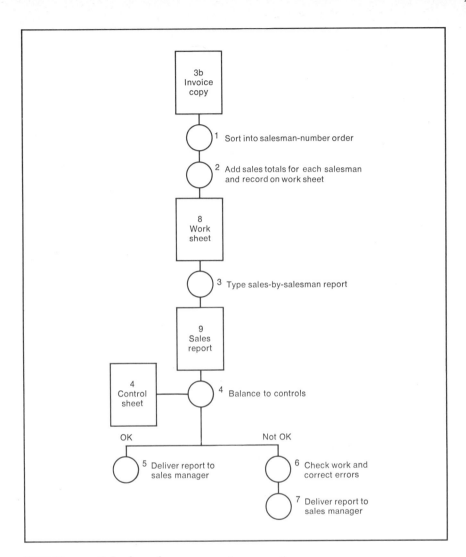

FIGURE 12-6   Sales-by-salesman report preparation

the sales-by-salesman report can be a very time-consuming procedure. In addition, the chance of error and the chance that the control sheet and sales total won't balance is increased as the number of invoices increases. To find an error, a clerk must check the typing, and, if this doesn't reveal the error, must redo the calculations. In short, the amount of work required to correct an error (or the cost of error correction) is almost as great as the amount of work (or cost) required to create the report. Thus, with a large number of invoices, it is probably better to summarize them on a daily or weekly, rather than a monthly, basis. This reduces the amount of time required to prepare the report at the end of the month, but the cost of error correction is still relatively high.

Because of the nature of manual operations, reports that involve great detail or extensive calculations become impractical to prepare on a manual system. For example, an aged trial balance, which is a routine report in an EDP system, becomes a very expensive report when using a manual system. As a result, a small business is likely to prepare an aged trial balance only once or twice a year, rather than monthly. Similarly, inventory reports, such as a sales-by-item report showing this-year-to-date and last-year-to-date totals, and financial reports, such as a budget analysis showing the percent of actual costs over or under budget, are too expensive to prepare regularly when using manual procedures.

OFFICE EQUIPMENT

To increase the speed and accuracy and to decrease the cost of manual procedures, many varieties of office equipment have been developed. The adding machine and calculator, for example, are designed to improve arithmetic operations. In general, an adding machine can add and subtract, while a calculator can add, subtract, multiply, and divide. The adding machine normally prints the results on a paper adding-machine tape, while calculators either print the results on a paper tape or display them in windows at the top of the machine. By using an adding machine or calculator, the speed and accuracy of operations such as totaling invoice charges and extending line items during billing can be improved.

To improve the efficiency of filing operations, many varieties of filing devices are available. *Tub files* have no tops, giving the effect of open file drawers at a height designed for filing efficiency. By eliminating the opening and closing of file drawers, records can be accessed more quickly. *Visible-record files,* such as the one in figure 12-7, are files in which the identifying information of records in a group is visible to the file clerk without any manual manipulation. After the clerk pulls out the appropriate group of records, he or she scans the visible portion of the records to find the required record, flips open the record, and reads or writes on it without removing it from the file. Since the record is never removed, there is no possiblity of misfiling. In addition to tub and visible-record files, there are many varieties of mechanized files in which a selected group of records is rotated to the clerk after he or she presses the appropriate control buttons.

Writing boards such as the one shown in figure 12-5 make use of the fact that the same business data is recorded on several different forms. By using carbon-backed paper or chemically treated transfer paper, a single recording by a clerk is transferred to two or more different documents. Thus, an accounts receivable charge is recorded on the monthly statement, the customer ledger, and the journal in a single operation; an

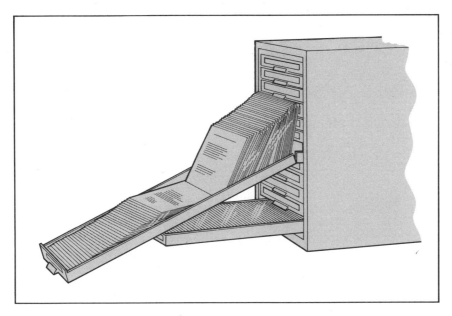

FIGURE 12-7   A visible-record file

employee's earnings and deduction data are recorded on his paycheck, the employee ledger, and the payroll journal in a single operation. By reducing the number of times a clerk records data, both speed and accuracy are increased.

Two office machines you will likely come in contact with since they are so widely used are the posting machine and the billing machine. The *posting machine,* one model of which is illustrated in figure 12-8, combines the principles of the writing board, adding machine, and typewriter. Two or more documents can be overlaid in the machine at any one time, adding and subtracting are done automatically using the numeric keyboard, and the typewriter keyboard can be used to type data on the documents. The posting machine has the ability to store a limited amount of information in storage units commonly called *counters,* so some information—the date, for example—can be keyed into storage at the start of a job and can be printed automatically on all documents that are prepared. These counters can also be used to accumulate totals throughout an operation; thus, control totals can be printed automatically at the end of a job.

To illustrate the use of a posting machine, consider a typical posting operation—posting charges to accounts receivable records. At the start of the job, the operator inserts the accounts receivable journal into the machine, where it remains throughout the job. The day's date is then keyed into one of the machine's counters. After this preparation, the operator goes through these steps for each invoice amount to be posted:

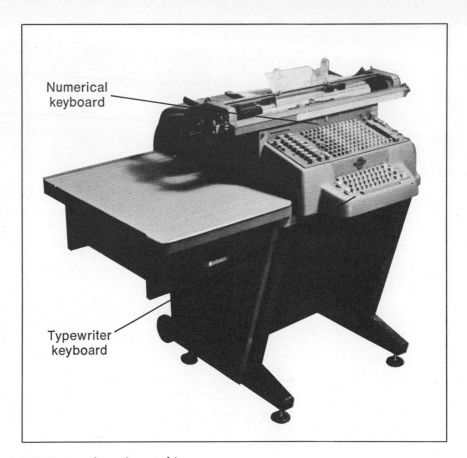

Numerical keyboard

Typewriter keyboard

FIGURE 12-8   A posting machine

1. The operator pulls the customer ledger card and monthly statement for the invoice to be posted from a file, usually some sort of tub file.
2. The operator inserts the ledger and the statement into the posting machine so that they overlay the journal as in figure 12-9. The posting machine normally has an adjustable chute, making it relatively easy to insert the documents. Since the documents are carbon-backed, any data recorded on the statement is also recorded on the ledger and the journal.
3. The operator keys the old balance read from the customer statement onto the numeric keyboard, thus entering it into one of the machine's counters and printing it in the lefthand column of the journal. Then, the machine automatically skips to the date column, prints the date, and skips to the reference-number column.
4. The operator keys the invoice number, which prints in the reference-number column.

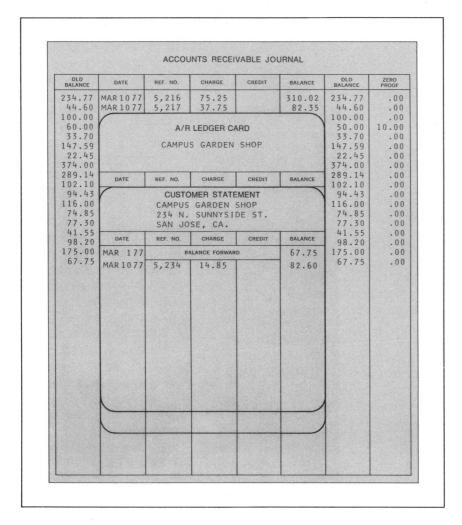

ACCOUNTS RECEIVABLE JOURNAL

OLD BALANCE	DATE	REF. NO.	CHARGE	CREDIT	BALANCE	OLD BALANCE	ZERO PROOF
234.77	MAR 10 77	5,216	75.25		310.02	234.77	.00
44.60	MAR 10 77	5,217	37.75		82.35	44.60	.00
100.00						100.00	.00
60.00						50.00	10.00
33.70						33.70	.00
147.59						147.59	.00
22.45						22.45	.00
374.00						374.00	.00
289.14						289.14	.00
102.10						102.10	.00
94.43						94.43	.00
116.00						116.00	.00
74.85						74.85	.00
77.30						77.30	.00
41.55						41.55	.00
98.20						98.20	.00
175.00	MAR 1 77		BALANCE FORWARD		67.75	175.00	.00
67.75	MAR 10 77	5,234	14.85		82.60	67.75	.00

A/R LEDGER CARD

CAMPUS GARDEN SHOP

CUSTOMER STATEMENT

CAMPUS GARDEN SHOP
234 N. SUNNYSIDE ST.
SAN JOSE, CA.

FIGURE 12-9 Alignment of documents in the posting machine

5. The operator then keys the invoice amount, which prints in the charge column and is entered into one of the machine's counters. This amount is automatically added to the daily total of charges in one of the counters and is automatically added to the old balance to derive the new balance. The machine then skips to the balance column and prints the new balance.

6. The operator keys the old balance again as a check on accuracy. The machine prints this amount in the second old-balance column, subtracts the second old balance from the first old balance to derive an amount called the *zero proof,* and prints the zero proof in the

zero-proof column. If the operator has keyed the old balance the same both times, the zero proof will be zero, thus indicating that the old balance has been keyed correctly.

7. The operator removes the ledger and the statement from the machine and returns them to the file.

The operator continues in this way until all of the charges for the day have been posted. Then, the operator aligns the machine at the charge column and presses a key that causes the final total of charges to print. At this time, the journal is used for balancing to controls. If the total charges balance to the total charges on the control sheet, all the amounts have been recorded correctly. If all zero proofs are zero, all old balances have been recorded correctly, so the new balances must be correct also.

A posting machine can also be used for other operations such as posting vendor charges to accounts payable or posting daily sales to salesman ledger cards. In addition, a posting machine can be used for summarizing expense or sales data. The document in figure 12-10, for example, is used to distribute sales into various categories. One line is recorded on the document for each invoice. Each of the amounts recorded in item classes 1 through 7 represents one line item of billing. Because a separate counter is used to total each column, the posting machine automatically prints the final total for each class at the bottom of the document. Because the number of counters available on a posting machine is limited, the number of classifications that can be used for summarizing data is also limited.

The automatic operations that a posting machine does—such as skipping, adding, and subtracting—are controlled in several different ways, depending on the machine model used. Two of the most common control mechanisms are the control bar and the control panel. These mechanisms are set up by the manufacturer's representative for each job the posting-machine user intends to do. Before each job, the operator inserts the appropriate bar or panel for the job to be done. Regardless of the mechanism used, transition from one job to another is accomplished in a short period of time, usually less than a minute.

The *billing machine*, which looks and operates much like a posting machine, can multiply and sometimes divide. When used in a billing operation, the operator uses the typewriter keyboard to type the heading of the invoice. Some heading data, such as the date and invoice number, can be made to print automatically from the storage units of the machine. For each line item, the opereator keys the quantity and unit price on the numeric keyboard, thus storing the data in counters. For item description and item number, the operator uses the typewriter keyboard. At the end of each line item, the machine automatically calculates the extension, prints it, and adds it to the invoice total. When all line items have been printed, the operator positions the machine at the total line, pushes a control button, and the invoice total is printed. Because one counter is

SALES SUMMARY

REF. NO.	TOTAL BILLED	ITEM CLASS 1	ITEM CLASS 2	ITEM CLASS 3	ITEM CLASS 4	ITEM CLASS 5	ITEM CLASS 6	ITEM CLASS 7
5,445	39.95	24.00		10.00				5.95
5,446	110.00					106.90	3.10	
5,447	40.00		40.00					
5,448	82.12		59.00		3.12		20.00	
5,449	31.00							31.00
5,450	173.90	112.00		2.90		40.00		19.00
5,451	12.00		12.00					
5,452	64.00			14.00	50.00			
TOTALS	552.97	136.00	111.00	26.90	53.12	146.90	23.10	55.95

Note: All totals are accumulated and printed out automatically.

FIGURE 12-10   Sales summary prepared by a posting machine

used to accumulate the invoice totals, the billing total for the day can be printed at the end of the job. If desired, hash totals of quantities and item numbers can also be accumulated during the operation and printed at the end of the job.

Because of its calculating ability, the billing machine is also used for operations such as writing paychecks and calculating commission amounts. In addition, it can be used for many of the jobs done by a posting machine. Some billing machines are equipped with features that allow them to do billing and posting to accounts receivable in a single operation. After the invoice total is printed, the machine skips to the statement, ledger, and journal, and prints the date, invoice number, and charge amount automatically. This eliminates a second keying of these data items during the posting operation. Posting then proceeds as if a posting machine were being used.

Posting and billing machines are continually being improved; they are being made quieter, with more efficient keyboards, with more electronic and fewer mechanical parts, and with more automatic operations, thus allowing more operations to be combined. Nevertheless, the speed and accuracy of these machines depend to a large extent on the operator, who can still misfile ledgers, key amounts incorrectly, and type addresses wrong. And one operator is still able to do far more work on her billing machine than another operator is able to do on hers. As a result, much of what has been said so far about the accuracy, speed, and information of manual procedures remains true as mechanical devices are incorporated into a system. In particular, checking and control balancing are an important part of any manual or mechanical procedure; the cost of error correction is likely to be relatively high; and the preparation of management information is likely to be time consuming and expensive.

DISCUSSION

Although some of the limitations of manual and mechanical procedures have been pointed out in this chapter, it does not mean that computer systems are right for all businesses. On the contrary, because of cost, manual and mechanical procedures are right for many thousands of small companies and for many operations within the largest of companies. Furthermore, it is very likely that these procedures can be improved without moving from manual procedures to a computer system. Thus, a business that is large enough to have significant data-processing problems should consider revising existing procedures at the same time that they consider installing a computer. It may well be that a procedure revision is a more profitable alternative than installing a computer system.

In general, there are four ways of improving the efficiency of paperwork procedures. After charting the procedures so that they can be analyzed, each of the following changes should be considered:

1. Eliminating a step.
2. Combining two or more steps.
3. Changing the sequence of two or more steps.
4. Installing office equipment to help improve the efficiency of one or more steps.

For example, steps 3 and 4 of figure 12-3 could perhaps be combined for greater efficiency. Or steps 2 through 5 of figure 12-4 could be replaced by a posting-machine operation. Because most office procedures have evolved, rather than being carefully planned, it is common during analysis to discover documents that are no longer being used, steps that can be eliminated, and operations that long ago should have been combined. As a result, it is not unreasonable to expect a significant improvement in paperwork procedures by a careful analysis and revision of existing procedures.

In discussing manual procedures, one question worth considering is why consumers have become so critical of computerized billing. In view of the likelihood of errors and delays in noncomputerized systems, it seems unfair. The major criticism, however, seems to be that it is more difficult to get an error corrected on a computer-printed bill. In a 1971 survey, for example, 24 percent of the people interviewed said that they had had trouble getting computerized billing errors corrected. The question is why?

With this chapter as background, it is easy to see how noncomputerized errors can be corrected. For instance, if a company uses a posting machine for accounts receivable, a customer-service clerk can check the invoice in question, verify or deny the error by checking the source documents involved, and fill out the appropriate error-adjustment form. Then, the next time transactions are posted to accounts receivable records, the adjustment is posted and the error is corrected.

But why can't this be done on a computer system as well? Source documents and invoices copies are kept in computer systems just as they are in other systems. In addition, cash-receipt and invoice registers are available to help trace an error. Thus, it should be easy to determine whether an error has occurred. And if so, after the adjustment form is completed, the correction data can be keypunched and processed, and the error should be corrected.

Apparently, though, many correction procedures in computerized billing systems are poorly designed and controlled. As a result, it often takes two (or more) letters or calls to get a computer error corrected. In extreme cases, the correspondence between consumer and company has gone on for months. Although the final blame, it seems, has always fallen on the computer system, it is of course the computer system design that should be blamed.

If the ledger-card system has an advantage over the computer system, it is the fact that all of a customer's past transactions are recorded on a single document, the ledger card. When a company moves to a computer sytem, this document is no longer prepared. Although the information recorded on the ledger card can be found on other documents prepared by the computer system—such as various registers and reports—the one-time ledger-card user often feels that he has lost a valuable source of information. "The information that I used to be able to find out in five minutes now takes two weeks."

Although this typical complaint is unfounded since the information can actually be found in a reasonably short period of time, the complaint should not be dismissed lightly. At the least, it indicates the resistance to new methods and the need for the retraining of personnel. Furthermore, there is no question that for some types of information searches, it is easier to consult one ledger card than to search through a series of documents. From a profit-making point of view, however, the speed, accuracy, and information capabilities of the computer system should more than offset the disadvantages resulting from the lost ledger card.

SUMMARY

1. Although speed and accuracy can be achieved using manual procedures, delays, errors, and costly error corrections are likely if procedures aren't well-planned and controlled. The major limitation of manual procedures, however, is the limited information capability.

2. There are many varieties of office equipment and machines to help improve the speed and accuracy of manual procedures. Four office machines in common use are the adding machine, the posting machine, the calculator, and the billing machine.

3. Because office procedures are often developed without overall planning, it is reasonable to expect a significant improvement in performance as a result of procedure analysis and revision. Four possibilities to consider are (1) eliminating a step, (2) combining steps, (3) resequencing steps, and (4) installing office equipment.

TERMINOLOGY

procedure chart
journal
pegboard
writing board
tub file

visible-record file
posting machine
counter
zeroproof
billing machine

QUESTIONS

1. Suppose a company does around 1000 line items of billing per day. Is it possible for the billing system charted in figure 12-1 to be faster than a computerized billing system? By faster we mean having less elapsed time between receipt of order and mailing of invoice. If it is possible, explain how.

2. One time a collections manager told me that their receivables system had almost perfect accuracy. He also said that he doubted that a computerized system could improve its accuracy. The system they used was a ledger card system with posting done by a posting machine. Do you think he was right? Explain.

3. An inventory control manager for a wholesale distributor once told me she was getting all the information she needed from their control system. It was a manual posting system using inventory ledger cards in a visible-record filing device. If the company had 2500 different inventory items, do you think she was correct? Discuss.

13 PUNCHED-CARD SYSTEMS

Punched-card systems date back to the late 1800s, when Dr. Herman Hollerith invented the punched card and a number of punched-card machines. Until the computer was commercially marketed in the 1950s, punched-card systems were used in thousands of businesses—both large and small. It was commonplace, in fact, for a large company to use dozens and even hundreds of punched-card machines in a punched-card system—for example, forty-five keypunches, twenty-six verifiers, eight sorters, and so on.

Today, the punched-card system has been replaced by the computer in all but the very small companies. In addition, the price of small computers continues to drop so the number of punched-card systems in use should continue to drop. Thus, this chapter is primarily of historical interest. It may be many years before the punched-card system disappears altogether—it is still in use in thousands of businesses—but there is no question that the punched card system will become obsolete. Consequently, this chapter is but a brief introduction to the nature of the punched-card system.

PUNCHED-CARD MACHINES

In chapter 2, you were introduced to two of the punched-card machines, the keypunch and the verifier. Then chapter 5 presented the characteristics of the 80-column card and the card sorter. If you haven't read this material, please do so before continuing with this chapter.

The keypunch, verifier, and sorter are essential to all punched-card systems, since all such systems record source data in punched cards and sort these cards into acceptable sequences for processing. In addition, however, there are several other punched-card machines; specifically, the collator, the interpreter, the reproducer, the calculator, and the accounting machine. All of these machines are controlled by wired control panels that are inserted into the control-panel housing before a job is run.

Punched-card systems can be made up of a few or many machines. The simplest punched-card system, for example, consists of a keypunch, a sorter, and an accounting machine. On the other hand, a punched-card system might consist of all of the machines mentioned above, including more than one keypunch and verifier. Because this chapter is but an introduction to punched-card systems, only the calculator and accounting machine will be described before presenting a simple billing procedure using punched-card machines.

The Calculator

The *calculator,* shown in figure 13-1, has one hopper and one stacker. This machine can add, subtract, multiply, and sometimes divide; and it can perform a series of these calculations on a deck of cards in a single

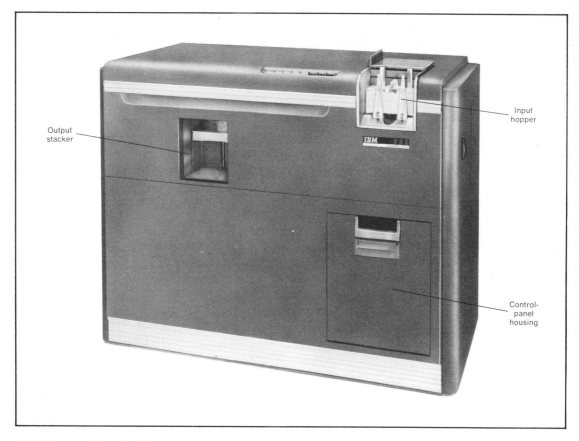

Output stacker

Input hopper

Control-panel housing

FIGURE 13-1   The calculator

pass through the machine. Calculations are performed on the input fields of one or more cards, and the results are punched into other fields of the same cards or other cards.

Although it is difficult to describe the exact capabilities of a calculator without getting into a lengthy explanation, a typical operation is illustrated in figure 13-2. Here, the calculator is used to extend costs and prices in a billing application. In a single pass of the cards through the machine, the calculator does the following:

1. Multiplies unit price by quantity, giving total price.
2. Multiplies unit cost by quantity, giving total cost.
3. Subtracts total cost from total price, giving gross profit.

The result fields—total cost, total price, and gross profit—are punched in the same card from which quantity, unit cost, and unit price were read.

Because of its ability to do a series of calculations in a single operation, the calculator is very useful in a payroll application. In a typical system,

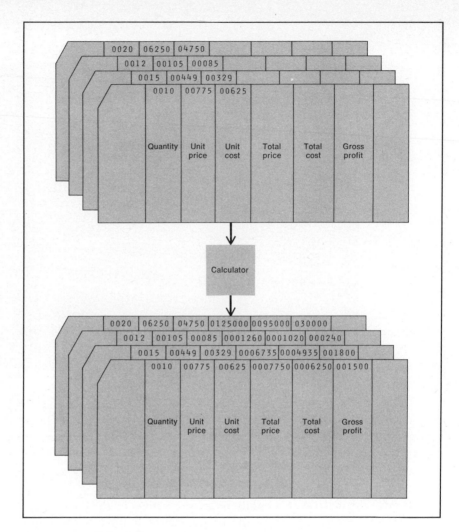

FIGURE 13-2 Calculating

employee earnings and year-to-date cards are passed through the calculator several times to derive gross pay, federal tax, social security tax,
state tax (if any), and net pay. Note, however, that the calculator cannot
print results; it can only punch them so that they can be printed by the
accounting machine.

The Accounting Machine

The *accounting machine,* shown in figure 13-3, reads an input deck and
prints on continuous-form output documents. By using a forms-control

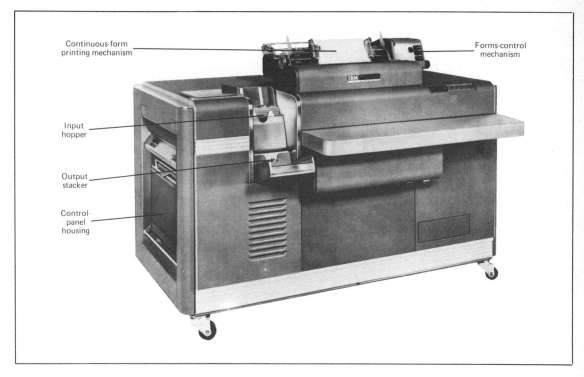

FIGURE 13-3   The accounting machine

tape similar to that used on printers of computer systems, the accounting machine is able to skip to appropriate parts of a form before printing a line. However, because the accounting machine is normally limited to printing one line per card, it by no means has the printing flexibility of a computer system. In addition, some models of the accounting machine can print only numeric data in positions after print position 44; some models cannot print decimal points or commas so, as shown in figure 13-4, a vertical line must be used on the output document to indicate the location of the decimal point.

Unlike the computer system, the accounting machine has limited arithmetic capabilities—it can only add or subtract—and it must process data in a rigidly prescribed way. In general, there are two types of documents that can be printed by the accounting machine, examples of which are given in figure 13-4. The first type of document, called a *detail-printed report* or *document,* consists of one output line for each input card. In addition, totals can be accumulated for selected fields of the input cards, and then printed when the number in the control field changes or after the last card has been processed. In contrast, the second type of document, called a *group-printed report* or *document,* consists of

SALES BY ITEM		
SHEET 2 OF 4		MONTH OF AUGUST

ITEM NO.	ITEM DESCRIPTION	SALES
11202	SQ SHANK SWIVEL	1349 20
11202	SQ SHANK SWIVEL	101 88
11202	SQ SHANK SWIVEL	250 00
11202	SQ SHANK SWIVEL	378 90
11202	SQ SHANK SWIVEL	2345 00
11202	SQ SHANK SWIVEL	221 25
11202	SQ SHANK SWIVEL	270 90
		4917 23 ✻
15102	CUSTOM BUILT	488 75
15102	CUSTOM BUILT	690 50
15102	CUSTOM BUILT	2890 00
15102	CUSTOM BUILT	2 80
		4072 05 ✻
16115	SQ SOCKET RIGID	112 50

DETAIL-PRINTED REPORT

SALES BY ITEM		
SHEET 2 OF 2		MONTH OF AUGUST

ITEM NO.	ITEM DESCRIPTION	SALES
11202	SQ SHANK SWIVEL	4916 23
15102	CUSTOM BUILT	4072 05
16115	SQ SOCKET RIGID	4981 42
17203	EXT SHANK WITH BRK	32 90
21103	SQ SHANK RIGID	6235 70
23302	EXTENSION SHANK	325 90
23702	ADJ ADAPTER SQUARE	4610 20
26104	HEX SOCKET RIGID	3995 76
26302	SQ SOCKET SWIVEL	4376 30
33202	FLAT TOP SWIVEL	563 70
33205	ROUND TOP SWIVEL	401 66
35105	HEX SHANK RIGID	3 81

GROUP-PRINTED REPORT

FIGURE 13-4   Detail- and group-printed reports

one summary line for each group of related input cards. Like the detail-printed document, this type of document may or may not have totals at the end of the report.

The Wired Control Panel

A wired control panel for an accounting machine is shown in figure 13-5. As you can see, the panel consists of dozens of little holes into which control wires are plugged. Because hundreds of wires are likely to be used for a simple accounting machine job, panel wiring can be a tedious and time-consuming job. For example, it may take two or three days to

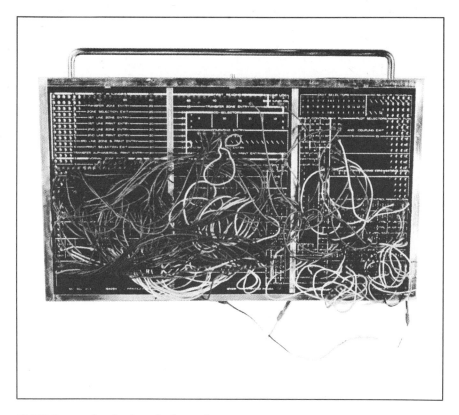

FIGURE 13-5   A wired control panel

wire and test a panel for a billing job. Although control panels for other machines are smaller, wiring can still be time consuming. Once wired and tested, of course, the panels are stored in panel racks, ready for use.

THE PUNCHED-CARD SYSTEM

To illustrate the design of a punched-card system, suppose a system consisting of a keypunch, a verifier, a sorter, a calculator, and an accounting machine is going to be used in a billing application. The flowchart in figure 13-6, then, represents the steps required to prepare invoices from shipping orders after they have been returned from the shipping department. The required card layouts are given in figure 13-7.

After control totals are accumulated and recorded in step 1, miscellaneous and item cards are keypunched and verified. The miscellaneous cards contain the data relating to the individual orders; the item cards contain the data pertinent to each line item of billing. Columns 1–64 are keypunched, and column 80 receives an X-punch whenever a line item is back-ordered.

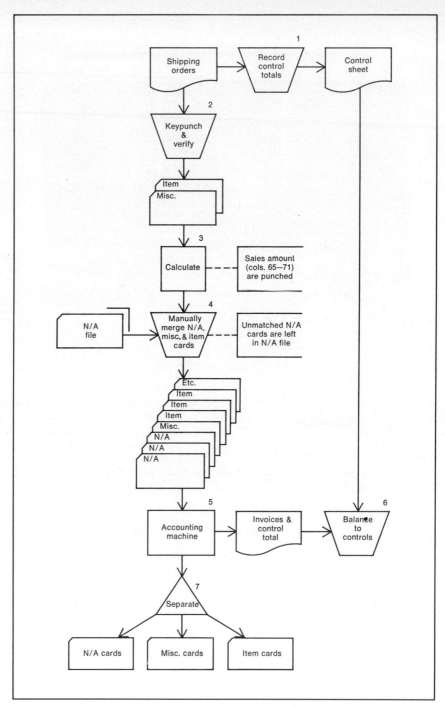

FIGURE 13-6 Flowchart for a billing system using the keypunch, verifier, sorter, calculator, and accounting machine

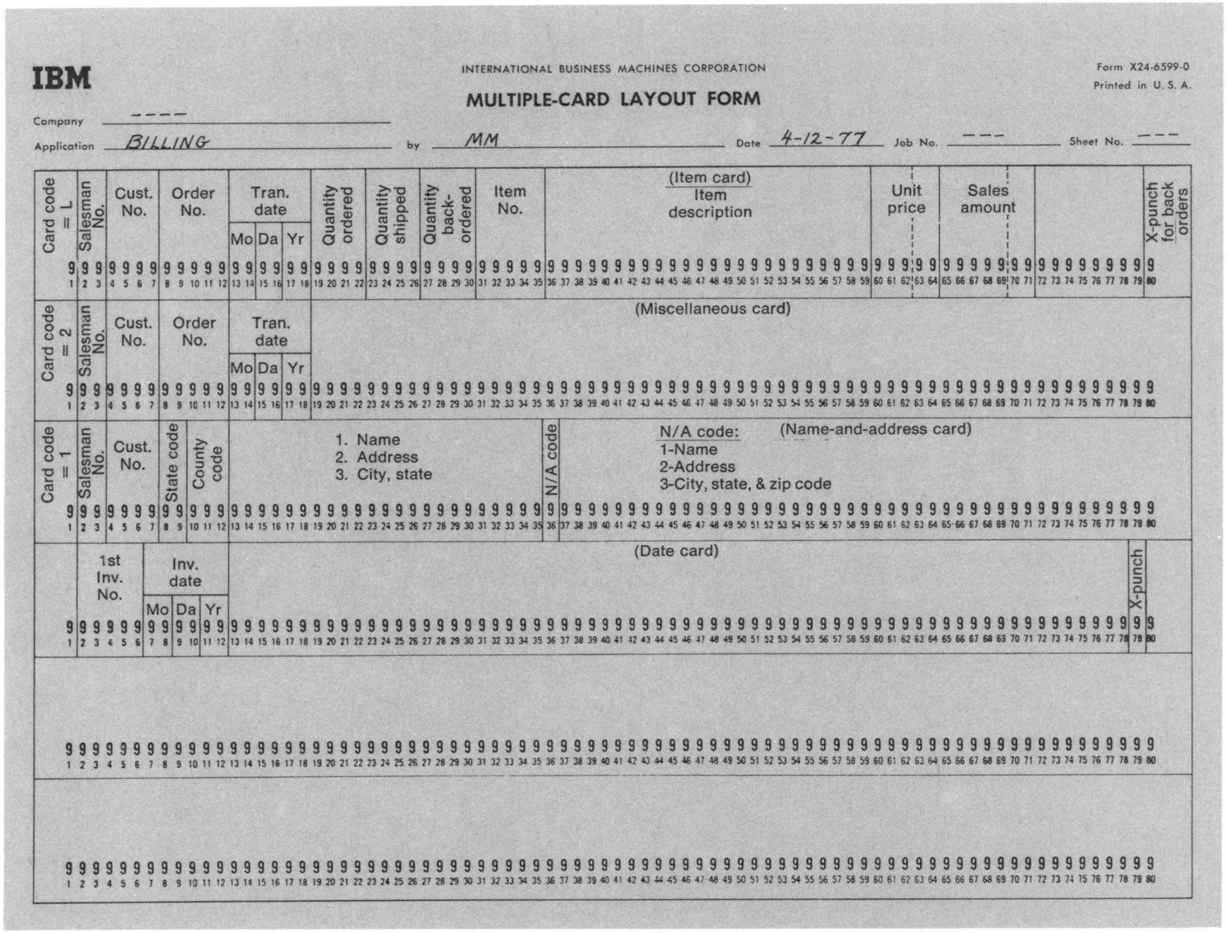

FIGURE 13-7 Card layouts for the billing application.

In step 3, the calculator extends the line items and punches the extensions in the sales-amount fields. Because the miscellaneous cards do not have an X-punch in column 1 but the item cards do (an L is the combination of an X-punch and a 3-punch), the calculator can be wired to ignore the miscellaneous cards. This makes it unnecessary to remove the miscellaneous cards from the deck before the calculating run.

In step 4, a clerk inserts the proper name-and-address (N/A) cards before the miscellaneous and item cards for each invoice. If a collator were available, this could be done by machine rather than manually. This step cannot be done on a sorter, however, since unmatched N/A cards must be removed from the deck prior to the invoicing run. Unlike the computer, the accounting machine cannot be wired to ignore un-matched master cards in a deck.

In step 5, the invoices are prepared as illustrated schematically in figure 13-8. Before putting the invoicing deck in the hopper of the accounting machine, a date card must be placed at the front of the deck so that the date and invoice number can be stored in counters and printed on each invoice. As each invoice is printed, the accounting machine will increase the invoice number by one. Note that, with the exception of the total line, there is one input card for each line that is printed on the invoice. Note also that decimal points and commas are not printed by the accounting machine. The only mathematical operation performed by the accounting machine is the addition required in deriving the invoice total and the control total of invoiced amounts for the day. After billing, control totals are balanced, the cards are separated by a sorter, and the cards are returned to files.

Although this has been only a brief introduction to punched-card systems, you can probably see their basic characteristics. First, the required data is punched into cards using machines like a keypunch or calculator. Second, the decks are arranged in proper sequence, either manually or by using a sorter. Finally, the accounting machine is used to print the documents required by the system.

In a larger punched-card system, the reproducer, collator, and inter-preter might be used in conjunction with the sorter, calculator, and accounting machine. In brief, the reproducer can punch data from one card or deck of cards into another card or card deck; the collator can merge two decks of cards while selecting out unmatched transaction or master cards; and the interpreter can print punched-card data on the front or back of the card. As a result, these machines don't alter the basic concepts described in this chapter. They simply provide other means for punching data, arranging decks, and printing results.

DISCUSSION

To appreciate why punched-card systems were replaced by computer systems, you need to consider the speed, accuracy, and information

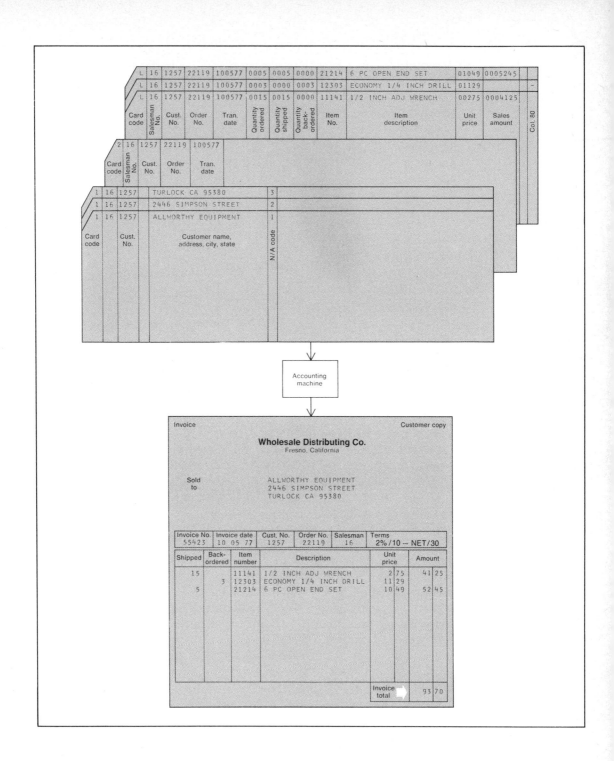

FIGURE 13-8   A billing operation on the accounting machine

capability for the punched-card system relative to the computer system. On the other hand, many small businesses have replaced manual or mechanical procedures with small punched-card systems. To appreciate why, you must again consider speed, accuracy, and information.

The speed of an accounting machine is normally between 50 and 150 cards per minute, depending on the model. Other punched-card machines—in particular, the calculator—may run even slower. For example, a calculator doing a state tax calculation may operate at a speed of 25 cards per minute or less. In comparison to small computer systems that print at 350 lines per minute and do calculations in milliseconds, this is of course quite slow. In addition, because of the many different steps required by a punched-card system, card handling by the machine operator is likely to slow down processing.

For two reasons, a punched-card system is likely to be less accurate than a computer system. First, because of the large amount of card handling required by the punched-card system, the chance of operator error—for example, leaving one transaction card in a sorter—is increased. Second, because punched-card machines are mechanical, it is possible for a machine malfunction to cause an error on an output document. For instance, a faulty punch die on a calculator could mean a punching error; a faulty counter on a calculator or accounting machine could mean an error in addition; a faulty printing mechanism on an accounting machine could mean a printing error. Although both of these types of errors are likely to be caught by various operating techniques, by document inspection, or by balancing to controls, some errors will slip through the system, and, at the least, the error-correction procedures will slow down the system.

As for information, you must consider the arithmetic and logic limitations of a punched-card system in comparison to those of a computer system. The calculations that can be done by an accounting machine or a calculator are decidedly limited. An accounting machine can only add and subtract, and a calculator is limited, at most, to a few dozen operations in sequence. As a result, calculating the economic order quantity for an inventory item or the standard deviation of its demand is beyond the capabilities of a punched-card system. And simpler calculations such as determining the efficiency percentage of a factory worker or the percent of actual to budgeted costs for a financial report, though possible to perform, often require enough additional machine time to be impractical. In contrast, a computer can do a lengthy series of calculations in a fraction of a second.

Similarly, the logic capabilities of a punched-card system are limited. Unlike a computer, the accounting machine cannot operate on different input records in totally different ways. Instead, all input records are processed using the same sequence of operations. Although the accounting machine can vary calculations and printing based on control punches in input cards and on the results of calculations (plus, minus, or zero), the variations are limited. In general, the options are to print a field in one group of print positions or another group; to not print the field; to add a field to, or subtract it from, one counter or another; or to not add or subtract it. One result of this fixed sequence of processing operations is that the accounting machine has only two options with regard to report format—group printing and detail printing. Because of these arithmetic and logic limitations, many forms of reports are difficult or impossible to prepare on a punched-card system.

In summary, the punched-card system is relatively slow, inaccurate, and has limited information capabilities when compared to a computer system. But, bear in mind that it's all relative. While 50 lines per minute may seem slow to the computer user, it is extremely fast compared to a typist. So, if an accounting machine turned out 3000 line items of billing in two hours, the users of the system were often well-pleased.

Similarly, the punched-card system is likely to be extremely accurate in comparison to manual or mechanical procedures. Because verified data is processed by machines rather than people and because control totals are automatically accumulated and printed, there is relatively little opportunity for error. In fact, it has often been the case that the installation of a punched-card system uncovered a large number of errors that went undetected by the paperwork procedures previously used.

As for information preparation, the punched-card system has a clear advantage over paperwork procedures. As in the computer system, information is an automatic by-product of other punched-card procedures. Once punched and verified, transaction data can be repeatedly processed by the punched-card machines to prepare a wide variety of management reports. The accounting machine, in fact, is designed to summarize data into reports. While these reports may seem unsophisticated to the computer user, they are quite elaborate to the user of a non-automated system.

SUMMARY

1. A punched-card system can consist of either a few machines or dozens of machines. In general, the keypunch, reproducer, and calculator are used to punch data into cards. Then, the sorter and collator are used to arrange decks into desired sequences for processing by the accounting machine.

2. Although the punched-card system may seem limited in comparison to the modern computer system, its previous importance should not be forgotten. For many years, the punched-card system was the most sophisticated method of processing data. The speed, accuracy, and

information that the punched-card system provided surpassed that of any alternative method of processing.

TERMINOLOGY

punched-card system
calculator
accounting machine
detail-printed report
group-printed report

QUESTIONS

1. How could you prepare monthly sales-by-salesman and sales-by-customer reports using the item cards prepared by the system in figure 13-6? Flowchart your procedures, using the sorter and accounting machine.

2. If you have already covered chapter 5, compare the punched-card billing system in figure 13-6 with the card computer system in figure 5-13. What differences do you see in these systems that would affect speed and accuracy? Also, how do you think increases in billing volume would affect each of these systems?

14 CPU CONCEPTS

There is certainly a question as to how much a programmer should be taught about the internal operation of a computer—particularly, in an introductory course. Theoretically, if a programmer is using a high-level language such as COBOL or FORTRAN, he doesn't need to know anything about internal computer operations. However, a basic understanding of the hardware characteristics of a computer will probably help in writing and debugging high-level language programs more efficiently.

This same question applies to system analysts and businesspeople: How much should they be taught about internal computer operations? Although the analyst is likely to require a certain amount of technical CPU knowledge for one project or another, such knowledge is irrelevant to those in business.

This chapter, then, presents some of the basic concepts and terminology that you would be likely to encounter as a programmer or analyst. The first topic includes an explanation of how data is stored within a typical computer and presents some common instructions used by it. The second topic considers the difficulty of drawing conclusions based on comparisons of hardware characteristics. Finally, the overlap of CPU operations with I/O operations is explained in the third topic.

TOPIC 1
STORAGE
ORGANIZATION AND
INSTRUCTION SETS

Each storage position in a computer is made up of a number of electronic components. These are called *binary components,* because they can be switched to either of two conditions. The two conditions are commonly referred to as "on" and "off."

The most commonly used storage component is the *magnetic core.* These tiny, doughnut-shaped components can be magnetized in either of two directions: clockwise or counterclockwise. When magnetized in one direction, a core is said to be *on;* when magnetized in the other direction, a core is said to be *off.* A string of cores makes up one storage position in a computer, and thousands of cores in planes make up a computer's storage. Because most storage consists of magnetic cores, you will often hear it referred to as *core storage.*

In order to represent data, the individual cores at a storage position are turned on or off in selected combinations by wires that run through the center of the cores. Each combination of on and off cores represents a digit or digits, a letter, or a special character. Figure 14-1, for example, might represent three storage positions of eight cores each. By decoding the combination at each storage position, it might be determined that the

FIGURE 14-1   Core storage

characters B, 2, and 9 are represented. (The shaded cores are on, and the white cores are off.)

Because the codes of a computer are represented by binary components, the *binary digits* 0 and 1 can be used to represent a binary code. If 1 is used to represent an on-core and 0 is used to represent an off-core, 11000010 represents the first string of cores in figure 14-1. Since a binary digit is referred to as a *bit* (a contraction of binary digit), magnetic cores are often called bits.

In some of the more recent computer systems, transistor-like solid materials—not magnetic cores—are used as the binary components.

Regardless of the components used, however, the principles are the same. A fixed number of binary components make up one storage position, and one or more storage positions represent one field in storage.

STORAGE ORGANIZATION

So you can appreciate the storage characteristics of an actual computer system, let's consider the System/360-370 in detail. It is the most widely used computer system, and it can operate on four different forms of data. Once you understand its data formats, it should be easy for you to understand the organization of other computers.

To begin with, each storage position of the System/360-370 is called a *byte* of data. Furthermore, this byte, and thus the storage position itself, is made up of nine bits—eight data bits plus one *parity bit*. The parity bit is used as a check on operations that take place within the CPU. Each time that a byte of data is moved into or out of storage during the execution of a program, the byte is *parity checked*. That is, the number of on-bits in the byte is checked to make sure that it is an odd number. If the number of on-bits is even, as in the code 011110011, an error is indicated and the system stops executing the program.

The parity bit at a storage position in the System/360-370 is used to make the on-bits for any bit combination odd in number. As a result, the complete code for the letter A is 011000001, where the leftmost bit is the parity bit and the eight rightmost bits are the data bits. Similarly, the complete code for the number 9 is 111111001, where the leftmost bit has been turned on to make the number of on-bits odd.

As mentioned earlier, there are four forms in which data can be stored in the System/360-370. Three of these are covered in this topic; they are *EBCDIC, packed decimal,* and *fixed-point binary* (or just *binary*). The fourth form, which is less frequently used and thus is not presented in this book, is called *floating-point binary.*

Regardless of the form of the data, the parity bit is used in each byte of storage. However, it is usually ignored when discussing specific codes or storage forms. For instance, the System/360-370 is usually said to have an 8-bit, rather than a 9-bit, byte. Consequently, no further mention of parity checking will be made in this chapter. After all, parity checking is simply an electronic check on the accuracy of internal operations.

Because it is difficult and awkward for a person to work with binary codes, *hexadecimal* notation is commonly used to represent the contents of System/360-370 storage. As a method of shorthand, the intent of hexadecimal is to replace a group of four binary digits with one hexadecimal character. Figure 14-2 shows the relationship between binary, decimal, and hexadecimal notation. Thus the binary 1111 is written as F in hexadecimal (or *hex*); the binary 1001 is a hex 9; and the binary 0110 is a hex 6.

Decimal	Binary	Hexadecimal
0	0000	0
1	0001	1
2	0010	2
3	0011	3
4	0100	4
5	0101	5
6	0110	6
7	0111	7
8	1000	8
9	1001	9
10	1010	A
11	1011	B
12	1100	C
13	1101	D
14	1110	E
15	1111	F
16	10000	10

FIGURE 14-2   Hexadecimal chart

EBCDIC

In EBCDIC code (pronounced eé-beé-dick or iɓ-si-dick), each byte of storage contains one character of data. Because eight bits can be arranged in 256 different combinations, 256 characters could be coded in EBCDIC. As a result, EBCDIC can be used to represent the letters of the alphabet (both upper- and lower-case), the decimal digits, and many special characters. However, not all of the 256 combinations are used.

Figure 14-3 gives the EBCDIC codes for the more commonly used characters. This table shows the binary bode, the punched-card code, and the hexadecimal code for each character. As indicated by the table, it is common to divide an EBCDIC code into two halves; the four leftmost bits representing the *zone bits* and the four rightmost bits representing the *digit bits*. When this is done, you can see a relationship between EBCDIC and the punched-card code that is described in chapter 5. For letters and numbers, the zone bits 1100 or hex C correspond to a 12-punch; the bits 1101 or hex D to an 11-punch; the bits 1110 or hex E to a 0-punch; and 1111 or hex F to no zone punch.

The digit bits correspond even more closely to the card punches. For example, hex 0 corresponds to a 0-punch, hex 1 to a 1-punch, and hex 9 to a 9-punch.

For special characters, other zone-bit combinations are used. Thus, 01011011 is used for the dollar sign ($) and 01001101 for the left parenthesis. Although it is sometimes helpful for a programmer to know the EBCDIC codes for numbers and letters, decoding special characters is usually unnecessary. However, if it is required, the codes can be looked up easily in a reference table such as the one in figure 14-3.

Character	EBCDIC		Punched Card Code	Hexadecimal Code
	Zone Bits	Digit Bits		
.	0100	1011	12–3–8	4B
(	0100	1101	12–5–8	4D
+	0100	1110	12–6–8	4E
&	0101	0000	12	50
$	0101	1011	11–3–8	5B
*	0101	1100	11–4–8	5C
)	0101	1101	11–5–8	5D
;	0101	1110	11–6–8	5E
-	0110	0000	11	60
/	0110	0001	0–1	61
,	0110	1011	0–3–8	6B
%	0110	1100	0–4–8	6C
?	0110	1111	0–7–8	6F
#	0111	1011	3–8	7B
'	0111	1101	5–8	7D
=	0111	1110	6–8	7E
''	0111	1111	7–8	7F
A	1100	0001	12–1	C1
B	1100	0010	12–2	C2
C	1100	0011	12–3	C3
D	1100	0100	12–4	C4
E	1100	0101	12–5	C5
F	1100	0110	12–6	C6
G	1100	0111	12–7	C7
H	1100	1000	12–8	C8
I	1100	1001	12–9	C9
J	1101	0001	11–1	D1
K	1101	0010	11–2	D2
L	1101	0011	11–3	D3
M	1101	0100	11–4	D4
N	1101	0101	11–5	D5
O	1101	0110	11–6	D6
P	1101	0111	11–7	D7
Q	1101	1000	11–8	D8
R	1101	1001	11–9	D9
S	1110	0010	0–2	E2
T	1110	0011	0–3	E3
U	1110	0100	0–4	E4
V	1110	0101	0–5	E5
W	1110	0110	0–6	E6
X	1110	0111	0–7	E7
Y	1110	1000	0–8	E8
Z	1110	1001	0–9	E9
0	1111	0000	0	F0
1	1111	0001	1	F1
2	1111	0010	2	F2
3	1111	0011	3	F3
4	1111	0100	4	F4
5	1111	0101	5	F5
6	1111	0110	6	F6
7	1111	0111	7	F7
8	1111	1000	8	F8
9	1111	1001	9	F9

FIGURE 14-3   EBCDIC coding

To represent EBCDIC data in storage, hex can be used as in this example:

E2 C1 D4 40 40 40 40 40 40 40

Here, the name SAM is stored in ten bytes. (Hex 40 represents a blank.) Similarly, a six-byte numeric EBCDIC field containing 1234 can be shown as

F0 F0 F1 F2 F3 F4

This EBCDIC form of representing numbers is often referred to as *zoned decimal*. (Notice that an alphanumeric field is normally left-justified with blanks filling out the unused bytes to the right of the data; a numeric field is normally right-justified with zeros filling out the unused bytes in the left portion of the field.)

To represent the sign of a zoned-decimal field, the zone portion of the rightmost byte of the field is used. If the zone portion of this byte is 1111 (hex F) or 1100 (hex C), the number is positive. If the zone portion is 1101 (hex D), the number is negative. Thus, a positive 1234 in four storage positions can be shown as

F1 F2 F3 C4

A negative 1234 can be shown as

F1 F2 F3 D4

Packed Decimal

In contrast to zoned decimal, packed decimal is a more compact form of System/360-370 storage. Except for the rightmost byte of a packed-decimal field, two decimal digits are stored in each eight-bit byte. The rightmost byte of a field contains a decimal digit in its zone portion and the sign of the field in its digit portion. Using hex notation, the number +12345 is stored in three bytes as follows:

12 34 5C

(Remember that either C or F is a valid sign for a positive field.) A −12345 is stored in four bytes like this:

00 12 34 5D

This illustrates that leading zeros must fill out the positions of a packed-decimal number if the number is fewer digits than the field provides for.

Packed decimal fields in hex are relatively easy to decode because the decimal digits 0 through 9 are also 0 through 9 in hex. The only problem, then, is determining the sign of the field by analyzing the digit portion of the rightmost byte of the field.

Binary

In System/360-370, two or four consecutive bytes are used for a binary field. Thus, sixteen or thirty-two bits are used to represent a binary number. The number can be converted to its decimal equivalent by assigning a *place value* to each bit. The place values start at the rightmost bit position with a value of 1 and double for each position to the left. Thus, the place values for a 32-bit binary number are 1, 2, 4, 8, 16, 32, 64, and so on, until the next to the leftmost bit, the thirty-first bit, which has a place value of 1,073,741,824. The leftmost bit is used to indicate the sign of the number—if 0, the number is positive; if 1, the number is negative. In a 16-bit binary number, fifteen bits are used for the number, while the leftmost bit indicates the sign.

To illustrate binary coding, consider the following binary number: 0010010000011011. Since the leftmost bit is 0, the number is positive. By adding the place values of the on-bits, you can determine that the decimal equivalent is 9243. The decoding process is illustrated in figure 14-4. The maximum value of a 16-bit binary number is +32,767; the maximum value of a 32-bit number is +2,147,483,647.

Using hex, the binary storage of decimal 9243 can be shown like this:

24 1B

If 9243 is stored as a four-byte binary number, it can be shown as this:

00 00 24 1B

Because negative binary numbers are not simply binary numbers with a 1-bit preceding them, you will not be able to decode negative hex

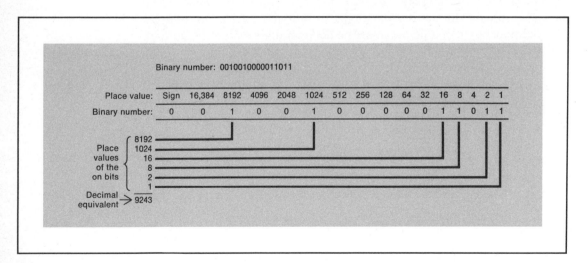

FIGURE 14-4   Fixed-point binary coding

numbers as shown in figure 14-4. Fortunately, you normally don't have to when using common business programming techniques. For the most part, then, it is enough to know that any binary number that has a 1 as its leftmost bit is a negative number.

On the System/360-370, a two-byte binary field is referred to as a *halfword* and a four-byte binary field as a *fullword.* For some conversion operations, an eight-byte field known as a *doubleword* is also used. These fields must have the proper *boundary alignment* before they can be operated upon by System/360 instructions; boundary alignment is not required by the System/370. A half-word, for example, must start at a storage address that is a multiple of two (such as address 2, 4, 6, 8, or 10). This is called a *halfword boundary.* Similarly, a fullword must start at a *fullword boundary,* an address that is a multiple of four, and a doubleword must start at a *doubleword boundary,* an address that is a multiple of eight. Figure 14-5 summarizes this terminology as applied to the first ten positions of storage.

With three different types of data representation, the number of storage positions required for a numeric field on the System/360-370 is determined by the number of digits in the field and the data format used. For example, if a field contains the number +205,597,474, it requires nine bytes of storage using zoned decimal, five bytes using packed decimal, and a fullword (four bytes) using binary. If a field consists of only one decimal digit such as +7, one byte of storage is required using zoned decimal, one byte using packed decimal, and a halfword (two bytes) using binary. Figure 14-6 summarizes these examples.

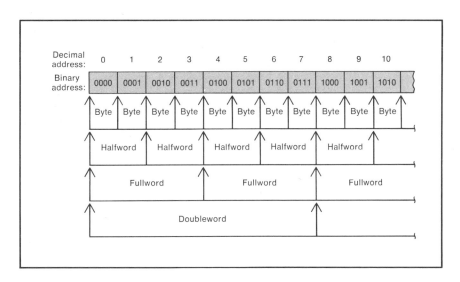

FIGURE 14-5   Storage boundaries

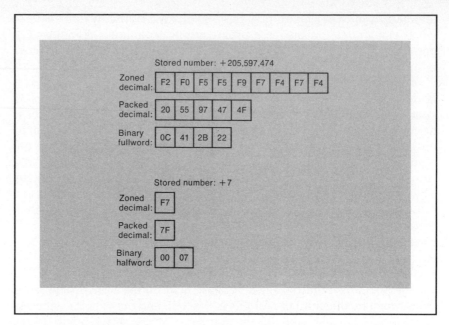

FIGURE 14-6   Storage use

INSTRUCTION FORMATS

While a program is being executed, both the instructions of the program and the data being processed are contained in storage. The instructions, in coded form, indicate the operations that are to be performed and give the addresses and lengths of the fields that are to be operated upon. In the System/360-370, instructions are two, four, or six storage positions in length depending on the function of the instruction.

To illustrate the parts of a typical instruction, consider one of the several System/360-370 move instructions. It is six bytes in length with this format:

Op code	Length factor	Address-1	Address-2
0 7	8 15	16 31	32 47

The first byte of the instruction (bits 0–7) is the operation code. There is a unique code for each of the System/360-370 instructions. For the basic move instruction, the code is 11010010, or hex D2. The second byte of the instruction (bits 8–15) is the length factor, an 8-bit binary number from 0 through 255 that indicates how many storage positions should be moved. The last four bytes represent two addresses that specify the starting locations of the fields involved in the instruction. If the length factor is a binary 9 (indicating that ten bytes should be moved), the ten bytes of data starting at the location specified as address-2 are moved to the ten bytes of storage starting at the location specified as address-1.

An address in a System/360-370 instruction is actually made up of two parts: four bits that specify a *base register* and twelve bits that represent a *displacement factor*. The base register can be any one of the sixteen *general-purpose registers* that are components of the System/360-370 CPU. These general-purpose registers consist of thirty-two bit positions—the equivalent of a fullword. When a register is used as a base register, the twenty-four rightmost bit positions are used to represent a base address, which is always a positive number. To get the actual address, the *base address* is added to the displacement factor specified in the instruction.

To be more specific, then, the format of the basic move instruction is this:

D2		L		B₁	D₁		B₂	D₂	
0	7	8	15	16 19	20	31	32 35	36	47

Here, D2 is the actual operation code in hex, L is the length factor, B1 and B2 are 4-bit binary numbers that specify one of the sixteen registers (numbered 0 through 15 or hex 0 through F), and D1 and D2 are 12-bit binary numbers that represent displacement factors.

With this background, you can understand that an instruction that moves bytes 1551–1555 to 1701–1705 might be represented in hex like this:

D20432A5320F

By breaking this down, you can determine that the operation code is D2, the number of bytes to be moved is 5 (hex 4), address-1 consists of a base address in register 3 plus a displacement of hex 2A5 (decimal 677), and address-2 consists of a base address in register 3 plus a displacement of hex 20F (decimal 527). If register 3 contains hex 400 (decimal 1024) at the time the instruction is executed, bytes 1551–1555 will be moved to bytes 1701–1705. Each time an instruction is executed, the CPU performs this type of decoding of the parts of an instruction.

Quite frankly, this is much more than a programmer needs to know about machine language. There is, however, one good reason for going into this much detail: it points out the need for symbolic languages in general and high-level languages, such as COBOL, in particular. Unlike some earlier computers, the System/360-370 machine language can't even be expressed in familiar notation. Instead, hexadecimal notation is used. As a result, programming in machine language would be a nightmare.

INSTRUCTION SET

The term *instruction set* applies to the collection of machine instructions—all valid operation codes—that a specific computer can execute. The NCR Century 100, for example, has 19 instructions in its instruction set. In contrast, the instruction set of the Control Data 3100 contains 164 different instructions. A typical System/360-370 has about 150 instructions in its instruction set.

Any computer's instruction set can be broken down into these functional groups:

1. Data-movement instructions
2. Arithmetic instructions
3. Logic instructions
4. Input/Output (I/O) instructions

To give you some appreciation of the instructions within a typical instruction set, the remainder of this topic presents examples of System/360-370 instructions in each group.

Data-Movement Instructions

Besides the basic move instruction just described, the System/360-370 has move instructions that move only the zone or digit portions of one field to another. There is also an edit instruction that can be used to zero-suppress insignificant zeros in a number and, at the same time, insert editing characters such as commas and a decimal point. For example, the packed-decimal number 0112389 can be edited as follows:

	Sending field	Receiving field
Before:	01 12 38 9C	40 20 20 6B 20 20 21 4B 20 20
After:	01 12 38 9C	40 40 F1 6B F1 F2 F3 4B F8 F9

Because the hex characters 40, 6B, and 4B are the blank, comma, and decimal point, the resulting field is equivalent to 1,123.89. Notice that the receiving field must contain certain editing characters before the edit instruction can be executed and that the sending field must be in packed-decimal format.

Other data-movement instructions convert numeric fields from one form to another. For example, the pack instruction moves and converts data from an EBCDIC field into a packed-decimal field as follows:

	Sending field	Receiving field
Before:	F1 F2 F3 F4 F5	?? ?? ??
After:	F1 F2 F3 F4 F5	12 34 5F

In contrast, the unpack instruction moves data from a sending field in packed-decimal format to a receiving field in EBCDIC format.

To convert a numeric field to and from binary format, the convert-to-binary and convert-to-decimal instructions are used. As shown in the following example, the convert-to-binary instruction moves data from a sending field in packed-decimal format to one of the sixteen general-purpose registers in binary format. The sending field must be eight bytes in length (a doubleword).

	Sending field	Receiving register
Before:	00 00 00 00 00 00 53 8C	?? ?? ?? ??
After:	00 00 00 00 00 00 53 8C	00 00 02 1A

If desired, the contents of a register can be moved to storage by using a store instruction as in this example:

	Register	Receiving field
Before:	00 00 02 1A	?? ?? ?? ??
After:	00 00 02 1A	00 00 02 1A

The load and convert-to-decimal instructions can be used to convert a field from binary to packed-decimal format. First, a binary fullword is loaded into a general register using a load instruction. Second, the contents of the register are converted to packed-decimal format and moved to a doubleword receiving field using the convert-to-decimal instruction.

Arithmetic Instructions

You may be wondering why the conversion instructions are necessary. When data is read into storage from a card, it is in the EBCDIC format. However, on the System/360-370, arithmetic can take place only on fields that are in packed-decimal or binary formats. Before the results of a calculation can be printed, they must be converted back to EBCDIC format.

When arithmetic operations are performed on packed-decimal fields, two fields are involved, with the result replacing one of the fields. As an example, consider the following decimal add instruction:

	Field-1	Field-2
Before:	10 00 0C	01 0C
After:	10 01 0C	01 0C

Here, 10 is added to 10000, and the result, 10010, replaces the contents of field-1. Similarly, decimal subtract, multiply, and divide instructions operate on two fields, with the result of the calculation being placed in field-1. In the divide instruction, both quotient and remainder are placed in the result field.

On System/360-370, binary arithmetic instructions typically involve one field in storage and the contents of a register. For example, a binary field can be added to a register as follows:

	Register	Storage field
Before:	00 00 00 10	00 00 00 0A
After:	00 00 00 1A	00 00 00 0A

Similarly, a field in storage can be subtracted from, multiplied by, or divided into the contents of a register, with the result being stored in the register. There are separate instruction codes for operating on halfwords or fullwords in storage.

Binary arithmetic can also be performed on the contents of registers only. For example, the contents of register 4 can be subtracted from the contents of register 5, with the answer being stored in register 5. Register-to-register calculation is the fastest form of fixed-point binary arithmetic on the System/360-370.

Which type of arithmetic is more efficient? It depends on the number of times a field is going to be arithmetically operated upon, the number of digits in the fields involved, and the amount of data conversion required. Although binary arithmetic instructions are normally executed faster than decimal arithmetic instructions, binary arithmetic usually requires more conversion. For example, if two EBCDIC fields are added using decimal arithmetic, the following sequence of instructions is required: (1) pack field-1, (2) pack field-2, and (3) add the two fields together. The result can then be unpacked or edited. To add two EBCDIC fields using binary arithmetic, however, the following sequence of instructions is required: (1) pack field-1, (2) convert packed field-1 to binary—the result is in a register, (3) pack field-2, (4) convert packed field-2 to binary—the result is in a register, and (5) add the contents of one register to the contents of the other register. If the result is then to be converted back to EBCDIC, two more instructions are required: (1) convert the contents of the register to packed decimal and (2) unpack or edit the field. Because of the additional conversion instructions required for binary operations, packed-decimal arithmetic is used for most business programs, while binary arithmetic is used for the lengthy series of calculations common to scientific and mathematical problems.

Logical Instructions

On System/360-370, compare instructions can be executed on EBCDIC, packed-decimal, or binary fields. There are separate operation codes for each type of comparison. When packed-decimal or binary fields are compared, the evaluation is done numerically. Thus $+123$ is greater than -580. When EBCDIC fields are compared, the fields are evaluated on the basis of the System/360-370 *collating sequence,* in which special characters come before (are less than) letters and letters come before numbers.

Thus $ is less than B, and B is less than 5. If two fields of different formats are compared, the results are unpredictable. For example, if an EBCDIC compare instruction (called a compare logical) compares an EBCDIC field containing decimal 123 (hex F1F2F3) with a packed-decimal field containing packed-decimal 58234 (hex 58234C), the EBCDIC field will be considered greater.

System/360-370 branch instructions branch based on the results of a comparison—field-1 is less than field-2, is equal to field-2, or is greater than field-2. A branch can also be based on the results of an arithmetic operation—the result is less than, equal to, or greater than zero, or the result is larger than the size of the result field (called arithmetic overflow). In addition, certain branch operations take place based on other conditions that result from the execution of a machine-language instruction.

I/O Instructions

The System/360-370 I/O instructions are perhaps the most complex in the instruction set. In fact, a computer user's program never executes I/O instructions. Instead, they are all initiated by the *supervisor program* supplied with the operating system. Whenever a user's program requires an I/O operation, it branches to the supervisor, which causes the appropriate instructions to be executed by *channels,* special components outside of the CPU that are designed for executing I/O instructions. This is explained more fully in topic 3. In general, however, a programmer need not be concerned with this complexity.

DISCUSSION

Although this has been but a brief introduction to storage organization and instruction sets, you may realize that the study of machine language can be a detailed and complex assignment. The question, then, is: Who needs to know this amount of detail? Although storage organization and instruction sets can affect the efficiency of internal computer operations, how do data-processing personnel use this knowledge?

The primary users of machine knowledge are assembler-language programmers. Because they are working with symbolic machine language, they must know the function of all the machine-language instructions of a computer. Since they debug their programs using machine language, they need to know the internal codes and storage organization of a computer.

Other than for the assembler-language programmer, though, machine knowledge is largely irrelevant. Since problem-oriented languages such as COBOL and FORTRAN are designed to be independent of the computer used, COBOL and FORTRAN programmers need little, if any, machine knowledge. Although a limited amount of knowledge—for example, knowing the data formats—may be helpful when coding or debugging, there are many high-level language programmers who don't have the background presented in this chapter.

As for system designers, the primary purpose of machine knowledge is to enable them to compare the capabilities of two different types of computers. For example, when making a decision as to which computer to buy, a system designer might be asked to compare the storage organization and instruction sets of two different computers. This is explained more fully in the next topic. In general, however, system designers make little use of CPU knowledge.

SUMMARY

1. The System/360 has eight data bits and one parity bit per storage position. It uses four formats for representing data, three of which are EBCDIC, packed decimal, and fixed-point binary.

2. The size of an instruction set varies by computer, but all have data-movement, arithmetic, logical, and I/O instructions.

TERMINOLOGY

binary component	zoned decimal
magnetic core	place value
core storage	halfword
binary digit	fullword
bit	doubleword
byte	boundary alignment
parity bit	halfword boundary
parity checking	fullword boundary
EBCDIC	doubleword boundary
packed decimal	base register
fixed-point binary	displacement factor
binary	general-purpose register
floating-point binary	base address
hexadecimal	instruction set
hex	collating sequence
zone bit	supervisor program
digit bit	channel

QUESTIONS

1. A computer has odd parity and one of its 8-bit bytes contains this bit configuration: 101111111. What does this mean? What would happen when the byte was moved into or out of storage?

2. In a simulation program, the same factors might be operated upon arithmetically hundreds of times in succession. Which type of System/360 arithmetic do you think would be most efficient for this program—packed decimal or binary? Why?

TOPIC 2
HARDWARE
COMPARISONS

When describing a computer system, a programmer or system designer often specifies the number of storage positions. For example, "We have a 32K Model 30 System/360 computer," meaning it has 32,000 storage positions. Similarly, a programmer or system designer may refer to a computer's speed: "Our system has an access-cycle time of 2 microseconds." These specifications, however, can be highly misleading. Unless all other factors are equal, it is possible that an 8K computer can store more data and instructions than a 16K machine. It is possible that a machine with an access-cycle time of 1 microsecond can be slower than a machine with an access-cycle time of 2 microseconds.

COMPARING STORAGE
CAPACITIES

As you have already seen, the effective storage of data depends on the storage organization of a computer. If a computer has forty-eight data bits per storage position, it can store up to six EBCDIC characters per storage position or a binary number up to a value in the trillions. In contrast, a machine such as the System/360 with an 8-bit byte can store only one EBCDIC character per storage position and requires eight storage positions to store a binary number with a value in the trillions.

When a program is being executed, though, the storage of a computer contains both data and instructions—perhaps 20 percent data and 80 percent instructions, depending on the type of program being run. As a result, the number of storage positions used for a program depends largely on how effectively the computer stores instructions. Two factors involved are (1) the average instruction length (how many positions required per instruction) and (2) the instruction set (how many instructions required per program).

To illustrate, suppose a System/360 program averages 4.5 bytes per instruction, while the same program on another computer averages 5.2 bytes per instruction. If both programs have 1000 instructions, the first program's instructions will require 4500 storage positions, while the second program's instructions will require 5200 storage positions.

In actuality, however, the same program written for different computers would require different numbers of instructions, depending on the instruction set used. If a computer has a large instruction set, its programs will likely be written with a minimum number of instructions. In contrast, a computer with a limited instruction set may require many extra instructions to accomplish the same processing.

To illustrate this with an obvious example, one fairly common computer of the past didn't have the multiply instruction. Thus if this operation was to be performed, it was accomplished with a series of add instructions. On computers with the multiply instruction, of course, this operation requires a single instruction.

If the instruction set of one computer allows its programs to be written using fewer instructions than another type of computer, there can be a considerable difference in the number of storage positions used. For example, if one computer requires only 1700 instructions for a program, another requires 2100 instructions for the same program, and both computers have an average instruction length of five bytes, the first computer will use 2000 less storage positions for its program.

In summary, the number of storage positions a computer has can be misleading. Effective use of storage depends on storage organization, instruction length, and instruction set. Only when these factors are equal can we say that a 32K machine has twice the memory capacity of a 16K machine.

COMPARING CPU SPEEDS

Access-cycle time is one measure of the speed of a CPU. To appreciate what this speed indicates, you must have a conceptual understanding of how a computer executes an instruction

Although a CPU consists of hundreds of thousands of electronic components, these components can be divided into three sections: (1) the *control unit,* (2) the *arithmetic and logic unit,* and (3) *main storage* (core storage). (Although some people maintain that main storage isn't part of the CPU, I think you'll agree that it's a trivial distinction.) When an instruction is executed, it is moved from the main storage into the control unit, and the data fields to be operated upon are moved into the arithmetic and logic unit. In some cases, the result of the operation is returned to storage from the arithmetic and logic unit.

To illustrate what takes place during the execution of an instruction, consider figure 14-7, which represents the execution of an add instruction operating upon two packed-decimal fields. First, the instruction is accessed from main storage into the control unit. Second, the two data fields are accessed into the arithmetic and logic unit and the addition is performed. Third, the result is returned from the arithmetic and logic unit to main storage.

Depending on the instruction and the computer model, there are many variations as to exactly how an instruction is executed. Some instructions, such as the branch, do not operate on data. As a result, only the instruction is accessed from storage and the arithmetic and logic unit isn't used. Other instructions involve only one data field; after the instruction is accessed, the data field is accessed from storage into the arithmetic and

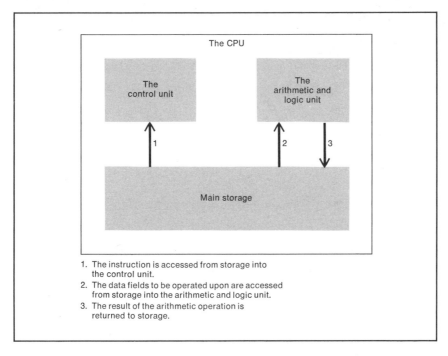

FIGURE 14-7 Data movement within the CPU (execution of an arithmetic operation involving two packed-decimal fields)

logic unit and the operation is performed. In all cases, however, the instruction is first accessed into the control unit; then the data fields, if any, are accessed to and from the arithmetic and logic unit.

When instructions or data are accessed to and from storage, *access cycles* are required. The exact number of cycles required depends on the *access width* of the computer being used. On the System/360 Model 40, for example, the access width is two storage positions (two bytes). This means that two bytes are moved to or from storage during each access cycle. If a six-byte instruction is to be executed, then, three access cycles are required to move the instruction to the control unit. Similarly, if two four-byte fields are going to be operated upon, two access cycles will be needed to move each field into the arithmetic and logic unit—a total of four access cycles.

Other machines, of course, have different access widths. Smaller machines such as the HIS H200/115 have access widths of one byte, so only one byte is accessed during each cycle. The Burroughs B6500 accesses one 48-bit storage position during each access cycle, the equivalent of six bytes. And a machine such as the System/370 Model 155 accesses eight bytes during each access cycle.

Each computer requires a fixed amount of time for an access cycle. This is called *access-cycle time,* or just *cycle time.* For example, the HIS H200/115 has a cycle time of 2.75 microseconds (2.75 millionths of a second); the B6500, 600 nanoseconds (600 billionths of a second); and the System/370 Model 155, 345 nanoseconds.

Once you know the cycle time and access width of a computer, you have some idea of a computer's speed. If you divide the cycle time by the access width, you derive a rough measure that is called the *access speed.* Thus, the H200/115 has an access speed of 2.75 microseconds per byte; the B6500 has an access speed of 600 nanoseconds per storage position, or about 83 nanoseconds per byte; and the System/370 Model 155 has an access speed of about 43 nanoseconds per byte.

Because access cycles account for the major portion of a CPU's processing time, access speed is a good indication of a computer's internal speed. Although the arithmetic and logic unit may require a certain amount of time to actually perform an operation—such as an addition or a comparison—this time is normally insignificant compared to the time required for accessing instructions and data to and from storage.

On the other hand, access speed can be misleading because different computers require different numbers of access cycles to perform the same processing functions. Just as effective use of storage capacity depends on storage organization, instruction length, and instruction set, so does the number of access cycles required by a program. If a computer stores data efficiently, if its instructions are short, if its instruction set is comprehensive so the resulting program is short—then program execution is likely to require a reasonable number of access cycles. If these conditions are not true, the computer is likely inefficient and may require more access cycles to run a program than the efficient computer. Thus it's possible that a computer with an access speed of 1.5 microseconds per byte will take longer to run a program than a computer with an access speed of 2.0 microseconds per byte.

The message? Although access speed is a good indication of CPU speed, it is not an exact measure and should be used only when all other factors are equal.

COMPUTER GENERATIONS

To give you an idea of how internal computer speeds have developed, consider what is referred to as the first three generations of computers. The *first generation* is usually considered to have begun with Univac I, the first commercially sold computer. In general, the machines in this generation used a type of drum storage (see chapter 7) for main storage and had access speeds that were measured in milliseconds (thousandths of a second). One of the major components of the CPU was the vacuum tube, which took up space, gave off heat, and was relatively unreliable.

The *second generation* of computers began in the late 1950s with the development of the IBM 1401 and the IBM 1620. These machines used transistors instead of vacuum tubes, core instead of drum storage, and consequently were smaller in size, gave off less heat, and were more reliable than first-generation machines. Their access speeds were measured in microseconds—for example, 11.5 microseconds per storage position on the 1401.

The *third generation,* starting in the mid-1960s with machines such as the System/360, continued the trend toward greater speed, greater reliability, and less heat. Instead of transistors and conventional wiring, these machines used microminiature components and solid logic components. Access speeds were now often measured in nanoseconds.

As these developments took place, the computer user got more and more processing capability for the dollar. In 1965, for example, if a computer user replaced an IBM 1401 with a System/360 or a Honeywell 200, he could run his 1401 object programs without reprogramming, run the programs in shorter amounts of time (often cutting run times by 50 percent or more), and pay less monthly rental for the new system. Technological development lowered computing costs, and thus, computers became practical for more users.

Because technological improvements—however marked—are often implemented somewhat gradually, there are no clear-cut definitions as to what is a second- and what is a third-generation computer. Some computers have components common to both generations and are therefore difficult to classify. In addition, many people classify generations based on more than just hardware technology. These people consider such factors as the I/O devices, the programming support provided by the manufacturer, and the data-communication capabilities—thus complicating the job of classifying a system.

In any event, we now are on the verge of, and in fact may have entered, the fourth generation of computers. Some people, for instance, classify the IBM System/370 as a fourth-generation machine, although others disagree. The problem is in determining what should make up a fourth-generation machine. Although the System/370 uses much third-generation technology, it is used in a more sophisticated way. For example, through a technique called *interleaving,* four access cycles from four different areas of main storage can take place at one time. Are developments such as this enough to mark fourth-generation equipment?

The question, of course, can't be settled until enough time has passed to gain some perspective. Perhaps a major technological development that clearly marks the fourth generation will take place. Or perhaps, unlike the industry's first twenty years, future developments will be gradual and distinctions between generations will be hazy.

DISCUSSION

As we have tried to point out in this topic, comparing storage capabilities and internal speeds requires a complicated analysis of storage organization, instruction lengths, and instruction sets. To further complicate the process, what may be true for one type of program—say a certain program on system A requires less storage and runs faster than it does on system B—may not be true for another type of program. Depending on design, one computer may be adapted for one type of program—for example, one involving extensive calculations—and another computer may be adapted for another type of program—for example, one involving high volumes of printed output.

In addition, program execution speed depends on many factors other than internal speeds. The I/O devices, the programming languages, the degree of overlap (see the next topic), and the operating system—these all have an effect on the time it takes to execute a program. As a result, it is almost impossible to determine which of two computers will execute programs faster based on technical specifications only. Instead, it has become common to try a series of *benchmark runs* (or just *benchmarks*) on the two computers to be compared.

A benchmark is a timed test run that approximates actual conditions as closely as possible. To make sure that the test doesn't favor one particular type of computer design, benchmarks are normally run using three or more different types of programs. After the benchmark runs, the system analyst has some actual data on which to base the choice of computer. Because of the effectiveness of the benchmark procedure and because of the increasing complexity of hardware, there is a trend away from the detailed hardware analysis that was once quite common when making a buying decision.

SUMMARY

1. The common measure of a computer's storage capacity is the number of storage positions it has. However, the efficiency of a computer in using its storage depends on its storage organization, instruction lengths, and instruction set.

2. Access cycles take up the major portion of CPU time during the execution of a program. Thus, access width, cycle time, and the resulting access speed are good measures of a computer's internal speed. Here again, however, storage organization, instruction lengths, and instruction set must be considered when comparing two computers.

3. The computer industry has already seen three generations of computers. These generations are distinguished by different types of electronic components, with resulting improvements in speed, reliability, size, and heat.

4. Because of the difficulty of hardware analysis based on technical specifications alone, benchmarks are commonly used.

control unit	access speed
arithmetic and logic unit	first generation
main storage	second generation
access cycle	third generation
access width	interleaving
access-cycle time	benchmark run
cycle time	benchmark

1. Two computers have 32K bytes of storage. What else would you want to know if you had to evaluate their relative storage capacities?

2. Two computers have 2.0 microsecond cycle times. What else would you want to know if you had to evaluate the relative speeds of these machines?

3. Two computers run the same benchmark series, consisting of a disk update run, a sort run, and a COBOL compilation. Computer A takes 8 minutes for all three runs; computer B takes 16 minutes. Is computer A twice as fast as computer B? Can you be sure computer A is faster than computer B? Explain.

TOPIC 3
OVERLAP

Until the mid-1960s, most computer systems could perform only one operation at a time. For instance, a typical card system read a card, processed it, and printed an output line on the printer. This sequence was then repeated for the next card record. Similarly, a typical tape system read input, processed it, and gave output—but only one operation at a time. The problem with this method of processing is that the components of the computer system are often idle, even though the system is running.

To illustrate, suppose a tape system executes a program that reads a tape record, processes it, and writes a tape record. Figure 14-8 might then represent the relative amounts of time that the CPU and the tape drives would be busy during execution of the program. (These percentages, of course, would vary depending on the speed of the components.) In this example, the CPU is busy 44 percent of the time that the system is running, while each tape drive is busy only 28 percent of the time.

To overcome this problem of idle components, systems were developed to *overlap* I/O operations with CPU processing. The difference between nonoverlapped and overlapped processing is illustrated in figure 14-9. On system A, the nonoverlapped system, nine time intervals are required to read, process, and write three records. On system B, the overlapped system, nine records have been read, eight have been processed, and seven have been written at the end of the nine time intervals. Although this example is based on the unlikely assumption that reading, processing, and writing each take equal amounts of time, the message is clear: overlap can significantly increase the amount of work that a computer system can do.

One reason earlier computers weren't able to overlap operations is that the CPU executed all of the instructions of a program, one after the other. In contrast, the CPU of an overlapped system doesn't execute I/O

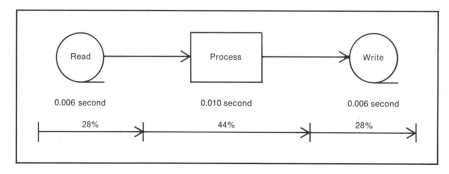

FIGURE 14-8   The problem of idle computer components

instructions. Instead, *channels* are used to execute the I/O instructions, while the CPU executes the arithmetic, logic, and data-movement instructions. The I/O instructions executed by the channels are called *channel commands*. Figure 14-10, then, illustrates the components of an overlapped system: one channel executes an input command, a second

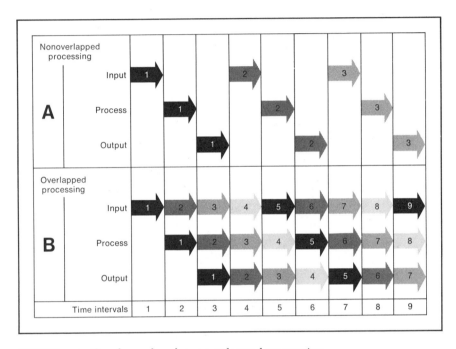

FIGURE 14-9   Overlapped and nonoverlapped processing

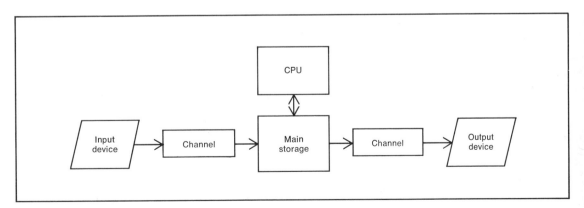

FIGURE 14-10   Computer system components with overlap capabilities

channel executes an output command, and the CPU executes other instructions of the program—all at the same time. (Although the CPU is generally considered to consist of storage and control circuitry, the CPU and storage are shown separately in the illustration to indicate that both CPU and channels access data from storage.)

Whenever data is transferred from a channel to storage or from storage to a channel, CPU processing is interrupted for one access cycle. Because of the tremendous difference between access-cycle speeds and I/O speeds, however, this is a minor interruption. To illustrate, suppose cards read by a 600-card-per-minute card reader are being processed by a computer that transfers one byte of data during each access cycle. If an access cycle takes 2 microseconds (millionths of a second), which is a typical access speed of a medium-sized computer, CPU processing will be interrupted for a total of 160 microseconds to read all eighty card columns. In contrast, the card reader takes 1/10 second, or 100,000 microseconds to read all eighty card columns. This means that while each card is read, the CPU can spend over 99 percent of its time, 99,840 out of 100,000 microseconds to be exact, executing other instructions of the program.

Although tape and disk devices are many times faster than card readers and printers, this same type of inequality is likely to exist between the speeds of these I/O devices and access-cycle speeds. For example, a tape drive with a 50,000-byte-per-second transfer rate reads or writes one byte of data every 20 microseconds. If the CPU requires 2 microseconds to transfer the byte to or from storage, 18 microseconds per byte are available for other processing. In other words, with overlap capability, the CPU can spend 90 percent of its time executing other instructions.

Since a channel, like a CPU, can execute only one operation at a time, the number of overlapped operations that a system can have is limited by the number of channels on the system. For instance, a one-channel system can overlap one I/O operation with CPU processing, and a three-channel system can overlap three I/O operations with CPU processing. The one exception to this is the *multiplexor channel,* which can read or write on two or more slow-speed I/O devices at one time.

The multiplexor channel has the ability to alternate between several I/O devices. For example, if a card reader, a card punch, and a printer are attached to a multiplexor channel, the channel can accept one byte of data from the card reader, send one byte to the card punch, send one byte to the printer, and then accept another byte from the card reader. By switching from one device to another, this single channel can overlap several different devices. Here again, the extreme difference in speeds between I/O devices and access cycles makes this possible.

Figure 14-11 shows a typical configuration of a tape system with four tape drives. All of its slow-speed devices—the card reader, card punch, printer, and console typewriter—are attached to a multiplexor channel,

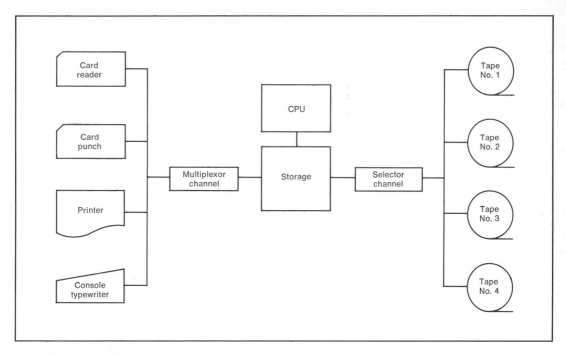

FIGURE 14-11   Configuration of a typical tape system

while the tape drives are attached to the other type of channel, a *selector channel*. This system, then, can overlap card reading, printing, punching, console-typewriter operations, and reading or writing on one tape drive. Because a selector channel can do only one operation at a time, however, reading from tape drive 1 and writing on tape drive 2 cannot be overlapped. Since tape drives are considerably faster than the slow-speed devices, it is more important that slow-speed operations be overlapped than tape operations. In general, a computer system consists of one multiplexor channel and one or more selector channels.

A programming complexity resulting from overlap is that two I/O areas in storage must be used for each I/O operation. If only one input area was used for a card-reading operation, for example, the second card would be moved into the input area while the first card was being processed—thus destroying the data from the first card. Instead, the second card is read into a second input area of storage while the first card is being processed in the first input area. Then, the third card is read into the first input area, while the second card is processed in the second input area. This switching from one input area to the other is continued throughout the program. Similarly, all other I/O operations that are overlapped must use dual I/O areas in storage.

So the programmer doesn't have to worry about the switching of I/O areas and the other complexities associated with overlap such as writing channel commands, a supervisor program is supplied with an overlapped system. This supervisor is loaded into storage at the start of a day's operations and remains in storage while all programs are executed. Two of the responsibilities of the supervisor are (1) handling the switching of I/O areas required for overlap and (2) initiating all I/O commands. The programmer, then, writes the programs as if no overlap were taking place. Whenever the source program issues an I/O statement, object code is compiled that causes a branch to the supervisor, which in turn sends the appropriate channel command to the selected channel.

I/O-BOUND AND
PROCESS-BOUND PROGRAMS

The illustration in figure 14-9 is, of course, unrealistic. Input, output, and processing times would never be equal; different input records would likely require different amounts of processing time; and few programs have such simple logic—read a record, process it, and write a record. Nevertheless, the illustration does demonstrate the idea of overlapped processing. With these same shortcomings, similar illustrations are used in figures 14-12 and 14-13 to represent two types of overlapped programs: *I/O-bound* and *process-bound* programs.

When an I/O-bound program is executed, the execution speed is limited by one or more I/O devices. For example, if figure 14-12 represents a program that reads a tape record, processes it, and writes a line on the printer, the printer is the limiting device. If the printer were replaced by a faster I/O device, the program could be speeded up. Thus, the program is said to be printer-bound, or I/O-bound. In general, most business programs are I/O-bound by one device or another.

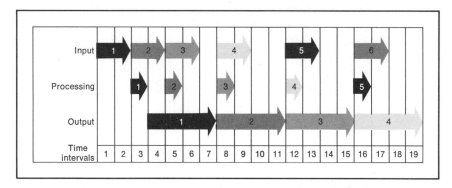

FIGURE 14-12   An I/O-bound program

In contrast, process-bound (sometimes called *CPU-bound*) refers to a program that is limited by internal processing speeds, as illustrated in figure 14-13. Here, the speed of the CPU would have to be increased in order to reduce the execution time of the program. Because they often require extensive calculations, scientific and engineering programs are commonly process-bound.

MULTIPROGRAMMING

To make better use of the components of a computer system when running I/O-bound and process-bound programs, a technique called *multiprogramming* was developed. When multiprogramming is used, two or more programs plus a supervisor program are loaded into storage at one time. Then, whenever the CPU is idle because it is waiting for an I/O operation to be completed, it branches to the supervisor, which branches to the next instruction to be executed in one of the other programs in storage. Because the supervisor must handle the switching between programs, a multiprogramming supervisor is more extensive than a supervisor for single-program processing.

Figure 14-4 illustrates how two I/O-bound programs might be executed using multiprogramming. If only program A were being executed, the CPU would have to wait for an I/O operation to finish at the end of the third interval. With multiprogramming, however, the program branches to the supervisor, which then branches to program B. By switching back and forth throughout program execution, the amount of processing done in nineteen intervals of time is increased considerably. In addition, the CPU is used for a much greater portion of the total execution time.

Depending on the size of the computer system, two, three, or more programs can be executed using multiprogramming. These programs can be either I/O- or process-bound. As each program is loaded into storage,

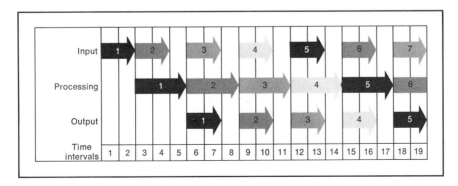

FIGURE 14-13   A process-bound program

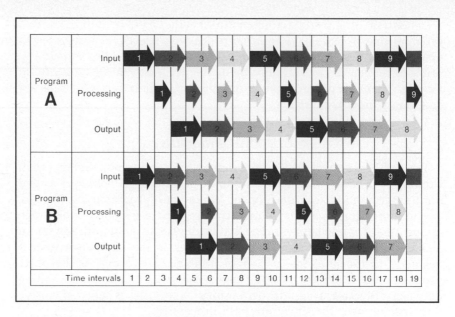

FIGURE 14-14   Multiprogramming two I/O-bound programs

it is given a priority number so that the supervisor can branch to the program with the highest priority whenever a program switch occurs. In this way, top priority programs receive the most attention from the CPU, while the lowest priority program is given use of the CPU only when all other programs are waiting for an I/O operation to end. If enough programs are loaded into storage and if enough I/O operations are overlapped, utilization of the CPU can approach 100 percent.

Some of the costs of multiprogramming include extra channels, relatively large amounts of main storage, and a relatively large supervisor program. Multiprogramming users, however, consider these costs to be well-justified. By reducing the idle time for the CPU and the I/O components, a multiprogramming system is capable of more processing per dollar spent than a system that uses single-program processing. In fact, multiprogramming is now the normal mode of operation for medium- and large-sized computers.

DISCUSSION

Depending on the computer manufacturer, overlap and channels may be referred to by other names. For example, some manufacturers refer to overlap as *simultaneity* and speak of eight simultaneous I/O operations in addition to CPU processing. Similarly, channels are sometimes referred to as *I/O trunks.* Regardless of the terminology, though, all major computer manufacturers provide systems with overlap capabilities.

The number of operations that can be overlapped by a system is another question. This, as has been said, depends on the channels available to the system. Some systems can overlap only a few operations; some can overlap dozens of operations. The overlap capability, in fact, can be one of the most critical factors in determining a system's speed. If two systems have comparable I/O devices, the one that has a higher degree of overlap is likely to be the faster machine. Because most business programs are I/O-bound, the internal processing speeds lose their significance.

SUMMARY

1. By use of channels and a supervisor program, I/O operations can be overlapped with CPU operations, thus increasing program execution speed. As a point of interest for programmers, two I/O areas must be available for each I/O device being overlapped.

2. In an I/O-bound program, speed is limited by the speed of one or more I/O operations. A process-bound program is limited by CPU speeds.

3. Multiprogramming attempts to better utilize the CPU by executing two or more programs at once. This requires extra channels, additional main storage, and an expanded supervisor program.

4. Because most business programs are I/O-bound, the degree of overlap achieved by a system is critical to the system's speed.

TERMINOLOGY

overlap	I/O-bound
channel	process-bound
channel command	CPU-bound
multiplexor channel	multiprogramming
selector channel	simultaneity
supervisor program	I/O trunk

QUESTIONS

1. An overlapped computer system is run three shifts per day, six days per week. It executes one program at a time, and these programs are almost always I/O bound. What changes might be made to this system that would shorten the total number of hours the computer is in use?

2. A multiprogramming system averages 2.3 programs in storage and has 75 percent CPU utilization. What hardware changes might be required in order to increase the multiprogramming average and the CPU utilization?

15 DATA ENTRY

The most common method of entering data into an EDP system is through punched cards. Because keypunching and verifying are manual operations, however, it is common for input preparation to take considerably longer than processing. For example, it may take three days to prepare employee job cards, but only three hours to process them and prepare payroll checks. Similarly, it may take several hours longer to prepare customer-order cards than it does to process them and print shipping orders and invoices. Because they are a primary source of delay within a system, keypunching and verifying are often referred to as the "keypunch bottleneck."

Input preparation can also be a significant cost in an EDP installation. A large computer user, for example, may have 150 or more keypunches and operators. At $600 or more per month per keypunch station (keypunch and operator), the keypunching budget may be well over $100,000 per year.

Because of its effect on the speed and cost of an EDP system, system designers have looked for alternatives to keypunching for many years. One of the traditional approaches has been to use *turnaround documents* such as the one in figure 15-1. This document is a premium notice issued by an insurance company, but when it is returned with the exact payment, it becomes input to the computer system as a record of payment. If you decode the holes punched in the card, you will see that customer number, payment period, due date, and amount due are

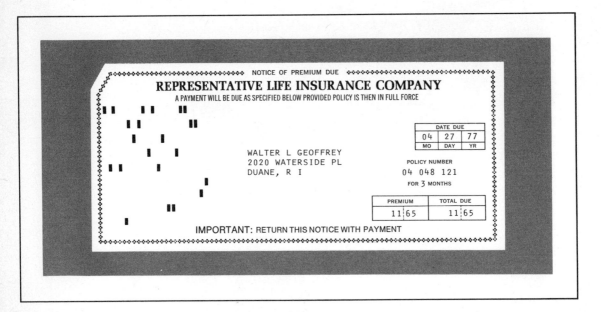

FIGURE 15-1 A turnaround premium notice

punched in the card as well as printed on it; thus, the data can be processed by a computer if the customer pays the full amount. If a partial payment is made or if the notice isn't returned with the payment, auxiliary procedures must be used.

A turnaround document can be prepared in a couple of ways. First, the cards can be punched and printed in a single step by using a computer system with a multifunction card machine as described in chapter 5. Second, the cards can be punched by the computer system in one step and printed by the computer system in another step. For this purpose, there are printers that print on punched cards as well as continuous-form documents. These printers also have the ability to read the data punched in the cards; thus, the program can check that the data is being printed on the correct cards.

Another traditional approach to reducing keypunching is the preparation of punched paper tape as a by-product of some manual operation. For instance, the device in figure 15-2 can be used to punch a paper tape while shipping orders are being typed on the typewriter keyboard. The punched paper tape, which contains order data in coded form, can be used as input to a computer system that has a paper-tape reader as input device. In addition to typewriter devices, paper-tape punches can be attached to adding machines and cash registers.

FIGURE 15-2 A document writer with paper-tape output

These traditional approaches are of course limited to certain restricted applications. To use a turnaround premium notice, for example, a company must have a high percentage of the premium notices returned with payment; otherwise, the technique loses its value. Similarly, if nothing is gained by typing shipping orders (such as a gain in order-writing speed), the user might be better off keypunching cards and having the computer system print the shipping orders. Obviously, then, other alternatives to keypunching are needed.

In recent years, considerable emphasis has been placed on developing these alternatives. The three alternatives that have been given the most attention are (1) replacing keypunches and verifiers with other key-operated devices such as key-to-tape devices or systems, (2) the use of machine-readable source documents, and (3) source-data automation.

KEYPUNCH REPLACEMENT

In 1965 Mohawk Data Sciences Corporation introduced a device, called a *data recorder,* that is a replacement for the keypunch and verifier. This device is shown in figure 15-3. When the operator keys data on the keyboard, it is recorded on a magnetic tape. To correct an error, the operator backspaces the tape and keys the correct data, which then replaces the incorrect data. Similarly, when the data recorder is used for verifying, errors are corrected when the correct data is keyed over the incorrect data.

The data recorder can improve operations in two ways. First, because tape can be read by a computer system at a speed many times faster than card reading, less computer time is required for reading the input data. Second, because card handling and card movement through the machine are eliminated and because of the ease of error correction, operator efficiency is improved. The disadvantage of using data recorders is that in many cases several tapes with a small amount of data on each—one tape for each operator—must be merged by the computer system into a single tape before the records can be sorted or edited.

Since the introduction of the Mohawk data recorder, other manufacturers have developed many varieties of key-to-tape devices and systems. Figure 15-4, for example, schematically illustrates one of the more common systems, a key-to-tape (or key-to-disk) system. Here, eight keyboards are connected to a small computer (a minicomputer) that has both magnetic-disk and magnetic-tape input and output. During operation, all eight operators can be working on the same job or different jobs. As data is keyed, it is read into the computer, which performs certain editing operations to determine whether the data is valid. If invalid data is detected, the operator is notified immediately so that it can be corrected at once. If the data is valid, it is stored on the disk. At various times during the day, data recorded on the disk by one or more operators

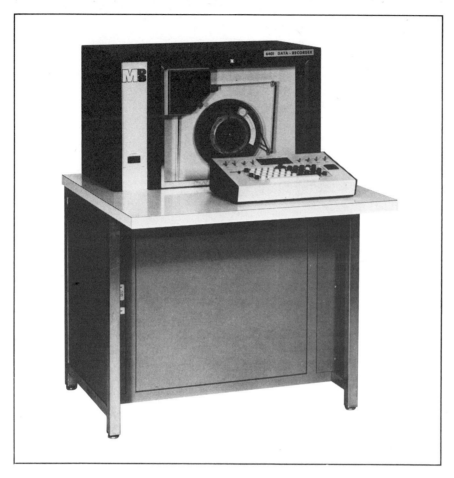

FIGURE 15-3   A Mohawk data recorder

is written onto one tape. The tape can then be processed by the main computer system.

In general, each key station in a system like this consists of a keyboard and some sort of visual-display unit. As the operator keys data, it is displayed on the television-like screen, so that it can be visually verified. If the operator keys data that doesn't conform to the data-entry program—for example, numeric data when alphabetic data is expected—error messages are displayed by the computer so the data can be re-entered.

There are several advantages of a key-to-tape system such as this. First, because editing routines are executed when the keying takes place, many types of invalid fields can be corrected immediately. In contrast, when editing is done independently of the keying operations, error correction

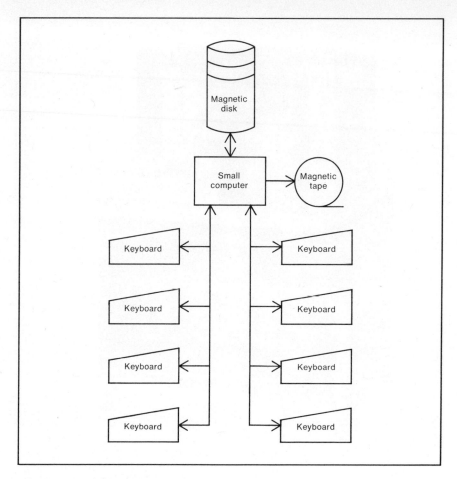

FIGURE 15-4   A key-to-tape system

can be a time-consuming and costly job. Second, because card handling and card movement are eliminated and error correction is simplified, operator speed is increased by 25 percent or more as compared to a keypunching and verifying operation. Finally, in contrast to data-recorder operations, several tapes do not have to be merged into one tape by the main computer system. Instead, records keyed by several different operators are consolidated by a disk-to-tape run executed by the key-to-tape system.

The disadvantage of a key-to-tape system is downtime. If the computer that is central to the system fails, all operators that are using the system—as many as sixty-four—will be idle. In actual practice, however, these systems have proven to be highly reliable. As a result, it is a rare occurrence when a system is down for more than an hour.

MACHINE-READABLE SOURCE DOCUMENTS

Although replacement of the keypunch can improve operations, the basic bottleneck remains. A more complete solution consists of eliminating keying operations altogether by using source documents that can be read by a computer system. Four types of data that are readable by both humans and computers are (1) magnetic-ink characters, (2) optical marks, (3) optical characters, and (4) handwritten characters.

Magnetic-Ink Characters

Magnetic-ink character recognition (MICR) refers to the reading of characters (sometimes called *MICR characters*) that are printed in magnetic ink. These characters are used in the banking industry for processing the checks used in checking accounts. When a customer opens an account, he is issued checks similar to those in figure 15-5 (part A). Printed near the bottom of the checks are the customer's name, bank number, and other routing data. Because the data is printed in ink that contains magnetic particles, it can be read by a MICR reader that is connected to a computer system. Figure 15-6 shows the fourteen MICR characters that can be used in magnetic-ink character recognition—the ten decimal digits plus four control characters.

When a person writes a check and it is deposited in a bank, the amount must be recorded on the check in MICR characters as shown in figure 15-5 (part B). This is done using a MICR inscriber such as the one shown in figure 15-7. As data is keyed on the keyboard, MICR characters are printed on the check, ready for reading by a computer system. You might note, then, that keying operations are not eliminated entirely by the use of MICR characters—the amount must still be keyed.

To read and process MICR characters, a reader/sorter such as the one in figure 15-8 is used. This device, which has sixteen pockets, is used to sort the checks by bank number so they can be returned to the issuing bank. When it is used for sorting, the reader/sorter can be independent of the computer system. This is referred to as offline operation. Then, when the checks are processed by the issuing bank, the reader/sorter is *online* to the computer system. As the checks are read, the data can be processed immediately or written on magnetic tapes for later processing. In the issuing bank, checks are sorted into account-number sequence so they can be returned to the customer with the monthly statement.

The use of MICR characters began in the late 1950s. Then in 1960 the American Banking Association (ABA) agreed on a standard shape for the MICR characters to be used throughout the industry. The use of MICR characters was so effective that in 1967 the Federal Reserve Banks announced that checks without magnetic-ink encoding would not be processed through the normal collection channels and might be subject to a service charge.

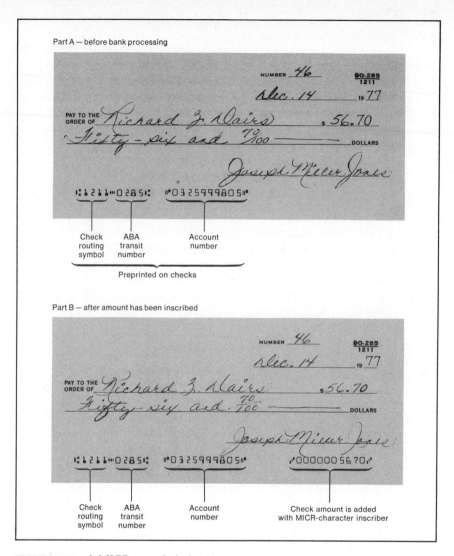

FIGURE 15-5   A MICR-encoded check

Optical Marks

A common use of *optical marks* is illustrated by the document in figure 15-9. This of course is a test scoring sheet on which a student makes marks indicating his answers. To read this type of document, an optical-mark page reader such as the one in figure 15-10 is used. When connected to a computer system, this reader reads the data directly into storage, thus eliminating keypunching entirely.

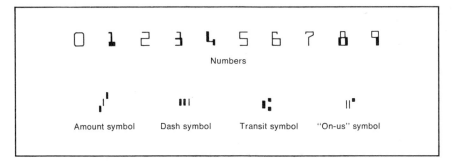

FIGURE 15-6 MICR characters

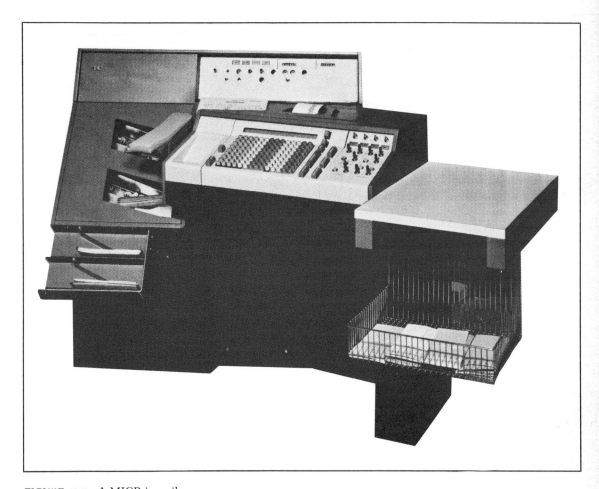

FIGURE 15-7 A MICR inscriber

FIGURE 15-8   A MICR reader/sorter

Although test scoring is a primary use of optical marks, they can also be used for many other applications in many different types of businesses. For example, the document in figure 15-11 can be used as an order form. When completed by a salesman or clerk, this source document becomes direct computer input. Similarly, optical-mark documents can be used for attendance reporting in schools, as insurance-policy applications, for marketing-research forms, for specifying inventory reorder amounts, and so on. In addition to full pages, optical marks can be recorded on and read from punched-card documents.

The main limitation of optical marks has been the increased possibility of error when recording the source data. Because accuracy depends on the location of the mark rather than the mark itself, errors are more

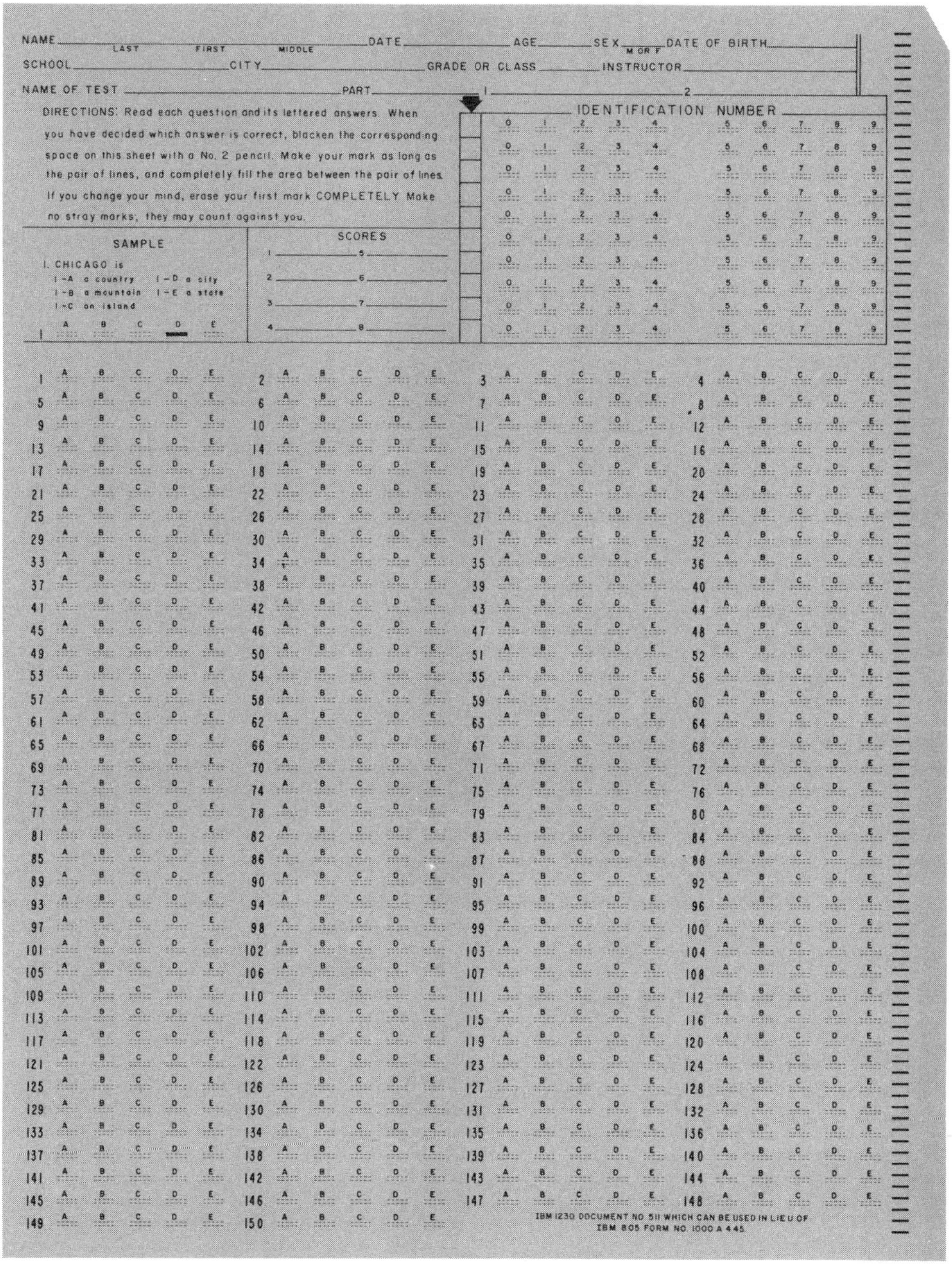

FIGURE 15-9   A test-scoring sheet

FIGURE 15-10   An optical-mark page reader

common when using optical marks than when using traditional characters to record data. This is particularly true if the form is complex and
many different items of data must be recorded. Furthermore, clerical
workers often object to using optical marks, thus compounding the
problems.

Nevertheless, optical marks have been used to great advantage by
many companies. One company, for example, claims a saving of $32,000 a
year in input preparation costs. This company uses optical marks for
preparing the equivalent of 125,000 job cards per month in a payroll
application.

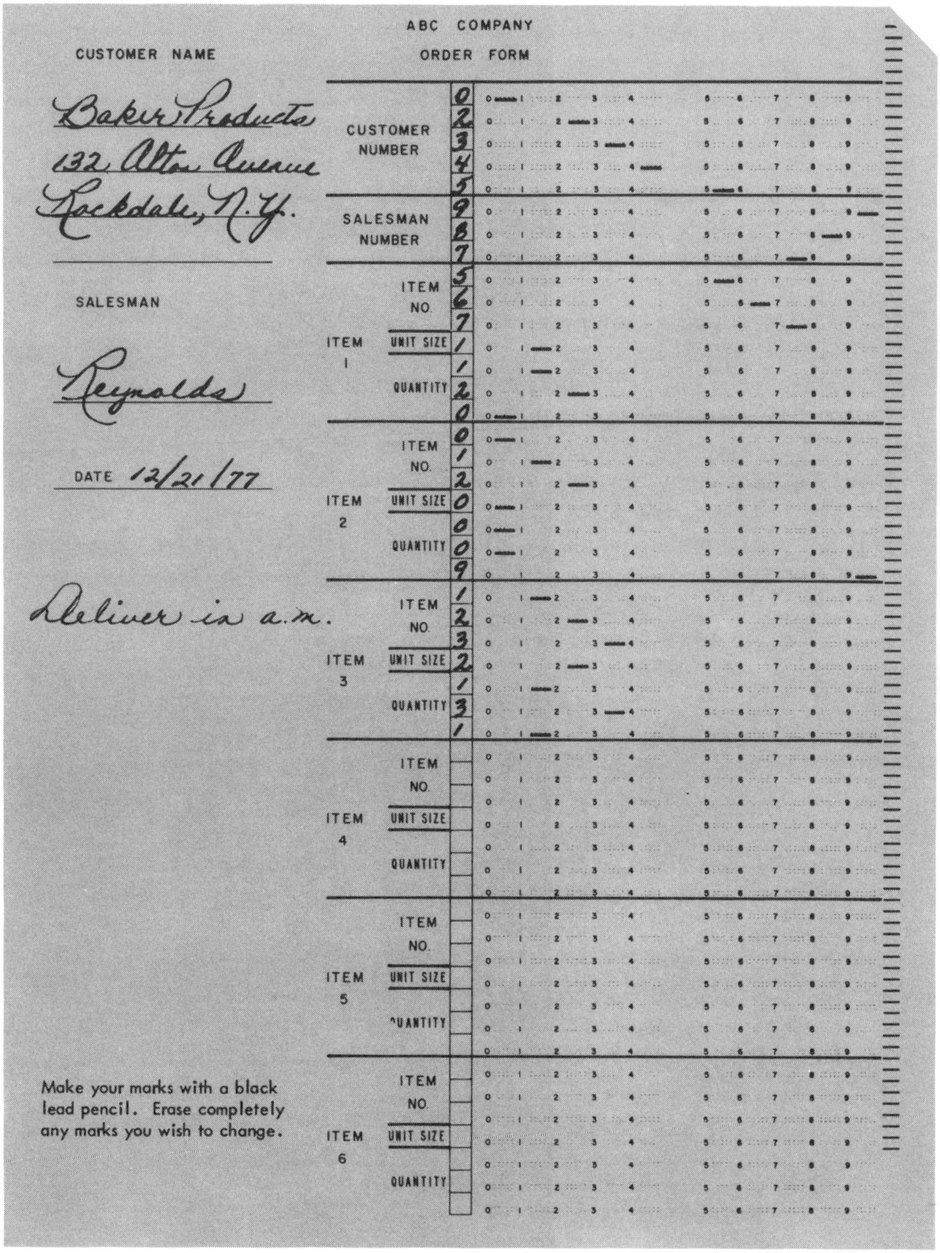

FIGURE 15-11   An order-writing form

Optical Characters

Optical-character recognition (OCR) refers to equipment that can read optical characters (or *OCR characters*) such as those in figure 15-12. OCR equipment reads these characters by using a mechanism that shines a bright light on the characters to be read and, with photocells, senses the reflected pattern of the characters. The same type of mechanism is used for reading optical marks. There are several different typefaces (fonts) that can be used for OCR characters, two of the most widely used being OCR-A and OCR-B. OCR-A characters, which are those shown in figure 15-12, have distinctive characteristics so they can be interpreted more easily by OCR equipment. In contrast, OCR-B characters are easier for people to read but more difficult for machines to interpret.

OCR documents can be printed by computer printers, typewriters, cash registers, and time clocks. These documents can be full sheets of paper (8½ inches by 11 inches), cut forms of various sizes, cash-register rolls, or time cards. The document in figure 15-13, for example, is a cut-form utility bill. When this bill, which was printed by a computer printer, is returned by the customer, it becomes input to the computer system. It can be read by an OCR reader such as the one in figure 15-14. If a partial payment is made, optical marks can be entered on the left side of the form and read by the same OCR reader. It is common, in fact, for an OCR reader to be able to read optical marks as well as optical characters.

FIGURE 15-12   OCR characters (Type OCR-A)

OCR characters can be used in a wide variety of applications. For example, if an item code is printed by a cash register along with the charge amount, the cash-register roll can be input to an inventory or sales-analysis application. On the other hand, documents such as the one in figure 15-15 can be used to record information about new checking and savings accounts in the banking industry. After the data is typed on the form, the form becomes direct input to the computer system. Note that keypunching has been entirely eliminated in all cases.

One of the primary problems with optical-character recognition is the reject rate. In most cases, when an OCR reader cannot interpret an OCR character, the document is stacked in a reject pocket. As an alternative, some readers stop with the unreadable character displayed in a window on the device. If the operator can recognize the character, he or she keys the correct character on the keyboard of the device and reading continues. In either case, if the reject rate is high—say as much as 5 percent—the value of optical-character recognition is reduced considerably.

One of the primary causes of rejects is the quality of printing on the source documents. The paper, the ink, the precision of the device used for printing—all can affect the reject rate. If the print quality is high, the reject rate should be low—perhaps less than 1 percent.

Although the potential of optical-character recognition seems to be high, it has yet to be adopted by a large percentage of the computer users. One of the major reasons for this is the cost of an OCR reader. A typical monthly rental, for example, is about $4000. At this price, a company has to displace about twelve keypunch operators in order to justify the

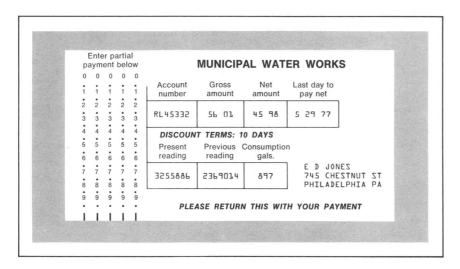

FIGURE 15-13   An OCR utility bill

FIGURE 15-14   An OCR reader

device based on cost. As a result, optical-character recognition is not yet economical for the small computer user.

Regardless of its limitations and price, there are many success stories that support the use of OCR equipment. One company claims replacement of thirty keypunch operators by using an OCR reader. In a controlled test, another company discovered that documents that had required twelve hours of keypunching and verifying could be read by an OCR reader in thirteen minutes.

Handwritten Characters

Handwritten characters can also be read by some models of OCR readers, though this capability was developed somewhat later than the ability to read machine-printed documents. Thus far, only handwritten numbers and a few control letters can be read, but it is expected that equipment that can read the entire alphabet will soon be available. When handwritten numbers are used, they must be carefully written, as indicated by the examples in figure 15-16.

Figure 15-17 illustrates a handwritten sales slip that could be used in a retail store. The boxes on the form indicate exactly where the data must be printed. After the form is filled out, it is read by a device such as the one in figure 15-14. Because an OCR reader that can read handwritten

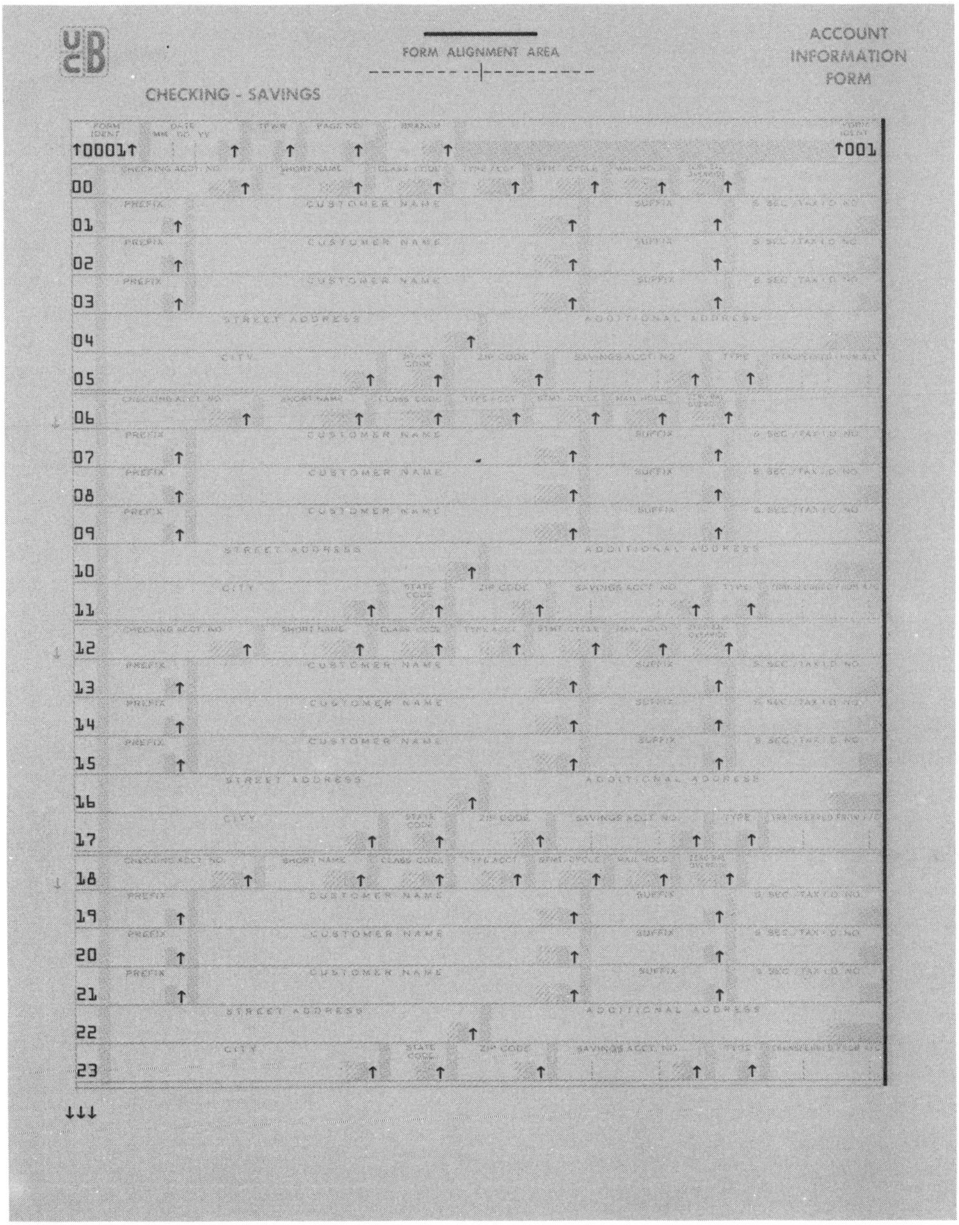

FIGURE 15-15 An OCR form for the banking industry

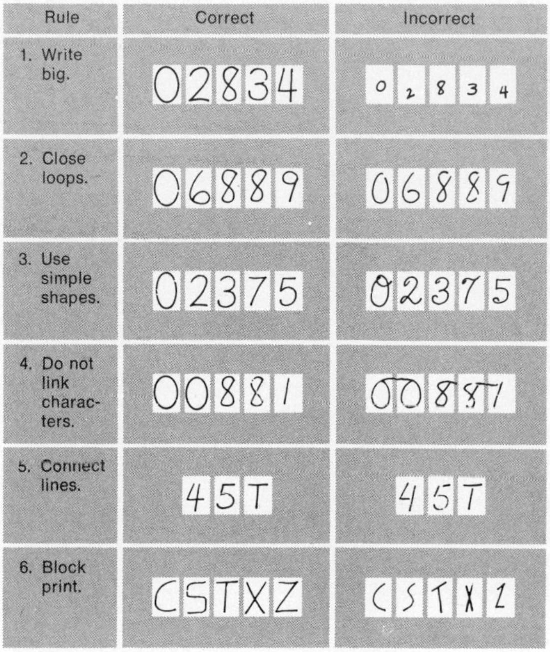

Rule	Correct	Incorrect
1. Write big.	02834	02834
2. Close loops.	06889	06889
3. Use simple shapes.	02375	02375
4. Do not link characters.	00881	00881
5. Connect lines.	45T	45T
6. Block print.	CSTXZ	CSTXZ

FIGURE 15-16   Handwritten characters

characters can also read machine-printed characters, both types of characters can be combined on one form.

As with machine-printed characters, the problem with handwritten characters is the reject rate. In addition, an OCR reader will sometimes misread a handwritten character, and thus an incorrect character is read into storage. This is referred to as a *substitution*—an incorrect character is substituted for the correct character. Needless to say, the reject rate and substitution rate is critical to the success of the system.

Here again, the major cause of rejections and substitutions is the printing itself. Some clerks, for example, will record data with low substitution and rejection rates, while others will record data with relatively high rejection and substitution rates. To cope with this problem requires adequate training of clerks, constant control of the handwriting quality, and retraining when necessary.

Because of the cost of OCR equipment and the human factors involved in quality control, handwritten characters are not used for computer input in a large number of businesses. Before handwritten characters will

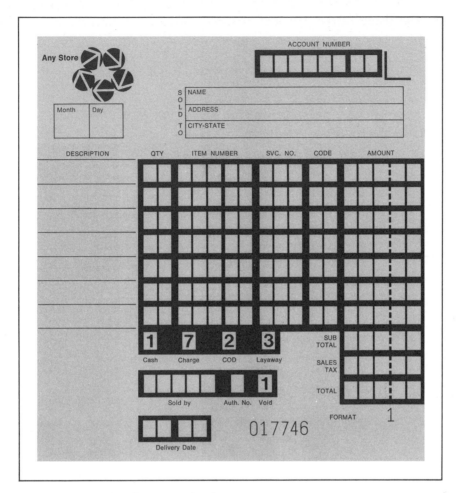

FIGURE 15-17   A handwritten sales document

be widely accepted, two factors must change. First, equipment must be developed with larger tolerances for variations in the printed characters, thus reducing the reject and substitution rate. Second, the cost of the devices must be lowered. Nevertheless, the possibilities for handwritten input seem endless. If technological developments continue as they have in the past, handwritten characters could become a major input form.

SOURCE-DATA AUTOMATION

Source-data automation is another approach to eliminating the keypunch bottleneck. This term refers to the use of automated devices at the point where source data originates; it refers to devices that operate independently of the computer system as well as to devices that are connected to the computer and interact with it.

Figure 15-18 illustrates a device used for recording order information in an inventory application in a retail store. As the clerk walks down the aisle, he or she enters the item code of the items to be reordered on the adding machine keyboard of the self-powered device. The data is then recorded on a magnetic-tape cassette stored within a unit attached to the adding machine. At the end of the day or at various times during the day, the cassette can be transferred to a transmitting device that is connected to a telephone line so the data can be transmitted to the company's computer and inventory reorders can be processed.

In the factory, source-data automation is used to collect data concerning production operations. These systems, commonly called *data-collection systems,* can be either offline or online to the computer system. In an offline system, the data-entry device (called a *terminal*) is normally connected to a card punch, as schematically illustrated in figure 15-19. As data is entered at the terminals located throughout the factory, cards are punched for use as input to the computer system.

The basic data entered into a data-collection system in the factory are employee number, job number, operation number, and quantity of pieces produced. This data is entered into a terminal such as the one shown in figure 15-20 by inserting an employee badge for employee number, by inserting a punched card giving job number and operation number, and by keying or using manual slides for entering quantity produced.

In a more sophisticated data-collection system, the terminals are connected (online) to the computer system so that data is entered directly into the system. This eliminates the punching of cards and allows production records to be updated shortly after operations are completed on the factory floor. In this case, there is one-way transmittal of data—from terminal to computer.

FIGURE 15-18   A reorder-entry device

The next level of sophistication is a two-way communication between terminals and computer. The terminals are online to the computer, and output from the computer system can be printed or displayed on the terminals. In this case, the computer can take over some of the functions of a foreman or supervisor. For example, if an employee enters data that indicates he is starting to work on the wrong job, the computer can indicate the job he should be doing. If an employee enters a quantity that is less than the required number of pieces for the job, the computer can indicate that more pieces must be completed. In other words, by checking the master production schedule stored on direct-access devices, the computer can monitor production. Because a system such as this gives a response in time to correct an operation that otherwise would be done in error, it is called a *real-time system*. (Online and real-time systems are explained more fully in chapter 16, Data-Communication Systems.)

In retail operations, source-data automation is used to capture data at the point of sale. Such systems are called point-of-sale (or POS) systems and can vary in sophistication in much the same way that data-collection systems vary. In a typical *POS system*, terminals such as the one in figure 15-21 are used. Inventory and sales data is entered on the keyboard and then transmitted over communication lines at the end of the day to the home-office computer. In advanced systems, a POS terminal can be used in a real-time system. For example, a terminal can be used to check a customer's credit rating when a credit transaction is being processed. Because the response from the computer is given in seconds, the customer may never be aware that the credit check has taken place.

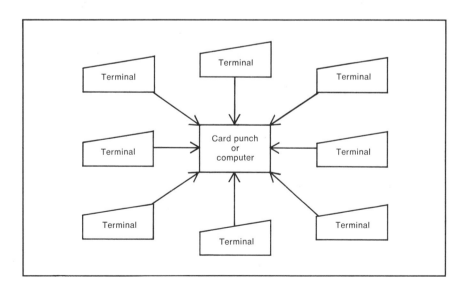

FIGURE 15-19   A data-collection system

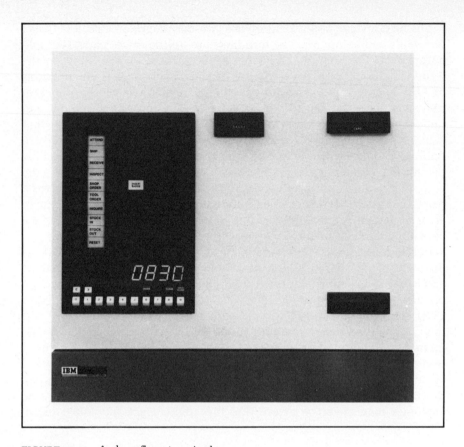

FIGURE 15-20   A shop-floor terminal

Similarly, the computer can automatically calculate and print sales taxes and give responses to clerks that indicate when invalid item codes have been entered.

Although these examples only begin to illustrate the range of applications for source-data automation, they do illustrate its potential. By entering data at its point of origin, the keypunch bottleneck is eliminated entirely. If speed is critical, the online or real-time system makes it possible to update files within seconds from the time a transaction takes place, and exception information can be printed or displayed on a manager's terminal seconds after that.

On the other hand, there are many problems pertinent to source-data automation systems—in particular, online systems. First, the cost of an online system is likely to be two or three times greater than that of a traditional system. This cost must therefore be justified by increased sales, reduced operating costs, or other benefits—a difficult justification

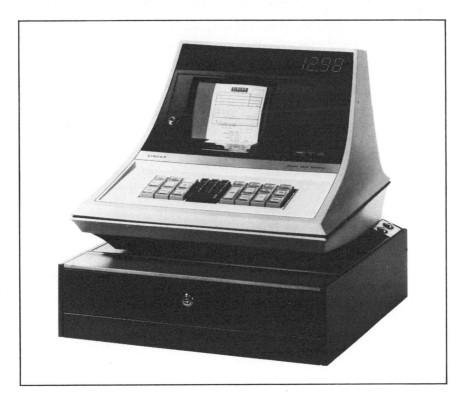

FIGURE 15-21   A POS terminal

to make. Second, if the equipment breaks down, backup procedures must
be available. In an online retail operation, for instance, it would be a
disaster if the computer broke down for even a few minutes and some
method of backup weren't available. These backup costs can be extensive, thus making it still harder to justify the system. Finally, source-data
automation is generally used in what system analysts call a "hostile
environment." Fear of computers, resistance to new methods, grease
smudges on punched cards that are inserted into factory terminals,
factory dust settling into terminals—all of these make it difficult to install
a successful system. As a result, many systems that looked good on paper
have failed upon installation.

DISCUSSION

Each of the three solutions to the keypunch problem described in this
chapter has advantages and limitations. Although keypunch replacement
is the most flexible of the solutions (since it can be used for any type of
source data), it is only a partial solution. Instead of the keypunch

bottleneck, the user takes on the key-tape bottleneck. On the other hand, though optical-character recognition and source-data automation can eliminate the bottleneck, they are expensive and limited in application. Optical-character recognition may have the greatest potential of the three as far as cost reduction is concerned, but source-data automation can provide immediate entry of source data into a system.

Because of these advantages and limitations, it is not unusual for a company to use all three solutions in solving the keypunch problem. For instance, a company may use optical-character recognition for order entry, an online data collection system for production control, and a key-to-tape system for all other input. Since most of the solutions for the input preparation problem are still developing, it remains to be seen as to which solutions will prove most profitable in the future.

SUMMARY

1. Keypunching and verifying are a major source of cost and delay within an EDP system. Traditional solutions to this problem include the use of turnaround documents and punched paper tape that is a by-product of a paperwork procedure.

2. Key-to-tape devices and systems are one alternative to keypunching. Although they increase the speed of keying operations and reduce the input time on the computer, the basic problem of input preparation remains.

3. MICR characters, optical marks, OCR characters, and some handwritten characters can be read by a computer system, thus eliminating keypunching. Because of their limitations, however, they are not used in most businesses.

4. Source-data automation refers to automating the original recording of source data. This source data is stored in tape cassettes, punched into cards, or transmitted directly to the computer system.

TERMINOLOGY

turnaround document
data recorder
MICR character
offline
online
optical mark
OCR character

substitution
source-data automation
data-collection system
terminal
real-time system
POS system

1. One of the problems with optical marks is morale. Clerks just don't like to use them. They call optical marking "coloring," and they would prefer to record data using traditional techniques. Can you justify the use of optical marks?

2. Suppose a small EDP department has only two full-time keypunch operators. Nevertheless, it would like to reduce the delays caused by keypunching. What are some possible solutions?

3. A large national company would like to cut its data-preparation costs for order processing and inventory control. At present, 97 percent of its orders are sent by customers on purchase orders; 3 percent are phone orders. What are some possible methods of lowering the costs of data entry?

16 DATA-COMMUNICATION SYSTEMS

This chapter is divided into two topics. In the first, the major types of data-communication systems and applications are described. Then, topic 2 describes the considerations for determining whether a real-time system—one type of data-communication system—is justifiable.

TOPIC 1
SYSTEMS AND
APPLICATIONS

In the last twenty years, there have been many developments that have increased the processing speed of computer systems. The speeds of CPUs and I/O devices have been increased tremendously by technological developments, direct-access devices have been developed and improved, and techniques have been developed for overlapping I/O operations with CPU operations. When you consider the entire data-processing cycle, however, you will see that source data must be *collected* before it can be processed, and processed data must be *distributed* before it can be used. Thus even if processing time is reduced to minutes, there can still be significant delays in a system.

To illustrate, suppose a wholesale distributing company consists of a home office, five branch sales offices, and a warehouse, all located in different cities. Customer orders, which are received in the branch offices, are collected in batches and mailed to the home office where they are processed. After the shipping orders are printed by the home-office computer, they are mailed to the warehouse for shipment. In this case, even if orders are processed immediately upon receipt in the home office, there is a delay of one or two days in collecting the orders and a delay of one or two days in distributing the shipping orders to the warehouse.

Data-communication systems are designed to reduce the delays in collecting and distributing data. The term *data communication* refers to the electronic transmission of data from one location to another, usually over *communication lines* such as telephone or telegraph wires. Although there are many forms of data-communication systems, they can be broken down into four classifications: offline, online batch-processing, online real-time, and time-sharing systems.

Offline Systems

Offline means that the transmission of data is not directly to or from the computer. An example of offline communications is illustrated in figure 16-1. Here, transaction cards are keypunched in the branch offices. When a batch of cards has accumulated, they are read by a card reader in the branch office and the data in the cards is transmitted over communication lines to the home office. The card reader is called a *terminal* since it

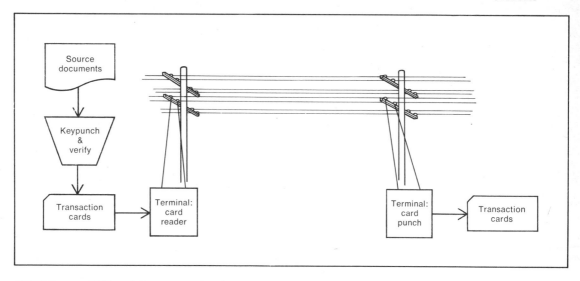

FIGURE 16-1   Offline data communication

is at one end of the communication line. The receiving device, or
terminal, in the home office is a card punch, which punches cards
identical to those in the branch. After the transaction cards from each
branch are transmitted and punched, they can be processed by the
computer.

Offline data communication, then, is simply a means of eliminating the
delays in sending data between two geographical points. In addition to
card readers and punches, other devices such as tape drives and printers
can be used as terminals. For example, if large volumes of data are to be
transmitted, a tape drive in a branch can transmit to a tape drive in the
home office. If a report is to be printed for branch-office management,
data can be read by a tape drive in the home office and printed on a
printer in the branch office.

One of the most widely used mediums for offline data communications
has been the punched *paper tape,* which is illustrated in figure 16-2.
Various coding schemes can be used, but the idea is that different
combinations of punched holes represent different characters of information. When a reel of punched paper tape is mounted on a paper-tape
reader, as illustrated in figure 16-3, it can be read and its data can be
transmitted over communication lines. Similarly, a paper-tape punch,
such as the one shown in figure 16-3, can be used as a receiving unit for
offline transmission of data. Thus, there are data transmissions that
convert data from paper tape to cards, card to tape, tape to printer, and
so on.

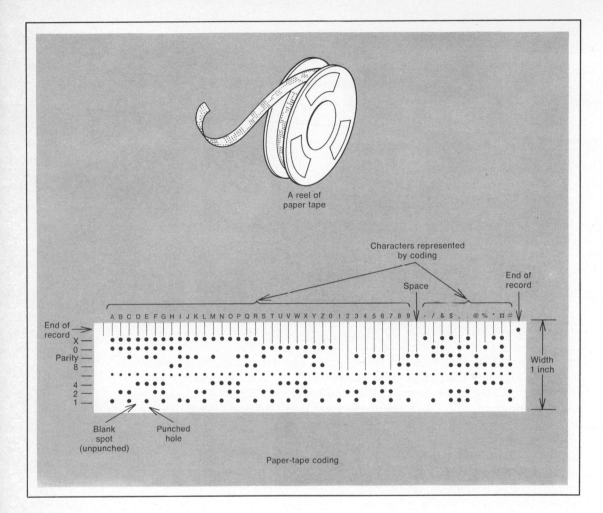

FIGURE 16-2   Paper tape

Paper-tape readers can be used as input devices on computer systems; however, they are slow input devices, generally, somewhat slower than punched-card readers. Because the records on paper tape can't be sorted, paper tape is limited in use when compared with punched cards.

Paper tape is a popular data-communication medium because it can be prepared as a by-product of other office operations. A paper-tape punch is often part of a typewriter-like device. As the operator types on the keyboard, a paper tape is punched containing selected portions of the data that was typed. For example, while an operator is typing invoices, data pertaining to each line item can be punched into a paper tape for use in a sales-analysis application. This paper tape can then be used to transmit the data via communication lines.

FIGURE 16-3   Paper-tape reading and punching terminals

Online Batch-Processing Systems

Online means that data is transmitted directly to the computer. Batch refers to the accumulation of transactions into groups or batches before transmission. An online batch-processing system is illustrated in figure 16-4. Here, a punched paper tape is prepared from customer orders, and then used as input to the computer system via phone lines. In the home office, the computer performs an editing run while writing the transactions on magnetic tape. After the transactions from all the branches are edited and written, the tapes can be merged and processed.

Figure 16-5 illustrates another type of online batch processing, called *remote job entry,* or *RJE.* Here, four RJE stations are connected to a central computer via communication lines. The RJE stations can be in the same building as the central computer or many miles away from it. As jobs are entered through the card reader in a RJE station, the data is processed by the central computer using central tape or direct-access

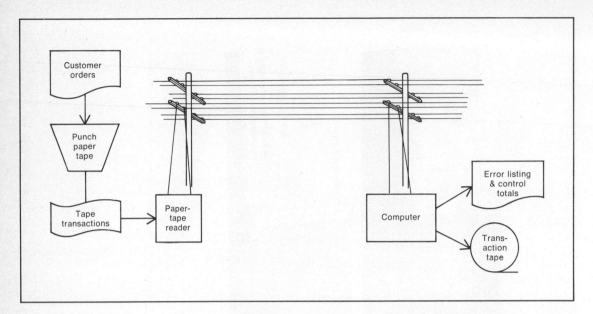

FIGURE 16-4 An online batch-processing system

files, and the results are printed on the RJE printer. Thus each RJE station seems to be a computer system in itself, even though one CPU does the processing for all four.

RJE is becoming popular because it can cut overall DP costs for any company that has multiple computer systems. For instance, a computer with one medium-sized and twelve small branch-office systems can usually save money by switching to one large system and twelve RJE stations. At the same time, processing capabilities are likely to be increased in the branches, because each RJE station has the CPU capabilities of the large system.

Of course, there are many variations of online batch processing. In general, a terminal or RJE station can consist of whatever I/O devices are necessary for the type and volume of data to be processed.

Online Real-Time Systems

Real-time systems are online communication systems that provide a two-way communication between terminal and computer. The term *real time* means that the computer gives responses to inquiries from a terminal so fast that these responses can be used to answer a customer's questions, control an operation, or modify a process.

To illustrate, suppose a customer calls a branch office to ask whether a certain replacement part for a lawn mower is available for immediate

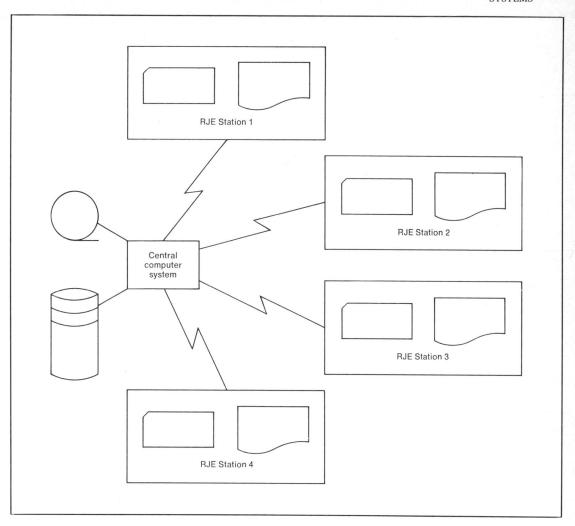

FIGURE 16-5 Remote job entry

delivery. Since the inventory records are kept in the home office, the branch office normally would call the home office to see if the part was available and then call the customer back. In a real-time system, however, the branch office communicates directly with the computer in the home office. With the customer still on the phone, the sales clerk types an inquiry on a typewriter-like terminal commonly called a *teletypewriter*. The inquiry might consist of a code indicating a request for inventory information, the part number of the item needed, and the quantity needed. This data is then transmitted to the computer, which searches a direct-access file for the selected inventory record, determines if the on-hand quantity is sufficient to fill the order, and then returns a response of yes or no to the teletypewriter; if no, it indicates when the part is expected to be in stock. Because of the high computing and transmission speeds of a data-communication system, this entire communication would take only a few seconds. Thus, the clerk can answer the customer's question after only a short pause.

If the part is available, the customer might then ask for immediate shipment. In a traditional system, this too would require a special call to the home office. In the real-time system, however, the order can be entered in much the same way that the inquiry was made. The clerk keys a code to indicate an order to be shipped, and then keys the customer number, the item number, and the quantity to be shipped. The computer processes the transaction data, updates the inventory records, and prepares a shipping order. If the warehouse has a printer terminal, the computer can transmit the data to the terminal so that the shipping order is printed in the warehouse within seconds from the time the customer placed the order. Think of the improvement in customer service!

An order-processing system is schematically shown in figure 16-6. Here, a typewriter terminal is located in every branch office, and a printer and typewriter terminal are located in the warehouse. As the transactions from the branch offices are processed, the inventory records are updated, the shipping orders are printed in the warehouse, accounts receivable records are updated, and a file of invoicing records is written. When shipments are received in the warehouse, the transactions are entered on the typewriter terminal, thus keeping inventory records constantly up to date. At the end of the day, the invoicing file is used to print invoices to be sent to the customers.

In actual practice, a real-time system often links many more than five terminals in a data-communication network. For example, Westinghouse Corporation has a real-time system that links more than 350 offices, factories, and warehouses. Within three seconds from the time that 90 percent of its 2000 daily orders are received, shipping instructions are printed on a terminal in the warehouse nearest the customer. As orders are processed, the system determines whether an inventory item should be manufactured or reordered. If it should be, a purchase order or production order is automatically prepared.

Time-Sharing Systems

A *time-sharing system* is an online real-time system in which many users with different processing needs share one central computer. In a university, for example, a half dozen or more typewriter terminals may be linked to a computer, as illustrated in figure 16-7. These terminals may be available to the engineering, math, and business departments. At any

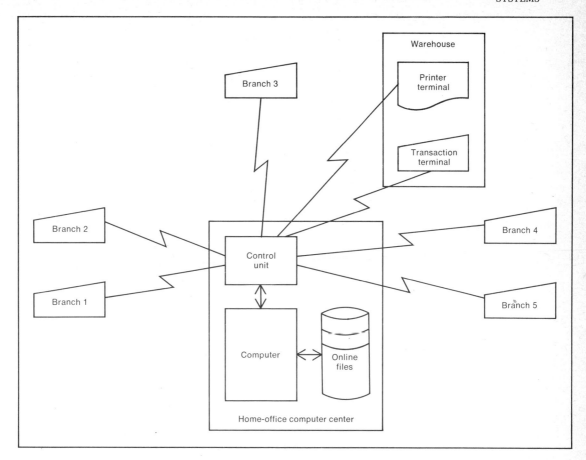

FIGURE 16-6   A real-time order-processing system

one time, a student in the engineering department may be writing a
FORTRAN program, a student in the math department may be executing
a program that solves systems of linear equations, and a student in the
business department may be developing a programming model that
projects profit and loss when any revenue or expense is varied. Because
the central computer moves from one terminal to another at fantastic
speeds, each person has the feeling that he or she alone is using the
central computer.

To give you a better appreciation of the difference between human and
computer speeds, consider that a typist working at 60 words per minute is
typing 5 characters per second. In contrast, a typical time-sharing CPU is
able to accept into storage over 1 million characters of data per second.
Thus, a computer could accept the data from 200,000 typists working at 60
words per minute. In a time-sharing system, therefore, a computer is able

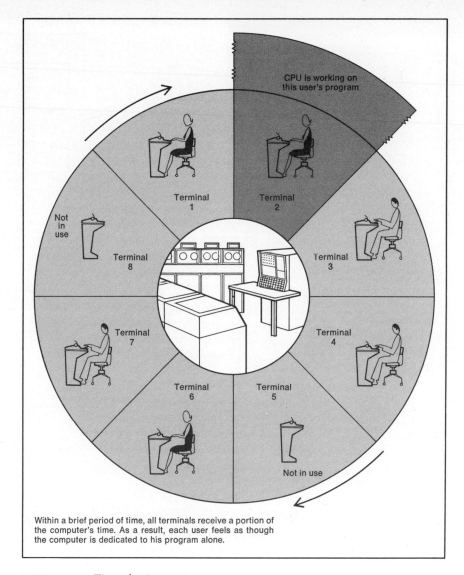

Within a brief period of time, all terminals receive a portion of the computer's time. As a result, each user feels as though the computer is dedicated to his program alone.

FIGURE 16-7   Time sharing

to accept input, process it, and return a response to a terminal so fast that many such terminals can be handled by a single computer.

Although many companies and institutions own and operate their own time-sharing systems (known as *inhouse systems*), it is also possible to rent a time-sharing service. For example, if a company needs only one terminal for the engineering department, it can rent this service from an outside source, usually known as a time-sharing service bureau. In this case, the terminal user pays a monthly rent for the terminal, plus a rate based on the amount of time the terminal is connected to the computer and the amount of time the CPU is actually used by the terminal. In a typical commercial system, the service bureau rents to many companies throughout the country.

To illustrate the use of a time-sharing service, suppose a printing company rents one terminal from a service bureau to calculate printing costs. Since this is a complicated calculation based on factors such as page size, type of paper used, and number of copies to be printed, the printing company figures that the cost of the time-sharing service is justified by increased accuracy and reduced clerical costs.

To calculate a printing cost, the costing clerk dials the computer's number on a phone located next to the typewriter terminal. When the computer answers with a beeping noise, the clerk places the phone in a coupler attached to the terminal, thus connecting the terminal to the computer. A conversation, as shown in figure 16-8, then begins between the computer and the clerk. In the illustration, the lines typed by the clerk are shaded.

After giving the date and time, the computer asks for the identification (ID?) of the user. Since the user code given in response is valid, MM044, the computer types READY. When the clerk replies RUN COSTING, which indicates that the costing program should be executed, the computer loads the program named COSTING, prints OUTPUT, and executes the program. It begins with a series of questions relating to the cost calculation. When all of the questions have been asked and answered, the cost summary is calculated and printed. The computer then types END OF OUTPUT and READY to indicate that it is ready for another job. Because the user does not have a second job, the clerk types LOGOFF. The computer then prints the time and the amount of CPU time the user will be charged for; and the terminal and computer are disconnected.

Remember that as the costing program is being executed, other terminals in the system are being used for other purposes. This, in fact, is what distinguishes a time-sharing system from other real-time systems. In a time-sharing system, the terminals in the system can be used for many different purposes. Thus, one terminal may be used for calculating printing costs, another terminal for making cash-flow projections, another for making an engineering calculation. In other real-time systems, all terminals are used as part of one integrated system, such as the order-processing system described earlier.

REAL-TIME APPLICATIONS

Although real-time systems can be used for basic business applications such as order writing, inventory, and payroll, they are more likely to be used for specialized applications in industries such as insurance, bank-

```
DATE 02/17/77  TIME 12.73  ID? MM044
READY  RUN COSTING
OUTPUT

              PRINTING BID

NUMBER OF PAGES?
384

PAGE SIZE?
7.125, 10.125

CODE FOR PAPER USED IN TEXT?
50CM

CODE FOR END SHEETS?
801
INVALID CODE--TRY AGAIN.
80K

CODE FOR COVER?
BL

NUMBER OF COLORS--TEXT?
2

NUMBER OF COLORS--COVER?
4

BINDING CODE?
C12

QUANTITY TO BE PRINTED?
10000

         COSTS

PREP        1,424.00
PLATES        858.00
PRESS       6,309.00
STOCK       5,924.00
BINDING     9,038.00

TOTAL... $23,553.00

END OF OUTPUT
READY  LOGOFF
TIME 12.91  CPU TIME 1.9 SECONDS
```

FIGURE 16-8   A time-sharing example

ing, air transportation, manufacturing, and retail distribution. In the insurance industry, for example, handling customer inquiries can be a major problem for the customer-service department. To illustrate, suppose a health insurance company with several million policyholders has a home office in Chicago and branch offices in twenty-one cities

FIGURE 16-9   A visual-display terminal

throughout the country. To minimize duplication of records, all policy records are kept in the home office. When a policyholder calls the Kansas City branch to find out details of coverage, the customer-service department must request the policy from the home office and then call the customer when the policy arrives. Because of mailing delays, the entire process is likely to take two or more days.

As an alternative, consider a real-time system in which all policy information is stored on direct-access devices in the home office and all branch offices are connected to the home office in a communication network. The terminals used in the branches are visual-display terminals as illustrated in figure 16-9. To make an inquiry, a clerk uses the keyboard of the terminal. When data is received, it is displayed on the screen. Thus when a customer calls a branch for information, the clerk types the request for information on the keyboard, giving proper codes and policy numbers. This inquiry is transmitted to the computer in the home office, where the appropriate records are accessed from direct-access files. The requested information is then displayed on the visual-display terminal. Since the entire process takes only a few seconds, the clerk is able to give a reply to the customer after only a short pause.

A typical real-time application in banking is savings-account processing. In this type of system, teller terminals such as the one in figure 16-10 are connected to a central computer. These special-purpose terminals can accept data via the keyboard; they can also print data on a continuous form and on passbooks inserted into the slot on the right side of the device. The terminals can be located in the same building as the

FIGURE 16-10   A teller terminal

computer or in distant branch offices. When a customer wishes to withdraw money from an account, the teller places the passbook in the terminal and keys data such as transaction code, teller code, account number, and amount of withdrawal. Besides being printed on a continuous-form register within the terminal, this transaction data is transmitted to the computer, which accesses the master record, updates the record, and prints the transaction data and new balance in the passbook. At the end of the day, control totals accumulated by the computer for each teller are available to assist in balancing cash. If control totals don't balance, the transaction register in the terminal is available to help locate errors.

One of the first real-time business applications was the airline reservation system. In this application, an inventory of the available seats for every flight in the country is kept by one central computer. When a customer requests a reservation on a flight, the clerk keys the request on a terminal designed specifically for this purpose. Upon receiving the request, the computer checks the direct-access record for the flight to determine if space is available. If so, the reservation is confirmed, the number of available seats is reduced, and a confirmation message is printed on the terminal. If space isn't available, the customer can be advised immediately to seek another flight.

Just as important as making a reservation in an airline system is processing a cancellation. Here again, the transaction can be processed and the master record updated in a few seconds, thus making the cancelled seats available to any other terminal in the country. Since there was no way of keeping records current in earlier nonmechanized systems, flights that were supposedly filled often took off filled to 80 percent or less capacity.

In manufacturing, real-time systems are used to control shop-floor production. For example, a shop-floor terminal such as the one in figure 16-11 can be used by factory workers to punch on and off a job. When a worker punches on a job, the input device reads an employee badge showing employee number and a punched card containing the number and description of the job he or she is to work on. The computer, which has a master production schedule available to it via direct-access files, can then compare the sequence of jobs done by a worker with the sequence of jobs scheduled. If a worker punches onto the wrong job, the computer responds with an immediate instruction on a printer terminal, indicating the job that should be done next. Thus any deviation from the master schedule can be corrected before a problem is created.

When a worker punches off a job, he or she inserts a badge and the punched card giving the job description, and then, using the slides at the top of the terminal, keys the number of pieces produced. The computer then updates production records so the current status of every job in the shop is always available. If a manager desires information about a particular job, the master record can be accessed and displayed on a

FIGURE 16-11 A shop-floor terminal

visual-display or typewriter terminal. This contrasts a traditional system in which an expediter may spend several hours tracking down the location and status of a job.

One of the problems of a retail department store is authorizing credit transactions at the point of sale. If it takes too long, a customer may become dissatisfied. On the other hand, if authorization procedures become lax, profits can be lessened because of bad debts. One alternative is a real-time system using ordinary touch telephones for input and audio response through the phones (the human voice) for output. As the sales clerk fills out the sales slip for a credit transaction, he or she picks up the phone and keys the number of the computer. When the computer answers with a beeping tone, the clerk keys the account number and the amount of the sale. The computer then accesses the customer's record and determines if the transaction is okay. If so, a prerecorded reply such as "Transaction is okay" is given over the phone. If the transaction is not okay, the computer can reply with the name of the manager for the customer to contact for further information. Because the inquiry is made and answered in seconds, more credit authorizations can be made with less customer dissatisfaction.

Although this sampling of applications barely touches on the diversity and significance of real-time applications, it should be clear that real-time systems make possible new dimensions in customer service and management control. Using real-time technology, it is possible to answer customer inquiries without making return calls. It is possible to check a customer's credit without delay. It is possible to provide management information within seconds from the time that exceptional conditions occur.

DISCUSSION

As you can now see, the term *data-communication system* covers a lot of ground. It can refer to an offline, online batch-processing, or online real-time system. It can refer to a system that uses offline terminals such as paper-tape readers or card readers; to a real-time system that uses general-purpose terminals such as teletypewriters, visual-display units, or telephones; or to a real-time system that uses special-purpose terminals such as teller terminals in banking or shop-floor terminals for production control. On the one hand, a data-communication system might involve only a simple offline connection between two branches of a company; on the other hand, it might involve 1600 terminals connected to an enormous computer system.

Multiprogramming, as described in chapter 10, is often essential to the real-time system. Multiprogramming means that two or more programs are executed by a computer in the same period of time. Since a computer (or its CPU) can execute only one instruction at a time, this means that two or more programs are loaded into storage and the CPU switches back and forth between the programs.

To illustrate the need for multiprogramming, suppose a company uses a real-time system for processing orders. Since orders can come in from any of the branches throughout the day, the order-processing program must always be available in storage to handle transactions. On the other hand, there may be very few orders at certain periods of the day—for example, the lunch hour—so the system is likely to be idle much of the time. If multiprogramming is used, however, the idle time is used for other applications such as payroll, sales analysis, or financial reporting.

Suppose, then, that a second program—such as a payroll check-writing program—is loaded into storage along with the order-processing program and the supervisor program. This is illustrated in figure 16-12. Now, whenever the order-processing program is idle, the computer branches to the supervisor program, which in turn branches to the next instruction to

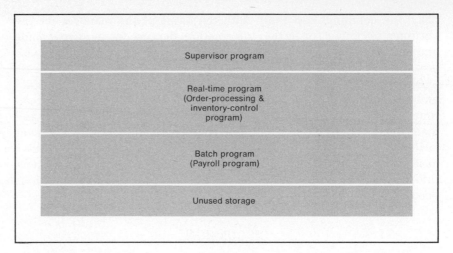

| Supervisor program |
| Real-time program (Order-processing & inventory-control program) |
| Batch program (Payroll program) |
| Unused storage |

FIGURE 16-12   Core storage during multiprogramming

be executed in the payroll program. Similarly, whenever a transaction is received from one of the branch offices, the payroll program is automatically interrupted and the location of the next instruction to be executed is stored for use by the supervisor. The computer then automatically branches to the supervisor, which branches to the proper instruction for handling the transaction in the order-processing program. By using multiprogramming, the real-time program is always available for handling transactions, and batch programs are executed whenever the real-time program is not in use. The result is a more productive computer system. In actual practice, two or more batch programs are likely to be multiprogrammed with the real-time program.

Although multiprogramming is common for real-time systems, I do not mean to imply that all real-time systems use it. On the contrary, there seems to be a trend toward somewhat smaller computer systems that deal with a single real-time application. These systems are referred to as *dedicated systems* since no attempt is made to run batch-processing programs while the real-time system is in operation. If batch programs are to be run, they are executed when the real-time system is not being used, such as during the second or third shifts.

Minicomputers, as described in chapter 17, are often associated with real-time systems. For instance, the control unit in figure 16-7 can be a minicomputer that takes care of some of the message-handling requirements of the system. This use is referred to as *front-end processing* and can take some of the workload off of the main computer.

Similarly, minicomputers can be used as *intelligent terminals*. That means that the terminal has the circuitry to do some of the processing, such as editing data, before it is sent to the central computer. For instance, a teller terminal could contain circuitry that checks savings-account transactions for validity before they are sent to the main computer. The intelligent terminal might also calculate the new balance before it is printed in the customer's passbook. Here again, the minicomputer reduces the workload of the main computer.

When analyzing the feasibility of data-communication systems, offline and remote batch systems are relatively straightforward. In general, the benefits of speed (turnaround time) and accuracy (resulting from better data control) can be weighed against any additional costs. And often these systems can be justified based on cost reductions. (Real-time systems, however, are a problem all their own. As a result, they are described in more detail in the next topic.)

1. Data-communication systems are intended to reduce the time spent in collecting and distributing data within a system. There is wide variation in the types of systems, which include offline, online batch-processing, online real-time, and time-sharing systems.

2. Although real-time systems can be used for basic applications such as order processing, they are more likely to be found in specialized applications in industries such as banking, insurance, and manufacturing. A wide range of general- and special-purpose terminals is available to make these applications possible.

SUMMARY

collecting data	real-time system
distributing data	real time
data-communication system	teletypewriter
data communication	time-sharing system
communication line	inhouse system
offline	multiprogramming
terminal	supervisor program
paper tape	supervisor
online	dedicated system
remote job entry	intelligent terminal
RJE	

TERMINOLOGY

1. What do you think the major cost additions of a batch system like the one in figure 16-4 are? List the benefits of this system, assuming that it is used solely for order entry.

2. Assume that RJE is used on three different campuses of a state college. The computer is located on the main campus. The RJE stations are used

QUESTIONS

for administrative data as well as for student programs. What are the benefits of a system like this?

3. What are the benefits of the real-time insurance inquiry system described in this chapter? Which do you think are most significant? Do you think they would justify the cost of a system like this?

4. List the benefits of the real-time teller system described in the chapter. Which do you think are the most significant? Do you think they would justify the cost of a system like this?

TOPIC 2
JUSTIFYING THE
REAL-TIME SYSTEM

To determine whether a real-time system is advantageous for a company to install, the cost of the proposed system must be balanced against the expected benefits. When you compare the costs of a real-time system with the costs of a traditional system, however, you normally find a significant cost increase. Real-time systems involve hardware, programming and system-design costs that have no counterpart in batch systems. These costs must therefore be offset by some unusual benefits.

Hardware Costs

Some of the obvious hardware costs of a real-time system are terminals, communication lines, and large-capacity, fast-access, direct-access devices. In addition, a real-time system requires some special components that make possible the transmission of data between terminals and a computer. Between each terminal and its communication line, for example, there is a *modem* (*modulator/demodulator*) that converts data from EDP code to communication-line code, and vice versa. Similarly, between the computer and the communication lines, there is usually a minicomputer (a front-end processor) that controls the order in which data is sent and received by each of the online terminals. In addition, the CPU itself must be equipped with certain features that facilitate real-time processing and multiprogramming. Because of these hardware requirements, a real-time system is likely to cost considerably more than a batch-processing system.

Programming Costs

Just as a real-time system requires more complicated hardware, it requires more complicated programming. As a result, a real-time system normally requires more programming hours than a comparable batch system, as well as higher paid (better-trained) programmers. The net result is significantly higher programming budgets for real-time systems.

To illustrate the programming demands of a real-time system, consider that the real-time program must be able to handle any condition that comes up when a transaction is being handled. In making an airline reservation, for example, there are over eighty different operations that might be involved. Thus the program must be able to handle all eighty operations in any combination. In contrast, many of the exceptional conditions in a batch-processing system can be handled through clerical procedures rather than programming routines.

In addition to the routines that are required by the application itself, though, a real-time system requires many hundreds of instructions that make possible the sending and receiving of data. For example, the controlling routines must be able to handle questions such as: Which terminal is next in line to send data? Did the transmission of data take place without error? Did the transaction contain a valid terminal address? If an incoming transmission contains an error, has the sending terminal been notified and the error corrected?

Because of the application and control routines required, real-time programs are likely to be exceptionally long and require several man-years of programming time. The real-time program for one company's airline reservation system, for example, consists of over 600,000 instructions. In practice, then, several programmers usually work together developing the routines for a single real-time program. This makes it possible to complete the program within a reasonable period of time, but it also increases the difficulties involved in testing and debugging the program.

System-Design Costs

The design costs for a real-time system are commonly several times more than those for a batch system. The problems of real-time design are such that they demand the best people in the computer industry, and thousands of hours of labor are required for the design of a typical system. In fact, real-time system design is becoming a study in itself. Many books have been written about the problems of real-time system design; these problems range from statistically projecting the volume of transactions to be handled by a system, to determining the best methods of file organization for the online files, to developing the most efficient operating procedures for the terminal operators. To give you some idea of the complexity and significance of real-time design problems, let me briefly describe just a few.

One of the major problems is determining the hardware requirements of a system. How many terminals are needed to handle the present volume of transactions and the volume expected in one, two, three, or more years? What type of communication lines should be used—telephone, telegraph, leased or purchased? If communication lines are to be purchased, which network of lines will keep costs to a minimum but still handle peak loads? Which direct-access devices are large enough and fast enough for the online files?

To complicate the problem, a computer user normally deals with three or more vendors when purchasing a real-time system—one for the computer, one for the communication lines, and one for the terminals. Thus, he must coordinate information from several sources. As an indication of how difficult this problem of determining hardware requirements can be, there have been some overwhelming mistakes made in the past. One airline company, for example, installed a system that required 50 percent more terminals and cost more than twice as much as originally expected. Unfortunately, because hardware planning is often done several years before a real-time system is actually installed, such gross errors are not uncommon.

A second problem is that of establishing accounting controls. In a system where all transactions are processed as they occur, how can you be sure at the end of the day that all transactions have been processed by the computer? And if processed, how can you be sure they've been processed correctly? Even more difficult, if the central computer fails (suppose a direct-access device isn't operating properly), how do you know which transactions have been processed correctly and which transactions need to be resubmitted?

This leads to another problem—that of backup. Since a real-time system is critical to a company's operations, alternative procedures must be available immediately if the main system should fail. In a small system, this may mean a return to manual procedures until the computer is repaired. Then, when the computer system is operating again, all transactions that have been processed manually can be processed by the computer system to update the files. In a large system such as an airline reservation system, however, a system failure would be a disaster. As a result, these systems are commonly made up of two or more complete computer systems (*duplexed computers*). Then, when one fails, the second system automatically takes over so that the real-time system never stops operating. In either case, however, there are many related problems to consider. How can you be sure that the switchover from one system to the next took place with no lost or incompletely processed transactions? How can each branch be notified as to which transaction was last to be processed and which transactions should be resubmitted when the system begins operating again?

In summary, the design of real-time systems is one of the most demanding problems in the computer industry today. In fact, it is fair to say that the lack of competent design personnel has been a major limitation in the development of real-time systems. Because of the cost of an experienced real-time system-design group, even deciding whether a real-time system is a practical consideration can be a significant expense.

The Benefits of Real-Time Systems

To determine whether a real-time system is economically justifiable, the benefits of the proposed system must, of course, be balanced against the cost of the system. All too often, however, the benefits are intangible or difficult to measure—such as improved customer service or increased control of operations or more timely management information. As a result, the system analyst must justify the system by balancing some hard-to-measure benefits against some very real hardware, programming, and system-design costs.

To illustrate, consider the real-time order-processing and inventory-control system described in topic 1. To justify the increased cost of the system, the analyst must evaluate characteristics such as improved customer service and its effect on sales, faster inventory updating and its effect on inventory levels, and greater order-handling efficiency and its effect on morale, absenteeism, and the employee turnover rate. In short, it is difficult, and at times impossible, to correctly estimate the effect on profits that a real-time system will have. Although this is also true for batch-processing systems, the problems are compounded when evaluating real-time systems.

This same type of reasoning applies to justifying time-sharing systems. In general, the cost of the system or service is compared with the increased productivity or morale of the persons using the service. For example, if an engineer making $1500 per month could increase his or her productivity 50 percent by using a time-sharing service that costs $300 per month, the service would be justified. Here again, though, the problem is in measuring something that is difficult to measure—in this case, increased productivity. Thus there is still much debate as to the extent to which time-sharing services are justifiable.

In some cases, however, the benefits of a real-time or a time-sharing system seem to more than justify the costs. For example, today no major airline could afford to be without an airline reservation system. Such a system not only affects customer service, but, more important, enables airlines to maintain higher loading rates than is otherwise possible. By keeping a more accurate and current inventory of available seats, airlines have been able to increase the average percentage of seats filled for each flight. Because this has a direct effect on profits, this benefit alone justifies a reservation system. One major airline, for instance, is reported to have increased revenues by over $1 million per year when it improved its load-planning capabilities. In addition, the airline claims that the reservation system has enabled clerks to increase their productivity by 30 percent, even though the cost of the entire system is only 1.5 percent of total operating expenses.

To give another example, consider a hospital that is in the process of installing a real-time accounting system. Thirty-eight terminals throughout the hospital will be online to a central computer so that charges can be entered into a patient's account as the charges are actually incurred. Because many of the separate charges are normally lost through the inefficiency of the old manual system, the hospital estimates an increase of $625,000 each year in patient billings, not to mention the reduction in paperwork for the hospital's 400 nurses. If these estimates hold true, the increased billings alone will more than pay for the real-time system.

DISCUSSION

Although real-time systems have tremendous fascination from both a technical and a management point of view, two critical questions have been raised in recent years as to their practicality and contribution to profits. For one thing, as mentioned before, some overwhelming errors have been made in the design and implementation of real-time systems: actual system costs have far exceeded the anticipated costs, and programming and system-design projects have fallen months and even years behind the original installation schedules. As a result, many companies question whether a real-time system can, in fact, be installed at a reasonable cost given the present hardware and communication-line costs and the present level of competency of design and programming personnel. Furthermore, many companies are questioning whether the actual benefits of real-time processing are as significant as they initially appeared to be.

The second question is whether or not several small dedicated systems aren't better than one large multipurpose system. The reasoning here is that large systems using multiprogramming and real-time updating of several online files tend to make extraordinary demands on programmers and system designers. They also tend to reduce the overall productivity of the computer systems themselves. (There are technical reasons for this that we don't need to get into.) As a result, hardware, programming, and system-design costs tend to increase at a rate that is out of proportion to the benefits of the system. In contrast, some analysts say that several small systems, each concerning itself with a single application or family of applications, is a more profitable alternative.

A third question that must be answered in the years ahead concerns a particular type of real-time system—the *total information system,* or the *management-information system (MIS)* as described in chapter 11. The idea of a total system or MIS became popular in the mid-1960s and continues to interest executives throughout the country. The theory behind the management-information system is that one of management's traditional problems has been getting information that is current. However, if the major files—such as inventory, accounts receivable, and general ledger—could be stored on direct-access devices and updated on a real-time basis, it would be possible to provide management the information it needs within minutes from the time of the request. For example, if the vice-president in charge of sales requests the year-to-date sales totals for each branch office, this sales report could be printed or displayed on a terminal in an office within minutes from the time that he or she keyed the request. If a credit manager keys a request for the credit history of an account, this information could likewise be printed or displayed within seconds. Thus by solving the problem of providing current information, the managers throughout a company will supposedly become more efficient and make business decisions that are more profitable. And this, of course, should give a company an advantage over its competitors.

The question concerning the management-information system is whether or not managers need real-time information at all. John Dearden, professor of Business Administration at the Harvard Business School, has stated this criticism in an article entitled "Myth of Real-time Management Information," *Harvard Business Review* (May–June 1966): "It is my personal opinion that, of all the ridiculous things that have been foisted on the long-suffering executive in the name of science and progress, the real-time management-information system is the silliest." He then describes what he considers to be the major duties of top management and shows why these duties do not require real-time information. If his analysis is correct (needless to say, there is much disagreement on the issue), the millions of dollars that have been spent on developing MIS systems are certainly cause for concern.

I mention these issues to point out that the application of real-time systems to business problems is a developing art that is barely out of its infancy. That's why these rather basic issues are still unsettled. In the next few years, hardware costs are certain to drop, and the level of programming and system-design expertise is sure to rise. However, it will be years before all the profitable real-time applications are discovered, and all the unprofitable applications have been tried and abandoned. Similarly, it will be years before standard operating procedures for design and implementation are developed. Until then, this area of the computer industry will continue to be one of the most challenging and dynamic in the entire world of business.

SUMMARY

1. Some extraordinary hardware, programming, and system-design costs put the burden of justifying the real-time system on correctly estimating the benefits of the system. In the past, some classic blunders have been made, both in estimating costs and benefits.

2. The fact that several major questions concerning the usefulness of real-time systems are still unsettled attests to the newness of real-time technology. These issues will contiue to be debated until the technology and the programming and system-design expertise are more fully developed.

TERMINOLOGY

modem
duplexed system
total information system
management-information system
MIS

QUESTIONS

1. Consider the time-sharing application in topic 1—the calculation of printing costs for sales estimates and for billing. Assume that estimates were usually done by sales personnel at a cost of about $20 per estimate. In addition, about 2 percent of the estimates were found to contain errors when recalculated for billing. What else would you want to know in order to determine feasibility?

2. A hospital estimates that it will increase billings by $625,000 per year by installing a real-time accounting system. If their yearly billing is $22,000,000, does this increase seem reasonable to you? How could a hospital lose $625,000 through faulty billing procedures? What data do you think the hospital had on which they based this estimate?

17 MINICOMPUTERS

Minicomputers are small computers. They are made up of one CPU, one or more input devices, and one or more output devices, and are controlled by a program stored in the main storage of the CPU. Perhaps the distinguishing characteristic of a minicomputer is its price. In general, it will cost less than $50,000. If this requirement isn't met, at least one model of a minicomputer family must cost less than $50,000 if the other models in it are to be classified as minicomputers. Because of the low cost, minicomputers are usually purchased rather than leased.

In an attempt to further define a minicomputer, other attributes have often been included in the minicomputer definition. For example, some say a minicomputer has from 4K to 64K storage positions. Others say the storage of a minicomputer must consist of addressable *words* rather than bytes. (A word of minicomputer storage usually consists of two bytes, so a 32K machine can store 64K bytes.) Still others say that a minicomputer must be general purpose (able to do a variety of jobs) rather than special purpose. But these and other attempts to narrow the definition of a minicomputer have met with debate.

In fact then, there is no general agreement on the definition of a minicomputer. So price is as good a guideline as any. When does a minicomputer become a small business computer? When it costs more than $50,000. Using this guideline, IBM's System/3, as described in chapter 5, is a small business computer; IBM's System/32 is a minicomputer, because the smallest System/32's cost less than $50,000.

In general, a minicomputer is like a maxicomputer in concept. As a result, this chapter should present no special difficulties for you. If you understand computers, you understand minicomputers. That's why this chapter will try primarily to show you how minicomputers differ from maxicomputers in terms of hardware, software, and applications.

HARDWARE

As computer technology advanced, the cost of circuitry and storage in the CPU was reduced severalfold—even though processing speeds increased. To get the price of the entire minicomputer system down, however, the cost of I/O devices had to be reduced accordingly. But card readers, printers, and tape and disk devices were high-priced indeed. As a result, the early minicomputers often used paper tape as input and typewriter as output. These limited I/O devices, of course, limited the use of the minicomputers.

In recent years, a number of I/O devices have been developed specifically for the minicomputer. The minicomputer in figure 17-1, for example, has a visual-display device for output, a keyboard for input, and *tape cassettes* for auxiliary, offline storage. The tape cassettes, which are similar to the ones used with home tape recorders, are inserted in the top of the system and can be used to store data or programs.

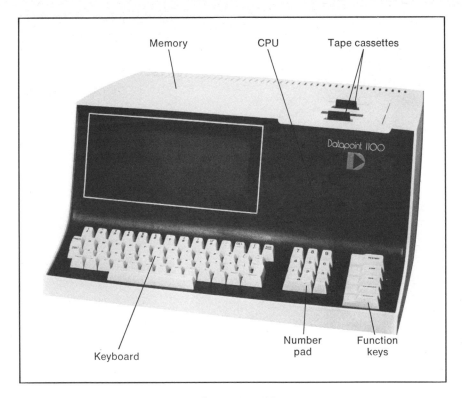

FIGURE 17-1   A minicomputer with cassette I/O

Just as the cassette provides inexpensive tape I/O, the *diskette* provides inexpensive disk I/O. These disks (often called *floppy disks*) resemble a 45 RPM record stored in an envelope. The entire envelope is placed in the disk unit as shown in figure 17-2, and data can be read from or written on the diskette. A typical diskette can store about 250,000 bytes of data. Although access speeds are generally slow in comparison to larger disk devices, they are fast enough for most minicomputer applications.

To keep costs down, many of the printers used on minicomputers are typewriter-like devices. That means they print one character at a time. As printing requirements increase, however, a line printer can be added to the system. These printers will range in speed from 100 to 600 lines per minute.

Visual-display units (also known as *cathode-ray tubes,* or *CRTs*) are commonly used for minicomputer output. They can be used to display any data that has been entered into the system. You might notice that neither of the systems in figure 17-1 or 17-2 has a card reader. Instead, data is entered through the keyboard of the computer. As data is entered,

FIGURE 17-2   A minicomputer with diskette I/O

it is displayed on the CRT so the operator can visually verify it. This method of data entry reduces cost, because auxiliary keying devices aren't needed.

As a firm grows, it can add data entry stations to the system, consisting of keyboard and CRT. For instance, the system illustrated schematically in figure 17-3, has three data-entry stations on line to the system that processes the data. Here again, the data is entered directly into the system under control of a data-entry program. The data is usually stored on a cassette or diskette before subsequent processing.

In addition to typewriter, CRT, cassette, diskette, and printer I/O, several other devices are often available with minicomputer systems. For instance, there are small card readers that use 96-column cards as described in chapter 5. There are tape devices that can read magnetic tapes like those used on maxicomputers. There are cartridge disk devices that provide enlarged disk capacities. And there are devices that can read

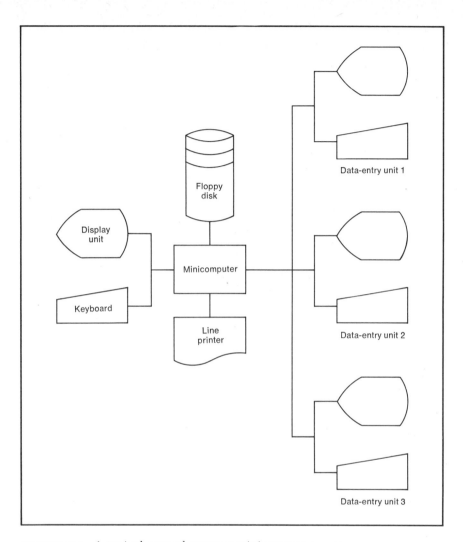

FIGURE 17-3   A typical general-purpose minicomputer system

data from magnetic strips mounted on ledger cards. In short, a minicomputer can usually be adapted to a wide range of processing requirements.

SOFTWARE

To some extent, software has been a major reason why minicomputer sales haven't grown more rapidly. Early systems often had to be programmed in machine language. And software that was supplied by the manufacturers was often limited and unreliable. Today, however, most minicomputers offer a range of software products that include operating systems and application packages.

The operating system of a minicomputer typically offers a monitor, or supervisor, program that controls the operation of the system, language translators, sort programs, and utilities. The operating system may also provide for multiprogramming as described in chapter 10. In comparison to the operating system of a maxicomputer, however, the facilities for the minicomputer will be more limited. For example, a multiprogramming system may provide for only two programs in storage, whereas a larger operating system will provide for many more.

Similarly, the number and scope of the language translators will be limited. And in some cases, compilation will have to be done by a larger system, after which the object programs can be run by the smaller system. On the smallest minicomputers, no language translators are available, and machine language is used.

The most common languages for minicomputers are assembler language, RPG II, BASIC, and FORTRAN (as described in chapter 8). In addition, some minicomputer manufacturers have developed special-purpose languages for their machines. For example, Datapoint Corporation has a language called *Databus,* which can be used for creating data-entry programs as well as processing programs. COBOL is available with some of the more recent minicomputer systems, but it hasn't received much use as yet.

Application packages are generalized programs designed for specific applications. For instance, payroll and accounts-receivable packages are quite common. Since these applications are similar regardless of the industry, these packages can be used in a wide range of businesses with only minor adjustments. Other application packages may be designed for a specific industry, such as a banking package. Use of these packages can lower the cost of system development significantly so that the minicomputer becomes more feasible.

APPLICATIONS

Because the definition of a minicomputer is imprecise, it is hard to say exactly which applications are minicomputer ones. If one uses a broad definition, minicomputer applications are described in several other areas of this book. In chapter 11, process control, which is often done by a minicomputer, is described. In chapter 15, key-to-tape data-entry systems, which are controlled by a minicomputer, are described. In chapter 16, intelligent terminals and front-end processors for data-communication systems are mentioned, both of which can be thought of as minicomputers. Many people, however, think of minicomputers as general-purpose machines, so to them these applications are not minicomputer applications at all.

In any event, minicomputers have expanded the range of computer applications considerably. Because of their size, they can be used in locations that are impractical for other systems. Because of their cost, they can be dedicated to uses that are impractical for other systems. Thus we find minicomputers used in the homes of engineers for computations, in schools for computer-assisted instruction, and in hospitals for collecting medical data.

If we try to classify general-purpose minicomputer systems by use, we might start with four classifications: (1) single-purpose systems, (2) multipurpose systems, (3) time-sharing systems, and (4) distributed processing systems. Although these classifications aren't clearcut, they should give you a better idea about the uses of minicomputers.

Single-Purpose Systems

In many cases, a minicomputer is purchased for one and only one application. For instance, a system like the one in figure 17-1 might be used for accounting projections. A series of programs might be involved, but all will deal with entering and processing data for projecting financial outcomes. Similarly, a computer might be purchased for use in a special research project. Because of its low cost, the benefits from the single application repay the cost of the system in a short period of time.

A single-purpose system is often installed as a *turnkey system*. That means that the user doesn't do any of the programming for the system. It is either done by the manufacturer or by an outside service group. When it is installed, the user (theoretically, at least) simply has to turn the key to get it to do the intended processing. To make this type of installation work effectively, users have to specify exactly what they want out of the system so they don't demand much change once it is installed.

An example of a turnkey system is one that was installed for a pharmacy in the East. This system keeps the prescription histories of several thousand patients of a nearby nursing home. The system prints labels to be applied to the prescription fulfillments and can be used to check past prescriptions. In addition, it automatically searches for potentially dangerous drug combinations and prints out warning messages. The system consists of CPU, keyboard, CRT, printer, and disk.

Multipurpose Batch Systems

A minicomputer is often used for a range of applications in a small business. A minicomputer like the one in figure 17-3, for example, might be used for billing, accounts receivable, inventory control, sales analysis, and payroll. Multiprogramming is used on a system like this; therefore, one program controls data entry while other programs process data on a batch basis. In brief, the minicomputer operates much like a maxicomputer—except for cost and method of data entry.

The use of minicomputers has allowed many small businesses to install their first computer. To attract this business, manufacturers try to make their systems so simple to operate that the transition from manual to computerized processing can be done with little confusion. To a great extent, they have been successful in recent years.

Time-Sharing Systems

Time-sharing systems are described in chapter 16. Quite simply, several users operating on typewriter or CRT terminals make use of one CPU. Because the CPU can process data many times faster than it can be entered through the keyboards, all users get the impression that they have the sole control of the computer system.

A typical minicomputer application using time sharing is *computer-assisted instruction,* or *CAI.* Here, the computer gives students instruction through the terminal, and the students make appropriate responses through the keyboards. Based on these responses, the computer program varies its instruction to meet the requirements of each individual. Needless to say, the effectiveness of this kind of system depends on the quality of the instructional programs. Nevertheless, CAI has proven effective in many different programs throughout the country. Another typical time-sharing application is engineering computation. Here, many engineers will have access to the computer through desk-top terminals. As a result, each engineer has powerful computational capabilities at his or her fingertips.

The minicomputer has made many time-sharing applications possible because it has lowered costs. For example, a dedicated CAI system within the school itself can eliminate the communication line costs associated with a larger centralized system that serves several schools. In addition, the minicomputer system is likely to be simpler and less costly than the comparable cost of sharing a larger one. In a recent case, one insurance company estimates its yearly savings at $100,000 as a result of switching from a time-sharing service to its own inhouse minicomputer time-sharing system.

In many cases, the minicomputer time-sharing system is a dedicated single-purpose system, such as the CAI system just described. In some cases, however, the time-sharing application is multiprogrammed with batch applications. As the system complexity increases, however, system cost rises, and a firm is often out of the minicomputer range. As a result, either the time-sharing operations or the batch operations are usually limited in complexity when minicomputers are used.

Distributed Processing Systems

Distributed processing means that the computing activities of an organization are done in several different locations. It is a recent term and has not yet received a narrow definition. The key point, however, is that data is actually processed at several different sites, not only at one central location.

For example, figure 17-4 illustrates a distributed processing network. Here, one central computer is supported by eight minicomputers in branch offices. During the day, each minicomputer collects data and does some branch-office processing. Then the minicomputers can transmit branch-office data to the central computer at night for further processing. If necessary, data can be transmitted back to the branch computers for report printing or display the next morning.

The primary intent of a distributed processing network is to reduce overall EDP costs. By dividing the total workload, the overall complexity of the system is reduced, and system design and programming costs are lowered. Since these have become a major portion of the data-processing budget, the overall data-processing costs are thus lowered, even if the

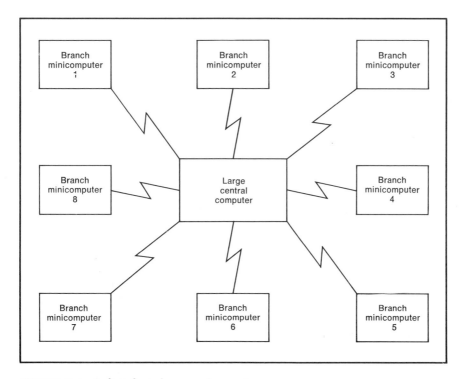

FIGURE 17-4   A distributed processing system

total hardware costs show a slight increase. In addition, each branch has greater control over their own data-processing functions.

There is now a trend toward distributed processing, or decentralization, of computer activities. This has taken place because the complexity of large central systems has often become unmanageable. As a result, programming and system-development costs have grown at an unacceptable rate. The minicomputer and distributed-processing systems offer a way to decrease system complexity.

The minicomputer sites in a distributed processing network can perform in a variety of ways. The minicomputers may be singlepurpose, but they are more likely to be multipurpose. They may offer time-sharing to the branch users. They may pass data to the central computer throughout the day or only during off hours. Regardless of the variations, the minicomputers must actually do some processing in a distributed-processing network; it is not enough that they collect data for processing by the central computer.

DISCUSSION

Although this has been a brief introduction to minicomputers, you probably can see their place in business data processing. First, they make small special-purpose applications possible. Second, they make it possible for small businesses to install general-purpose computers for business data processing. Third, they make specialized time-sharing systems practical. Fourth, they make distributed data processing practical—an area with large potential for cost reductions.

Although minicomputers have been around since the 1950s, the growth of the minicomputer industry was limited for many years by software and I/O devices. Once these problems were solved, the sales of minicomputers leaped. For instance, one study shows that 90,000 minicomputers were in use in 1973, and 50,000 more were installed in 1974. That's a growth rate of 56 percent.

To look at it another way, about one-fourth of the installed computers in 1967 were minicomputers. By 1975, however, over half of the computers were. This reflects the use of minicomputers in businesses that could never before afford a computer, as well as their use in distributed data-processing systems. With the recent trend toward decentralization, the minicomputer industry should continue to grow at a rate faster than the rest of the computer industry.

SUMMARY   1. Conceptually, a minicomputer is like a maxicomputer. The primary difference is cost. To keep costs down, minicomputers often use special I/O devices, such as cassette and diskette units.

2. Because of size and cost, the minicomputer can be used in many applications in which a maxicomputer would be impractical. In large companies, minicomputers are used in distributed processing systems in an attempt to reduce the complexity and cost of the overall system.

TERMINOLOGY

minicomputer	CRT
tape cassette	turnkey system
diskette	time-sharing system
floppy disk	computer-assisted instruction
visual-display unit	CAI
cathode-ray tube	distributed processing

QUESTIONS

1. If a general-purpose minicomputer costs $40,000, how small a business might consider computerizing some of their data-processing applications? Think in terms of annual revenue and number of employees.

2. Some people in the data-processing industry now recommend complete decentralization of computer operations. In other words, they recommend a minicomputer network with no central computer at all. Each minicomputer would perform specific applications, so it is possible more than one minicomputer might be used at a single location. It's also possible that the minicomputers would communicate with one another. This type of network is intended to eliminate the complexity of a large central computer entirely. But does the approach seem feasible to you? Why or why not?

18 PERSONNEL WITHIN THE COMPUTER INSTALLATION

The term *computer installation* refers to the EDP department within a company. Although a large percentage of the budget of a computer installation is spent on equipment, the largest portion is spent on personnel. A 1971 survey of the nation's largest computer users, for example, showed that 44.6 percent of the average installation's budget was for personnel, while only 34.2 percent was spent on equipment. In recent years, the personnel cost has continued to increase relative to equipment costs. Some of the personnel requirements of a computer user are thus described in this chapter.

In general, there are three major types of activities within a computer installation: system analysis, programming, and operations. As a result, a computer user requires one or more employees skilled in each of these disciplines.

System Analysis

The term *system analysis* covers a lot of ground. From the time that a company decides that some particular operation might be a profitable computer application until the time the application is actually running on the computer, there are many tasks required by the system-analysis function. These tasks include: (1) problem definition; (2) determining feasibility; (3) equipment evaluation; (4) system design; and (5) system implementation.

Three job titles commonly found on the system-analysis staff are system-analysis manager, senior system analyst, and system analyst. The system-analysis manager is in charge of a company's system-analysis activities. The senior system analyst, usually one of the more experienced members of the staff, directs various system-analysis projects. He or she normally works with one or more system analysts in meeting the objectives of the projects.

Because system analysis has such a major effect on the success of a system, good system analysts are a must for an EDP department. In general, system analysts must be able to communicate with and get information from employees at all levels within a company—from a clerk to the top executive; they must be familiar with a wide range of equipment and programming support; they must have some background in programming (often, they have worked one or two years as programmers before becoming analysts); they must be able to develop plans, solutions, and systems from the available data; and if they have any background in accounting, statistics, or industrial engineering, that helps too. In short, system analysts should have a broad range of abilities and still be strong enough technically to research hardware or software developments pertinent to the project on which they are working. Because it is difficult to find people with these capabilities, there is a lack of competent system analysts; this has been one of the major limitations to progress within the computer industry.

Programming

Within a typical computer installation, there are likely to be three different types of programmers. The programmer who writes programs for business applications—such as inventory or payroll programs—is commonly referred to as an *applications programmer*. The other two types of programmers are maintenance and systems programmers.

The *maintenance programmer* is responsible for making changes to programs that are already in use. For example, if a payroll program needs to be modified because of a change in tax laws, a maintenance programmer will be assigned to the job. By using maintenance programmers, applications programmers are free to develop new programs without being interrupted.

The *systems programmer* (also known as a software programmer) writes *systems programs* such as compilers, assemblers, sort programs, and other programs of an operating system. Because these are likely to be written in assembler language and require advanced programming techniques, the job of a systems programmer is considerably more technical than that of an applications programmer. Although systems programs have traditionally been supplied by computer manufacturers and other software suppliers, the majority of large computer users now employ one or more systems programmers of their own. These programmers usually don't write complete systems programs, but they may modify the system software supplied to them in order to make it more applicable to the requirements of their company. They are also responsible for seeing that the software runs as efficiently as possible.

Within a programming department, there are also job titles that indicate rank or tenure. For instance, senior programmer, programmer, junior programmer, and programmer trainee are commonly used titles that indicate the amount of experience a programmer has. After a person has done programming for a few years, he or she can advance in either of two directions: within the programming department—from junior programmer to programmer to senior programmer to programming manager—or switch to the system-analysis department. In some companies, the term programmer/analyst is used to indicate that a person has both system-analysis and programming responsibilities.

Operations

Operations refers to the daily production activities of an EDP department. This includes preparing data (usually, keypunching and verifying), scheduling and controlling the jobs to be run, operating the computer and associated equipment, and keeping a library of system and programming documentation, magnetic tapes, disk packs, and other records essential to the system. The various job titles within the operations department include manager or supervisor of operations, computer operator, punched-card equipment operator, keypunch supervisor, keypunch operator, scheduler, control clerk, and librarian. As you might guess, one of the responsibilities of the control clerk is to record and balance control totals that are kept within the EDP department.

While many of the jobs in operations are narrowly defined and thus routine, that of a computer operator can be quite demanding—particularly, with large computer systems. In addition to loading cards, mounting tapes and disk packs, and operating the computer console, the computer operator must be able to use job-control language and to locate and correct error conditions that occur during processing. Since this often requires knowledge of programming and operating systems, a good computer operator is likely to be promoted to a position as a programmer.

THE ORGANIZATION OF AN
EDP DEPARTMENT

An EDP department can be organized in several ways, depending on the size and goals of the department. For example, the EDP department of a small company may be organized as shown in figure 18-1. This department consists of one programmer/analyst, one programmer, one machine operator, and a data-preparation group—all reporting directly to the data-processing manager.

In contrast, a large computer installation might be organized as shown in figure 18-2. Here, the department manager will likely be referred to as the director of information systems rather than the data-processing manager. Reporting to the director are the system-analysis, programming, and operations managers who direct the activities of the department.

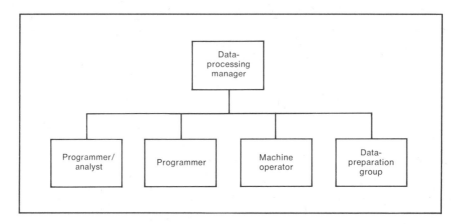

FIGURE 18-1   Organization of a small EDP staff

Needless to say, there are many other ways in which a department can be organized. It is common, for example, for system analysis and programming to be managed by a systems and programming manager. It is also common for maintenance programmers to report to the operations manager rather than the programming manager. Regardless of the variations, however, figures 18-1 and 18-2 are typical of small and large EDP departments.

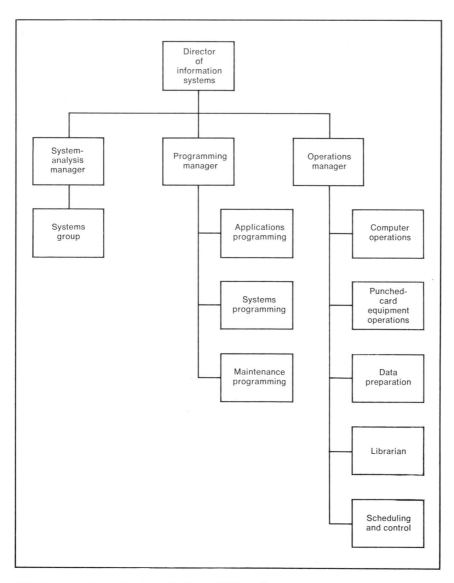

FIGURE 18-2   Organization of a large EDP staff

DISCUSSION

In addition to the normal computer user such as a bank or wholesale distributor, there are many other types of companies that require people trained in system analysis, programming, and operations. Computer manufacturers, for example, employ thousands of people trained in system analysis as marketing representatives. Software houses employ systems programmers to develop system software that can be marketed to computer users. When one company operates another company's computer system on a fee basis, it is referred to as *facilities management*. Facilities-management companies, therefore, require complete EDP staffs. The advantage of working for companies such as these is that in a relatively short period of time, you are exposed to the data-processing problems of many companies.

Regardless of the type of company, pay levels vary considerably for each kind of job. For example, the range of salaries for programmers in 1975 was from below $6000 per year to over $25,000 per year. In general, the pay level for a job depends on two factors: (1) the sophistication of the computer system used and (2) the type of problem or application being worked on. For instance, a programmer writing a real-time production-control program for a large direct-access system will be paid considerably more than a programmer working on a payroll application for a tape system. Similarly, an operator of a large, multiprogrammed disk system will be paid more than an operator of a card system.

SUMMARY

In general, the jobs within an EDP department center around three types of activity: system analysis, programming, and operations. Within any given company, there can be several levels of jobs and pay for each type of activity.

TERMINOLOGY

computer installation
applications programmer
maintenance programmer
systems programmer

systems program
operations
facilities management

QUESTIONS

1. A programmer is given the task of writing a program that projects sales for each of a company's inventory items based on sales for the last twelve months. Is this the job of an applications or systems programmer?

2. A programmer is given the task of modifying the job-control cards for a sort run so that it will execute more quickly. Is this the job of an applications or systems programmer?

SECTION FIVE

BASIC

This section introduces you to BASIC, a language that is widely used by people who have little background in computing. If you master all of the material in this section, you should attain a significant programming skill. Chapter 19 presents the critical material, so you should be prepared to put your major effort there.

(The teaching approach for this section was developed by Gerald Wohl of Pace University in New York City. My thanks to Jerry for letting me adapt it to the purposes of this book.)

19 AN INTRODUCTION TO BASIC

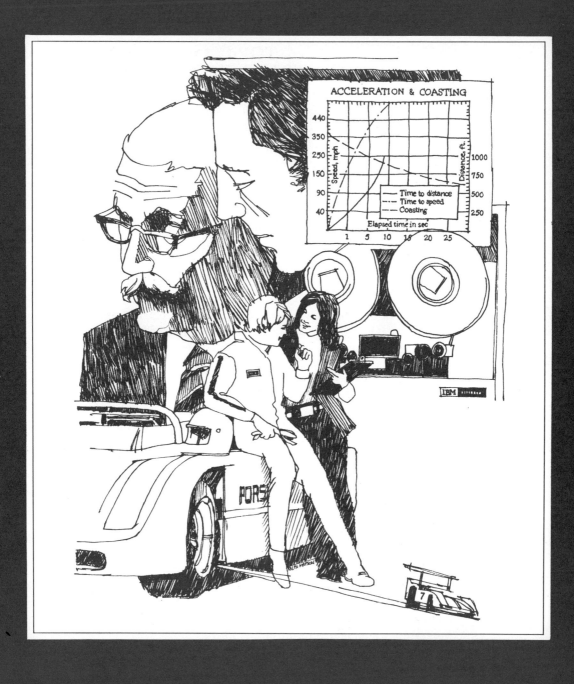

This chapter is divided into four topics. The first describes the operational procedures for using BASIC. The second presents a collection of BASIC statements that will get you started programming. The third illustrates how these statements are used in a series of sample programs. Then, the last topic explains how to test and debug your programs. When you complete this chapter, you should be able to write BASIC programs for a wide range of processing activities.

TOPIC 1
WRITING A PROGRAM
IN BASIC

BASIC, which stands for Beginner's All-purpose Symbolic Instruction Code, was developed at Dartmouth College for the GE 235 computer system. Today it is available on a wide range of computer systems. The language is easy to learn—even by people with little computer knowledge—and it is growing rapidly in popularity.

Although the BASIC language is usually used for time-sharing (or interactive) programming, it can also be used for batch programming. The general procedures for each method of programming are described in the remainder of this topic.

INTERACTIVE PROGRAMMING

To program on a *time-sharing* basis means that two or more users are sharing a central computer via remote terminals. The *terminals* are either keyboard devices like the teletypewriter terminal in figure 19-1 or visual-display units like the one in figure 19-2. The programmer enters code through the keyboard of the teletypewriter or visual-display unit, after which the program is compiled and executed. The output from the program is either printed by the teletypewriter or displayed on the visual-display unit. Because one computer can handle many terminals, it appears to each user as if he or she has complete control of the computer system. (Time-sharing is described in more detail in chapters 11 and 16.)

Programming on a time-sharing basis is also called *interactive programming*, because the computer interacts with the programmer. If, for example, an illegal statement is typed on the keyboard, the computer will respond with an appropriate error message. The programmer can then correct the error before the program is compiled. As you proceed through this section, you will see other examples of how the programmer and computer interact when time-sharing is used.

In general, there are two phases of an interactive programming session. In the first phase the user establishes contact between the computer and the terminal and "signs on" to the system. In the second phase, the user communicates with the computer through control commands and the programming language he or she is using.

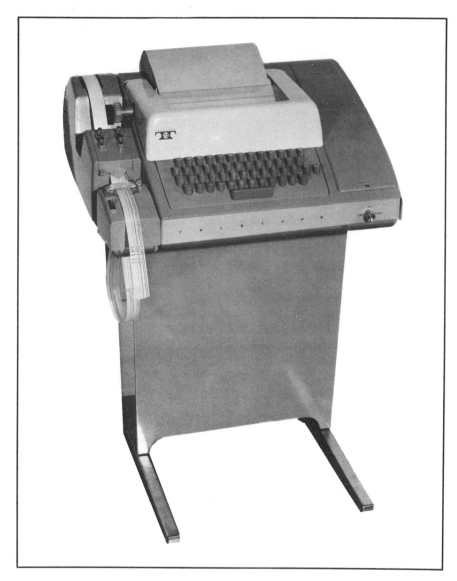

FIGURE 19–1 A teletypewriter terminal for interactive programming

Signing on

Signing on varies considerably from one computer system to another. Using a terminal like the one in figure 19-1, the user turns on the terminal and the modem and dials the phone number of the computer. (The *modem* is the device that converts data from digital form to one that can be transmitted over telephone lines and vice versa.) If the phone responds with a beeping or whining sound, the user places the phone in the modem to

FIGURE 19–2   A visual-display terminal for interactive programming

connect the terminal to the computer. If a connection takes place, a light on the terminal will turn on, indicating that the terminal is ready for operation. If the phone doesn't respond properly, or if the connection isn't successfully completed, the user hangs up and tries again.

On other systems, the terminal may be permanently connected to the computer by inhouse lines (the computer and terminal are in the same building). Then the user simply turns on the terminal, and it is ready for operation.

After the computer has been connected to the terminal, it will usually print a greeting and will certainly print a message asking for the user's code. This code tells the computer that an authorized person is using the terminal. Before using a time-sharing system, then, you must get a proper code from your instructor or supervisor. So when the computer prints a message like:

```
USER NUMBER---
```

you can respond with a valid code. Once your code has been accepted, you are ready for your interactive programming session.

Command	Meaning
NEW	I would like to work on a new program. Erase whatever I have been working on.
OLD	I would like to work on an old program. Erase whatever I have been working on.
SAVE	Save the program in my library for later use.
UNSAVE-SAMPLE	Remove the program from my library.
RENAME-SAMPLE	Change the name of the program I'm working on, but don't destroy the program.
CATALOG	List the names of all programs in my library.
SCRATCH	Erase the program I have been working on, but leave the name and user code intact (I'm going to start over).
RUN	Execute the program.
RUNNH	Execute the program without heading information.
STOP	Stop computation at once. This can be entered while the computer is typing. (On some systems there is a key on the keyboard that will have the same effect.)
LIST	List the entire program.
LISTNH	List the entire program without heading information.
LIST XXX-YYY	List the program beginning with statement XXX and ending with statement YYY.
DELETE XXX-YYY	Delete the statements beginning with statement XXX and ending with statement YYY.
RENUMBER	Renumber the program beginning with 100 and counting by tens.
BYE or GOODBYE	I'm finished; stop the service.

FIGURE 19–3   Some typical control commands for interactive programming

Using Control Commands

During the interactive session, the programmer communicates with the computer by using *control commands* like those in figure 19-3. Although these commands may vary from one system to another, all systems have commands that perform the basic functions listed. For instance, SAVE means to save a program in a library for later use; LIST means to list all of the statements within a program. And all systems will have Save and List functions.

To give you a better idea of how to use the control commands, look at figure 19-4. It is a listing of a simple interactive session. Here the commands and statements entered by the programmer are shaded; the messages or data printed by the computer are not. On the left side of the figure are comments to help describe what is happening.

	Remarks	Terminal Printout

1. The user identifies himself, the language he will be using, and the program he will be working on.

```
USER NUMBER---MM0401,DP50S5,ACAD
SYSTEM---BASIC
NEW OR OLD---OLD
OLD PROGRAM NAME---GRPAY

READY
```

2. The programmer requests a listing without a heading and the computer lists GRPAY.

```
LISTNH

100   REM PROGRAM TO CALCULATE GROSS PAY
110   REM E IS EMPLOYEE NUMBER
120   REM H IS HOURS WORKED
130   REM R IS HOURLY RATE
140   REM G IS GROSS PAY
150   READ E,H,R
160   IF E = -999 THEN 200
170   LET G = H * R
180   PRINT "EMP NO ="; E, "GROSS PAY ="; G
190   GO TO 150
200   STOP
210   DATA 101,40.0,3.00,102,43.1,2.27
220   DATA 103,37.3,2.12,-999,0,0
230   END

READY
```

3. The programmer requests that the program be executed without a heading and the program is executed.

```
RUNNH

EMP NO = 101    GROSS PAY = 120
EMP NO = 102    GROSS PAY = 97.837
EMP NO = 103    GROSS PAY = 79.076

READY
```

4. The programmer adds statement 175 to the program so the results are rounded to two decimal places. He then requests that statements 150–200 be listed to make sure the program was changed as he intended.

```
175 LET G = INT(G*100+.5)/100

LIST 150-200

150   READ E,H,R
160   IF E = -999 THEN 200
170   LET G = H * R
175   LET G = INT(G*100+.5)/100
180   PRINT "EMP NO ="; E, "GROSS PAY ="; G
190   GO TO 150
200   STOP

READY
```

5. The programmer requests that the program be executed without a heading and the new results print. The program works as intended.

```
RUNNH

EMP NO = 101    GROSS PAY = 120
EMP NO = 102    GROSS PAY = 97.84
EMP NO = 103    GROSS PAY = 79.08

READY
```

6. The programmer requests that the program be saved in his library.

```
SAVE

READY
```

7. The programmer requests a listing of all programs in his library. There is only one, GRPAY.

```
CATALOG

GRPAY

READY
```

8. The programmer signs off.

```
GOODBYE

OFF AT 2:10
```

FIGURE 19–4 Interactive session—example 1

In part 1, the user identifies himself with a proper user code, then responds to the word SYSTEM (meaning what language system) with the word BASIC. Finally, he tells the computer he will be working on an old program named GRPAY (a short form of GROSS PAY).

In parts 2 through 8, the programmer requests a listing of the program with no heading information (LISTNH), requests execution with no heading (RUNNH), adds a line to his program, requests a listing of statements 150-200 (LIST), requests execution (RUNNH), requests that the program be saved (SAVE), requests a listing of the names of all programs in his library (CATALOG), and signs off (GOODBYE). At the end of each command or statement entered by the programmer, the carriage-control key is pressed to indicate that the computer can now act upon the command. After the computer executes each command, it prints READY. The programmer can then enter another control command.

Figure 19-5 illustrates work on a new program in another interactive session. After the user identifies himself and his language in part 1, he indicates that he will be working on a new program. When the computer requests the name of this program, he responds with MNHTTN. Although the rules for forming program names will vary from one system to another, a safe rule is to form names from six or less alphabetic characters.

In part 2, the programmer enters a BASIC program (statements 100 through 500). Then in part 3 he decides to change statement 300. He does this by retyping the statement, and the computer substitutes new statement 300 for the old. After making this correction, the programmer requests a new listing, followed by program execution (part 5).

During program execution, something goes wrong. The computer repeatedly prints the question, WHAT YEAR IS IT? As a result, the programmer interrupts execution by entering STOP. Rather than waste time trying to determine what the error is, he saves this program so he can correct it later (part 7) and requests a switch to an old program (part 9). He will then continue until he has completed his interactive session.

In some cases a control command must supply a program name to be interpreted correctly. For instance, the UNSAVE command must specify the name of the program to be removed from the program library. Although the exact form will vary from system to system, the command is usually followed by a hyphen and then the program name, as in this example:

```
UNSAVE-PROGA
```

Similarly, the RENAME command might assign the name PROGB to a program as follows:

```
RENAME-PROGB
```

And the NEW and OLD commands might provide names as follows:

Remarks	Terminal Printout
| 1. User identifies himself, the language, and the program. | ```
USER NUMBER---MM0401,DP5055,ACAD
SYSTEM--BASIC
NEW OR OLD---NEW
NEW PROGRAM NAME--MNHTTN

READY
``` |
| 2. User enters a new program. | ```
100  REM MANHATTAN PROBLEM
200  PRINT "WHAT YEAR IS IT";
210  INPUT C
220  LET P = 24.00
230  LET Y = 1627
300  LET P = P+(P*.065)
310  LET Y = Y+1
320  If Y < C THEN 200
400  PRINT "ANSWER IS"; P
500  END

READY
``` |
| 3. User changes a statement. | ```
300  LET P = 1.065*P
``` |
| 4. User requests a new program listing without a heading. | ```
LISTNH

100  REM MANHATTAN PROBLEM
200  PRINT "WHAT YEAR IS IT";
210  INPUT C
220  LET P = 24.00
230  LET Y = 1627
300  LET P = 1.065*P
310  LET Y = Y+1
320  IF Y < C THEN 200
400  PRINT "ANSWER IS"; P
500  END

READY
``` |
| 5. User requests program execution without a heading. | ```
RUNNH

WHAT YEAR IS IT?1977
WHAT YEAR IS IT?1977
WHAT YEAR IS IT?
``` |
| 6. User interrupts processing by entering STOP. There is an obvious program error. | ```
STOP

READY
``` |
| 7. User requests that program be saved in his library so it can be corrected later. | ```
SAVE

READY
``` |
| 8. User requests a listing of all programs in the library. There are now two, GRPAY and MNHTTN. | ```
CATALOG

GRPAY
MNHTTN

READY
``` |
| 9. User tells system that he would like to work on an old program. System asks for program name, and user replies with GRPAY. | ```
OLD
OLD PROGRAM NAME---GRPAY

READY
``` |
| 10. User requests listing of GRPAY without a heading. | ```
LISTNH

100  REM PROGRAM TO CALCULATE GROSS PAY
110  REM E IS EMPLOYEE NUMBER
 .
 .
 .
``` |

FIGURE 19–5 Interactive session—example 2

```
NEW-PAYREG
OLD-MNHTTN
```

In any event, find out what the coding rules are for your system and use them.

Making Correction to Commands
or Statements

One question that often comes up is, what happens if you spell a command or statement wrong? The answer is to not worry about it. The computer will be unable to interpret the words and will print an appropriate error message. You can then enter the command or statement again.

In general, there are three ways to correct a command or statement. First, if you detect the error before you press the carriage-return key, you can press the backspace key once for each character that needs to be corrected. The carriage doesn't actually backspace, but the characters in storage are erased. After backspacing, you can continue as though the errors were never made. (On some systems, the underline key or some other key will have the same effect as the backspace key. Find out what it is on your system.)

Second, if you want to delete the line you are keying and start over, there is usually a key for line deletion. On teletypewriter terminals, this key is often labeled ESC or ALT MODE. In any event, find out if this key is available to you, and if so, how it is labeled. After you delete the line, you simply rekey it correctly.

Third, if you want to change a BASIC program statement after you have pressed the carriage-return key, you can simply rekey it, using the appropriate line number. As you have seen in the sample conversations in figure 19-4 and 19-5, the computer will automatically substitute the new line for the old.

BATCH PROGRAMMING

As I said, most BASIC programming is done on an interactive basis. In some cases, however, there aren't enough terminals to go around. When this happens, BASIC can be run on a batch basis, thus eliminating the need for terminals.

To run on a batch basis, you keypunch the source code of the BASIC program into an object deck. Then you keypunch one or more job-control cards that tell the operating system to compile and execute the source program. If program execution requires input data, you keypunch the data decks—if they aren't provided for you. You then assemble the job-control, source, and data decks in a sequence that conforms to the requirements of the operating system.

Since each operating system has different job-control requirements, you must learn the requirements of the system you will be using. In most cases, you will be able to use the same job-control cards for all of your programs. When your deck is assembled, you leave it at the computer center for processing. Normally you can pick up your deck and the resulting printout the following day, and perhaps even sooner.

When you examine your printout, you will first find a listing of the source code. If any errors were detected during compilation, you will find a list of diagnostic error messages after the source code. In this case, the object program will not be executed, and you must correct the source deck and try again. On the other hand, if no error messages were detected, your object program will be executed, and the execution output will be printed after the source listing. You can then examine this output to see whether the program ran properly.

DISCUSSION

Since this has been a general introduction to programming in BASIC, you may run into many variations of the procedures described. The main purpose of this topic, then, is to give you an idea of what you need to know in order to use BASIC. If you are batch programming, you need to find out the format and sequence of the job-control cards for your system. If you are using interactive programming, you need to learn the sign-on procedures and the control commands. In the next topic, you will learn the BASIC language itself.

SUMMARY

1. When BASIC is used on an interactive basis, the programmer communicates with the computer using control commands. If any errors are made when keying commands or program statements, the computer will respond with an appropriate error message.

2. When BASIC is used on a batch basis, the programmer uses job-control cards to instruct the computer to compile and execute the program. If the source deck contains any errors, the error messages will print out after compilation, and the object program won't be executed.

TERMINOLOGY

time-sharing
terminal
interactive programming
signing on
control command

QUESTIONS

1. Suppose you are the programmer in the interactive session illustrated in figure 19-5. Take over where the listing leaves off and change the name of the old program GRPAY to PRCALC. What command would you enter?

2. What command would you enter if you wanted to rewrite the program entirely but keep the same name?

3. What command would you enter to erase the program from your library?

TOPIC 2
A SUBSET OF THE
BASIC LANGUAGE

This chapter presents eleven statements of the BASIC language. After you learn the function of each statement, you should be able to understand programs like the one in figure 19-6. You should also be able to write programs of your own when you complete this topic. (Then you can learn about other BASIC statements in chapter 20 and in supplementary reading materials.)

Because the program in figure 19-6 will be referred to throughout this topic, let me briefly describe it. This program calculates an employee's gross pay when hours worked and hourly pay rate are supplied to it. It also requires the employee's identification number, and the program will end when an identification number of -999 (that's minus 999) is entered. To calculate gross pay, the program simply multiplies hours worked times pay rate.

The remainder of this topic is divided into two parts. First, some background information is given about BASIC. Second, the eleven statements of the introductory BASIC subset are presented.

```
100   REM PROGRAM TO CALCULATE GROSS PAY
110   REM E IS EMPLOYEE NUMBER
120   REM H IS HOURS WORKED
130   REM R IS HOURLY RATE
140   REM G IS GROSS PAY

150   READ E,H,R
160   IF E = -999 THEN 200
170   LET G = H * R
180   PRINT "EMP NO ="; E, "GROSS PAY ="; G
190   GO TO 150
200   STOP

210   DATA 101,40.0,3.00,102,43.1,2.27
220   DATA 103,37.3,2.12,-999,0,0

230   END
```

FIGURE 19-6 A BASIC program that calculates gross pay

SOME BACKGROUND
INFORMATION

A BASIC program is made up of a series of *statements*. For instance, the program in figure 19-6 consists of fourteen statements. These statements are known as the REM statement, the READ statement, the IF statement, and so on.

Statement Numbers

When writing a BASIC program, each statement must be given a *statement number*. For instance, the statements in figure 19-6 are numbered starting with 100 and counting by tens. These statement numbers indicate the sequence of the source statements. Later on, if a statement or two needs to be added to the program, it can be done by choosing statement numbers that represent the proper sequence. For instance, statement numbers 162, 164, and 166 could be inserted between statements 160 and 170. Although any statement numbers from 0 to 99999 can be used, I recommend for now that you start with 100 and number by tens. This is a common programming practice.

Statement Length

A BASIC statement ends when the typewriter's carriage is returned. As a result, the statement can be as long as the line length on the terminal. (In most cases, this is about 72 characters, but it may be more on your terminal.)

Statement Formats

As you will soon see, each statement must be written using a rigidly prescribed sequence of elements. For instance, the GO TO statement must consist of a statement number, the words GO TO, and the statement number of another statement in the program. On the other hand, blanks are optional within a statement. As a result,

```
GOTO150
```

and

```
GO TO 150
```

are both valid statements. (To make your programs easy to read and understand, however, you should use blanks whenever they improve clarity.)

Numeric Values

As you write your programs, you will often need to express numeric values. In figure 19-6, for example, the programmer uses a value of -999 in statement 160. During the execution of some of your programs, you will also be required to supply input to the program. In either case, the ways of expressing numeric values are identical.

There are three forms in which BASIC accepts and displays numeric values. These are illustrated in figure 19-7. In the first two forms (integer and decimal), the values are written using our familiar notation (an integer value is simply a whole number). If the values are negative, they are preceded by a minus sign.

In the exponential form, an E is used to indicate what power of ten the number should be multiplied by to get the actual value. Thus 153E3 means 153 times 10^3, or 153 times 1000. And 2154E-5 means 2154 times 10^{-5}, or 2154 times .00001. This is a common notation for scientific problems.

To think of it another way, the E notation tells where the decimal point should be placed to get the actual value. If the E-value is plus, the decimal point should be moved to the right the number of places specified. If the E-value is minus, the decimal point should be moved to the left the number of places indicated. (For most business problems, however, you shouldn't need to use the exponential form.)

When a BASIC program prints out numbers, it may use any of the three forms shown in figure 19-7. For most computers, it determines which form to use based on these rules:

Form	Examples	Value
Integer	5	As expressed
	-999	
	12876	
Decimal	6.7	As expressed
	-492.76	
	3.141659	
	.0951	
Exponential	153E3	153,000
	153E$+3$	153,000
	2154E-8	.00002154
	2154E-5	.02154

FIGURE 19–7   Numeric data in BASIC

1. If the number to be printed has no fractional portion and has less than seven significant digits, integer form is used.
2. If the number has a fractional portion and has less than seven significant digits, decimal form is used.
3. If the number has seven or more significant digits, exponential form is used.

Because some of your programs may print results with more than six significant digits, you may encounter output in exponential form even though you didn't use it in your program or your input data.

(In case you don't know what a *significant digit* is, it is a digit within a number that actually contributes to its accuracy. For instance, the leading and trailing zeros in the number 012.500 aren't significant. If they are dropped, the value of the number doesn't change. On the other hand, the zeros in 153,000 are significant. The number of significant digits printed will vary somewhat from one system to another, but six is most common. Find out what it is on your system.)

When a numeric value is used in a BASIC statement like

```
IF E = -999 THEN 200
```

the value can be called a *constant,* or *numeric constant.* It is called a constant, because the value won't change as the program is executed.

String Values

String values are non-numeric values that consist of any combination of letters (A-Z), digits (0-9), and special characters (commas, periods, dollar signs, etc.). When string values are used in a BASIC statement, they must be enclosed within quotation marks as in these examples:

```
"END OF PROGRAM"
"SEQUENCE ERROR"
"GROSS PAY ="
```

In general, when string values are used as input to a program, they do not require quotation marks unless they (1) start with a blank, (2) start with a digit, or (3) contain a comma. Then the string value will start with the first character keyed and end with the first comma or carriage return. In the beginning, however, you may want to use quotation marks around all string input that your programs require.

When a string value is specified in a BASIC statement, it can be called a *constant,* or a *string constant.* For instance, NONE is a constant in this statement:

```
IF E$ = "NONE" THEN 220
```

Like numeric constants, a string constant can't be changed during the execution of a program.

Most computers limit the length of string variables, but the limit is usually more than you need. On some systems, however, the limit is as low as 18 characters, and on at least one system the limit is one character. So find out what your system's limit is.

Variable Names

As you write a program, you will give names to fields in storage that will change during the execution of the program. These fields are called *variables,* and their names are called *variable names.* For instance, E, H, R, and G are variable names given to fields used in the program in figure 19-6. The rules for forming variable names differ, depending on whether the name represents numeric or string data.

Numeric variable names are made up of one letter (A-Z) or one letter followed by one digit (0-9). Thus A, X, D, D1, G2, and V9 are all valid names for numeric fields. Similarly, 9V, AB, and B+ are not valid. String variable names are made up of a single letter followed by the dollar sign. Thus X$, B$, and C$ are valid, whereas $X, 3$, and GC$ are not. On some of the more advanced BASIC compilers, a string variable name can also consist of a letter, digit, and dollar sign, as in D1$ or X9$. You'll have to check to find out whether these are valid on your system.

Arithmetic Expressions

An *arithmetic expression* (or just *expression*) can be made up of variable names, numeric constants, and *arithmetic operators.* The arithmetic operators are as follows:

Operator	Operation
+	Addition
−	Subtraction
*	Multiplication
/	Division
↑	Exponentiation

Since exponentiation means "raise to the power of," 10↑2 is equivalent to 10^2.

An arithmetic expression can be as simple as a single constant or variable name, and it can be as complex as one line of coding will permit. Figure 19-8 gives some examples of some typical expressions and the evaluation of them. Thus 1.23 is an expression, H is an expression, and

```
(2↑E*((D1/4) + (5-X)))/2
```

is an expression.

To evaluate an expression, you need to know the current values of the variables. In figure 19-8, assumed values are given for each variable name in the column headed "variable values." In addition, however, you need to know in what sequence the operations are performed when an expression is evaluated. For instance, 2 + 3 * 4 is 20 if addition is done first, and it is 14 if multiplication is done first. Here, then, are the sequence rules for evaluating an expression:

1. Exponentiation is done first.
2. Multiplication and division are done second.
3. Addition and subtraction are done third.
4. If more than one operation at the same level is specified (such as one division and two multiplications), the operations are done in sequence, from left to right.

Using these rules, the resulting value of 2 + 3 * 4 is 14.

When parentheses are used, the operations within parentheses are performed before operations outside parentheses. When there are parentheses within parentheses, the operations in the innermost set of parentheses are performed first. Because parentheses help to clarify the order of operations, they should be used whenever there might be a chance of confusion.

With this as background, you should be able to see how the expression values in figure 19-8 were derived. In examples 5 and 6, you can see how the use of parentheses can change the value of an expression. In example 9, you can see parentheses within parentheses within parentheses. And in example 10, you should see that E↑.5 is the same as $E^{.5}$ or the square root of E ($\sqrt{E}$).

Example	Expression	Variable Values	Expression Value
1	1.23	none	1.23
2	(−4)	none	−4
3	H	H=43.1	43.1
4	H * R	H=43.1,R=2.91	125.421
5	5 + H * R	H=43.1,R=2.91	130.421
6	(5+H) * R	H=43.1,R=2.91	139.971
7	5 + H * 3 * R / 2	H=40.0,R=2.00	125
8	(5+H) * (3*R/2)	H=40.0,R=2.00	135
9	(2↑E*((D1/4)+(5−X)))/2	E=3,D1=−12,X=3	−4
10	E↑.5	E=16	4

FIGURE 19–8 Arithmetic expressions in BASIC

When writing arithmetic expressions, you must be sure that no expression contains two consecutive operators. Thus

$$2 + -E$$

is "illegal." You should also avoid starting an expression with a minus sign as in

$$-E + 2$$

since the evaluation of an expression like this will vary from one system to another.

Functions Supplied by BASIC

To aid in performing calculations, most BASIC compilers supply a number of *functions* that can be used in an arithmetic expression. For instance, the table in figure 19-9 describes the ones that are commonly available. Of these, normally only the first four are of use to the BASIC programmer in business applications. The others are used for scientific applications.

To use a function, you code the three-character function name, followed by an *argument* within parentheses. The argument can be any arithmetic expression. Thus

$$SQR \ (E2)$$

Function	Definition
ABS(X)	Determine the absolute value of X. If X is negative, convert it to a positive value. If X is positive, leave it as is.
SGN(X)	Determine the sign of X. If X is positive, SGN(X) has a value of +1; if X is zero, SGN(X) has a value of zero; if X is negative, SGN(X) has a value of −1.
INT(X)	Derive the integer portion of X; that is, the largest integer value that is not greater than X. Thus, INT(17.9) is 17; INT(−6.1) is −7.
SQR(X)	Calculate the square root of X.
EXP(X)	Calculate the natural exponent of X (e^x).
LOG(X)	Calculate the natural logarithm of X ($\log_e X$).
SIN(X)	Calculate the sine of X. The angle X must be expressed in radians (there are 2 pi radians in a circle).
COS(X)	Calculate the cosine of X. The angle X must be expressed in radians (there are 2 pi radians in a circle).
TAN(X)	Calculate the tangent of X. The angle X must be expressed in radians (there are 2 pi radians in a circle).
ATN(X)	Calculate the arctangent of X. The answer is expressed in radians (there are 2 pi radians in a circle).

FIGURE 19–9 Functions normally available with BASIC

means take the square root of the variable named E2. And

$$INT \ (G \ * \ 100 \ + \ .5)$$

means take the integer portion of G * 100 + .5. In this case, if the expression has a value of 17.9, the function will derive a value of 17. If the expression has a value of −5.3, the function will derive a value of −6 (the INT function determines the largest integer not greater than the argument).

As you will see, functions are often used within arithmetic statements. When they are, the functions are evaluated before any other operations on a left-to-right basis. Parentheses, however, can still be used to indicate which portions of an expression are to be evaluated first.

THE STATEMENTS OF THE
BASIC SUBSET

With this as background, you should have no trouble learning how the statements of BASIC function when executed. Following are eleven statements that will allow you to write programs of considerable complexity.

The REM Statement

The REM (remark) statement is used to place remarks and explanations within a program. In figure 19-6, for example, the first statement describes the function of the program. Then the next four statements tell what the variable names E, H, R, and G stand for. REM statements are never executed, so the program in figure 19-6 will execute the same with or without statements 100-140.

REM statements are important because they help document a program. Without them, a program becomes much more difficult to follow. In general, remarks should be used (1) to identify the overall purpose of the program, (2) to identify variable names used within the program, and (3) to identify the function of various segments of code within the program. You will see all three of these uses in the programs in topic 3.

The LET Statement

The LET statement evaluates an arithmetic expression and places the result in a variable. To illustrate, consider this statement:

$$LET \ X \ = \ 3 \ * \ D$$

When the statement is executed, the value of 3 * D will be placed in the field named X. As a result, if D has a value of 4, a value of 12 will be placed in X.

In general, there are four ways in which the LET statement is used. First, it can be used to set a variable to an initial value as follows:

```
100 REM SET X, R, G1, AND D$ TO INITIAL VALUES
110 LET X = 1
120 LET R = .0585
130 LET G1 = -5.3
140 LET D$ = "SEQ"
```

After LET statements are executed, X, R, G1, and D$ have values of 1, .0585, −5.3 and "SEQ", regardless of what values they might have had previously. Notice that both numeric and string variables can be set to initial values using the LET statement.

A second use is to set a variable equal to the result of a calculation. You have already seen this in the statement LET X = 3 * D. The expression to the right of the equals sign can be as complex as the statement length of the system you are using will permit. Here, string variables are illegal.

A third use is to move a value from one field to another as in this example:

```
LET B = H
```

If, for example, H has a value of 465 when the statement is executed, both B and H will have a value of 465 after execution. When used for this purpose, string variables are okay, as in this statement:

```
LET B$ = T$
```

A fourth use is to increase or decrease a value by a constant amount, as follows:

```
LET A = A + 1
LET G = G - 2
```

In the first example, A is increased by 1, and the result is stored back in A. As a result, if A had a value of 12 before the statement was executed, it will have a value of 13 after execution. Similarly, in the second example, if G had a value of 10 before execution, it will have a value of 8 after execution. Note here that the same variable can be named on both sides of the equals sign; that is, it can receive the results of the statement execution, and it can also be part of the calculation.

The READ and DATA Statements

The READ and DATA statements work together. The READ statement requests that data be placed in one or more variables. The DATA statement supplies the data. In the program in figure 19-6, the READ statement specifies three variable names as follows:

```
150 READ E,H,R
```

When this statement is executed, it will take the first three values from the first data statement and place them in E, H, and R. Since the first DATA statement is coded as

```
210 DATA 101,40.0,3.00,102,43.1,2.27
```

E, H, and R will receive values of 101, 40.0, and 3.00 the first time the READ statement is executed. The next time a READ statement is executed, it will receive the next values in sequence from the first DATA statement. When all the values of the first DATA statement are used up, subsequent READ statements will take values from the next DATA statements in sequence.

To illustrate, suppose the sequence of statements shown in figure 19-10 is executed. The data to the right of these statements indicate the values of A, B, C, D, E as the instructions are executed. Can you see how the data is taken in sequence from successive DATA statements and how the data replaces whatever was previously stored in a variable? If a READ statement is executed and there are no more DATA values available to it, an error message like

```
OUT OF DATA
```

is printed, and the program ends.

The RESTORE Statement

The RESTORE statement allows the values within a DATA statement to be read more than once. This is useful when the same input data must be processed in several different ways. After the RESTORE statement is executed, the next READ statement will receive data starting with the

BASIC Statements	Variable Values				
	A	B	C	D	E
200 READ A	1	?	?	?	?
210 READ B,C,D,E	1	2	−3	5	10
220 READ A,D,E	1.416	2	−3	9	−9.2
230 READ A,B,C,D,E	41	12	−5	−9	1
240 DATA 1,2,−3,5,10,1.416					
250 DATA 9,−9.2,41					
260 DATA 12					
270 DATA −5,−9,1					

FIGURE 19–10 The READ and DATA statements

first value specified in the first DATA statement. To illustrate, consider these statements:

```
200 READ A
210 READ B, C, D, E
220 READ A, D, E
225 RESTORE
230 READ A, B, C, D, E
240 DATA 1, 2, -3, 5, 10, 1.416
250 DATA 9, -9.2, 41
```

After the first three READ statements receive the first eight values from the DATA statements, the RESTORE statement is executed. Then the next READ statement (statement 230) will receive the first five data values in statement 240.

The PRINT Statement

The PRINT statement is used to print the values of constants, variables, and expressions. In its simplest form,

```
PRINT
```

it doesn't print anything; it only causes the paper to be moved up one line.

Figure 19-11 gives several examples of PRINT statements along with the resulting output. For instance, statement 110 prints the data from three numeric variables, statement 130 prints a numeric variable and a numeric constant, statement 140 prints a string constant and a numeric variable, statement 150 prints a string variable and a numeric variable, and statement 160 prints the value of an expression. In brief, a single PRINT statement can print as many values as the length of the print line will permit.

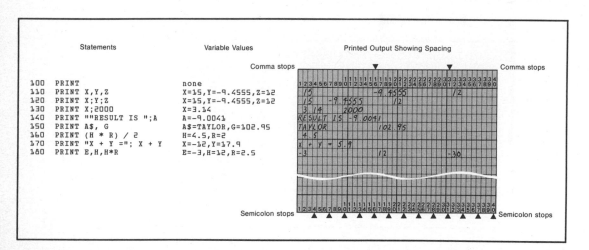

FIGURE 19–11   Examples of printed output in BASIC

The spacing of printed output in BASIC is determined by the commas and semicolons in the PRINT statement. When commas are used, you can think of tab stops like those on a typewriter set every fifteen print positions. So comma tabs are set at positions 1, 16, 31, 46, and so on. After one value is printed, the comma indicates that the printer should skip to the next comma tab stop before printing the next value. Thus statement 110 in figure 19-11 prints the variables named X, Y, and Z, starting in print positions 1, 16, and 31. If you check closely, however, you will see that X actually starts in position 2, and Z actually starts in position 32. This happens with numeric data because the first position is reserved for the sign of the number, if negative. As a result, a negative value starts exactly on the comma tab; a positive number starts one position to the right.

When semicolons are used to separate the elements of a PRINT statement, the spacing of output is closer together. Specifically, semicolon tabs are set every three positions: position 1, 4, 7, 10, and so on. Then, after one element is printed, the printer skips to the next semicolon tab—provided it is three or more positions away. If the next tab is less than three positions away, the printer skips to the second tab over. This accounts for the printing shown for statement 120 of figure 19-11. Here again, the first printing position for each value is reserved for the sign of the number. When a semicolon is used after string output, no skipping takes place after printing. This accounts for the printing for statement 140 of figure 19-11.

After a line is printed, the paper is normally moved up one line. If you want to print the data from two or more PRINT statements on a single line, however, you can do so by ending a PRINT statement with a comma or semicolon. For instance, all three of the following statements will print on the same line:

```
PRINT A; B;
PRINT X$; Y$,
PRINT C, D
```

After the first statement is executed, the printer will skip to the proper semicolon tab and print the data for the second statement. After the second statement is printed, the printer will skip to the next comma tab and print the data for the third statement.

Although the format of printed output in BASIC may at first confuse you, it usually doesn't cause much trouble. In most cases, the form of BASIC output isn't that important, as long as it's readable. And if the output must be in a rigidly specified format, you can experiment with some test data to make sure your program prints as intended.

The INPUT Statement

When the READ and DATA statements are used, the data is part of the program. Then, if the program is to be used on new data, the programmer must change the DATA statements. In many cases, however, you may want to supply data to the program as it is executed. If so, the INPUT statement must be used. When the INPUT statement is executed, the system prints or displays a question mark on the terminal. The user must then enter as many values as the INPUT statement has specified variables for. This is illustrated by these statements:

```
100 REM PARTIAL PROGRAM TO SUM 3 VALUES
110 PRINT "ENTER THREE NUMBERS"
120 INPUT A,B,C
130 PRINT "A + B + C ="; A + B + C
```

When the statements are executed, the program will print the following lines and then wait for input from the user:

```
ENTER THREE NUMBERS
?
```

Because the INPUT statement gives three variable names, the user must respond with three values separated by commas. When he or she is finished, the user carriage returns and the program proceeds with the next statement in sequence. Assuming that the user enters 4, 8, and −1.5, the complete printout for the four statements shown above would be like this:

```
ENTER 3 NUMBERS
?4,8,-1.5
A + B + C = 10.5
```

An INPUT statement can also request that a string value be supplied to the program. In this case, the user should enclose the string data in quotation marks, unless the data doesn't start with a blank or a number and doesn't contain a comma. Then quotation marks are optional.

The GO TO Statement

Normally, the statements of a program are executed in sequence from the lowest to the highest number statement. When the GO TO statement is executed, however, it causes a branch to the statement number specified. In the program in figure 19-6, statement number 190 causes a branch to statement 150, so more data can be read and processed. Since most programs require the same operations to be repeated many times, most BASIC programs will have one or more GO TO statements.

The IF-THEN Statement

One of the important features of a computer is its ability to perform different operations under different conditions. For instance, a payroll program may perform one series of operations if an employee has worked 40 or fewer hours in a week, another series of operations if the employee has worked more than 40 hours. In BASIC, the ability to select appropriate routines is accomplished by the IF-THEN statement.

In figure 19-6, an IF statement is used to determine when all the data has been processed:

```
IF E = -999 THEN 200
```

When this statement is executed, it will cause a branch to statement 200 if the value of E is equal to −999. If E doesn't equal −999, processing will continue with the next statement in sequence, statement 170. When coding an IF-THEN statement, you can use any of these *relational operators:*

Operator	Meaning
=	is equal to
<	is less than
< = or = <	is less than or equal to
>	is greater than
>= or =>	is greater than or equal to
<>	is not equal to

These operators can be used to compare any two arithmetic expressions, as in these examples:

```
IF A <> 6 THEN 260
IF A > = B + 5.2 THEN 360
IF (A + B)↑5 < (X + Y + Z)/2 THEN 460
```

In general, the only limit to the complexity of the arithmetic expressions in the IF-THEN statement is the length of the print line. In any case, if the relationship expression is true, the program branches to the statement named; otherwise, processing continues with the next instruction in sequence.

String variables and constants can also be used in an IF-THEN statement, as in these examples:

```
IF A$ =  "NONE" THEN 200
IF A$ <> B$ THEN 250
IF D$ >  X$ THEN 300
```

If the string data contains only letters and blanks, the relationship will be evaluated just as we might alphabetize name cards. Thus MICHAEL comes before (or is "less than") MIKE, and ANDY comes after (is "greater than") ANDI.

When strings contain numbers and special characters, however, the relationship will depend on the *collating sequence* of the computer being used. Rather than worry about this now, I suggest that you confine yourself to equal and not equal relationships when using string data. For the purposes of this course, at least, this should be as much flexibility as you will ever require.

The STOP Statement

The STOP statement will cause the program to end. It is coded in statement 200 of figure 19-6. In other words, after all data has been processed (an employee number of −999 has been read), the program should stop, and control should return to the terminal user.

The END Statement

Every program must have one and only one END statement. It must be the last statement in the program and have the highest sequence number. It tells the compiler where the source program ends. The END statement also causes program execution to stop. As a result, the IF-THEN statement in figure 19-6 could also be coded as

```
IF E = -999 THEN 230
```

Then the STOP statement wouldn't be required.

DISCUSSION

You have now been introduced to a complete subset of the BASIC language. Once you master this information, you will be able to read and understand a wide range of programs. And you should be able to write programs of your own. Because this topic presented a large amount of information, I doubt that anyone will remember it all after even a few readings. Consequently, refer to this topic repeatedly as you study the programs in the next topic and as you write your own programs.

At this stage, however, you should understand the program in figure 19-6 completely. Do you? If so, see if you can predict the output of this program when executed. After you have recorded what you think will print out, turn to portion 3 of figure 19-4 to see the actual results.

SUMMARY   This topic has introduced eleven BASIC statements. These statements can be used to perform I/O operations (READ, DATA, RESTORE, PRINT, and INPUT), to perform arithmetic operations (LET), and to control the sequence of operations (GO TO, IF-THEN, STOP, and END). You will be able to write complex programs when you master these statements.

TERMINOLOGY

statement	constant
statement number	numeric constant
numeric value	string value
significant digit	string constant

variable   a function
variable name   argument
arithmetic expression   relational operator
arithmetic operator

1. Give the values of A, B, C, X, and Y, as determined by these statements:

```
200 LET A = 2
210 LET B = A + 1.5
220 LET C = (2*A + 3.5/B) * 3
230 LET X = A * (B + 2↑A) - 7.1
240 LET Y = (A + B + C)↑A * 10↑3
```

2. Given the values assigned by the LET statements in question 1, show the output that would result from these PRINT statements, including the proper spacing:

```
300 PRINT A,B,C,X,Y
310 PRINT A;B;C;X;Y;
320 PRINT "END OF DATA"
330 PRINT "VALUES ARE"; A, B, C, X, Y
```

3. Consider this program:

```
100 READ A, B, C, D, E
110 READ X, Y, Z
120 GO TO 100
130 DATA 1.2,-2.3,4.6,3.7,9.124,10.11,-17.9
140 DATA 941,1017,621,320
150 DATA 40.8,32.9,-63,29,-1.01,117
160 END
```

   a. What will cause this program to stop?
   b. What will A, B, C, D, E, X, Y, and Z contain when the program ends?

4. Refer to the program in figure 19-6.
   a. What is the value of G the first time the LET statement is executed? The second time? The third time?
   b. What are the values of E, H, R, and G when the program ends?
   c. List the statement numbers of all statements that will be executed when this program is tested. List them in sequence from the start of program execution to completion (start with statement number 150, end with 200).

TOPIC 3
SOME SAMPLE
PROGRAMS

With topic 2 as background, you should now be able to understand the four programs presented in this chapter. Each of these programs is presented with sample input data and output results. The programs are designed to show how the statements presented in topic 2 are used in business programs. As you study these programs, refer to topic 2 whenever you are in doubt about the precise execution of a statement.

Example 1: Gross-Pay Calculation

The program in figure 19-12 is a refined version of the gross-pay program in figure 19-6. Here, an employee gets time-and-a-half for overtime hours (those hours over 40). The output is printed in four columns, including a column of string data containing the employee's last name. As part of the gross pay calculation, the result is rounded to two decimal places. Some highlights follow.

1. This program is divided into several blocks of code that start with a statement number that is a multiple of 100. Thus the remarks block starts with statement number 100, the housekeeping routine starts with 200, the main routine with 300, etc. This is a good programming practice, because it makes it easy for you to add statements to a block of code.

2. The executable statements of this program are divided into three segments: (1) the housekeeping routine, which prints the output headings and sets initial values; (2) the mainline routine, which does the main processing of the program; and (3) the end of job routine, which prints total lines and ends the program. It is good to divide a program into functional segments like this, because it can increase your efficiency when coding and debugging. (These segments of code are normally called *modules*, and modular program design is described in chapter 9.)

3. Gross pay for an employee who worked more than forty hours is calculated, using a technique that involves premium wages. The idea here is that normal wages are derived by multiplying hours worked times hourly rate. Then, if an employee has worked more than forty hours, the hours over forty are multiplied by pay rate and by .5. This result is called premium wages—that is, the extra pay that an employee receives for working overtime hours. When normal wages and premium wages are added together, gross pay is the result.

4. Statement 395 rounds gross pay to two decimal places, using the INT function. To see how this works, assume that the actual value of G

```
100    REM GROSS PAY CALCULATION WITH OVERTIME
110    REM E$ IS LAST NAME OF EMPLOYEE
120    REM H  IS HOURS WORKED
130    REM R  IS HOURLY RATE
140    REM P  IS PREMIUM WAGES
150    REM G  IS GROSS PAY
160    REM T  IS TOTAL GROSS PAY

200    REM HOUSEKEEPING ROUTINE
210    PRINT "NAME", "HOURS", "RATE", "GROSS"
220    LET T = 0

300    REM MAIN ROUTINE
310    READ E$,H,R
320    IF E$ = "NONE" THEN 500
330    REM NORMAL WAGES
340    LET G = H*R
350    IF H < = 40 THEN 390
360    REM PREMIUM WAGES
370    LET P = (H-40) * (R*.5)
380    LET G = G + P
390    REM PRINT ROUTINE
395    LET G = INT(G*1))+.5)/100
400    PRINT E$,H,R,G
410    LET T = T + G
420    GO TO 300

500    REM END OF JOB ROUTINE
510    PRINT
520    PRINT "TOTAL PAY ="; T
530    GO TO 700

600    DATA "DALEY",37.5,2.25
610    DATA "TAYLOR",42.5,3.13
620    DATA "HECTENBERGER",40.1,7.77
630    DATA "NONE",0,0

700    END

READY

RUNNH

NAME                    HOURS          RATE           GROSS
DALEY                   37.5           2.25           84.38
TAYLOR                  42.5           3.13           136.94
HECTENBERGER            40.1           7.77           311.97
TOTAL PAY = 533.29

READY
```

FIGURE 19–12 Gross-pay program with overtime calculations

before statement 395 is executed is 84.375. The LET statement then determines the value of this expression:

```
INT (84.375 * 100 + .5)/100
```

Since 84.375 times 100 plus .5 is 8438.0, the INT function determines a value of 8438. When this value is divided by 100, the result is 84.38 (the rounded value for gross pay). If you experiment with other values, you will see that the LET statement will always round properly.

Since you will find rounding useful in many programs, here is a general statement for rounding a value X to any number of decimal positions:

```
LET X = INT(X*10↑d+.5)/10↑d
```

In this arithmetic expression, d is the number of decimal places that you want to round to. If, for example, you want to round X to five decimal places, this statement will work:

```
LET X = INT(X*10↑5+.5)/10↑5
```

5. You might notice that the data printed in the GROSS column of output does not have its decimal points in vertical alignment. This happens because BASIC begins printing at the appropriate tab stop— without regard for decimal points. In contrast, a programming language like COBOL will usually print data with decimal points aligned. This can improve the clarity of the output.

Example 2: Determining
Economic Order Quantity

The program in figure 19-13 determines the *economic order quantity* (EOQ) for an inventory item after the user supplies the item number, annual sales in units, the cost of reordering the item, its unit cost, and the carrying cost as a decimal fraction. The EOQ for an item should be the order quantity that is most profitable for that particular item. It tries to establish a balance between the cost of carrying inventory and the cost of placing orders. Because the formula for determining EOQ's is complex, EOQ's are generally not used by companies without automated processing methods. Some of the highlights of this program follow:

1. This program consists of one functional module. It is a "conversation" between the system and the user (statements 200 through 380). When the user enters "N", which means no more EOQ calculations are needed; the program ends.
2. After each PRINT statement that asks the user to enter data, the programmer has placed a semicolon. This causes the question mark from the INPUT statement that follows to print on the same line as

```
100    REM DETERMINE ECONOMIC ORDER QUANTITY
110    REM N IS ITEM NUMBER
120    REM U IS ANNUAL USAGE IN UNITS
130    REM O IS COST OF PLACING ONE ORDER
140    REM I IS COST OF ONE ORDER
150    REM C IS CARRYING COST AS A DECIMAL FRACTION
160    REM E IS THE EOQ
170    REM R$ IS THE OPERATORS RESPONSE

200    REM THE BASIC CONVERSATION
210    PRINT "ITEM NUMBER";
220    INPUT N
230    PRINT "UNITS SOLD IN LAST 12 MONTHS";
240    INPUT U
250    PRINT "COST OF PLACING ONE ORDER";
260    INPUT O
270    PRINT "COST OF ONE ITEM";
280    INPUT I
290    PRINT "CARRYING COST OF ITEM AS A DECIMAL FRACTION";
300    INPUT C
310    LET E = SQR((2*U*O)/(I*C))
315    LET E = INT(E+.5)
320    PRINT "EOQ =";E
330    PRINT
340    PRINT "OTHER EOQS NEEDED? Y OR N";
350    INPUT R$
360    PRINT
370    IF R$ = "Y" THEN 200
380    END

READY

RUNNH

ITEM NUMBER?735
UNITS SOLD IN LAST 12 MONTHS?4120
COST OF PLACING ONE ORDER?12.00
COST OF ONE ITEM?2.25
CARRYING COST AS A DECIMAL FRACTION?.11
EOQ = 632

OTHER EOQS NEEDED? Y OR N?"Y"

ITEM NUMBER?810
UNITS SOLD IN LAST 12 MONTHS?369
COST OF PLACING ONE ORDER?25.50
COST OF ONE ITEM?62.50
CARRYING COST AS A DECIMAL FRACTION?.26
EOQ = 34

OTHER EOQS NEEDED? Y OR N?N

READY
```

FIGURE 19–13 Program for determining economic order quantities

the PRINT statement. The user then enters data immediately following the question mark.
3. The formula for determining the economic order quantity is this:

$$EOQ = \sqrt{\frac{2(\text{annual usage}) \ (\text{cost of placing one order})}{(\text{unit cost of item}) \ (\text{carrying cost as a decimal fraction})}}$$

Can you see how this has been translated into BASIC in figure 19-13?
(Incidentally, carrying cost as a decimal fraction means that a 25
percent annual carrying cost would be entered as .25.)

Example 3: Print a
Depreciation Schedule

The program in figure 19-14 prints a depreciation schedule after the
user enters the cost, estimated life, and salvage value of the item. After
printing one schedule, the program asks the user if he or she wants
schedules for other items. If the user enters a zero, the program ends.
Otherwise the computer asks the user for new input values.

This program is divided into four functional modules. The first one gets
the facts about the depreciable item; the second skips a space and sets
four variables to their initial values; the third prints the depreciation
schedule; and the fourth asks the user whether other schedules are
needed. You should now see how these modular divisions make the program easier to read and understand.

Example 4: Calculate Average
Sales and Average Deviation

The program in figure 19-15 calculates the average monthly sales for an
item, as well as the average monthly deviation from this average. It
demonstrates the use of the RESTORE statement, because the data supplied in the DATA statements is processed twice. The DATA statements
supply twelve values that represent the number of units sold for an
inventory item in each of the last twelve months.

In the first module (statements 200-280), the program determines the
average monthly sales. It does this by executing statements 230 through
260 twelve times each, after which T contains the total sales for the year.
Then statement 270 divides T by 12, giving the average monthly sales, and
rounds the result to the nearest whole number using the INT function.
When statement 280 is executed, the average monthly sales figure is
printed.

In the second module (statements 300-400), the program determines the
average deviation of monthly sales. It does this by first restoring the data
via the RESTORE statement and resetting the initial values in T and C.
Then statements 340 through 390 are executed 12 times, after which T

```
100   REM PRINT A DEPRECIATION SCHEDULE
110   REM C = COST
120   REM S = SALVAGE VALUE
130   REM L = ESTIMATED LIFE IN YEARS
140   REM Y = YEAR
150   REM D = DEPRECIATION PER YEAR
160   REM A = ACCUMULATED DEPRECIATION
170   REM B = BOOK VALUE OR C - A
180   REM R = OPERATORS RESPONSE

200   REM GET FACTS ABOUT ITEM
210   PRINT "COST";
220   INPUT C
230   PRINT "SALVAGE VALUE";
240   INPUT S
250   PRINT "ESTIMATED LIFE";
260   INPUT L

300   REM SETUP FOR DEPRECIATION TABLE
310   PRINT
320   LET Y = 1
330   LET A = 0
340   LET B = 0
350   LET D = (C-S)/L

400   REM PRINT DEPRECIATION SCHEDULE
410   PRINT "YEAR","COST","DEPN EXP","ACCUM DEP","BOOK VALUE"
420   LET A = A+D
430   LET B = C-A
440   PRINT Y,C,D,A,B
450   LET Y = Y + 1
460   IF Y <= L THEN 420

500   REM MORE DATA?
505   PRINT
510   PRINT "OTHER SCHEDULES NEEDED? ENTER 1 FOR YES, 0 FOR NO";
520   INPUT R
530   PRINT
540   IF R = 1 THEN 200
550   END

READY

RUNNH


COST?5000.00
SALVAGE VALUE?1000.00
ESTIMATED LIFE?5

YEAR        COST        DEPN EXP        ACCUM DEP        BOOK VALUE
  1         5000          800              800             4200
  2         5000          800             1600             3400
  3         5000          800             2400             2600
  4         5000          800             3200             1800
  5         5000          800             4000             1000

OTHER SCHEDULES NEEDED? ENTER 1 FOR YES, 0 FOR NO?0

READY
```

FIGURE 19–14 Program for printing depreciation schedules

```
100   REM CALCULATE AVERAGE MONTHLY SALES
110   REM   AND AVERAGE DEVIATION
120   REM T = TOTAL OF SALES AND DEVIATIONS
130   REM C = COUNTER
140   REM M = MONTHLY SALES IN UNITS
150   REM A = AVERAGE MONTHLY SALES
160   REM D = MONTHLY DEVIATION FROM AVERAGE

200   REM CALCULATE AVERAGE MONTHLY SALES
210   LET T = 0
220   LET C = 0
230   LET C = C+1
240   READ M
250   LET T = T+M
260   IF C < 12 THEN 230
270   LET A = INT(T/12+.5)
280   PRINT "AVERAGE MONTHLY SALES ="; A

300   REM CALCULATE AVERAGE DEVIATION
310   RESTORE
320   LET T = 0
330   LET C = 0
340   LET C = C+1
350   READ M
360   LET D = ABS(A-M)
370   LET T = T+D
380   IF C < 12 THEN 340
390   PRINT "AVERAGE DEVIATION ="; INT(T/12*10+.5)/10
400   STOP

600   DATA 125,257,178,191,361,402
610   DATA 373,253,282,126,87,99

700   END

READY

RUNNH

AVERAGE MONTHLY SALES = 228
AVERAGE DEVIATION = 93.5

READY
```

FIGURE 19–15   Program for calculating average monthly sales and average monthly deviations

contains the sum of the deviations for the year. In statement 360, the ABS function is used to convert a negative deviation to a positive value. When statement 390 is executed, the average deviation rounded to one decimal position is calculated and printed.

This topic has presented four typical business programs. Perhaps the main point to note is how these programs were divided into modules. In general, when programs are designed and coded in this way, they are easier to read and debug.

SUMMARY

module

TERMINOLOGY

QUESTIONS

1. Refer to the program in figure 19-12. What would happen if an employee's last name was NONE?

2. Refer to the program in figure 19-13. After the program prints

OTHER EOQS NEEDED? Y OR N?

what would happen if the operator entered YES?

3. Refer to the program in figure 19-14.
   a. Given the input data shown, list the numbers in sequence of all statements that would be executed before the program ends. (For example, the program starts with 210, 220, 230, 240, 250, 260, 310, etc.)
   b. Show the schedule that would print if the operator entered 1000, 100, and 3 for cost, salvage value, and estimated life.

4. Refer to the program in figure 19-15.
   a. What is the value of C when statement 270 is executed?
   b. How many times is statement 240 executed when this program is run?
   c. What is the value of C when statement 390 is executed?
   d. How many times is statement 350 executed when this program is run?
   e. What is the value of M when statement 350 is executed for the first time?

5. Add statements to the program in figure 19-12 so a second total line will print like this:

AVERAGE PAY = XXX.XX

Use appropriate statement numbers for statement insertions.

6. Could you convert the program in figure 19-15 so that the operator could enter input only one time via INPUT statements rather than using READ, DATA, and RESTORE statements? Explain how.

TOPIC 4
DIAGNOSTICS AND
DEBUGGING

After you have coded a program, you must complete several other phases before you have a tested program. First, you must create some test data (if you haven't already done this as part of the program via DATA statements). Second, you should desk-check your program for clerical and logical errors. Third, you should enter your program into the system through an interactive terminal or through punched cards on a batch basis. Fourth, the program should be executed on the test data. And fifth, any errors discovered during testing should be corrected (this is called debugging).

TEST DATA, DESK-CHECKING,
AND DIAGNOSTICS

When you create test data, you should be sure that it tests all the conditions that might come up during the execution of your program. As you create this data, you may realize that your program does not provide for some condition that is likely to come up. In addition to all conditions, the test data should provide data that covers the full range of values that might be processed by the program. For instance, if variable E might range from zero through 999999, then one test value for E should be zero and another should be 999999.

For the early test runs, be sure to keep your test data simple enough so that you can do the required calculations manually. Otherwise, you won't be able to tell whether the program ran correctly. In the EOQ program in figure 19-13, for example, it would be very difficult for you to manually do the calculations, given the input data shown.

After creating your initial test data and before entering your source program into the system, you should *desk-check* your program. This saves computer and programmer time, because desk-checking usually will catch an error or two. As you go through your program, check each statement to be sure it is coded correctly. You may also want to pretend you're the computer and operate on some of the test data you have created. Perform each operation specified by your program to see if it operates as you intended.

After you have desk-checked your program, you can enter your program into the system. If you are using a terminal, the system may give you error messages as you enter statements. It may also give you error messages when you tell the computer to RUN the program. In either case, these messages are called *diagnostics,* and the errors they call attention to must be corrected. To do this, you simply rekey the statement in its corrected form using the same statement number.

If you are running on a batch basis, you must keypunch your program after desk-checking. You will also keypunch job-control cards and any test data required for INPUT statements. After your deck is arranged in a suitable sequence for compilation and testing, you can submit it to the computer center. Then, if errors are detected during compilation, a *diagnostic listing* will be returned to you when you pick up your program. After you correct these errors, you can submit the program again for testing.

TESTING AND DEBUGGING

After a test run, you compare the actual output with the expected output. If they are the same, you can assume that your program ran without errors. You can then test the program on a more complete set of test data.

But what if the actual output isn't the same as that expected? In figure 19-12, for example, what if the gross-pay amounts didn't agree with your manual calculations? Or what if the columns of printed data weren't under the appropriate column headings? You would then have to find the cause of these errors (or bugs) and correct (or debug) them.

Debugging is one of the most challenging jobs of the programmer. In a complex program, debugging an error can be much like solving a mystery. To determine what happened, you begin with clues and trace backward until you find the culprit: a coding error or invalid input data.

In some cases, your bugs may be so difficult to find that a *tracing* technique is useful. To illustrate, consider the program in figure 19-16. This program calculates how much the $24.00 paid for Manhattan Island in 1627 would be worth today if it had been placed in a savings account at $6\frac{1}{2}$ percent simple interest. As you can see, the answer prints out in exponential form, since it has more than six significant digits. This is equivalent to 8.96550 times 10^{10}, or 89,655,000,000. But how do you know if this is correct? Performing these calculations manually would take you weeks.

One way of checking accuracy would be to run it the first time entering 1630 as the current year. The result would then print after only three repetitions of the calculation loop, and you could perform these operations manually in a few minutes. If the printed answer and the answer you derive manually are the same, you can assume the program will also work if you enter the correct current year.

Another way of testing the accuracy of this program is to insert a tracing statement. For instance, suppose this statement were inserted into the program before execution:

```
305 PRINT "Y="; Y; "P="; P
```

Then the values of Y and P would print for each year from 1627 to the present. Based on this tracing data, you can determine whether or not

```
100   REM MANHATTAN PROBLEM
110   REM THIS PROGRAM DETERMINES HOW MUCH $24 WOULD BE WORTH IF
120   REM DEPOSITED IN A SAVINGS ACCOUNT IN 1627 AT 6-1/2% SIMPLE
130   REM INTEREST.
140   REM C = CURRENT YEAR
150   REM P = PRINCIPAL
160   REM Y = YEAR OF CALCULATION

200   REM HOUSEKEEPING AND INPUT
210   PRINT "WHAT YEAR IS IT";
220   INPUT C
230   LET P = 24.00
240   LET Y = 1627

300   REM CALCULATION LOOP
310   LET P = P+(P*.065)
320   LET Y = Y+1
330   IF Y < C THEN 300

400   REM PRINT RESULT
410   PRINT "PRINCIPAL IS NOW"; P

500   END

READY

RUN

WHAT YEAR IS IT?1977
PRINCIPAL IS NOW 8.96550E+10

READY
```

FIGURE 19-16   The Manhattan program

the program is performing as intended. Because this would cause hundreds of lines of data to be printed for this program, you would want to stop the program by entering STOP after a dozen or so lines had printed. On some systems there is a key that can be used to stop runaway programs.

PRINT statements can be used for tracing the execution of statements as well as value changes. For instance, these statements could be entered into the program to determine the order in which the modules are executed:

```
305 PRINT 305
405 PRINT 405
```

Then, when the program is tested, this data would print:

```
WHAT YEAR IS IT?1630
      305
      305
      305
      405
PRINCIPAL IS NOW 28.9908
```

Here you can see that the modules were executed in their proper sequence.

By using PRINT statements to trace value changes and execution sequence, you should be able to isolate any program bug. After the bugs are corrected, you can remove the tracing statements. Then your program will run as intended.

Although the tracing technique just described can be effective, it is also time consuming. That's why a TRACE statement is available on some systems. This statement traces the execution of all statements that change the values of variables. It is normally the first statement of a program, so it can easily be removed after the program is debugged. Thus this TRACE statement in the Manhattan program

```
50 TRACE
```

will cause output like this when the program is executed.

```
WHAT YEAR IS IT? 1630
AT 220, C = 1630
AT 230, P = 24.
AT 240, Y = 1627
AT 310, P = 25.56
AT 320, Y = 1628
AT 310, P = 27.2214
AT 320, Y = 1629
AT 310, P = 28.9908
AT 320, Y = 1630
PRINCIPAL IS NOW 28.9908
```

As you can see, it gives you all the debugging data you need with little effort on your part. As a result, find out if the TRACE statement is available on your system, and if it is, use it as needed.

SUMMARY

1. After coding a program, the programmer must enter the program into the system and correct any errors detected during compilation. After this, the programmer must test and debug, using test data that tries all the conditions that are likely to come up when the program is actually used.

2. Tracing is useful during debugging, because it can show the sequence of statement execution as well as variable changes. On some systems,

a TRACE statement is available, so tracing can be done with little programmer effort.

TERMINOLOGY

desk checking
diagnostics
diagnostic listing
debugging
tracing

QUESTIONS

1. Refer to figure 19-12. Suppose the hourly rates are printed under the HOURS heading and the hours-worked values are printed under the RATE heading. What type of coding error could cause this bug?

2. Refer to figure 19-12. Suppose the program prints the heading line and the total line (nothing else) and then stops. What types of coding errors could cause this?

3. Refer to figure 19-12. Suppose the gross-pay amounts don't agree with your manual calculations.
   a. What PRINT statements could be inserted into the program to trace value changes and the sequence of module executions?
   b. How could the TRACE statement be used to trace execution sequence and variable changes?

20 EXPANDING THE INTRODUCTORY BASIC SUBSET

This chapter expands the introductory language subset presented in chapter 19. Topic 1 presents the BASIC elements for working with lists and tables. Topic 2 presents the BASIC elements for using subroutines.

TOPIC 1
LISTS AND TABLES

Lists and tables are used in many data-processing applications. For example, a tax table may be used to look up the amount of income tax based on the gross pay to be withheld from paychecks. Rating tables are often used to find the premium to be charged for an insurance policy. And in many statistical analyses, tables are printed to show how data breaks down into categories.

Figure 20-1 gives an example of a *list* (also known as a *vector*). As you can see, it is one dimensional and contains ten pay rates. Each of these rates may represent a different pay class, numbered from pay class 1 to pay class 10.

Figure 20-2 gives an example of a *table* (also known as a *matrix*). In contrast to a list, a table has two dimensions. The table in figure 20-2 gives insurance rates based on (1) age and (2) risk classification. Although other languages provide for tables that have more than two dimensions, most BASIC compilers provide for a maximum of two.

Subscripts

The variables in a list or table are called *elements*. To refer to an individual element, the programmer uses *subscripts*. For example, if

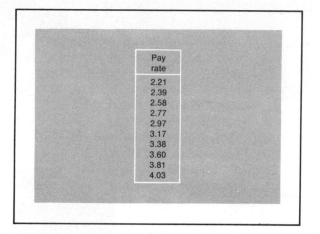

FIGURE 20-1   A list

R is the name given to the pay rate list in figure 20-1, the elements in the list can be referred to as R(1), R(2), R(3), and so on. In each case, the integer constant in parentheses following the list name is called the subscript. The subscript must always be positive and less than or equal to the total number of elements in the list.

To illustrate the use of subscripts for a table or matrix, consider the table in figure 20-3. Here the table represents monthly sales figures for twelve months in each of the last five years, and the name of the table is M. Rather than giving the monthly values, this figure shows the subscript

Age	Class 1	Class 2	Class 3	Class 4
18–34	$23.50	$27.05	$35.25	$52.90
35–39	24.00	27.55	35.75	53.40
40–44	24.60	28.15	36.35	54.00
45–49	25.30	28.85	37.05	54.70
50–54	26.30	29.85	38.05	55.70
55–59	28.00	31.55	39.75	57.40

FIGURE 20–2   A table

Month \ Year	1	2	3	4	5	
1	M(1,1)	M(1,2)	M(1,3)	M(1,4)	M(1,5)	← one row
2	M(2,1)	M(2,2)	M(2,3)	M(2,4)	M(2,5)	
3	M(3,1)	M(3,2)	M(3,3)	M(3,4)	M(3,5)	
4	M(4,1)	M(4,2)	M(4,3)	M(4,4)	M(4,5)	
5	M(5,1)	M(5,2)	M(5,3)	M(5,4)	M(5,5)	
6	M(6,1)	M(6,2)	M(6,3)	M(6,4)	M(6,5)	
7	M(7,1)	M(7,2)	M(7,3)	M(7,4)	M(7,5)	
8	M(8,1)	M(8,2)	M(8,3)	M(8,4)	M(8,5)	
9	M(9,1)	M(9,2)	M(9,3)	M(9,4)	M(9,5)	
10	M(10,1)	M(10,2)	M(10,3)	M(10,4)	M(10,5)	
11	M(11,1)	M(11,2)	M(11,3)	M(11,4)	M(11,5)	
12	M(12,1)	M(12,2)	M(12,3)	M(12,4)	M(12,5)	

↑
one
column

FIGURE 20–3   A table named M, showing subscripts

values for each of the 60 elements. It also shows you that a horizontal list of elements in a table is referred to as a *row*; a vertical list is referred to as a *column*.

In figure 20-3, the subscripts are numbered beginning with one. On some systems, however, subscripts must start with a value of zero. Thus the elements in figure 20-1 could be referred to as R(0), R(1), R(2), and so on. Because this will seriously affect your programs, find out whether subscripts on your system should start with zero or one and program accordingly. (All of the examples in this chapter assume a starting value of one.)

In general, you can use a constant or an arithmetic expression for a subscript in a BASIC program. Thus the subscripted variables M(7), X(A), A(X + Y), and B(2 * A + 9) are all valid. If the value of an expression used as a subscript isn't an integer, the decimal portion of the value will be dropped.

Array Names

Array is a general name for a list or a table. In most BASIC systems, *array names* are made up of one and only one letter. Thus A, B, C, and so on are valid names for arrays. When these array names are used in your program, they are always followed by subscripts.

It is legal to name a variable and an array with the same letter. Thus M could represent a variable, and M followed by a subscript could represent one of the elements of an array. Since this is confusing, it should be avoided.

The DIM Statement

The dimension (DIM) statement is used to tell the compiler how many elements a list or table will contain. For instance, the statement

```
100 DIM M(12),A(5,20)
```

tells the compiler that the program will use two arrays: one is a list named M that contains 12 elements; the other is a table named A that contains 5 rows and 20 columns. Although the DIM statement can be placed anywhere within a program, it is usually placed near the start of the program.

When the dimension statement is omitted, the compiler assumes that all lists consist of 10 elements, and all tables consist of 10 rows and 10 columns, or 100 elements. As a result, if your lists or tables are smaller than these assumptions, you can omit the DIM statement. However, it is good programming practice to use the DIM statement whenever you use an array. At the least, it documents the size of your arrays for reference later on.

The FOR-NEXT Statement

Figure 20-4 illustrates the use of the FOR-NEXT statement, which is often used for manipulating the elements in a list or a table. This simple program adds ten values taken from the DATA statement and prints out their sum. The arrow on the left of this listing indicates that the program repeatedly executes the statements that start with the FOR statement (110) and end with the NEXT statement (140). In fact, these statements are executed ten different times. The first time the statements are executed, I has a value of 1, the second time I has a value of 2, the third time a value of 3, and so on until I has a value of 10. Then the program continues with the first instruction following the NEXT statement.

In most cases, the variable named in a FOR statement will start with a value of one and increase by ones until the end value is reached. However, the starting value or step size can be other than one as in this statement:

```
FOR M = 2 TO 20 STEP 2
```

Here, the FOR-NEXT loop will be executed ten times, with M varying from 2 to 20 by twos; that is, 2, 4, 6, and so on. In a similar fashion, other starting values and step sizes can be used. If the STEP phrase isn't coded, the compiler assumes a step size of one.

Although constant starting values, ending values, and step sizes have been illustrated so far, they can also be variable. For instance, the statements that follow read in starting, ending, and step-size values before the FOR-NEXT loop is entered:

```
100    LET T=0
110    FOR I = 1 TO 10
120    READ X
130    LET T = T+X
140    NEXT I
150    PRINT "SUM ="; T
160    STOP
170    DATA 5,2,9,8,7,11,15,22,93,1,-2,8,16
180    END
```

FIGURE 20–4 A simple program showing the use of FOR-NEXT statements

```
210 READ S1,E,S2
220 FOR V = S1 TO E STEP S2
       .
       .
       .
300 NEXT V
```

Here, the number of times that the FOR-NEXT loop is executed will depend on the values of S1, E, and S2. Expressions can also be used to supply the starting, ending, and step values.

If one FOR-NEXT loop is contained within another, they are referred to as *nested FOR-NEXT loops*. This is legal as long as the inner loop is contained entirely within the outer loop. Thus figure 20-5 illustrates both legal and illegal nested FOR-NEXT loops. In the second example, the NEXT statement for the second loop comes after the NEXT statement for the first loop; therefore, it isn't properly contained. Note that a NEXT statement is related to its FOR statement by the variable that follows the words FOR and NEXT; they must be the same.

Although FOR-NEXT statements are particularly useful for manipulating subscript values, they can also be used to control repetitive processing loops. For instance, figure 20-6 illustrates two ways of coding a routine that prints a depreciation schedule (this is part of the program originally presented in figure 19-14). In version A, the programmer creates his own loop control by using a counter named Y. In version B, the programmer uses a FOR-NEXT loop to change the values of Y from 1 by ones, until Y reaches the value of the variable L. Although both versions contain the same number of statements, I think you'll find that version

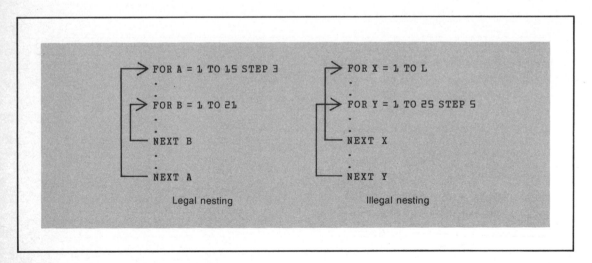

FIGURE 20–5 Nested FOR-NEXT loops

B is easier to read and follow (once you become used to FOR-NEXT loops).

USING LISTS

To illustrate the use of subscripts and FOR-NEXT loops for list processing, consider the program in figure 20-7. This is a revised version of the sales-averaging program originally presented in figure 19-15. In the 200 block of code, a FOR-NEXT loop reads and adds 12 monthly sales values. The loop is coded as follows:

```
220 FOR C = 1 TO 12
230 READ M(C)
240 LET T = T + M (C)
250 NEXT C
```

As a result, the loop is executed 12 times, and C is varied from one through twelve. The first time the loop is executed, a value is read into M(1), the first element of the array named M, and this value is added to T. The second time a value is read into M(2), and this value is added to T; and so on. When the loop is finished, twelve values are stored in the list named M, and all twelve values have been added to T.

```
400  REM PRINT DEPRECIATION SCHEDULE
410  PRINT "YEAR","COST","DEPN EXP","ACCUM DEP","BOOK VALUE"
420  LET A = A+D
430  LET B = C-A
440  PRINT Y,C,D,A,B
450  LET Y = Y + 1
460  IF Y <= L THEN 400

                         Version A

400  REM PRINT DEPRECIATION SCHEDULE
410  PRINT "YEAR","COST","DEPN EXP","ACCUM DEP","BOOK VALUE"
420  FOR Y = 1 TO L
430  LET A = A+D
440  LET B = C-A
450  PRINT Y,C,D,A,B
460  NEXT Y

                         Version B
```

FIGURE 20–6   A portion of a program that prints a depreciation schedule

```
 50   DIM M(12)
100   REM CALCULATE AVERAGE MONTHLY SALES
110   REM    AND AVERAGE DEVIATION
120   REM T = TOTAL OF SALES AND DEVIATIONS
130   REM C = COUNTER
140   REM M = LIST OF MONTHLY SALES--12 VALUES
150   REM A = AVERAGE MONTHLY SALES
160   REM D = MONTHLY DEVIATION FROM AVERAGE

200   REM CALCULATE AVERAGE MONTHLY SALES
210   LET T = 0
220   FOR C = 1 TO 12
230   READ M(C)
240   LET T = T + M(C)
250   NEXT C
260   LET A = INT(T/12+.5)
270   PRINT "AVERAGE MONTHLY SALES ="; A

300 REM CALCULATE AVERAGE DEVIATION
310   LET T = 0
320   FOR C = 1 TO 12
330   LET D = ABS(A-M(C))
340   LET T = T+D
350   NEXT C
360   PRINT "AVERAGE DEVIATION ="; INT(T/12*10+.5)/10
370   STOP

600   DATA 125,257,178,191,361,402
610   DATA 373,253,282,126,87,99

700   END
```

FIGURE 20–7   A revised version of the program that calculates average monthly sales and average deviation

In the 300 block of code, the program uses a FOR-NEXT loop to determine the deviation of each of the twelve values in the list M from the average monthly sales value. After this loop is executed twelve times with twelve different values for M(C), the average deviation is printed, and the program ends. Unlike the earlier version of this program, the RESTORE statement isn't needed, because the monthly sales values were stored in the list M after the first reading.

Figure 20-8 illustrates another version of this sales-averaging program. Here, up to 60 different monthly sales values can be entered for processing, using the INPUT statement. Note, then, that the DIM statement specifies an array named M with 60 elements. Because the actual

```
50   DIM M(60)
100  REM CALCULATE AVERAGE MONTHLY SALES
110  REM   AND AVERAGE DEVIATION
120  REM T = TOTAL OF SALES AND DEVIATIONS
130  REM C = COUNTER
140  REM M = LIST OF MONTHLY SALES--12 VALUES
150  REM A = AVERAGE MONTHLY SALES
160  REM D = MONTHLY DEVIATION FROM AVERAGE

200  REM PRELIMINARY CONVERSATION
210  PRINT "WHAT IS THE ITEM NUMBER";
220  INPUT I
230  PRINT "HOW MANY MONTHS SALES ARE YOU SUPPLYING";
240  INPUT L

300  REM GET VALUES AND PRINT AVERAGE MONTHLY SALES
310  LET T = 0
320  FOR C = 1 TO L
330  PRINT "MONTH"; C;
340  INPUT M(C)
350  LET T = T+M(C)
360  NEXT C
370  LET A = INT(T/L+.5)
380  PRINT "AVERAGE MONTHLY SALES ="; A

400  REM CALCULATE AVERAGE DEVIATION
410  LET T = 0
420  FOR C = 1 TO L
430  LET D = ABS(A-M(C))
440  LET T = T+D
450  NEXT C
460  PRINT "AVERAGE DEVIATION ="; INT(T/L*10+.5)/10

500  REM CLOSING CONVERSATION
510  PRINT
520  PRINT "MORE ITEMS FOR AVERAGING? Y OR N";
530  INPUT R$
540  PRINT
550  IF R$ = "Y" THEN 200
560  END

READY

RUNNH

WHAT IS THE ITEM NUMBER?49801
HOW MANY MONTHS SALES ARE YOU SUPPLYING?3
MONTH 1  ?341
MONTH 2  ?200
MONTH 3  ?150
AVERAGE MONTHLY SALES = 230
AVERAGE DEVIATION  73.7

MORE ITEMS FOR AVERAGING? Y OR N?N

READY
```

FIGURE 20–8 The averaging program using a variable number of monthly sales received via the INPUT statement

number of elements may vary from 1 to 60, the entire list may not be used.

You should be able to understand this program based on the information presented thus far. The FOR-NEXT statements use the variable L to specify the end value of the loop variable named C. In the 300 block of code, the loop variable is printed to indicate which month data should be supplied for:

```
330 PRINT "MONTH"; C;
```

Because a semicolon follows the C, the question mark from the INPUT statement prints, and the data is entered, on the same line.

USING TABLES

To illustrate the use of tables in BASIC, consider the program in figure 20-9. This averaging program will accept 12 monthly sales values for up to ten years, or a total of 120 values. As a result, the DIM statement specifies an array named M with 12 rows and 10 columns. Because data may be entered for from one to ten years, all of the elements in the array may not be used when the program is executed.

In the 200 block of the program, 12 input values for each year are requested. Here, the INPUT statement uses a constant subscript for rows and the variable subscript Y for columns as in

$$M(4,Y)$$

The FOR-NEXT loop that controls the input varies Y from 1 to the value of L, the number of years for which data is being entered.

The 300 block of code has nested FOR-NEXT loops. Here, the inner loop varies J from 1 through 12, and the outer loop varies Y from 1 through the value of L. As a result, if L equals 5, statement 330 is executed 60 times. The first time, $M(J,Y)$ will represent element $M(1,1)$, the second time it will represent element $M(2,1)$, the thirteenth time it will represent element $M(1,2)$, and so on.

The 400 block of code also has nested FOR-NEXT loops. This time, however, the outer loop varies the month subscript, and the inner loop varies the year subscript. Either way, the subscripts cover all elements of the table, so the results are correct. Notice in statement 430 that a subscripted variable is used within a function.

MAT STATEMENTS

To make it easy to manipulate lists and matrixes, most versions of BASIC provide MAT statements. For instance, figure 20-10 presents four MAT statements that are useful for business applications. These can be used to read or input data into a matrix, to print the contents of a matrix,

```
100    DIM M(12,10)
110    REM PROGRAM TO CALCULATE MONTHLY SALES AVERAGE
120    REM    AND AVERAGE DEVIATION
130    REM M IS A TABLE OF SALES BY MONTH AND YEAR
140    REM T IS USED TO TOTAL SALES AND DEVIATIONS
150    REM A IS AVERAGE MONTHLY SALES
160    REM D IS MONTHLY DEVIATION FROM AVERAGE

200    REM PRELIMINARY CONVERSATION
210    PRINT "WHAT IS THE ITEM NUMBER";
220    INPUT I
230    PRINT "HOW MANY YEARS SALES ARE YOU SUPPLYING";
240    INPUT L
250    FOR Y = 1 TO L
255    PRINT "ENTER FIRST SIX MONTHS SALES FOR YEAR"; Y
260    INPUT M(1,Y),M(2,Y),M(3,Y),M(4,Y),M(5,Y),M(6,Y)
270    PRINT "ENTER SECOND SIX MONTHS SALES FOR YEAR"; Y
280    INPUT M(7,Y),M(8,Y),M(9,Y),M(10,Y),M(11,Y),M(12,Y)
290    NEXT Y

300    REM CALCULATE AVERAGE MONTHLY SALES
305    LET T = 0
310    FOR Y = 1 TO L
320    FOR J = 1 TO 12
330    LET T = T + M(J,Y)
340    NEXT J
350    NEXT Y
360    LET A = INT(T/(12*L)+.5)
370    PRINT "AVERAGE MONTHLY SALES ="; A

400    REM CALCULATE AVERAGE DEVIATION
405    LET T = 0
410    FOR J = 1 TO 12
420    FOR Y = 1 TO L
430    LET D = ABS(A-M(J,Y))
440    LET T = T+D
450    NEXT Y
460    NEXT J
470    PRINT "AVERAGE DEVIATION ="; INT(T/(12*L)*10+.5)/10

500    REM CLOSING CONVERSATION
510    PRINT
520    PRINT "MORE ITEMS FOR AVERAGING? Y OR N";
530    INPUT R$
540    PRINT
550    IF R$ = "Y" THEN 200
560    END
```

FIGURE 20–9 A program that averages monthly sales over a period of years and calculates average deviation

MAT Statement	Operation
MAT PRINT X	Print the contents of the matrix in row sequence.
MAT READ X	Read data into the matrix in row sequence until the matrix is filled.
MAT INPUT X	Input data into the matrix in row sequence until the matrix is filled.
MAT X = ZER	Set all elements in the matrix to a value of zero.

FIGURE 20–10   Some useful MAT statements

or to set all the elements within a matrix to zero. In addition, most BASIC compilers provide MAT statements that are used in mathematical applications (matrix algebra).

Figure 20-11 is a short program that illustrates the use of two MAT statements. It reads five values into a list, reads 15 values into a 5 by 3 matrix, and prints the contents of the list and the matrix. If you study the output, you can figure out how these statements work. In general, the MAT PRINT statement prints five values per line, 15 print positions apart. However, if the array name is followed by a semicolon, the values are printed in a tightly packed format.

The MAT PRINT statement is particularly useful for debugging. If you have any doubt that your matrixes have been loaded correctly, you can insert a MAT PRINT statement into your program to see what values the matrix contains. After you are assured that the matrixes contain the intended values, you can remove the MAT PRINT statement.

DISCUSSION

Although this has been a relatively brief introduction to list and table handling in BASIC, you should now be able to use the DIM, FOR-NEXT, and MAT statements. Because they can improve the clarity of a program, you should use them whenever they correspond to the logic of the program.

SUMMARY

1. A list or vector is one dimensional; a table or matrix is two dimensional. BASIC provides language for processing the elements within a list or table.

```
       100    DIM A(5),B(3,5)
       110    MAT READ A,B
       120    MAT PRINT A;B
       130    STOP
       140    DATA -1,-2,-3,-4,-5
       150    DATA 1,2,3,4,5,6,7,8,9,10
       160    DATA 11,12,13,14,15
       170    END

     READY

     RUNNH

     -1     -2     -3     -4     -5
       1             2             3
       4             5             6
       7             8             9
      10            11            12
      13            14            15

     READY
```

FIGURE 20–11   A program to illustrate the operation of MAT statements

2. The DIM, FOR-NEXT, and MAT statements are used for processing lists or tables. They are used in conjunction with one or two dimensional subscripts.

TERMINOLOGY

list

vector

table

matrix

element

subscript

row

column

array

array name

nested FOR-NEXT loops

QUESTIONS

1. Refer to figure 20-7.
   a. Write a MAT statement that will read 12 values into the M array.
   b. Write a MAT statement that will print the M array.

2. Refer to figure 20-9. Assume that the user has entered 7 for the number of years that data will be supplied for.

    a.   What will statement 255 print the third time it is executed?

    b. Which elements of the array will be filled when statement 280 receives data for the fifth year?

    c. Write a MAT statement that will print the contents of the M array.

TOPIC 2
SUBROUTINES

A *subroutine* is a group of statements that are related by function. In a sense, then, all programs are made up of subroutines. If a subroutine is used in two or more modules of your program, you can set it off from the modules and branch to and from the subroutine using the GOSUB and RETURN statements.

Figure 20-12 schematically illustrates the use of the GOSUB and RETURN statements. When the GOSUB statement is executed, it branches to the statement number specified. Thus

```
360 GOSUB 1000
```

causes a branch to statement 1000. The program then executes the statements in sequence, until it encounters a RETURN statement such as this:

```
1120 RETURN
```

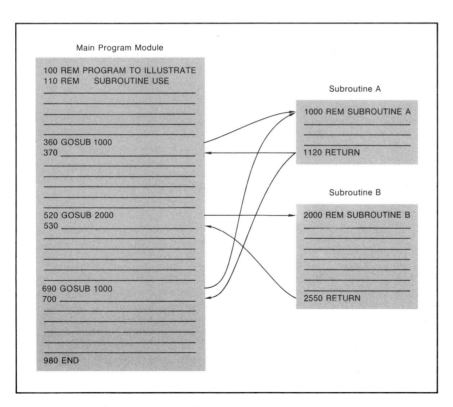

FIGURE 20–12   The concept of subroutines

The RETURN statement causes a branch to the statement following the GOSUB that transferred control to the subroutine.

In figure 20-12, the subroutine starting at statement 1000 is *called* by two different GOSUB statements. As a result, the subroutine will return to two different statements in the main routine, depending on which GOSUB transferred control to the subroutine. By using the subroutine, the programmer saved coding; otherwise, the statements of the subroutine would have been placed in the main routine twice.

The use of subroutines can also contribute to program clarity. (This has to do with the notion of modular program design as described in chapter 9.) If you think of your program as a structure of subroutines, you can divide your program into manageable modules. This becomes more important as the programs you work on become larger and more complex.

To illustrate the use of subroutines for simplifying program logic, consider the program in figure 20-13. This is a revised version of the program in figure 19-14, which prints a depreciation schedule after getting

```
200   REM MAIN ROUTINE
210   GOSUB 300
220   GOSUB 400
230   GOSUB 500
240   IF R = 1 THEN 200
250   STOP

300   REM GET FACTS SUBROUTINE
         .
         .
         .
      RETURN

400   REM PRINT TABLE SUBROUTINE
         .
         .
         .
      RETURN

500   REM CLOSING CONVERSATION SUBROUTINE
         .
         .
         .
      RETURN
```

FIGURE 20–13   Simplifying a main module by using subroutines

the required facts about a depreciable item. Here the main routine has been reduced to five executable statements by using subroutines. The first three are GOSUB statements that call the primary modules or subroutines of the program. As a result, although each of these subroutines may be extremely complex, the main routine is kept simple.

To further simplify program logic, one subroutine can call another one. This is referred to as *nested subroutines*. Although each compiler will have a limit as to how many levels of nested subroutines are legal, the limit is usually far more than you are likely to require. So use nested subroutines whenever they can improve program clarity.

When using subroutines, you should always start execution with the first statement and end execution with the last statement. This simplifies the program logic and will make it easier to debug later on.

Also, be sure that no subroutines are entered unless they are called by GOSUB statements. In other words, all subroutines should be preceded by STOP, GO TO, or RETURN statements so that there is no possibility of illegal entry. If a program enters a subroutine other than through a GOSUB statement, the computer won't know what to do when it encounters the RETURN statement. For this reason, subroutines are normally placed near the end of a program after the main processing modules.

SUMMARY

The GOSUB and RETURN statements can simplify logic and reduce duplication of code. The GOSUB statement causes a branch to a subroutine, and the RETURN causes a branch back to the statement following the calling GOSUB.

TERMINOLOGY

subroutine
calling a subroutine
nested subroutines

QUESTIONS

1. Do you think the program in figure 20-13 is easier to understand than the earlier version in figure 19-14? Discuss.

2. Since the programs in this section are all short, there isn't a good example of a program that could be simplified by structuring it into two or more subroutines. When a module becomes too long, however, you should analyze it to see whether or not it could be simplified by dividing it into two or more subfunctions and treating these as subroutines. But how long is too long? At what length do you think a module starts to become unwieldy? Discuss.

SECTION SIX

FORTRAN

This section introduces you to FORTRAN, one of the oldest and most widely used languages currently available. If you master all of the material in this section, you will have a significant programming skill. Chapter 21 presents the critical material, so you should be prepared to put your major efforts there.

21 AN INTRODUCTION TO FORTRAN

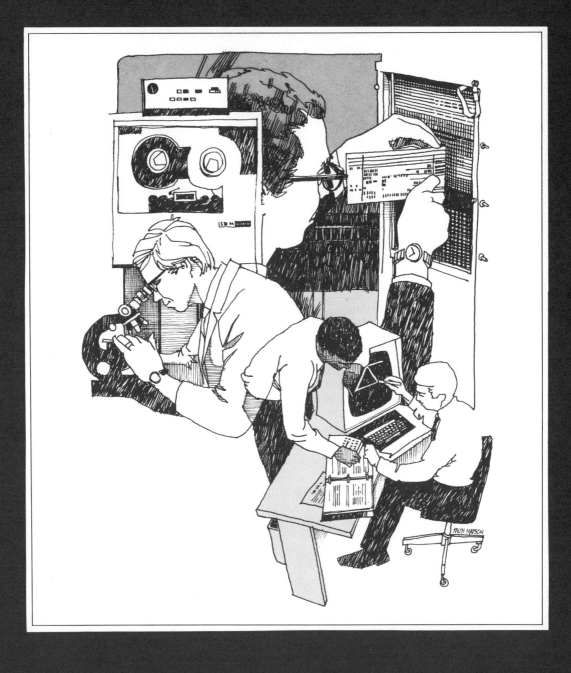

FORTRAN is the most widely used of all programming languages. It is also one of the oldest programming languages, first introduced in 1956. Because the language is essentially mathematical, FORTRAN, which stands for FORmula TRANslator, can be easily learned by scientists, engineers, and mathematicians. One of the attractions of FORTRAN is that a FORTRAN compiler is available for nearly all major computer systems.

Although all FORTRAN compilers are based on similar specifications, each computer manufacturer's version of FORTRAN traditionally has had its own peculiarities. In an attempt to standardize FORTRAN—to make it easier to switch from one computer to another—the American National Standards Institute developed specifications for a standard FORTRAN in 1966. This standard gives specifications for a Basic FORTRAN and a full FORTRAN, so standard FORTRAN can be used on relatively small computers as well as on medium- and large-sized computers.

Because Basic FORTRAN consists of selected elements of the full FORTRAN, it is said to be a *subset* of full FORTRAN. Thus, a Basic FORTRAN program can be compiled by a full FORTRAN compiler, but a full FORTRAN program using some of the advanced FORTRAN elements cannot be compiled by a Basic compiler. Some computers have both Basic and full compilers, in which case the Basic compiler (because it allows fewer elements) compiles at higher speeds than the full compiler.

For the most part, this book presents standard Basic FORTRAN. Whenever an element from full FORTRAN is presented, it is identified as such. If the computer you are using has only a Basic compiler, you must avoid the full FORTRAN elements.

This chapter is divided into three topics. The first presents ten FORTRAN statements that will get you started programming in this language. The second illustrates how these statements are used in two typical FORTRAN programs. The last topic explains how to prepare, test, and debug your program. When you complete this chapter, you should be able to write FORTRAN programs for a wide range of processing activities.

TOPIC 1
A SUBSET OF THE
FORTRAN LANGUAGE

This topic presents ten statements of the FORTRAN language. After you learn the function of each statement, you should be able to understand programs like the one in figure 21-1. You should also be able to write programs of your own when you finish this topic. Then, you can learn about other FORTRAN statements in chapter 22 and in supplementary reading materials.

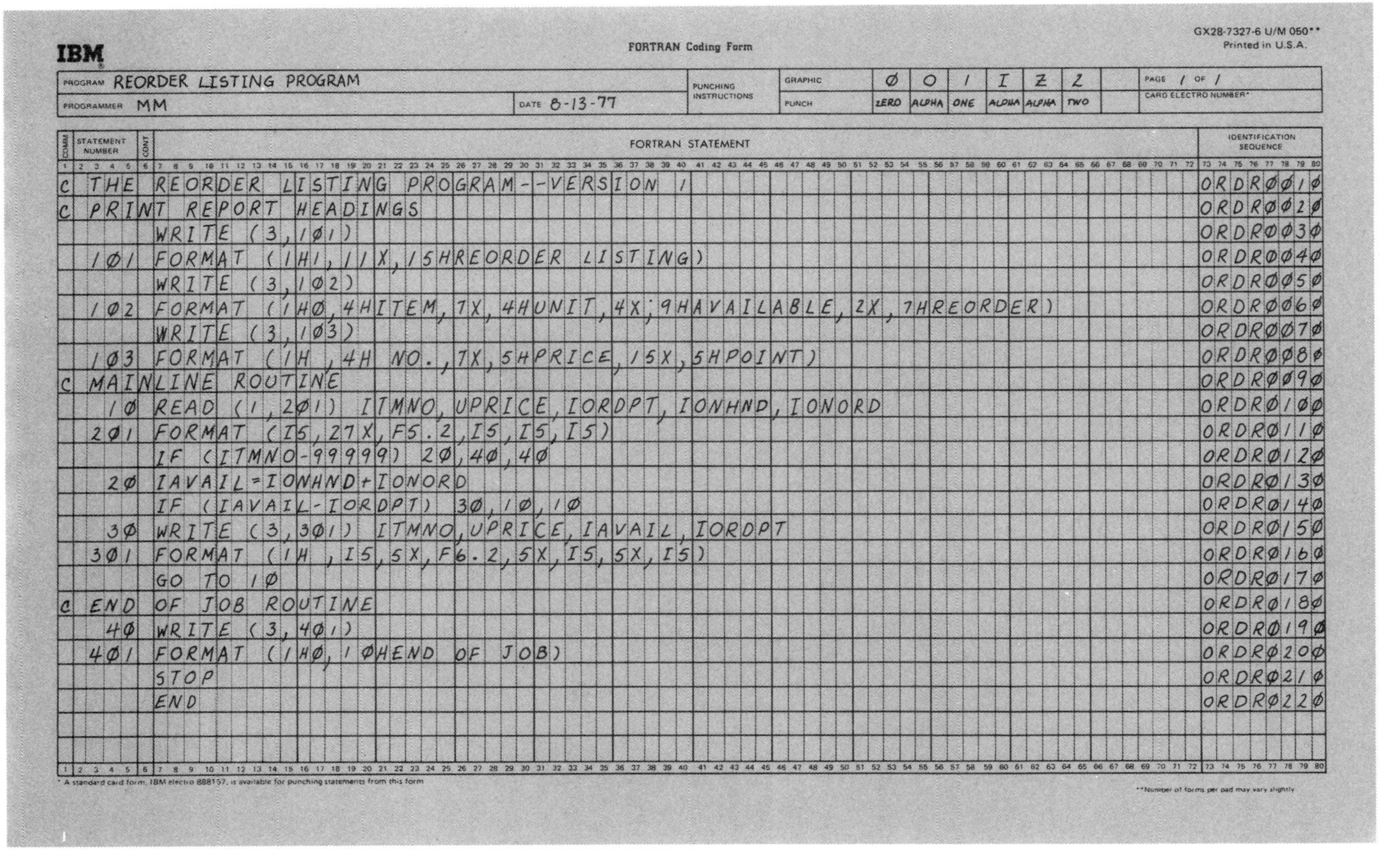

IBM — FORTRAN Coding Form — GX28-7327-6 U/M 050** Printed in U.S.A.

PROGRAM REORDER LISTING PROGRAM — PROGRAMMER MM — DATE 8-13-77

PUNCHING INSTRUCTIONS — GRAPHIC: Ø O I I Z Z — PUNCH: ZERO ALPHA ONE ALPHA ALPHA TWO — PAGE 1 OF 1 — CARD ELECTRO NUMBER*

```
C THE  REORDER LISTING PROGRAM--VERSION 1                           ORDRØØ1Ø
C PRINT REPORT HEADINGS                                             ORDRØØ2Ø
       WRITE (3,1Ø1)                                                ORDRØØ3Ø
  1Ø1  FORMAT (1H1,11X,15HREORDER LISTING)                          ORDRØØ4Ø
       WRITE (3,1Ø2)                                                ORDRØØ5Ø
  1Ø2  FORMAT (1HØ,4HITEM,7X,4HUNIT,4X,9HAVAILABLE,2X,7HREORDER)    ORDRØØ6Ø
       WRITE (3,1Ø3)                                                ORDRØØ7Ø
  1Ø3  FORMAT (1H ,4H NO.,7X,5HPRICE,15X,5HPOINT)                   ORDRØØ8Ø
C MAINLINE ROUTINE                                                  ORDRØØ9Ø
   1Ø  READ (1,2Ø1) ITMNO,UPRICE,IORDPT,IONHND,IONORD               ORDRØ1ØØ
  2Ø1  FORMAT (I5,27X,F5.2,I5,I5,I5)                                ORDRØ11Ø
       IF (ITMNO-99999) 2Ø,4Ø,4Ø                                    ORDRØ12Ø
   2Ø  IAVAIL=IONHND+IONORD                                         ORDRØ13Ø
       IF (IAVAIL-IORDPT) 3Ø,1Ø,1Ø                                  ORDRØ14Ø
   3Ø  WRITE (3,3Ø1) ITMNO,UPRICE,IAVAIL,IORDPT                     ORDRØ15Ø
  3Ø1  FORMAT (1H ,I5,5X,F6.2,5X,I5,5X,I5)                          ORDRØ16Ø
       GO TO 1Ø                                                     ORDRØ17Ø
C END OF JOB ROUTINE                                                ORDRØ18Ø
   4Ø  WRITE (3,4Ø1)                                                ORDRØ19Ø
  4Ø1  FORMAT (1HØ,1ØHEND OF JOB)                                   ORDRØ2ØØ
       STOP                                                         ORDRØ21Ø
       END                                                          ORDRØ22Ø
```

* A standard card form, IBM electro 888157, is available for punching statements from this form

**Number of forms per pad may vary slightly

FIGURE 21–1 The reorder-listing program on a FORTRAN coding form

Because the program in figure 21-1 is referred to throughout this topic, let me briefly describe it. The basic problem definition is given by the card layout form and print chart in figure 21-2. This program reads inventory cards and prints a listing of those items that need to be reordered. An item is listed only if the on-hand quantity plus the on-order quantity is less than the reorder point.

Figure 21-3 gives a flowchart for this program. As you can see, an item number of 99999 means that there are no more cards in the input deck.

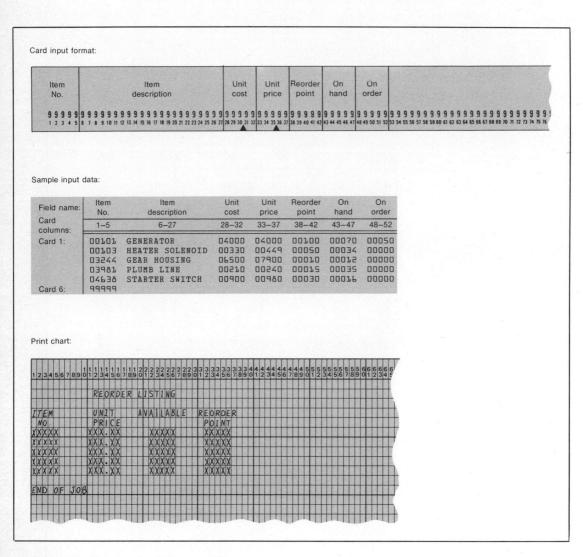

FIGURE 21-2   The reorder-listing problem

The program then prints an END OF JOB message and ends. Otherwise, the program loops through a calculate, decision, and print block, printing one line whenever an item should be reordered.

Figure 21-4 shows the reorder-listing program as it will appear when printed by the computer during compilation. In the remainder of this

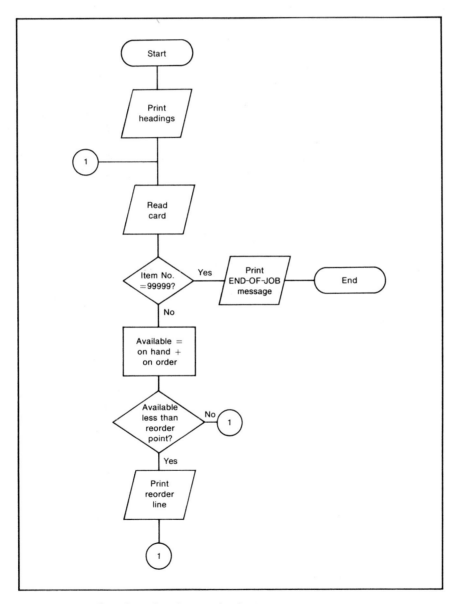

FIGURE 21-3   Flowchart for the reorder-listing program

```
C THE REORDER LISTING PROGRAM--VERSION 1

C PRINT REPORT HEADINGS
      WRITE (3,101)
  101 FORMAT (1H1,11X,15HREORDER LISTING)
      WRITE (3,102)
  102 FORMAT (1H0,4HITEM,7X,4HUNIT,4X,9HAVAILABLE,2X,7HREORDER)
      WRITE (3,103)
  103 FORMAT (1H ,4H NO.,7X,5HPRICE,15X,5HPOINT)

C MAINLINE ROUTINE
   10 READ (1,201) ITMNO,UPRICE,IORDPT,IONHND,IONORD
  201 FORMAT (I5,27X,F5.2,I5,I5,I5)
      IF (ITMNO-99999) 20,40,40
   20 IAVAIL = IONHND+IONORD
      IF (IAVAIL-IORDPT) 30,10,10
   30 WRITE (3,301) ITMNO,UPRICE,IAVAIL,IORDPT
  301 FORMAT (1H ,I5,5X,F6.2,5X,I5,5X,I5)
      GO TO 10

C END OF JOB ROUTINE
   40 WRITE (3,401)
  401 FORMAT (1H0,10HEND OF JOB)
      STOP
      END
```

FIGURE 21-4 Printout of the reorder-listing program

section, all programs will be illustrated in this form. In this case, the far-left print position represents column 1 of a source card.

The remainder of this topic is divided into two parts. First, some background information is given about FORTRAN. Second, the ten statements of the introductory FORTRAN subset are presented.

SOME BACKGROUND INFORMATION

The FORTRAN Coding Form

When a FORTRAN programmer codes a program, he usually uses coding forms such as the one in figure 21-1. The form in the illustration, in fact, contains the complete reorder-listing program. If you study the coding form, you will find eighty columns are indicated from left to right. When the program is completed, one source-deck card is keypunched for each coding line.

Because it is difficult to distinguish between some handwritten letters and numerals, programmers usually write certain characters in a distinctive way. In figure 21-1, for example, zeros have a slash through them (Ø) while the letter O does not. It is also common for programmers to write the letter Z with a bar through it (Ƶ) to distinguish it from the numeral 2 and to write the numeral 1 as a simple vertical (I) but the letter I with top and bottom cross members (I).

As far as the FORTRAN compiler is concerned, only columns 1-72 of the coding form are significant. Columns 73-80 can be used to identify the source-deck cards or to give them sequence numbers, but they are not processed by the compiler. Their use is at the option of the programmer. In figure 21-1 I have used columns 77–80 to sequentially number the source deck from 10 to 220; I have used columns 73–76 to identify the source deck with the code ORDR.

Comments

Comment cards, or *comments*, are identified by a C in column 1 of a source card. Thus the program in figure 21-1 has four comments. When C is coded in column 1, any characters may be coded in columns 2–80 without affecting the execution of the program. As a result, comments are for the convenience of the programmer only.

Comments are important because they help document a program. Without them, a program is much more difficult to follow. In general, comments should be used (1) to identify the overall purpose of the program and (2) to identify the function of various blocks of coding within the program. Thus the first comment in figure 21-1 identifies the program; the next three comments identify functional segments within it.

Statements and Statement Numbers

A FORTRAN program is made up of a series of *statements*. For instance, the program in figure 21-1 consists of 18 statements and four comments (each line that doesn't have a C in column 1 represents a statement). Although comments are optional, each statement is critical to the successful execution of a program.

Columns 1–5 of the coding form are used to give a statement a *statement number*. As you can see, not all statements are numbered. (You will find out later when you should number a statement.) On most FORTRAN systems, the statement number can range from 0 to 99999, but on some the maximum number is 9999. Find out what the maximum is for your system and don't exceed it. Incidentally, blanks that precede or follow a statement number are ignored, so the number can be punched anywhere in columns 1–5.

Statement Formats

As you will soon see, each FORTRAN statement must be coded in a rigidly prescribed way. For instance, the GO TO statement must consist of the words GO TO followed by the number of some other statement in the program.

On the other hand, spacing doesn't affect a FORTRAN statement in any way. As a result,

```
GO TO 150
```

and

```
GOTO150
```

are both valid statements. The FORTRAN compiler simply ignores blanks when compiling a source deck. To make your programs easy to read and understand, however, you should use blanks whenever you can improve clarity.

Statement Length and
Continuation Lines

In general, a FORTRAN statement can be as long as it needs to be. If a statement is too long to fit on one card, it can be continued on the next card. In this case, the second card is called a *continuation card,* or *continuation line.*

When a continuation line is used, some character other than zero or a blank must be coded in column 6 of the coding form. I recommend a 1 for the first continuation line, a 2 for the next continuation line, etc. Continuation lines may be used for any FORTRAN statement. Although all compilers place some limit on the number of continuation lines that are allowed, it is usually five or more—more than enough for most purposes.

Constants

As you write arithmetic expressions in FORTRAN, you will often need to express constant values. For example, the numbers 1, −12, +4.1567, and −7.1 are all *constants.* In the expression,

```
M + N - 120
```

120 is a constant. As you can see, constants will not change in value during the execution of a program.

In FORTRAN, constants may be integer or real. An *integer constant* is a constant that doesn't contain a decimal point. A *real constant* is one that does contain a decimal point. As a result, 7, +4599, and −10870 are integer constants, while these are real constants:

```
12077.
 -3.02
+0.0428967
```

As you can see, a constant can have a leading plus or minus sign, but it cannot contain commas. Note that a real constant doesn't necessarily have to have a decimal fraction; if it has a decimal point, it is real.

Variables and Variable Names

As you write a program, you will give names to fields in storage that will change during the execution of the program. These fields are called *variables,* and their names are called *variable names.* For instance, ITMNO, UPRICE, and IAVAIL are variable names used in the program in figure 21-1.

Quite simply, variable names in FORTRAN are made up of six or less letters or numbers and they must start with a letter. Thus, H24, SLSRTE, and N0045L are valid variable names, but 3X24, N#35, and DEDUCTION are not. In general, a variable name is chosen to be indicative of the data it represents. For example, UCOST is a much better name for a unit-cost field than H24. (Incidentally, some compilers limit names to five characters, but six are used in this book.)

In FORTRAN, there are three different types of variables: *integer variables, real variables,* and *alphanumeric variables.* An integer variable will contain integer data, a real variable will contain real data, and an alphanumeric variable can contain any characters. On most computer systems, each type of variable has its own form of internal storage. storage.

Although you don't have to know about the different forms of internal storage, you must be careful to assign proper names for each type of variable. To name an integer variable, you must create a name that starts with one of the letters I through N (that's I–N as in INteger). To name a real variable, you must create a name that starts with one of the letters A–H or O–Z (that's all of the letters other than I–N). And a variable name for an alphanumeric variable can start with any letter of the alphabet. You create the name, then, based on the type of data you want the variable to store.

Arithmetic Expressions

An *arithmetic expression* (or simply *expression*) can be made up of variable names, constants, and *arithmetic operators.* The arithmetic operators in FORTRAN are as follows:

Operator	Meaning
+	Addition
−	Subtraction
*	Multiplication
/	Division
**	Exponentiation

Since exponentiation means "raise to the power of," the FORTRAN expression

$$X**2$$

is equivalent to X^2. And the FORTRAN expression X**.5 is equivalent to $X^{1/2}$, or $\sqrt{X}$ (the square root of X).

An arithmetic expression can be as simple as a single constant or variable name, and it can be as complex as continuation lines will permit. Figure 21-5 gives some examples of some typical expressions and the evaluation of them. Thus 1.23 is an expression, H is an expression, and

$$(2.**X*((DVAL/4.0)+(5.0-X)))/2.$$

is an expression.

To evaluate an expression, you need to know the current values of the variables. In figure 21-5, assumed values are given for each variable name in the column headed "variable values." In addition, however, you need to know in what sequence the operations are performed when an expression is evaluated. For instance, 2 + 3 * 4 is 20 if addition is done first, and it is 14 if multiplication is done first.

Example	Expression	Variable Values	Expression Value
1	1.23	none	1.23
2	(−4)	none	−4
3	·HOURS	HOURS = 43.1	43.1
4	HOURS*RATE	HOURS = 43.1,RATE = 2.91	125.421
5	5.+HOURS*RATE	HOURS = 43.1,RATE = 2.91	130.421
6	(5.+HOURS)*RATE	HOURS = 43.1,RATE = 2.91	139.971
7	5.+HOURS*3.*RATE/2.	HOURS = 40.0,RATE = 2.00	125.
8	(5.+HOURS)*(3.*RATE/2.)	HOURS = 40.0,RATE = 2.00	135.
9	(2.***X*((DVAL/4.0)+(5.0−X)))/2.	E = 3.,DVAL = −12.,X = 3.	−4.
10	E**.5	E = 16.0	4.

FIGURE 21–5 Arithmetic expressions in FORTRAN

Here, then, are the sequence rules for evaluating an expression:

1. Exponentiation is done first.
2. Multiplication and division are done second.
3. Addition and subtraction are done third.
4. If more than one operation at the same level is specified (such as one division and two multiplications), the operations are done in sequence from left to right.

Using these rules, the value of 2 + 3 * 4 is 14.

When parentheses are used, the operations within parentheses are performed before operations outside parentheses. When there are parentheses within parentheses, the operations in the innermost set of parentheses are performed first. Because parentheses help to clarify the order of operations, they should be used whenever there might be a chance for confusion.

With this as background, you should be able to see how the expression values in figure 21-5 were derived. In examples 5 and 6, you can see how the use of parentheses can change the value of an expression. In example 9, you see parentheses within parentheses within parentheses.

When writing arithmetic expressions, you must be sure that no expression contains two consecutive operators. Thus

```
2.+ -E
```

is illegal. This expression can be made legal, however, by using parentheses as follows:

```
2.+ (-E)
```

You should note in figure 21-5 that all of the expressions are consistent as to *mode*. This means that each expression is made up of either real constants and variables, in which case it is said to be in the *real mode,* or of integer constants and variables, in which case it is said to be in the *integer mode*. This is a requirement of standard FORTRAN, which prohibits *mixed-mode* expressions.

Since standard FORTRAN allows an exponent in a real expression to be in either the real or integer mode, both

```
X**3 + X**5 and X**3. + X**5.
```

are in the real mode. Similarly, the expression

```
X**I+X**J
```

is in the real mode. Integer exponents should be used whenever possible since they lead to faster object-program execution.

One question you might be asking is when to use real and when to use integer expressions. Generally, use a real expression if one of the variables or constants in the expression requires decimal positions or if the calculated value of the expression might require decimal positions. An integer expression should be used only in relatively simple expressions involving whole numbers, and even then, a real expression will normally lead to the same results.

THE STATEMENTS OF
THE FORTRAN SUBSET

With this background, you should have little trouble learning how the statements of FORTRAN work. Here, then, are ten statements that will allow you to write programs of considerable complexity.

The Arithmetic
Assignment Statement

The *arithmetic assignment statement* (or just *assignment statement*) evaluates an arithmetic expression and places the result in a variable. To illustrate, consider this statement:

```
I = 3 * M
```

When the statement is executed, the value of 3 * M will be placed in the field named I. As a result, if M has a value of 4, a value of 12 will be placed in I. The value of M is unchanged by the execution of the statement.

In general, there are four ways the assignment statement is used. First, it can be used to set a variable to an initial value as in this examples:

```
X = 1.5
REM = -.0585
IYEAR = 1977
```

After the assignment statements are executed, X, REM, and IYEAR will have values of 1.5, −.0585, and 1977, regardless of what values they might have had previously.

A second use is to set a variable equal to the result of a calculation. You have already seen this in the statement I = 3 * M. The expression to the right of the equals sign can be any valid arithmetic expression.

A third use is to move a value from one field to another as in this example:

```
STVAL = OLDVAL
```

If, for example, OLDVAL has a value of 465.32 when the statement is executed, both STVAL and OLDVAL will have a value of 465.32 after execution.

A fourth use is to increase or decrease an integer value by a constant amount as in these examples:

```
I = I + 1
J = J - 2
```

In the first example, I is increased by 1, and the result is stored back in I. Consequently, if I had a value of 12 before the statement was executed, it will have a value of 13 after execution. Similarly, in the second example, if J had a value of 10 before execution, it will have a value of 8 after execution. Note here that a variable can be named on both sides of the equals sign; that is, it can receive the results of the statement execution, and it can also be part of the calculation.

One thing to watch for is this: Before a variable name can be used on the right side of an equation, it must be defined. One way of *defining a variable* is to use it on the left side of the equals sign in an arithmetic statement. The other way, as you will soon see, is to use the variable name in a READ statement. In other words, data must be stored in a variable before that variable can be operated upon in an assignment statement. If you don't define all variables before operating upon them, it will lead to programming errors.

Here are some other examples of assignment statements:

```
AREA = 3.00
VALUE = -.045*VARX
Y = X**2 + 2.*X + 7.533
NEWVAL = IVAL1 - IVAL2
J = K
```

In all of these statements, the variable to the left of the equals sign and the expression to the right are in the same mode. However, this is not a requirement of FORTRAN.

In some cases, you will want to use an expression in one mode and the variable to the left of the equals sign in another. Then the execution of the statement takes place in three stages. First, the value of the arithmetic expression is calculated. Second, the value is converted to the mode of the variable. Third, the converted value is placed in the variable to the left of the equals sign.

Since the conversion from one mode to another can significantly change the value of an expression, it is important to know what takes place during conversion. For example, when the statement

```
K = 9.88799
```

is executed, the value 9 is placed in the variable K. In other words, the decimal positions in the real constant 9.88799 are dropped when converting to integer mode. On the other hand, if the statement

```
X = M/N
```

is executed at a time when M has a value of 5 and N has a value of 2, X will receive the value of 2.0. Here, 5 is divided by 2 giving 2.5, but since the expression is in the integer mode, the .5 is dropped. Then when 2 is converted to the real mode, it becomes 2.0.

You can see that converting from one mode to another can lead to truncated decimal fractions. If the value of the expression does not involve decimal fractions, however, converting to another mode changes only the form of a variable, not its value; thus,

$$X = -2$$

causes X to receive a value of -2.0, and

$$I = 5.00$$

gives a value of 5 to I.

The READ Statement

When a READ statement is executed, one input record is read and data from that record is stored in the variables named. For instance, the program in figure 21-4 uses this READ statement:

```
10 READ (1,201) ITMNO,UPRICE,IORDPT,IONHND,IONORD
```

Within the parentheses following the word READ, two numbers are given, separated by a comma. The first of these numbers indicates the I/O device to be used. Although the numbers used for various devices depend on the system being used, a common convention is to use 1 for the card reader, 2 for the card punch, and 3 for the printer. Since this convention is followed in this text, the device referred to by the READ statement above is the card reader.

The second number in the parentheses is the statement number associated with a FORMAT statement. Since the number 201 is given, the FORMAT statement following the READ statement is specified. As you will soon see, the FORMAT statement gives detailed specifications for the location and type of data found in the input record.

Following the parentheses in the READ statement is a list of variable names. These names refer in sequence to the fields of the input cards that are to be used. Thus ITMNO is an integer variable name for the first field in the input card to be used by the program, the item-number field; UPRICE is a real variable name for the second input field to be used, the unit-price field; IORDPT is an integer variable name for the third field to be used, the reorder-point field; and so on. (Since the item-description and unit-cost fields aren't going to be used by this program, they are not given names in this list.)

The programmer selects integer or real names for the fields based on (1) whether or not the input field contains decimal positions, and (2) the extent to which the field will be involved in arithmetic statements. Since this program involves only simple arithmetic—the addition of two whole numbers—and since only unit price has decimal positions, all fields except unit price are given integer names.

The FORMAT Statement
(Input Description)

The FORMAT statement is used to describe the fields in both input and output records. Right now, I will present only the use of the FORMAT statement for input descriptions. Then, after you have been introduced to the WRITE statement, I will explain the use of the FORMAT statement for output descriptions.

If you check the program in figure 21-4, you can see that the FORMAT statement referred to by the READ statement is this:

```
201 FORMAT (I5,27X,F5.2,I5,I5,I5)
```

In the parentheses of the FORMAT statement, codes are given so the compiler knows in which card columns each of the variables named in the READ statement can be found. The first specification given is I5, indicating a five-column integer (I) field. In other words, the first variable named in the READ statement list (ITMNO) is located in card columns 1–5. The FORMAT statement indicates next that 27 card columns are to be skipped (27X); item description and unit price are in these card columns. The third code given is F5.2. This indicates that the next variable named in the READ list is a real number that is five-card columns long and has two decimal positions. Thus the location and the nature of the UPRICE field are given. In a similar manner, the FORMAT statement specifies that the next three variables named in the READ list are five-position integer fields (I5,I5,I5).

Do you see the relationship between the READ and FORMAT statements? The variables listed in the READ statement are given in the same sequence that they are found in the FORMAT statement and in the input record. For each variable named, the FORMAT statement must have one I or F specification, and the codes and names should be of the same mode— integer (I) or real (F). To show that input columns are to be skipped, the X code is used. In both the READ and the FORMAT statements, the use of parentheses and commas is significant. If they are omitted or misplaced, the statement will not perform as intended.

There are actually four different type codes that you will want to use for describing input fields in a FORMAT statement. They are as follows:

Code	Meaning
I	Integer variable
F	Real variable
A	Alphanumeric variable
X	Skipped position

After each I, F, or A code, you specify the width of the field and the number of decimal positions it contains (if any).

If a number is specified before the type code, it is a *repeat count*. The repeat count indicates the number of times that the field is repeated in succession in the input record. Thus, 3I5 means that three five-digit integer fields in succession are to be found in the input record. And 5F8.4 specifies five real fields in succession, each eight positions long with four decimal positions. (You will see repeat counts illustrated in one of the programs in topic 2 of this chapter.)

When numeric input data is keypunched for FORTRAN programs, there is considerable flexibility as to its form. In an integer field, for example, blanks are automatically converted to zeros, so bb12bbb (where b is a blank) and 0012000 in an I7 field will both be treated as a value of 12000. In contrast, when using other languages, a blank in a numeric field is often considered an invalid character that can't be processed.

If an integer field is signed, the sign is punched preceding the digits, so $-$bb47 or bb$-$47 in an I5 field is treated as -47. This contrasts with languages that require an X-punch in the rightmost position of a numeric field to indicate that it is negative.

Similarly, blanks in an F format input field are treated as zeros, and a leading plus or minus sign can be used to indicate the sign of the field. In addition, a decimal point can be punched in a real input field, in which case it overrides the specifications used in the associated FORMAT statement. To illustrate, suppose a real variable named FLD1 is punched in columns 1–10 of a card and the format statement is

```
FORMAT (F10.3)
```

Then, the following table represents data punched in the card and the value given to the stored variable (b = blank):

Punched Data	Value of FLD1 (F10.3)
bbb1234567	$+1234.567$
bbbbb382.9	$+382.9$
-112.5678b	-112.5678
bb201147bb	$+20114.700$
$+1.2$bbbbbb	$+1.2$

Because it is easier to left-justify than to right-justify when keypunching, it is common to left-justify all real fields for FORTRAN programs and to actually punch the decimal point. This tends to reduce the number of input errors.

Alphanumeric input fields are keypunched just as they would be when using any other language, but each alphanumeric variable can hold only a limited number of characters. This depends on the computer being used. For example, each variable on a System/370 can hold up to four alphanumeric characters, whereas each variable on the Burroughs B5500 and the Univac 1108 can hold up to six characters. As a result, several different variable names must be used for a twenty-character field such as item description or employee name.

To illustrate, suppose a card with the following format is to be read:

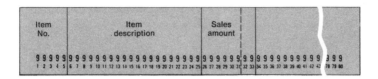

Then, READ and FORMAT statements such as the following are needed in System/370 FORTRAN:

```
      READ (1,101) ITMNO,DES1,DES2,DES3,DES4,DES5,SLSAMT
  101 FORMAT (I5,5A4,F8.2)
```

Here, the format code A is used for each alphanumeric variable. This code is followed by a number that is not larger than the maximum number of characters each alphanumeric variable can hold on a specific computer system. The number preceding code A indicates how many times the specification is to be repeated.

If an alphanumeric input field is smaller than the number of characters each variable can hold, the format specification is made accordingly. For example, a three-column input field is specified as A3. Similarly, a 22-character field can be treated as six variables with these format specifications: 5A4,A2. (You will see alphanumeric input fields operated upon by one of the sample programs in topic 2.)

It is interesting to note that the A format is not included in the standards for Basic FORTRAN. As a result, alphanumeric input and output fields cannot be processed using Basic FORTRAN. This gives you an idea of how inadequate some versions of FORTRAN are when used for business applications.

The WRITE Statement

The WRITE statement corresponds closely to the READ statement. When it is executed, one output record is written consisting of the fields named in the statement. For instance, the program in figure 21-4 uses this WRITE statement:

```
   30 WRITE (3,301) ITMNO,UPRICE,IAVAIL,IORDPT
```

The numbers in the parentheses following the word WRITE specify that device number 3 is going to be used, and that FORMAT statement number 301 is used to describe the output fields. Since device number 3 is used for the printer in this book, this WRITE statement will cause one line to be printed each time it is executed. The fields to be printed are given in sequence following the parentheses. In order, they are ITMNO, UPRICE, IAVAIL, and IORDPT.

The program in figure 21-4 also uses this WRITE statement:

WRITE (3,101)

This means that one line will be printed, based on the field descriptions given in FORMAT statement 101. Since no variables are named, however, no variable data will be printed by this statement. In a case like this, constant data is usually taken from the FORMAT statement itself—as you will now see.

The FORMAT Statement
(Output Description)

When a FORMAT statement is used for output descriptions, these type codes are commonly used:

Code	Meaning
H	Alphanumeric constant data
X	Blanks
I	Integer variable
F	Real variable
A	Alphanumeric variable

The only one that is new to you is H, since X, I, F, and A are also used for input descriptions. H means that an *alphanumeric constant* made up of any valid characters will follow. Then, when the related WRITE statement is executed, this constant will be printed.

To illustrate, consider the first FORMAT statement in figure 21-4.

101 FORMAT (1H1,11X,15HREORDER LISTING)

This describes an alphanumeric constant that is one character long, containing the number 1 (1H1). This is followed by 11 blanks (11X). And this is followed by an alphanumeric constant that is 15 characters long containing these characters:

REORDER LISTING

In other words, the heading, REORDER LISTING, will print when the first WRITE statement is executed.

But what about the first field description, 1H1? What does it do? The first position described in any FORMAT statement for a printed output line tells how the form should be skipped or spaced before printing. In the standards for full FORTRAN, the following characters can be used:

Character	Meaning
blank	Advance one line before printing
0 (zero)	Advance two lines before printing
1	Skip to the first line of the next page before printing
+	No advance before printing

As a result, FORMAT statement 101 tells the computer to skip the printer to the first line of the next page before printing the report title, REORDER LISTING.

The second FORMAT statement in figure 21-4 is this:

```
102 FORMAT (1H0,4HITEM,7X,4HUNIT,4X,9HAVAILABLE,2X,7HREORDER)
```

Can you interpret this one by yourself? It says advance two lines before printing, then print these column headings: ITEM, UNIT, AVAILABLE, and REORDER. The X descriptions between the alphanumeric constants indicate the proper spacing for these headings.

The fifth FORMAT statement in figure 21-4 along with the related WRITE statement follows:

```
30 WRITE (3,301) ITMNO,UPRICE,IAVAIL,IORDPT
301 FORMAT (1H ,I5,5X,F6.2,5X,I5,5X,I5)
```

Since the first character specified by the FORMAT statement is a blank, the form will be advanced one line before the line is printed. Then, since I5 reserves five print positions for an integer variable, the contents of ITMNO will be printed in print positions 1–5. The next five positions are specified as blanks by the FORMAT statement, followed by a six-position real field with two decimal positions. Thus the contents of UPRICE will be printed in print positions 11–16. Since the decimal point is actually printed for a real variable, the output field is given a length of six. If, for example, the input field contains 12345, it will print as 123.45. Finally, the specifications 5X,I5,5X,I5 give the spacing for the last two variables in the WRITE list. Thus IAVAIL and IORDPT will print in positions 22–26 and 32–36.

In FORTRAN, when numeric variables are printed, leading zeros are suppressed, the decimal point is properly placed, and a leading minus sign is printed if the field is negative. In addition, the output field is automatically rounded if less decimal positions are specified for the output field than are stored in the variable. Thus a variable with a value of −12.1176 printed with the format F8.2 will print as bb−12.12, where b is a blank. Similarly, a value of 00125 printed in an I5 field will print as bb125.

When coding FORMAT statements, you must be careful to use a format for each output field that is large enough to accommodate the full number plus the decimal point and minus sign (if any). If the output field is too small, errors will result. For instance, a variable with a value of 12345.67 printed with the format F7.2 will print as asterisks (*******) on the System 370.

If the format specified for a numeric field is too large for the number of digits in the variable, it causes no problems. FORTRAN simply fills the field with blanks to the left of the data. Thus an input field described as F6.2 printed in an output field described as F11.2 will be printed with five leading blanks. In other words, the effect of

```
FORMAT (1H ,I5,5X,F6.2,5X,I5,5X,I5)
```

and

```
FORMAT (1H ,I5,F11.2,2I10)
```

is the same if all of the variables contain five or fewer digits. Both statements will cause the four variables to print in the print positions shown by the print chart in figure 21-2. Because this coding technique is efficient, you will probably want to use it when you begin to write your own programs.

The GO TO Statement

Normally the statements of a program are executed in sequence, one statement after the other. When the GO TO statement is executed, however, it causes a branch to the statement number specified. In figure 21-4, for example, the GO TO statement in the mainline routine causes a branch to statement 10 so more data can be read and processed. Since most programs require the same operations to be repeated many times, most FORTRAN programs will have one or more GO TO statements.

The Arithmetic IF Statement

One of the important features of a computer is its ability to perform different operations under different conditions. For instance, a payroll program may perform one series of operations if an employee has worked 40 or fewer hours in a week, another series of operations if the employee has worked more than 40 hours. In FORTRAN, the IF statement gives a program the ability to select appropriate routines based on conditions that develop during program execution. There are two kinds of IF statements: (1) the arithmetic IF statement, and (2) the logical IF statement.

The program in figure 21-4 uses arithmetic IF statements. For instance, this IF statement is used to determine whether or not the last input card has been read:

```
IF (ITMNO-99999) 20,40,40
```

In the parentheses following the word IF, an arithmetic expression is written. This expression, which can be either real or integer mode, can be as simple as X or as complex as you wish it. Following the parentheses, three statement numbers are given, separated by commas.

When the IF statement is executed, it is done in two stages: first, the arithmetic expression is evaluated; second, the program branches to one of the statement numbers listed. If the value of the arithmetic expression is negative, the program branches to the first statement number in the list; if the value is zero, it branches to the second statement number; if the value is positive, it branches to the third statement number.

In the IF statement, the arithmetic expression is

```
ITMNO-99999
```

This is an integer expression that subtracts the constant 99999 from the value of the item-number field. If the item number is less than 99999, the value of the expression is negative and the program branches to statement number 20. If the item number is 99999, as it will be when the last input card is read, the value of the expression is zero and the program will branch to statement number 40. Since a five-digit field can't be greater than 99999, the expression will never be positive; thus, any statement number can be used as the third number in the list.

The second IF statement in figure 21-4 is this:

```
IF (IAVAIL-IORDPT) 30,10,10
```

It determines whether an output line should be printed. Since the arithmetic expression is IAVAIL-IORDPT, its value will be negative when the available stock is less than the reorder point. For example, if available is 34 and the reorder point is 50, the value of IAVAIL-IORDPT is −16 (minus 16), and the program branches to statement number 30, which causes a line to be printed. If the value of the expression is zero or positive, meaning available is *not* less than the reorder point, the program branches to statement number 10, which is the start of the program, and another input card is read.

Quite frankly, the arithmetic IF statement can be confusing and lead to programming errors. As a result, if your FORTRAN compiler has the logical IF statement, you should use it exclusively. It is much easier to code and to understand.

The Logical IF Statement

Although the logical IF statement is not in the Basic FORTRAN standards, it is available on most compilers. Its format is this:

IF (logical-expression) statement

For instance, the following are valid logical IF statements:

```
IF (X.LT.Y) GO TO 105
IF (A+B+7.5.GE.10.-X) GO TO 10
IF (M.EQ.5) X=20.5
```

The first example is read: if X is less than Y, go to statement number 105. The second statement is read: if A + B+7.5 is greater than or equal to 10. − X, go to statement number 10. The third is read as: if M is equal to 15, then X equals 20.5.

To form a *logical expression,* the following *logical operators* can be used:

Operator	Means
.LT.	Less than
.LE.	Less than or equal to
.EQ.	Equal to
.NE.	Not equal to
.GT.	Greater than
.GE.	Greater than or equal to

These operators separate two real or two integer arithmetic expressions (both expressions must be of the same model). Either expression can be as simple as a single variable name or constant or it can be as complex as is required by the logic of the program.

When the logical IF statement is executed, first the logical expression is evaluated. If it is true, the statement following the expression is executed. If it is not true, the statement following the expression is skipped, and the program continues with the statement following the logical IF statement.

In the program in figure 21-4, the mainline routine could be rewritten using logical IF statements as follows:

```
C MAINLINE ROUTINE
   10 READ (1,201) ITMNO,UPRICE,IORDPT,IONHND,IONORD
  201 FORMAT (I5,27X,F5.2,I5,I5,I5)
      IF (ITMNO.EQ.99999) GO TO 40
      IAVAIL=IONHND+IONORD
      IF (IAVAIL.GE.IORDPT) GO TO 10
      WRITE (3,301) ITMNO,UPRICE IAVAIL,IORDPT
  301 FORMAT (1H ,I5,5X,F6.2,5X,I5,5X,I5)
```

I think you'll agree that this code is much easier to follow than the version that uses arithmetic IF statements.

The STOP Statement

The STOP statement causes the program to end. It is the next to the last statement of the program in figure 21-4. In other words, after all data has been processed, the program ends.

The END Statement

The last statement of every FORTRAN program must be the END statement. It consists of one word, END. It is used to tell the compiler that there are no more statements in the source deck. Unlike the STOP statement, the END statement doesn't cause object code to be compiled.

DISCUSSION

You have now been introduced to a complete subset of FORTRAN. Once you master this information, you will be able to read and understand a wide range of programs. And you should be able to write programs of your own.

Because this topic has presented a large volume of information, I doubt that anyone can remember it all after just a few readings. Therefore, you will have to refer to this topic repeatedly as you study the programs in the next topic and as you write your own programs.

At this stage, however, you should understand the program in figure 21-4 completely. If you do, see if you can predict the output of this program when executed. Take the role of the computer and operate upon the test data given in figure 21-2, as prescribed by the program statements. Whenever the WRITE statement is executed, record the output that you think will print.

SUMMARY

1. In 1966 the American National Standards Institute published standards for Basic and full FORTRAN. These standards are intended to reduce the variations in FORTRAN as you go from one manufacturer's equipment to another's.

2. This topic has introduced you to ten FORTRAN statements. These statements can be used to perform I/O operations (READ and WRITE), to perform arithmetic operations (the assignment statement), and to control the sequence of operations (GO TO, arithmetic IF, logical IF, and STOP). The FORMAT and END statements give information to the compiler, but they do not cause any object code to be compiled.

TERMINOLOGY

subset
comment card
comment
statement
statement number
continuation card
continuation line

constant
integer constant
real constant
variable
variable name
integer variable
real variable

defining a variable
alphanumeric constant
logical expression
logical operator

alphanumeric variable
arithmetic expression
expression
arithmetic operator

QUESTIONS

1. What is the mode of each of the expressions in figure 21-5?

2. Give the values of A, B, C, X, and Y, as determined by these statements:

```
A = 2.
B = A + 1.5
C = (2.*A+3.5/B)*3.
X = A * (B+2.**A) - 7.1
Y = (A+B+C)**A*10.**3
```

3. Refer to the program in figure 21-4 and assume that it is tested on the sample data given in figure 21-2.
   a. What is the value of IORDPT after the READ statement is executed for each input card?
   b. What does the value of IAVAIL become each time the assignment statement (statement 20) is executed?
   c. For which cards will a reorder line be printed?

TOPIC 2
TWO EXAMPLE PROGRAMS

With topic 1 as background, you should now be able to understand the two programs in this topic. As you study the programs, you should feel free to refer to topic 1 whenever you are in doubt about the precise execution of a statement.

Example 1: Version 2 of the
Reorder-Listing Program

The program in figure 21-6 is a refined version of the reorder listing program of figure 21-4. It will print output data in the form given by the print chart in figure 21-7. As you can see, alphanumeric input data is printed (the item-description field), and a page number is printed in the heading for each page of the report. This program will print a maximum of 50 reorder lines on each page of output, after which it will skip to the top of the next page and repeat the headings. (This is practical, of course, because otherwise a computer would print right over the perforation between two pages of a long report!)

Some of the highlights of this program follow:

1. All of the FORMAT statements are grouped at the start of the program. Since FORMAT statements can be placed anywhere within a program, this is at the option of the programmer. In general, you will find FORMAT statements grouped at the start, grouped before the END statement, or immediately following the READ or WRITE statement they relate to.

2. FORMAT statement 602 is so long that it requires a continuation line. As a result, you can see a 1 in column 6 of the continuation line.

3. If you look at FORMAT statements 501 and 604, you can see repeat counts used to describe input and output fields. Also, you can see that the item-description field is described as

$$5A4,A2$$

Consequently, it is 22 card columns long. If you check the READ and WRITE statements, you can see that six variable names are required to read and write this single alphanumeric field.

4. Logical IF statements are used in this program to improve program clarity. In the third IF statement, the program checks to see whether the line count is less than 50. If it is, the next reorder line is printed. Otherwise the form is skipped to the top of the next page, headings are printed, and LINE is reset to zero; then the next reorder line is printed.

```
C THE REORDER LISTING PROGRAM--VERSION 2
C THIS VERSION PRINTS ALPHANUMERIC DATA,
C     USES THE LOGICAL IF STATEMENT,
C     AND WILL PRINT ONLY 50 LINES PER PAGE.

C THE FORMAT FOR THE INPUT CARDS FOLLOWS
  501 FORMAT (I5,5A4,A2,5X,F5.2,3I5)

C THE FORMATS OF THE PRINT LINES FOLLOW
  601 FORMAT (5H1PAGE,I3,16X,15HREORDER LISTING)
  602 FORMAT (5H0ITEM,12X,4HITEM,17X,4HUNIT,5X,9HAVAILABLE,
    1           2X,7HREORDER)
  603 FORMAT (5H  NO.,9X,11HDESCRIPTION,13X,5HPRICE,16X,5HPOINT)
  604 FORMAT (1X,I5,5X,5A4,A2,F11.2,2I10)
  605 FORMAT (11H0END OF JOB)

C HOUSEKEEPING ROUTINE
      IPAGE = 1
      LINE = 50

C MAINLINE ROUTINE
   10 READ (1,501) ITMNO,D1,D2,D3,D4,D5,D6,UPRICE,IORDPT,IONHND,IONORD
      IF (ITMNO.EQ.99999) GO TO 999
      IAVAIL = IONHND+IONORD
      IF (IAVAIL.GE.IORDPT) GO TO 10

C PRINT AND PAGE OVERFLOW ROUTINE
      IF (LINE.LT.50) GO TO 20
          WRITE (3,601) IPAGE
          WRITE (3,602)
          WRITE (3,603)
          IPAGE = IPAGE+1
          LINE = 0
   20 WRITE (3,604) ITMNO,D1,D2,D3,D4,D5,D6,UPRICE,IAVAIL,IORDPT
      LINE = LINE+1
      GO TO 10

C END OF JOB ROUTINE
  999 WRITE (3,605)
      STOP
      END
```

FIGURE 21–6   The reorder-listing program (version 2)

5. Indentation is used in the print and page-overflow routine to help show related blocks of code. Specifically, the five statements following the IF statement are indented four spaces to show that all are executed if the line count isn't less than 50. Since blanks don't affect FORTRAN statements, indentation can be used any time you think it will improve clarity.

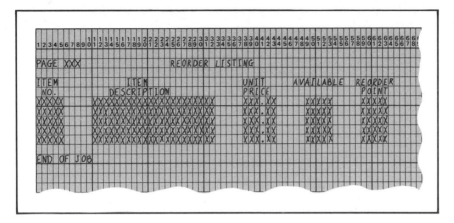

FIGURE 21–7   Print chart for version 2 of the reorder-listing program

Example 2: The Manhattan Program

The program in figure 21-8 illustrates the use of FORTRAN in another type of problem. This program determines how much the $24.00 paid for Manhattan Island in 1627 would be worth today if it had been placed in a savings account at 4½ percent annual interest. For this program, the current year is punched into columns 1–4 of a card that is read at the start of the program.

Since this program presents nothing new, you should be able to follow it without too much trouble. After reading the single input card, the program enters a main loop that is executed once for each year between 1627 and the present. A counter named I is used to keep track of the years (it is increased by one for each execution of the loop) and when I equals the current year, the current principal is printed.

This program, however, does raise one question. That is, how large can FORTRAN variables be? If the loop is repeated long enough, will PRINC become so large that the computer can no longer store the answer? And then what happens?

The answer is that each computer has a limit as to the size of integer and real variables. This is referred to as the *range* of a variable. On the System/370, for example, the allowable range of integer variables is from $-2{,}147{,}483{,}647$ to $+2{,}147{,}483{,}647$. On other systems, the maximum integer size may vary from 7 to 18 digits.

For real variables, the range is usually very large, so it is never a problem in business applications. However, real variables also have a limitation as to *precision*. The precision of a number indicates how many digits are actually significant. On the System/370, for example, a real variable has approximately seven significant digits. Therefore, a value like

$$79{,}812{,}533{,}101$$

```
C THE MANHATTAN PROBLEM
C GET CURRENT YEAR AND SET INITIAL VALUES
      READ (1,101) IYEAR
  101 FORMAT (I4)
      PRINC = 24.00
      I = 1627
C THE MAIN PROCESSING LOOP
   10 PRINC = PRINC*1.045
      I = I+1
      IF (I.LT.IYEAR) GO TO 10
C PRINT THE ANSWER
      WRITE (3,201) PRINC
  201 FORMAT (17H PRINCIPAL IS NOW,F15.2)
      STOP
      END
```

FIGURE 21–8   The Manhattan program

is treated as a value of

79,812,530,000

In other words, a computer's precision limits the degree to which an exact result can be computed. If the precision of a computer is seven digits, the results of the calculations can have only seven significant digits.

This brings us back to the Manhattan problem. Since the calculation is done in the real mode and the answer is ten or more significant digits— for example, the answer was 98,701,004.67 in 1973—the precision of many computers will be exceeded. Thus the answer will not be exact. On System/370, for instance, the answer line in 1973 would print as

```
PRINCIPAL IS NOW    98695744.00
```

(In actuality, the precision of System/370 is slightly more than seven decimal digits; that's why eight are printed here.)

Admittedly, this is a small degree of error in relationship to the size of the answer, and for that reason, the lack of precision can often be ignored. However, if a more precise answer is required, FORTRAN provides the DOUBLE PRECISION statement. This statement consists of the words DOUBLE PRECISION, followed by a list of variable names separated by commas, as in this example:

```
DOUBLE PRECISION X,Y, XINT,PAYMENT
```

By placing this statement at the start of a program, the variables named are stored in *double-precision* format, which means they have at least twice as many significant digits as they would otherwise have. On System/370, a double-precision number has 16 significant digits in contrast to the seven of single precision. (Single and double precision numbers have the same range, however.)

To get an exact answer to the Manhattan problem, then, this statement should be placed at the start of the program:

```
DOUBLE PRECISION PRINC
```

You should know, however, that the DOUBLE PRECISION statement is not available on all compilers. In fact, it is not included in the standards for the Basic FORTRAN subset.

Because many computers have limited precision for real variables, the DOUBLE PRECISION statement is often used for business programs. If a computer has a precision of only seven digits, sales figures in the millions will require double precision if they must be expressed exactly. As a result, you should be prepared to use this statement for business applications.

DISCUSSION

Although the explanations in this topic are brief, you should none-theless be able to follow these programs without too much difficulty. And you should now be more than ready to start writing programs of your own.

SUMMARY

1. This topic has presented two typical FORTRAN programs. The first performs the same operations on many different input records. The second performs repetitive calculations on a single set of starting values.

2. All compilers have a limit as to the range and precision of variables. Although the range doesn't usually affect business programs, the precision might. In this case, the DOUBLE PRECISION statement can be used.

TERMINOLOGY

range
precision

QUESTIONS

1. Refer to figure 21-6.
   a. Draw a program flowchart for this program.
   b. How does the program determine when to skip to the top of the next page and repeat the headings?

c. How many reorder lines will this program print per output page?

d. If the reorder-listing report requires three pages of output, what is the value of IPAGE when the program ends?

e. Add statements that will count the total number of cards processed and the total number of reorder lines printed and print these counts at the end of the program in this format:

```
XXXXX CARDS PROCESSED
XXXXX REORDER LINES PRINTED
END OF JOB
```

2. Refer to figure 21-8.

a. What are the values of IYEAR, I, and PRINC for the first three executions of the main processing loop?

b. How many times will the main processing loop be executed if the current year entered is 1977?

c. If the answer is 1,234,567.89, show how the final output line will be printed, giving the exact spacing.

d. If the answer is 1,234,567.89, will it be exactly correct if the program is run on System/370 without using the DOUBLE PRECISION statement? Explain.

TOPIC 3
DIAGNOSTICS AND DEBUGGING

After you have coded a FORTRAN program, you must complete several other phases before you have a tested program. First, you must create some test data. Second, you should desk-check your program for clerical and logical errors. Third, you must have your program keypunched. Fourth, the program should be executed on the test data. And fifth, any errors discovered during testing should be corrected (this is called debugging).

CREATING TEST DATA,
DESK-CHECKING, AND
CORRECTING DIAGNOSTICS

When you create test data, you should be sure that it tests all of the conditions that might come up during the execution of your program. As you create this data, you may realize that your program does not provide for some condition that is likely to come up. In addition to testing all conditions, the test data should provide data that covers the full range of values that might be processed by the program. For instance, if an input field may range from zero through 99999, then one test value for the field should be zero and another should be 99999. For the early test runs, be sure to keep your test data simple enough so that you can do the required calculations manually. Otherwise you won't be able to tell whether or not the program ran correctly.

After creating your initial test data—and before entering your source program into the system—you should *desk-check* your program. This saves computer and programmer time because desk-checking usually will catch an error or two. As you go through your program, check each statement to be sure that it is coded correctly. You may also want to "play computer" and operate on some of the test data you have created. Perform each operation specified by your program to see if it operates as you intended.

After you have desk-checked your program, you must keypunch your program. You will also keypunch job-control cards and any test data required. After your deck is arranged in a suitable sequence for compilation and testing, you can submit it to the computer center. Then, if errors are detected during compilation, a *diagnostic listing* will be returned to you when you pick up your program. Depending on the compiler used, the diagnostic messages vary from being quite brief and confusing to quite understandable. In either case, it is the programmer's job to decode the error messages and to make the necessary corrections.

TESTING AND DEBUGGING

After a test run, you compare the actual output with the expected output. If they are the same, you can assume that your program ran without errors. You can then test the program on a more complete set of test data. But what if the actual output isn't the same as the expected output? For instance, when the reorder listing program is executed, what if the available amounts don't agree with your manual calculations? Or what if the columns of printed data aren't under the appropriate column headings? You would then have to find the cause of these errors (or bugs) and correct (or debug) them.

Debugging is one of the most challenging jobs of a programmer. In a complex program, debugging an error can be much like solving a mystery. To determine what happened, you begin with clues and trace backward until you find the culprit: a coding error or invalid input data. After all bugs have been corrected and the program has been tested on complete test data, the program is ready to use.

SUMMARY

After coding a program, the programmer must keypunch the program, have it compiled, and correct any errors detected during compilation. After this, the programmer must test and debug using test data that tries all the conditions that are likely to come up when the program is actually used.

TERMINOLOGY

desk checking
diagnostic listing
debugging

QUESTIONS

1. Refer to figure 21-2. What conditions or input value ranges won't be tested by the sample data shown?

2. Refer to figure 21-6.
    a. Suppose the program prints the heading lines, prints one reorder line, prints the END OF JOB line, and stops. What types of coding errors could cause this?
    b. Suppose the reorder-point quantities print under the AVAILABLE heading and the available quantities print under the REORDER POINT heading. What types of coding errors could cause this?

3. Refer to figure 21-8. Suppose the program reads the input card and starts to execute. However, it runs for a longer time than expected and finally prints out a message that says that arithmetic overflow took place and the program is unable to continue. What do you think this would mean and what is a likely cause of the error?

22 FORTRAN FOR TABLES AND ARRAYS

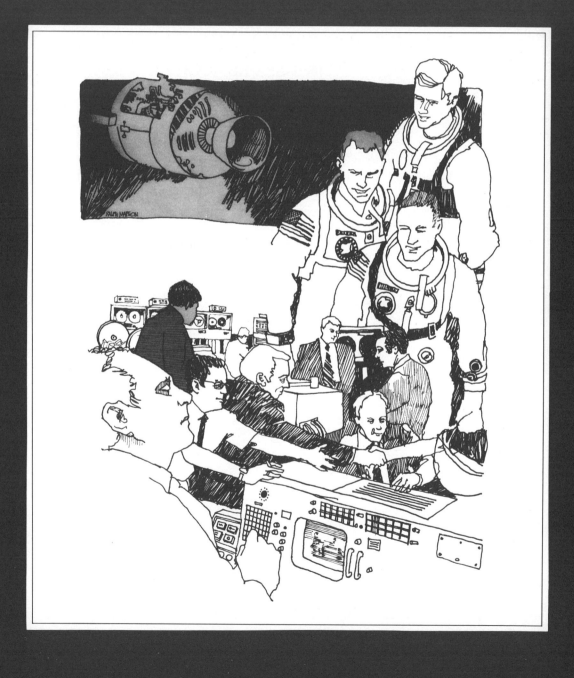

Tables are used in many data-processing applications. For example, a tax table may be used to look up the amount of income tax to be withheld from paychecks. Rating tables are often used to find the premium to be charged for an insurance policy. And in many statistical analyses, tables are printed to show how data breaks down into categories. Topic 1 of this chapter covers the FORTRAN elements used for handling one-level tables, while topic 2 covers the elements for two- and three-level tables.

TOPIC 1
ONE-LEVEL TABLES

Figure 22-1 is an example of a one-level table. (It can also be called a one-dimensional *array*.) As you can see, it contains ten pay rates. Each of these rates may correspond to a different pay class, numbered from 1 to 10.

When an array is stored in the computer as part of a FORTRAN program, one variable name, such as RATE, is used to refer to the entire array. It is then called an *array name*. The array name can be either integer or real, depending on the type of variable to be stored in the array.

Subscripts

The variables in an array are called *array elements*. To refer to these elements, the programmer uses *subscripts*. If, for example, the pay-rate array is given the name RATE, the first rate can be referred to as RATE(1), the second as RATE(2), and so on, as shown in figure 22-2. In each case,

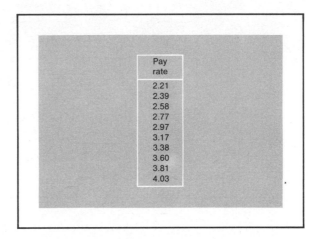

Pay rate
2.21
2.39
2.58
2.77
2.97
3.17
3.38
3.60
3.81
4.03

FIGURE 22–1 A one-level array

the integer constant in parentheses following the array name is called the subscript. The subscript must always be greater than zero and less than, or equal to, the total number of elements in the array.

An integer variable name can be used as a subscript in the same way that an integer constant is. Then, the array element that is referred to depends on the value of the subscript field at the time the statement is executed. For example, ICLASS is the subscript in the following arithmetic statement:

```
GROSS = RATE(ICLASS)*HRSWKD
```

If ICLASS contains a 1 when the statement is executed, 2.21 in figure 22-2 is referred to; if ICLASS contains a 2, then 2.39 is referred to; and so on.

Certain arithmetic expressions can also be used as subscripts. If IVALUE is the name of an array, IVALUE(K+1) is a legal subscripted variable. Then, if K equals 5, the sixth element in the array is referred to. Note, however, that the expression must be in the integer mode, and it must be in one of the following forms.

Constant * Variable + Constant
Constant * Variable − Constant
Constant * Variable
Variable + Constant
Variable − Constant

Thus, IVALUE(4 * NUM − 2) and IVALUE(2 * N) are valid subscripted variables, but IVALUE(NUM/4 + 3) is not.

Array Name = RATE	
Variable Name	Value
RATE(1)	2.21
RATE(2)	2.39
RATE(3)	2.58
RATE(4)	2.77
RATE(5)	2.97
RATE(6)	3.17
RATE(7)	3.38
RATE(8)	3.60
RATE(9)	3.81
RATE(10)	4.03

FIGURE 22–2   Subscripts used to reference the elements of an array

The DIMENSION Statement

The DIMENSION statement is required near the start of any FORTRAN program that uses arrays. It tells the compiler the number of locations in storage to set aside for each array used. For example, the statement

```
DIMENSION ARRAY1(120),ARRAY2(50),IARRAY(12)
```

specifies that the program is going to use three arrays: the first, named ARRAY1, consists of 120 real elements; the second, named ARRAY2, consists of 50 real elements; and the third, named IARRAY, consists of 12 integer elements. The DIMENSION statement does not cause any object code to be compiled, and one DIMENSION statement can be used for all arrays used by a program. This statement is usually found at the start of the source deck and must always be ahead of any of the executable FORTRAN statements.

The DO and CONTINUE Statements

The DO statement is used to cause one or more statements to be executed a specified number of times. It is particularly helpful when processing arrays because it automatically increases the value of a variable that can be used as a subscript.

To illustrate the DO statement, consider the simple program in figure 22-3. This program determines how much $1000 placed in a savings account at 6½ percent would be worth after accumulating simple interest for five years. The main processing loop follows:

```
      DO 10 N=1,5
      PRINC=PRINC*(1.+XINT)
   10 CONTINUE
```

It is called a *DO loop* because it is controlled by the DO statement. In this case, the loop will be executed five times.

Specifically, the DO statement says to execute all statements up to—and including—the statement number given (in this case, 10) and to execute the statements once for each value of the *index* (in this case, the index is N). The index is an integer variable that will change values while the DO loop is executed. In this case, N is varied from 1 to 5, after which the program leaves the loop and prints the result. The first time the loop is executed, N has a value of one, the second time it has a value of two, and so on, until it reaches a value of five.

It is the *index definition* within the DO statement that prescribes how the index values should be varied. In the DO statement above, the index definition is this:

```
      N=1,5
```

```
            C PROGRAM TO DETERMINE PRINCIPAL INCREASES IN A
            C      SAVINGS ACCOUNT

            C SET INITIAL VALUES
                  PRINC=1000.
                  XINT=.065

            C MAIN PROCESSING LOOP
                  DO 10 N=1,5
DO loop           PRINC=PRINC*(1.+XINT)
                10 CONTINUE

            C PRINT ENDING VALUE OF PRINCIPAL
                  WRITE (3,201) PRINC
               201 FORMAT (18H ENDING PRINCIPAL=,F10.2)
                  STOP
                  END
```

FIGURE 22-3   Program to illustrate the use of a DO loop

This means to give N a starting value of one, increase this value by 1 each time the DO loop is executed, and leave the loop when N reaches a value of 5.

The CONTINUE statement simply marks the end of a DO loop. It causes no object code to be compiled. Its statement number must be the same as the one given in the related DO statement.

In most cases, the index will start with a value of one and increase by one's, until the end value is reached. However, the starting value or increment size can be other than one as in this statement's index definition:

$$DO\ 50\ I=2,20,2$$

Here, the DO loop will be executed ten times with I varying from 2 to 20, counting by 2's (that is, 2, 4, 6, and so on). In a similar fashion, other starting values and increment sizes can be used. If the increment size isn't coded in the index definition, the compiler assumes a value of one.

Although constant starting values, ending values, and increment sizes have been illustrated so far, they can also be variable. For instance, the index definition below specifies a variable named IYEARS that is read before entering the DO loop.

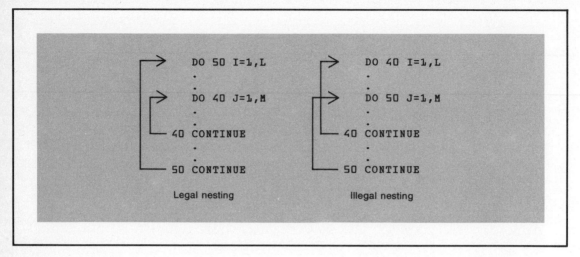

FIGURE 22–4   Nested DO loops

```
        READ (1,101) PRINC,XINT,IYEARS
101 FORMAT (F10.2,F3.3,I2)
        DO 10 N=1,IYEARS
        PRINC=PRINC*(1.+XINT)
 10 CONTINUE
```

Similarly, variables can be used for the starting value and increment size as in this DO statement:

```
DO 60 I=ISTRT,IEND,INC
```

All variables used in the DO statement should, of course, be integer variables.

If one DO loop is contained within another, they are referred to as *nested DO loops*. This is legal as long as the inner loop is contained entirely within the outer loop. Figure 22-4 illustrates both legal and illegal DO loops. In the second example, the CONTINUE statement for the second loop comes after the CONTINUE statement for the first loop, so it isn't properly contained. (The use of nested DO loops will be illustrated several times in topic 2.)

To illustrate the use of DO loops for subscript manipulation, suppose the rate array in figure 22-1 is punched into cards, one rate per card in columns 1–3. Following the ten rate cards in the data deck are employee payroll cards with this format:

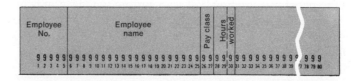

```
C USING A PAY RATE TABLE
      DIMENSION RATE(10)

C READ ARRAY NAMED RATE
      DO 10 I=1,10
      READ (1,101) RATE(I)
  101 FORMAT (F3.2)
   10 CONTINUE

C PRINT REPORT HEADING
      WRITE (3,201)
  201 FORMAT (1X,4HEMP.,1X,3HNO.,3X,5HCLASS,3X,5HHOURS,
     1            3X,4HRATE,5X,5HGROSS)

C PROCESS DATA CARDS
   20 READ (1,301) IEMPNO,ICLASS,HRSWKD
  301 FORMAT (I5,20X,I2,F3.1)
      IF (IEMPNO.EQ.99999) GO TO 30
      GROSS=RATE(ICLASS)*HRSWKD
      WRITE (3,401) IEMPNO,ICLASS,HRSWKD,RATE(ICLASS),GROSS
  401 FORMAT (2X,I5,I9,F9.1,F7.2,F11.2)
      GO TO 20

C END OF JOB ROUTINE
   30 WRITE (3,501)
  501 FORMAT (11H0END OF JOB)
      STOP
      END
```

FIGURE 22–5 A program using a one-level pay-rate table

The program to be written is supposed to read an employee card, look up the correct pay rate in the rate table, calculate the gross pay for an employee (hours worked times rate of pay), and print a listing of the results.

Figure 22-5 shows a FORTRAN program that accomplishes the processing using the DO statement, the DIMENSION statement, and subscripts. The first statement of the program, the DIMENSION statement, gives the name RATE to the rate array and indicates that it consists of ten elements. The DO statement is then used to read the rates from rate cards into the RATE array, as follows:

```
      DO 10 I=1,10
      READ (1,101) RATE (I)
  101 FORMAT (F3.2)
   10 CONTINUE
```

During the first execution of the DO loop, I has a value of 1; during the second execution, I has a value of 2; and so forth. As a result, the rate from the first card is stored in RATE(1), the rate from the second card is stored in RATE(2), and so on, until the rate from the tenth card is stored in RATE(10).

After the ten rates have been stored in the rate array, the program processes the data cards. Notice the use of the input variable named ICLASS as a subscript in this arithmetic statement:

```
GROSS=RATE(ICLASS)*HRSWKD
```

and in this WRITE statement:

```
WRITE (3,401) IEMPNO,ICLASS,HRSWKD,RATE(ICLASS),GROSS
```

Thus the proper pay rate is used to calculate the gross pay for each employee. If, for example, ICLASS has a value of five, the fifth value in the array will be used for the calculation.

One point to remember when using DO-loops is that a program cannot branch into the middle of a loop from outside the loop. If it did, the counter would not be set up properly and the results would be unpredictable. On the other hand, it is perfectly legal to branch out of a DO-loop before the test end value is reached. In this case, the value of the index is available to subsequent statements of the program.

To illustrate the technique of branching out of a DO loop, consider a program that uses a table like the one in figure 22-6 for calculating the premium to be charged for an insurance policy. After the rate is found by searching for the appropriate age bracket, the total premium is derived by multiplying this base rate by the number of hundreds of dollars of coverage applied for. Thus, $300-per-month coverage for a 41-year-old person costs $3.50 times 3, or $10.50

Age	Rate	Array Name = MAXAGE		Array Name = RATE	
		Variable Name	Value	Variable Name	Value
18–34	$3.00	MAXAGE(1)	34	RATE(1)	3.00
35–39	3.25	MAXAGE(2)	39	RATE(2)	3.25
40–44	3.50	MAXAGE(3)	44	RATE(3)	3.50
45–49	3.75	MAXAGE(4)	49	RATE(4)	3.75
50–54	4.00	MAXAGE(5)	54	RATE(5)	4.00
55–59	4.50	MAXAGE(6)	59	RATE(6)	4.50

FIGURE 22–6   Rating table and related arrays used by the program in figure 22–7

Using FORTRAN, the insurance table could be treated as two separate arrays. In the first array, the elements would be the maximum ages for each age bracket. In the second array, the elements would be the rates. These arrays are illustrated in figure 22-6.

The input arrays could be punched into input cards in several different formats. One way would be to punch two numbers, one value from each array, into each input card, as follows:

Max age	Rate
59	450
54	400
49	375
44	350
39	325
34	300
1—2	3—5

Here, the maximum age for each bracket is punched in columns 1 and 2, and the rate in columns 3–5.

After the arrays are read into storage, application cards containing the applicant's account number, amount of insurance applied for, and age are read and processed. If the applicant is between the ages of 18 and 59 and does not apply for over $500-per-month coverage, the program prints out the premium to be charged. Otherwise, the program prints the account number, age, and amount of insurance applied for, along with the message UNINSURABLE.

The program to accomplish this processing is listed in figure 22-7. Note that the statements within the DO loops are indented, so you can tell at a glance which statements are part of the loops. This is a good programming practice, so use indentation whenever you use DO loops.

To make it easier to follow the listing, the program flowchart is given in figure 22-8. After the table cards are read into storage and the report headings are printed, the program reads one card and determines if the applicant's age is less than 18 or if the coverage applied for is over $500 per month. If not, the program enters the following lookup routine:

```
C TABLE LOOKUP
  30 DO 40 I=1,6
          IF (IAGE.LE.MAXAGE(I)) GO TO 50
  40      CONTINUE
```

This DO loop will be executed up to six times, depending on the value of the applicant's age (IAGE). Each time through the loop, IAGE is sub-

```
C ONE LEVEL INSURANCE RATE TABLE LOOKUP
      DIMENSION MAXAGE(6),RATE(6)

C READ ARRAYS NAMED MAXAGE AND RATE
      DO 10 I=1,6
          READ (1,1) MAXAGE(I),RATE(I)
    1     FORMAT (I2,F3.2)
   10     CONTINUE

C PRINT REPORT HEADINGS
      WRITE (3,2)
    2 FORMAT (10H ACCT. NO.,3X,3HAGE,3X,9HPOL. AMT.,3X,
    1          3X,8HRATE/100,4X,4HRATE)

C READ APPLICANT CARD AND CHECK FOR VALIDITY
   20 READ (1,3) IACCT,AMOUNT,IAGE
    3 FORMAT (I5,F3.0,I2)
      IF (IACCT.EQ.99999) GO TO 99
      IF (IAGE.LT.18) GO TO 98
      IF (AMOUNT.GT.500) GO TO 98

C TABLE LOOKUP
   30 DO 40 I=1,6
          IF (IAGE.LE.MAXAGE(I)) GO TO 50
   40     CONTINUE

C APPLICANT IS UNINSURABLE--AGE IS UNDER 18, OVER 59,
C     OR AMOUNT APPLIED FOR IS OVER $500
   98 WRITE (3,4) IACCT,IAGE,AMOUNT
    4 FORMAT (1H ,I7,I8,F10.2,4X,11HUNINSURABLE)
      GO TO 20

C CALCULATE AND PRINT APPLICANT'S RATE
   50 PLRATE=RATE(I)*(AMOUNT/100.)
      WRITE (3,5) IACCT,IAGE,AMOUNT,RATE(I),PLRATE
    5 FORMAT (1X,I7,I8,F10.2,F11.2,F11.2)
      GO TO 20

C END OF JOB ROUTINE
   99 WRITE (3,6)
    6 FORMAT (11HOEND OF JOB)
      STOP
      END
```

FIGURE 22–7   One-level rating program

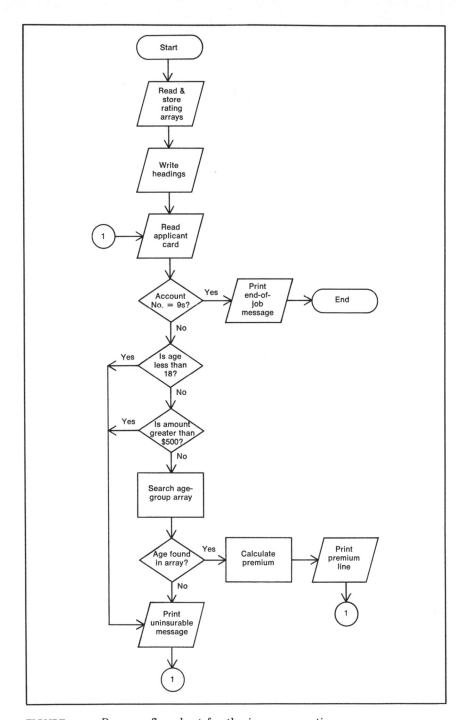

FIGURE 22–8   Program flowchart for the insurance-rating program

tracted from one of the values in the MAXAGE array. If IAGE is equal to or less than MAXAGE(I), the program branches to statement number 50, thus leaving the DO-loop.

To show more explicitly how the DO-loop operates, suppose IAGE has a value of 48. The following table then shows the values for the variables involved each time the DO-loop is executed:

I	IAGE	MAXAGE(I)
1	48	34
2	48	39
3	48	44
4	48	49

Since IAGE is less than MAXAGE(I) when I is equal to 4, the program leaves the DO-loop at this time. On the other hand, if IAGE has a value of 68, the DO-loop is executed the maximum of six times, and the program then continues with statement number 98.

When an IF or GO TO statement branches out of a DO loop before it has been executed the maximum number of times, the value of the index is available to subsequent program statements. When IAGE is 48, for instance, the program branches to statement number 50 when I equals 4. Statement number 50 then uses this value as a subscript:

```
PLRATE=RATE(I)*(AMOUNT/100.)
```

In other words, the fourth element in the RATE array is used as the base rate for calculating the total rate to be paid for the policy.

DO-Implied READ and WRITE Statements

In the program in figure 22-5, the pay rates are punched one per input card and read using this code:

```
    DO 10 I=1,10
    READ (1,101) RATE(I)
101 FORMAT (F3.2)
 10 CONTINUE
```

By using a DO-implied READ statement, the same results can be accomplished using less coding, as follows:

```
    READ (1,101) (RATE(I),I=1,10)
101 FORMAT (F3.2)
```

Here, the READ statement itself specifies a DO-loop. Following the variable named RATE(I), the index definition I=1,10 is given just as in a DO statement. This means that the READ statement should be repeated until ten values are placed into the array named RATE. Since the associated FORMAT statement specifies only one value per card (F3.2), ten cards are read as a result of the *DO-implied statement*. When coding a DO-implied loop, the index definition and the variable or variables to which it applies must be enclosed in parentheses.

Now suppose that the ten pay rates are punched five per card. Then, the same READ statement with a modified FORMAT statement would read two cards and store all ten values:

```
        READ (1,101) (RATE(I),I=1,10)
    101 FORMAT (5F3.2)
```

The advantage of the READ statement is that it gives the programmer increased flexibility since it will read as few or as many records as is necessary to fill the array elements specified.

If elements from two or more arrays are punched in one input card, this too can be specified in a DO-implied statement. For example, this statement would read the arrays used in the program in figure 22-7:

```
      READ (1,1) (MAXAGE(I),RATE(I),I=1,6)
    1 FORMAT (I2,F3.2)
```

If all six values of each array are punched into one card, as shown here:

34	300	39	325	44	350	49	375	54	400	59	450
Age	Rate	Age	Rate	Age	Rate	Age	Rate	Age	Rate	Age	Rate

the same READ statement could be used with this FORMAT statement.

```
    1 FORMAT (6(I2,F3.2))
```

By using parentheses within the FORMAT statement, the compiler is told that the two-column integer field and the three-column real field are repeated six times in one card. As a result, this statement is equivalent to

```
1 FORMAT (I2,F3.2,I2,F3.2,I2,F3.2,I2,F3.2,I2,F3.2,I2,F3.2)
```

Like an index definition in a DO statement, a DO-implied index definition can be given an increment value as follows:

```
      READ (1,1) (A(J),J=1,100,2)
```

This statement would read values into the odd-numbered elements of the array named A. Thus, positions 1, 3, 5, and so on would be filled.

In some cases, the number of elements in an array is not known at the time a program is coded. Then, an integer variable must be used as the test value in an index definition. For example, if 200 or less values are to be read and stored in an array, a lead card can be used as follows to give the test value for the index definition:

```
        DIMENSION X(200)
        . . .
        . . .
        READ (1,1) LIMIT
      1 FORMAT (I3)
        READ (1,2) (X(K),K=1,LIMIT)
      2 FORMAT (10F8.2)
```

If the lead card contains 177 in columns 1–3, the program will read eighteen cards. It will take ten values from the first seventeen cards and seven from the eighteenth card. Note that the DIMENSION statement must give a range for the X array that is larger than the value of LIMIT.

In certain cases, other variables can be recorded in the same card as the elements of one or more arrays. For example, an alphanumeric field in a typical card record can be treated as an array in the following manner:

```
        READ (1,1) IEMPNO,(NAME(I),I=1,5),ICLASS,HRSWKD
      1 FORMAT (I5,5A4,F3.2)
```

Here, the DO loop within the READ statement is used to read the five parts of a name field into a five-element array. Note again that the variable or variables in the DO loop, as well as the index definition, must be enclosed in parentheses.

The principles of the DO-implied READ statement can also be used in a WRITE statement. For example, if the table used in the program in figure 22-7 is to be printed with one pair of values per output line, this WRITE statement could be used:

```
        WRITE (3,7) (MAXAGE(I),RATE(I),I=1,6)
      7 FORMAT (1X,I5,F9.2)
```

And, if the six rates are to be printed, three per line, this coding could be used:

```
        WRITE (3,7) (RATE(I),I=1,6)
      7 FORMAT (1X,3F10.2)
```

DISCUSSION

Although this has been a relatively brief introduction to table handling in FORTRAN, you should now be able to use the DIMENSION, DO, and CONTINUE statements. You should also be able to use DO-implied READ and WRITE statements.

SUMMARY

In order to store or process arrays, FORTRAN provides subscripts, the DIMENSION statement, the DO statement, the CONTINUE statement, and DO-implied READ and WRITE statements. These FORTRAN elements give the capability of looking up values in an array, as well as the capability of changing values in an array.

array	index
array elements	index definition
array name	nested DO loops
subscript	DO-implied statement
DO loop	

1. Refer to figure 22-5. Add statements to this program that will print out the pay rate table in the end-of-job routine. One rate value should be printed per line.
   a. Use a DO loop.
   b. Use a DO-implied loop.

2. Refer to figure 22-7. Assume that a card is read by statement 20 and IACCT equals 12345, AMOUNT equals 300, and IAGE equals 51.
   a. What statements will be executed before branching back to statement number 20? (Don't write them down, but follow the statement execution through for the entire processing loop.)
   b. What data will be printed for this input card?

TOPIC 2
TWO- AND
THREE-LEVEL
TABLES

Many tables used in data-processing applications involve two or three variables. The insurance rates in the rating table in part A of figure 22-9, for example, vary based on an applicant's age and his job classification. Because two variables are involved, this is called a two-level table. Similarly, the table in part A of figure 22-10 can be called a three-level table since its rates vary by age group, sex (male or female), and job classification.

In FORTRAN, two- and three-level tables are stored as two- and three-dimensional arrays. Basic FORTRAN allows two-dimensional arrays; full FORTRAN allows two- and three-dimensional arrays. To process these arrays, nested DO-loops are commonly used.

To illustrate the subscripts used for a two-dimensional array, consider part B of figure 22-9. This indicates the normal way in which the array elements are referenced using subscripts. Thus, the rate for a 42-year-old man in class 2 can be referred to as RATE(3,2), and the rate for a 32-year-old man in class 4 can be referred to as RATE(1,4).

Part B of figure 22-10 indicates the way in which subscripts are used to refer to elements in a three-dimensional array. Thus, the rate for a 53-

Age	Class 1	Class 2	Class 3	Class 4
18—34	$23.50	$27.05	$35.25	$52.90
35—39	24.00	27.55	35.75	53.40
40—44	24.60	28.15	36.35	54.00
45—49	25.30	28.85	37.05	54.70
50—54	26.30	29.85	38.05	55.70
55—59	28.00	31.55	39.75	57.40

Part A — Rating table

Age	Class 1	Class 2	Class 3	Class 4
18—34	RATE (1,1)	RATE (1,2)	RATE (1,3)	RATE (1,4)
35—39	RATE (2,1)	RATE (2,2)	RATE (2,3)	RATE (2,4)
40—44	RATE (3,1)	RATE (3,2)	RATE (3,3)	RATE (3,4)
45—49	RATE (4,1)	RATE (4,2)	RATE (4,3)	RATE (4,4)
50—54	RATE (5,1)	RATE (5,2)	RATE (5,3)	RATE (5,4)
55—59	RATE (6,1)	RATE (6,2)	RATE (6,3)	RATE (6,4)

Part B — Subscript notation

FIGURE 22–9   A two-level rating table and subscript notation

year-old woman in class 2 can be referred to as RATE(5,2,2). And RATE (6,1,1) indicates a man in class 1 between the ages of 55 and 59.

In a FORTRAN program the subscript used can be an integer, an integer variable, or any of several limited arithmetic expressions in the integer mode. As a result, RATE(I,J+1) and ARRAY1(2,IVAL1,2*IVAL2−3) are valid two- and three-dimensional subscripted variables. The array element that is referenced depends on the value of the variables used in the subscript at the time a statement is executed. The forms of the arithmetic expressions that can be used for two- and three-dimensional subscripts are the same as those acceptable for one-dimensional subscripts.

PROCESSING A TWO-LEVEL TABLE

Figure 22-11 is a program listing that illustrates how FORTRAN is used to process the two-level table in figure 22-9. This program treats the table as two arrays: a one-dimensional array called MAXAGE that contains the maximum age for each age group, and a two-dimensional array that contains the rates for six age groups and four job classifications. At the start of the program, the table is read into storage; then application cards are read, and the table is used to print the appropriate rate for each applicant. At the end of the program, the average rate in the table is calculated and printed, and the values in the RATE array are printed.

Age	Men		Women	
	Class 1	Class 2	Class 1	Class 2
18—34	$23.50	$27.05	$24.75	$28.45
35—39	24.00	27.55	25.80	29.50
40—44	24.60	28.15	27.10	30.80
45—49	25.30	28.85	29.10	32.80
50—54	26.30	29.85	31.55	35.25
55—59	28.00	31.55	35.00	38.70

Part A — Rating table

Age	Men		Women	
	Class 1	Class 2	Class 1	Class 2
18—34	RATE (1,1,1)	RATE (1,1,2)	RATE (1,2,1)	RATE (1,2,2)
35—39	RATE (2,1,1)	RATE (2,1,2)	RATE (2,2,1)	RATE (2,2,2)
40—44	RATE (3,1,1)	RATE (3,1,2)	RATE (3,2,1)	RATE (3,2,2)
45—49	RATE (4,1,1)	RATE (4,1,2)	RATE (4,2,1)	RATE (4,2,2)
50—54	RATE (5,1,1)	RATE (5,1,2)	RATE (5,2,1)	RATE (5,2,2)
55—59	RATE (6,1,1)	RATE (6,1,2)	RATE (6,2,1)	RATE (6,2,2)

Part B — Subscript notation

FIGURE 22–10 A three-level table and subscript notation

```
C TWO LEVEL INSURANCE RATING PROGRAM (AGE,CLASS)
      DIMENSION MAXAGE(6),RATE(6,4),NAME(5)

C READ AND STORE INPUT ARRAYS
      DO 10 I=1,6
          READ (1,1) MAXAGE(I),(RATE(I,J),J=1,4)
    1     FORMAT (I2,4F4.2)
   10     CONTINUE

C PRINT REPORT HEADINGS
      WRITE (3,2)
    2 FORMAT (8X,4HNAME,14X,4HRATE)

C READ AND PROCESS APPLICATION CARDS
   20 READ (1,3) (NAME(I),I=1,5),IAGE,ICLASS
    3 FORMAT (5A4,I2,I1)
      IF (IAGE.EQ.99) GO TO 99
      IF (IAGE.LT.18) GO TO 98

C SEARCH MAXAGE TABLE FOR PROPER AGE GROUP
      DO 30 I=1,6
          IF (IAGE.LE.MAXAGE(I)) GO TO 40
   30     CONTINUE

C PRINT UNINSURABLE MESSAGE FOR APPLICANTS UNDER 18 OR OVER 59
   98 WRITE (3,4) (NAME(I),I=1,5)
    4 FORMAT (1X,5A4,15H IS UNINSURABLE)
      GO TO 20

C PRINT APPROPRIATE RATE FOR APPLICANTS BETWEEN 18 AND 59
   40 IAGEGR=I
      WRITE (3,5) (NAME(I),I=1,5),RATE(IAGEGR,ICLASS)
    5 FORMAT (1X,5A4,F10.2)
      GO TO 20

C CALCULATE RATE SUM AFTER PROCESSING INPUT CARDS
   99 RTESUM=0.
      DO 60 I=1,6
          DO 50 J=1,4
          RTESUM=RTESUM+RATE(I,J)
   50     CONTINUE
   60 CONTINUE

C PRINT AVERAGE RATE
      RTEAVE=RTESUM/24.
      WRITE (3,6) RTEAVE
    6 FORMAT (17HOAVERAGE RATE IS ,F5.2)

C PRINT RATE ARRAY
      WRITE (3,7) ((RATE(I,J),J=1,4),I=1,6)
    7 FORMAT (1X,4F10.2)

C END OF JOB ROUTINE
      WRITE (3,8)
    8 FORMAT (11HOEND OF JOB)
      STOP
      END
```

FIGURE 22–11   A two-level rating program

In the DIMENSION statement, the dimensions for the arrays used are given as follows:

```
DIMENSION MAXAGE(6),RATE(6,4),NAME(5)
```

This indicates that the MAXAGE array consists of six elements and that the RATE array is a two-dimensional array consisting of six rows of four elements each. A third array called NAME is used to store the name field from the application cards.

The table for this program is punched into six cards as follows:

59	2800	3155	3975	5740		
54	2630	2985	3805	5570		
49	2530	2885	3705	5470		
44	2460	2815	3635	5400		
39	2400	2755	3575	5340		
34	2350	2705	3525	5290		

This means that one value from the MAXAGE array and four values from the RATE array are punched into each table card. Thus, the following code is required to read the table:

```
      DO 10 I=1,6
          READ (1,1) MAXAGE(I),(RATE(I,J),J=1,4)
    1     FORMAT (I2,4F4.2)
   10     CONTINUE
```

Here, the variable J is moved from 1 through 4 each time the READ statement is executed. Because the READ statement is in a DO-loop, it is executed six times, once for each value of I. Note that RATE in the READ statement has a two-value subscript, one value varied by the DO-implied loop of the READ statement, and the other value varied by the DO-loop itself.

This, of course, is only one of the forms that the input table could be in. Another typical form, for example, would be to punch the age-group maximums into one card, followed by cards with the rates punched four to a card as follows:

2800	3155	3975	5740			
2630	2985	3805	5570			
2530	2885	3705	5470			
2460	2815	3635	5400			
2400	2755	3575	5340			
2350	2705	3525	5290			
34	39	44	49	54	59	

The following code could then be used to store the arrays:

```
      READ (1,1) (MAXAGE(I),I=1,6)
    1 FORMAT (6I2)
      READ (1,2) ((RATE(I,J),J=1,4),I=1,6)
    2 FORMAT (4F4.2)
```

After the MAXAGE array is stored using a one-dimensional DO-implied READ statement, the RATE array is stored using a two-dimensional DO-implied READ statement. In the two-dimensional statement, J is varied from 1 through 4 for each value of I, as I is varied from 1 through 6. In other words, the effect is that of nested DO-loops. The index definition specified in the inner parentheses represents the inner loop; the index definition within the outer parentheses represents the outer loop. As with all FORTRAN statements, note the placement of the parentheses and commas since they are critical to the operation of the statement.

After the report heading is printed, the program reads the first application card, which has this format:

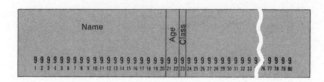

The NAME array is used for the name field, and four columns of the field are read into each of the five elements of the array. After a card is read, two IF statements test to determine whether the last input card has been read (9s in the age field) and whether the applicant is less than 18 years old. If neither condition is true, the program searches the MAXAGE array to find the applicant's age group by using this coding:

```
      DO 30 I=1,6
          IF (IAGE.LE.MAXAGE(I)) GO TO 40
   30     CONTINUE
```

If the age is equal to or less than the maximum age for a group, the program branches out of the loop to statement number 40. If the program finishes the loop, a message indicating that the applicant is uninsurable is printed, and the program reads another application card.

Beginning with statement 40, the program sets the value of IAGEGR to I, the value of the index at the time the program left the previous DO-loop. RATE(IAGEGR,ICLASS) then indicates the appropriate rate for the application being processed. After the applicant's name and rate are printed, the program reads the next application card.

When the last application card is read, the program branches to statement 99. Here, the rates in the rate table are added together as follows:

```
99 RTESUM=0.
   DO 60 I=1,6
      DO 50 J=1,4
      RTESUM=RTESUM+RATE(I,J)
50    CONTINUE
60 CONTINUE
```

Using nested DO loops, the twenty-four values of the RATE array are added to RTESUM in this order:

> RATE(1,1)
> RATE(1,2)
> RATE(1,3)
> RATE(1,4)
> RATE(2,1)
> and so on.

In other words, J is varied from 1 through 4 for each value of I. After the DO-loops have been completed, RTESUM is divided by 24 to give the average rate, RTEAVE.

The final statements in the program print the average rate, print the values in the RATE array using nested DO-implied loops in a WRITE statement, print an end-of-job message, and stop the program. In the DO-implied WRITE statement, the important thing to note is the order in which the index definitions are given. Because the index J is in the inner parentheses, the values are printed as follows:

```
RATE(1,1)  RATE(1,2)  RATE(1,3)  RATE(1,4)
RATE(2,1)  RATE(2,2)  RATE(2,3)  RATE(2,4)
and so on.
```

However, if the index definitions were reversed as in

```
WRITE (3,6) ((RATE(I,J),I=1,6),J=1,4)
```

the table would print like this:

```
RATE(1,1)  RATE(2,1)  RATE(3,1)  RATE(4,1)
RATE(5,1)  RATE(6,1)  RATE(1,2)  RATE(2,2)
RATE(3,2)  RATE(4,2)  and so on.
```

This, of course, would not be the intent of the programmer.

PROCESSING A
THREE-LEVEL TABLE

Figure 22-12 is a program listing that processes the three-level table given in figure 22-10. The processing is similar to that of the previous program: the table is read into storage, a listing of applicants and rates is printed, the average rate is calculated and printed, the RATE array is printed, an end-of-job message is printed, and the program ends. The

```
C THREE DIMENSIONAL INSURANCE RATING PROGRAM (AGE,SEX,CLASS)
      DIMENSION MAXAGE(6),RATE(6,2,2),NAME(5)

C READ AND STORE INPUT ARRAYS
      READ (1,1) (MAXAGE(I),I=1,6)
    1 FORMAT (6I2)
      READ (1,2) (((RATE(I,J,K),K=1,2),J=1,2),I=1,6)
    2 FORMAT (4F4.2)

C PRINT REPORT HEADINGS
      WRITE (3,3)
    3 FORMAT (8X,4HNAME,14X,4HRATE)

C READ AND PROCESS APPLICATION CARDS
   10 READ (1,4) ((NAME(I),I=1,5),IAGE,ICLASS,ISEX)
    4 FORMAT (5A4,I2,2I1)
      IF (IAGE.EQ.99) GO TO 99
      IF (IAGE.LT.18) GO TO 98

C SEARCH MAXAGE TABLE FOR PROPER AGE GROUP
      DO 20 I=1,6
         IF (IAGE.LE.MAXAGE(I)) GO TO 30
   20    CONTINUE

C PRINT UNINSURABLE MESSAGE FOR APPLICANTS UNDER 18 OR OVER 59
   98 WRITE (3,5) (NAME(I),I=1,5)
    5 FORMAT (1X,5A4,15H IS UNINSURABLE)
      GO TO 10

C PRINT APPROPRIATE RATE FOR APPLICANTS BETWEEN 18 AND 59
   30 IAGEGR=I
      WRITE (3,6) (NAME(I),I=1,5),RATE(IAGEGR,ISEX,ICLASS)
    6 FORMAT (1X,5A4,F10.2)
      GO TO 10

C CALCULATE RATE SUM AFTER PROCESSING INPUT CARDS
   99 RTESUM=0.
      DO 60 I=1,6
         DO 50 J=1,2
            DO 40 K=1,2
            RTESUM=RTESUM+RATE(I,J,K)
   40       CONTINUE
   40    CONTINUE
   60 CONTINUE

C PRINT AVERAGE RATE
      RTEAVE=RTESUM/24.
      WRITE (3,7) RTEAVE
    7 FORMAT (17HOAVERAGE RATE IS ,F5.2)

C PRINT RATE ARRAY
      WRITE (3,8) (((RATE(I,J,K),I=1,6),J=1,2),K=1,2)
    8 FORMAT (1X,6F10.2)

C END OF JOB ROUTINE
      WRITE (3,9)
    9 FORMAT (11HOEND OF JOB)
      STOP
      END
```

FIGURE 22–12   A three-level rating program

main difference between this and the previous program is that the rates are treated as a three-dimensional array. Thus, three-dimensional subscripts are used and three levels of nested DO-loops and nested DO-implied loops are used.

As the comment line at the start of the program indicates, the subscript values for the RATE array represent in order the age group, the sex code, and the job classification. Thus, the DIMENSION statement gives the RATE dimension as (6,2,2). Because the MAXAGE elements are punched into one card and the RATE elements are punched four per card into the next six cards, the following code is used to read the rating table:

```
    READ (1,1) (MAXAGE(I),I=1,6)
  1 FORMAT (6I2)
    READ (1,2) (((RATE(I,J,K),K=1,2),J=1,2),I=1,6)
  2 FORMAT (4F4.2)
```

Here, the second READ statement has three DO-implied loops that vary the subscript values in this order: class, sex, and age group. Thus, the RATE elements are filled in this order:

$$RATE(1,1,1)$$
$$RATE(1,1,2)$$
$$RATE(1,2,1)$$
$$RATE(1,2,2)$$
$$RATE(2,1,1)$$
$$RATE(2,1,2)$$
$$RATE(2,2,1)$$
$$RATE(2,2,2)$$
$$RATE(3,1,1)$$

and so on.

Note again the use of the commas and the parentheses in the DO-implied portion of the READ statement.

The remainder of the program should be self-explanatory. Three levels of nested DO loops are used to total the rates in the table before the average-rate calculation; three levels of DO-implied loops are used in printing the RATE array near the end of the program. Because the WRITE statement varies the subscript values in reverse order from the way the input array is read and because the FORMAT statement specifies 6F10.2 for the output line, the table will print as follows:

```
    23.50    24.00    24.60    25.30    26.30    28.00
    24.75    25.80    27.10    29.10    31.55    35.00
    27.05    27.55    28.15    28.85    29.85    31.55
    28.45    29.50    30.80    32.80    35.25    38.70
```

One of the most difficult aspects of handling three-dimensional arrays is maintaining consistency in the use of subscripts. In other words, if you read an array into storage with the subscript values in order representing age group, sex, and job classification, you must be careful to keep this order throughout the program. If you reference an array element thinking that the subscript values in order are age group, job classification, and sex code, a programming error will result.

SUMMARY

Basically, two- and three-dimensional arrays are processed using the same FORTRAN elements that are used for one-dimensional arrays. However, nested DO loops and DO-implied loops are more prominent, and two- and three-value subscripts must be used.

QUESTIONS

1. Refer to figure 22-11. Add statements to the program that will increase all rates by 10 percent after they are stored in the RATE array.

2. Refer to figure 22-12. Add statements to the program that will increase all rates by 10 percent after they are stored in the RATE array.

SECTION SEVEN

APPENDIXES

APPENDIX A STANDARD SYSTEM FLOWCHART SYMBOLS

BASIC SYMBOLS
Input/output
Process
Annotation, comment
SPECIALIZED INPUT/OUTPUT SYMBOLS
Punched card
Punched tape
Document
Deck of cards
Magnetic drum
Manual input
File of cards
Magnetic disk
Display
Online storage
Communication link
Magnetic tape
Core
Offline storage
SPECIALIZED PROCESS SYMBOLS
Auxiliary operation
Collate
Extract
Manual operation
Merge
Sort
ADDITIONAL SYMBOLS
Connector
Terminal

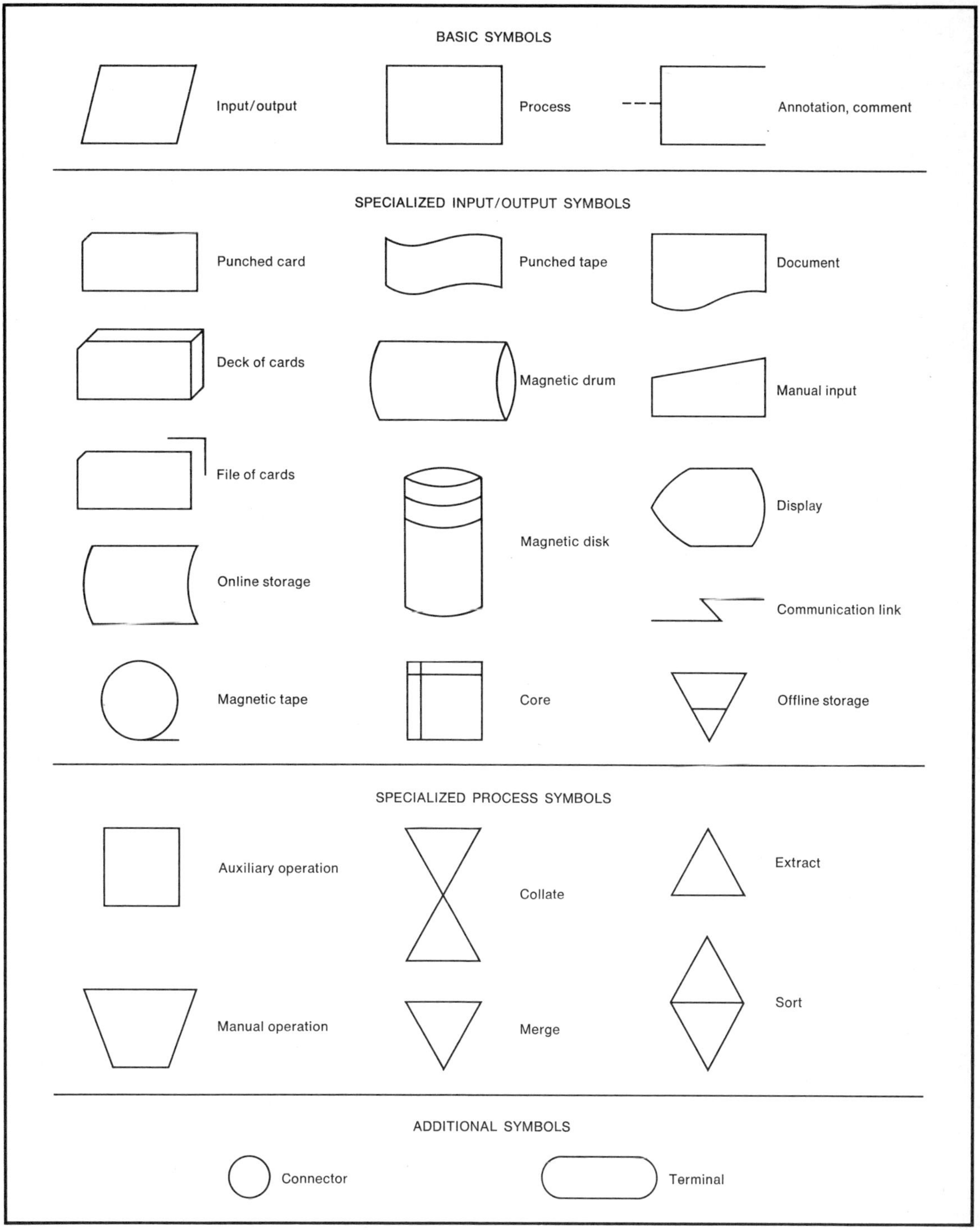

APPENDIX B
STANDARD
PROGRAM
FLOWCHART
SYMBOLS

SYMBOL	SYMBOL NAME	MEANING
	Terminal	Start or end of a sequence of operations
	Input/Output	I/O operation
	Process	Any kind of processing function
	Decision	A logical or branching operation
	Connector	Connection between parts of a flowchart
	Annotation	Explanatory comments
	Predefined Process	A routine or function described in another set of flowcharts
	Preparation	Modification of a field or instruction that changes the sequence of processing in the program itself.

As you read through these procedures, use figures C-1 and C-2 to locate parts of the 029 keypunch.

MANUAL OPERATION OF THE 029 KEYPUNCH

Setup

1. Turn on the power switch located beneath the desklike surface of the keypunch.

2. Place blank cards in the input hopper.

3. Depress the FEED key twice to move a card to the punching station.

4. Push the program-control lever to the right so that program control is off.

5. Set the switches located above the keyboard so that AUTO FEED and PRINT are on and AUTO SKIP DUP and LZ PRINT are off. (The positions of the other switches don't matter.)

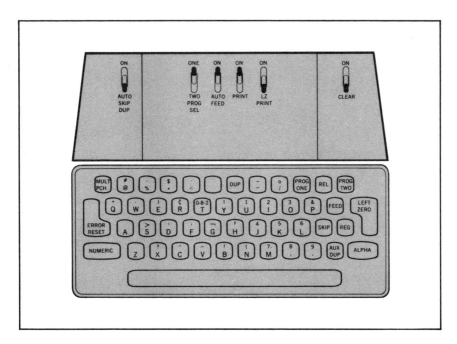

FIGURE C-1   Keyboard of the 029 keypunch

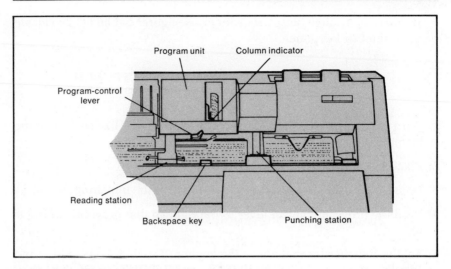

FIGURE C-2   Features of the 029 keypunch

Operating Procedures

1. Key the data. The keyboard is in alphabetic shift. If numbers or other upper-shift characters are to be punched, the NUMERIC key must be used. The column indicator shows the next column to be punched. When all columns to be punched have been keyed, push the REL (release) key.

2. The backspace key can be used to move back one column at a time.

3. To duplicate data from one card to the next, press the DUP key for those columns.

4. When you are finished keypunching, flip the CLEAR switch to the ON position to clear the reading and punching stations of cards.

PROGRAM-CONTROL OPERATION OF THE 029 KEYPUNCH

Simple Program Card for FORTRAN Source Deck

This card assumes columns 73–80 of the source cards are not used for identification or sequence codes.

Columns	Punches	Meaning
1–6	b&&&&& (b = blank)	Columns 1–6 are in numeric shift.
7–80	1 followed by 73 As	Columns 7–80 are in alphabetic shift.

Setup

1. Raise the starwheels in the program unit by pushing the program-control lever to the right.

2. Pull the cover of the program unit forward.

3. Lift the program drum from its spindle.

4. At the top of the program drum is a clamping-strip handle. Remove the old program card by moving this handle all the way to the left (counterclockwise).

5. Put the drum back on its spindle in the program unit, making sure that the alignment pin on the bottom of the drum is in the alignment hole in the program unit.

6. Close the cover of the program unit and lower the starwheels by pushing the program-control lever to the left. Then, press the REL key. This causes the program drum to rotate once, thus engaging the starwheels in the holes of the program card.

7. Place blank cards in the input hopper.

8. Depress the FEED key twice to move a card to the punching station.

9. Set the switches located above the keyboard so that AUTO FEED, PRINT, and AUTO SKIP DUP are on and LZ PRINT is off.

Operating Procedures

1. Skipping and shifting of the keyboard are now under program control as dictated by the program card. To punch alphabetic data in a numeric field, use the ALPHA key. To punch numeric data in an alphabetic field, use the NUMERIC key. To skip to the end of a field, press the SKIP key.

2. If you want to avoid automatic skipping or duplication, turn the AUTO SKIP DUP key off before the start of the automatic field. For example, if you want to use a continuation punch in column 7, turn AUTO SKIP DUP off before the end of the preceding card. Then, columns 1–7 can be punched using manual operations.

3. If you make an error, it can be corrected in this way. First, push the REL key, thus releasing the error card to the reading station. Second, turn off the AUTO SKIP DUP switch. Third, press the DUP key until the keypunch reaches the column that contains the error. This duplicates all data that was punched correctly before the error was made. Now, correct the error, turn AUTO SKIP DUP back on, and continue punching as usual. Be sure, however, that you remove the error card from the source deck.

VARIATIONS WHEN USING THE 026 KEYPUNCH

1. The 026 keypunch requires a warmup period of about half a minute after the mainline switch is turned on. As a result, it is customary to press the REL key after turning the machine on. When the warmup period is over, the program drum rotates once (because the REL key was depressed), thus indicating that the machine is ready for operation.

2. There is no CLEAR switch on the 026 keypunch. To move cards to the output stacker, the AUTO FEED switch must be turned off. Then the release and register (REG) keys are pressed alternately—REL, REG, REL, REG, REL, REG—until all cards are moved to the stacker.

3. The 026 keyboard, illustrated in figure C-3, does not have all of the special characters that the 029 has. For example, it does not have the semicolon (;), the single quotation mark ('), and the equals sign (=). To punch these on the 026, the MULT PCH key must be used. When it is depressed, the keyboard is in numeric shift and the card does not advance until the MULT PCH key is released. To punch a single quotation mark, which consists of a 5- and an 8-punch, the MULT PCH key is pressed and the 5 and 8 keys are struck. When the MULT PCH key is released, the card moves to the next card column. The following are the special characters for which MULT PCH must be used:

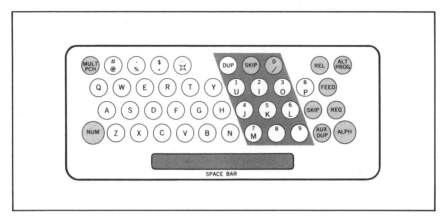

FIGURE C-3   Keyboard of the 026 keypunch

Character	Card code
$<$	12,4,8
(	12,5,8
+	12,6,8
)	11,5,8
;	11,6,8
− (minus)	0,5,8
$>$	0,6,8
?	0,7,8
'	5,8
$=$	6,8

SPECIAL PROCEDURES

Resetting a Locked Keyboard

In some cases, the keyboard will lock because of an error; for example, keying a non-numeric character such as the letter A in a numeric field. On the 026 keypunch, the keyboard can be unlocked by pressing either the REL or the backspace key; on the 029 keypunch, the ERROR RESET key must be pressed.

Duplicating a Damaged Card

1. Turn off AUTO FEED and AUTO SKIP DUP, and clear the machine of cards. (Cards may be left in the stacker, however.)

2. Smooth the card and insert it through the plastic guides at the reading station. Slide the card forward as far as it will go, and then pull it back about one-quarter inch.

3. Place a blank card through the guides at the punching station. Again, slide the card forward until it stops, and then pull it back about one-quarter inch.

4. Press the REG key to register the cards at the reading and punching stations.

5. Press the DUP key until all of the data in the damaged card is punched into the new card. Then, press the REL key to release both cards.

6. Clear the cards from the machine.

Correcting a Few Columns of an Error Card

1. Follow steps 2–4 above for duplicating a damaged card.

2. Push the DUP key for all correct card columns; rekey the error columns.

Adding Data to a Card

1. Insert the card through the guides at the punching station. Slide the card forward as far as it will go; then pull it back about one-quarter inch.

2. Press the REG key to register the card at the punching station.

3. Using the space bar, space over the punched columns to the columns that need to be punched.

4. Key the additional data in the indicated columns.

The language summary that follows gives the format for each of the 16 statements presented in this text. It also gives examples of use for each type of statement.

Statement Format	Examples of Use
DATA constant	DATA 1.5
DATA constant,constant, . . .	DATA 3.2,-7.9,4.16,-21
DIM letter(integer-constant)	DIM X(17)
DIM letter(integer-constant, integer-constant)	DIM A(25,100)
END	END
FOR variable=expression TO expression	FOR X=A TO 15
FOR variable−expression TO expression STEP expression	FOR Y=2 TO L STEP 5
.	.
.	.
.	.
NEXT variable	NEXT Y
	NEXT X
GOSUB statement-number	GOSUB 3000
.	.
.	.
RETURN	RETURN
GO TO statement-number	GO TO 150
IF relational-expression THEN statement-number	IF Y$="NO" THEN 1000
	IF X+Y <=74 THEN 770
INPUT variable	INPUT D$
	INPUT D1
INPUT variable,variable, . . .	INPUT S5,D$,N,N5
LET variable = expression	LET X = A*Y+.5
	LET I = I+1
	LET A = B
	LET M = 3.1416
PRINT	PRINT

PRINT constant	```PRINT 3500``` ```PRINT "END OF JOB"```
PRINT expression	```PRINT X*Y/3```
PRINT $\begin{Bmatrix} \text{expression} \\ \text{constant} \end{Bmatrix}$'$\begin{Bmatrix} \text{expression} \\ \text{constant} \end{Bmatrix}$',...,	```PRINT X,2000,F$,Y4,H*R```
$\begin{Bmatrix} \text{expression} \\ \text{constant} \end{Bmatrix}$'$\begin{Bmatrix} \text{blank} \\ , \\ ; \end{Bmatrix}$	```PRINT "ANSWER IS";```
READ variable	```READ A```
READ variable,variable, . . .	```READ A,B,D,F4,G$```
REM any-text	```REM LOOP TO FOLLOW```
RESTORE	```RESTORE```
STOP	```STOP```

The American National Standards Institute (ANSI) provides two sets of FORTRAN specifications. One is referred to as Basic FORTRAN; the other as FORTRAN, or full FORTRAN. Because Basic FORTRAN is a subset of full FORTRAN, a Basic FORTRAN program can be compiled by a full FORTRAN compiler. The reverse, however, is not true.

The summary that follows is divided into these sections:

General FORTRAN Information
FORTRAN Statements

To the left of each FORTRAN specification is a column that indicates whether the specification applies to a Basic or a full FORTRAN compiler: B indicates Basic, while F indicates full. This summary includes only those elements or variations of elements covered in this book.

GENERAL FORTRAN INFORMATION

ANS Level	
	Character set:
B	A–Z
B	0–9
B	Blank = + − * / ( ) , .
F	$
B	Arithmetic operators: + − * / **
F	Relational operators:

	.LT.	Less than
	.LE.	Less than or equal to
	.EQ.	Equal to
	.NE.	Not equal to
	.GT.	Greater than
	.GE.	Greater than or equal to

Rules for forming variable names:

B	1. Five or less letters or numbers, starting with a letter.
F	2. Six or less letters or numbers, starting with a letter.
B	3. Names starting with the letters I–N are integer variables; names beginning with other letters are real variables.

F	Double precision variables: Specifying a variable as double precision by using the DOUBLE PRECISION statement doubles the number of

ANS
Level

significant digits in a real variable, but does not change the range of the variable. Only real variables can be double precision.

B   Rules for forming integer constants:
1. Can have a leading + or − sign; if omitted, constant is assumed to be positive.
2. Other than a lead sign, it must consist entirely of decimal digits.

B   Rules for forming real constants:
1. Can have a leading + or − sign; if omitted, constant is assumed to be positive.
2. Must have one and only one decimal point within a decimal number.

Rules for statement numbers:

B   From 1 to 4 decimal digits located anywhere in columns 1–5 of the coding form. Leading zeros are not significant.

F   From 1 to 5 decimal digits located anywhere in columns 1–5 of the coding form. Leading zeros are not significant.

Subscripting and arrays:

B   One- or two-dimensional arrays only.

F   One-, two-, or three-dimensional arrays.

B   All subscripts must be integers or integer expressions.

B   Allowable subscript expressions:
Constant * Variable ± Constant
Constant * Variable
Variable ± Constant

B   Order of source deck:
DOUBLE PRECISION and DIMENSION Statements
FORMAT Statements
Executable Statements
END Statement
(Note: FORMAT statements may also be placed anywhere within the executable statements.)

B   Use of coding form:
1. Use of program identification (columns 73–80) is optional.
2. Blanks are ignored by the compiler.

ANS
<u>Level</u>

B Comment lines:
   1. The letter C is required in column 1.
   2. Any other characters can be punched in columns 2–80 since they are ignored by the compiler.

B Continuation lines:
   1. If a FORTRAN statement requires more than one coding line, column 6 of the continuation line must receive a character other than zero or blank.
B 2. Up to five continuation lines are allowed.
F 3. Up to nineteen continuation lines are allowed.

FORTRAN STATEMENTS

I/O and FORMAT Statements

READ statement:
B   READ (device-number, format-statement-number) list

WRITE statement:
B   WRITE (device-number, format-statement-number) list

FORMAT statement:
B   FORMAT list

Field descriptors:
B   rFw.d   (Real variable, no exponent)
B   rIw   (Integer variable)
B   nHcharacter-string   (Alphanumeric constant data)
B   nX   (Skipped data or blanks)
F   rAw   (Alphanumeric variable)
      r = repeat count
      n = number of characters in string
      w = field width
      d = number of decimal positions

Carriage-control characters:
B   blank   One line spaced before printing
F   0   Two lines spaced before printing
F   1   Skip to first line of next page before printing
F   +   No advance

DO-implied lists in READ and WRITE statements:
B   1. One-dimensional:
         (variable-list,index-definition)

ANS Level	
B	2. Two-dimensional: ((variable-list,index-definition-1),index-definition-2)
F	3. Three-dimensional: (((variable-list,index-definition-1),index-definition-2), index-definition-3)

Arithmetic Statements

B	Arithmetic assignment statement: variable-name = arithmetic-expression

Control Statements

B	Unconditional GO TO statement: GO TO statement number
B	Arithmetic IF statement: IF (arithmetic-expression) statement-no.-1,statement-no.-2, statement-no.-3
F	Logical IF statement: IF (logical-expression) statement-no.
B	DO statement:

DO statement-number $i = m_1, m_2, m_3$
where i = integer variable
m_1 = starting parameter
m_2 = ending parameter
m_3 = incrementation parameter

B	STOP statement: STOP

Nonexecutable Statements

B	CONTINUE statement: CONTINUE
B	DIMENSION statement: DIMENSION array-name(array-declarator). . .
F	DOUBLE PRECISION statement: DOUBLE PRECISION variable-list
B	END statement: END